DANIEL STIH'S
ROCK CLIMBING
IN ZION
NATIONAL PARK

Copyright ©2023, 2024, 2026 by Daniel Stih

All rights reserved.

ISBN: 978-1-7365856-0-3

No part of this book may be reproduced or transmitted in any form, electronic or mechanical, including photocopying, without written permission of the author, except for brief passages in a magazine or newspaper review.

Inquiries regarding requests to reprint parts should be addressed to:

Daniel Stih
P.O. Box 32
Springdale, UT 84767

Warning and Disclaimer

Climb at your own risk. Please don't consider this book a road map. Use it as a history book to see what's been climbed, where, and how. Find your own way. Make a new way. In doing so, please do not add bolts to existing climbs. It alters the experience for everyone. If in doubt, turn around and go down. If you're scared and think you need to place a bolt, consider what an experienced climber told me when I was a teenager, attempting a climb more dangerous than anything I had done before, and not up to the task: "You're not ready for this." We went down, something that was a learning experience for me. I learned how to get down when I got in over my head. Years later, I returned and had a fun time climbing that mountain.

Sentinel Canyon.

Acknowledgments

Thank you Vince Bert, my partner on my first climb in Zion; Bill Paul for teaching me about big wall climbing and safety; Ron Raimond for teaching me how to place pitons, the concept of alpine climbing, and doing traverses; Dave Everett for letting me drag him out on epic first ascents in the backcountry. His first two climbs in Zion were with me on big projects, when I'm sure he would rather have climbed Prodigal Sun like everyone else does for their first climb in Zion; My nephew Nathaniel Stih, for playing hooky and walking many miles with me to where it's better out there; D.B, for her suggestion to C.P. to show me the pages in his guidebook that contained pictures of two unclimbed mountains; Steffan Gregory for keeping me out of trouble; My sister-in-law Geri, an emergency contact who answers her phone; my brother John, for telling me not to make decisions based on how things appear on satellite images; my brother Todd, for feedback as I was writing *Because You Can*; the park rangers and staff in the backcountry office; the flowers - I never knew what surprises I might find; the trees and bushes I used to clip my rope into for anchors. Thank you for letting me use you. Grow big and strong; the spirit of the mountains and the spirits that dwell in the canyons, some lost, some found, for sharing the mountains with me and letting me pass safely; to my guardian angel Nick and to his helpers; to a spirit that can't be named, one that has no name, one that encompasses the mountain in each of us.

CONTENTS

Introduction
Sand 101	11
Who This Book is For	12
Permits	14
Rescue	14
Ethics	15
Logistics	16
Surviving Hot Weather	19
Exercise in Eliminating Excess	21
Dangerous Dan Tips	21

We Are Learning
Prodigal Sun	28
Space Shot	31
Moonlight Buttress	32
Interlude	34
My First Solo	39
My Second Solo	40
Touchstone	45
Days of Future	46
The Lowe Route	48
The Search for Something New	51
Sun, Snow, and Ticks	52
The First Modern Climbing Fatality in Zion National Park	54

Introduction to My Routes
Ratings	64
Favorite Routes	64

First Ascents of Mountains Named on Maps
The Altar of Sacrifice	68
The Sun Dial	80
Abraham	84
Cliff Dwelling Mountain	92
The Bishopric East	97
The North Bishopric	104
The Meridian Tower	117
The Inclined Temple	125
Ivins Mountain	131
Castle Dome	145
Gregory Butte	153

First Climbing Ascents of Mountains Named on Maps

Cable Mountain	161
Death Point	174

First Ascents of Peaks Not Previously Named on Maps

The Witch Head	180
Broken Tooth & Rotten Tooth	184
Chameleon	186
Middle Cathedral	190
Cats Tail Ridge	197
The Blob	198
The King	206
The Queen	209
Lancelot	212
Corbin Castle	218
Joyous Gard	221
Sky Island	227
The Finger	234
Center Point	235
The North Eye	246
Magic Rabbit Peak	254
Birthday Cake	258
Lucky Charm	259
The Unicorn	263
The Little Bishop	265
Red Tooth	268
Battle Ship Rock	270
Nipples Peak	274
The Subdial	282
The Princess Spires	285
Big Red	304
Rosebud	315
The Point	316
Triangle Peak	319
Cats Crown	334
Gabriel	335
The Droids	339

Other First Ascents

Nice Line	341
East Temple Direct	347
The Sentinel - The North Face	354
Jacob - The North Face	362
Isaac - The North Face	364
Good Times on the West Temple	368

Cathedral Mountain, The Iron Curtain 5.10 A3+	371
Red Arch Mountain (By Descent)	380

Other Notable Ascents
Checkerboard Mesa	386
Hidden Canyon	392
Arch Gully (Natural Bridge)	397

Traverses
Traverse of the Towers of the Virgin	405
Traverse of the Beehives	473

Closed Loop Traverses
Traverse of the Court of the Patriarchs	421
Traverse of the Three Bishoprics	434
Traverse of the Sanctuary, King, and Queen	443
Traverse Around the Emerald Pools	447
Traverse of Kolob Canyons	461
Traverse of the Time Machine	481
The Cat Walk - Traversing the Gregory Butte Massif	485

Canyon Descents
Inclined Canyon (North Side of Inclined Temple)	490
Meridian Tower Plateau into Oak Creek	492
Chipmunk Cliff (Birch Creek into the Court of the Patriarchs)	494
Descent from Jacob / Lady Mountain into Isaac Canyon	496
Goose Canyon	498
Sentinel Canyon	502
Mars Canyon	510

Time for a Break	512
Bibliography	514

Bird Beak Spire as seen on my ascent of Triangle Peak.

Introduction

In the United States, the traditional way of documenting climbs is the *American Alpine Journal*. Due to space limitations, some of my trip reports were given little space or omitted. I wanted to provide a place for climbers to access the missing information and decided to write the book you are reading.

The rope wearing a groove in the rock.

As I was developing a draft, friends told me they were more interested in the stories than climbing routes. One does not wake up one day and decide to do the first ascent of a mountain that has never been climbed. There's a learning curve. A spark lights a fire, that burns and fuels a desire, propelling one to achieve things they thought weren't possible. The first chapters are stories of me climbing existing routes in Zion, before I started exploring and climbing mountains that had not been climbed. When I started climbing I was the voted the least likely to succeed. They had to drag me up a 5.6 (on a scale of difficulty from 5.1 to 5.15). I was terrified. Like most, I climbed the trade routes in Zion before embarking on climbing peaks that had not been climbed. I spent years learning my craft before one day I found myself ready to explore and climb the unknown. I hope that my stories inspire you. I include my hand-written notes as originally penned after completing an adventure, and print-photos from photo albums. Many of these climbs were first done before digital cameras were available.

SAND 101

Unlike the solid granite in Yosemite, the rock in Zion is composed of grains of sand, held loosely together by friction. It's even more difficult to climb in Zion when the rock (sand) gets wet. Sand absorbs water. As water is absorbed, there is the less friction between the grains to keep them from sliding apart. It's like trying to keep your car on the road in a heavy down-pour, driving fast with bald tires. When grains of sand slide, the rock falls apart.

Scientists who study this phenomenon refer to it as the coefficient of friction and as surface energy. It's my opinion they don't really know how it works. What is known is that climbing 1,000 feet of sandstone can feel like climbing 3,000 feet of granite.

Even when the rock in Zion appears to be dry, it may not be. This is due to capillary action. Sand holds different amounts of moisture, based on time and elevation. Contrary to what seems logical, the sandstone on exposed faces may be weaker (wetter) months AFTER it rains or snows. This is because it takes time for water, with the help of gravity, to settle to lower elevations. As it settles, water takes the path of least resistance, and is pushed sideways. This results in springs, weeps, and seeps that magically come out of the rock. The general consensus is you should wait two days after it rains before climbing; three days on north facing routes with less sunlight. You won't know the actual condition of a route until you start.

WHO THIS BOOK IS FOR

If you are not a climber, sit back and enjoy. I climbed these mountains so you don't have to. Witness places few have gone, and gleam insight into the eternal question: Why?

Zion was once underwater. I found crustaceans near the summit of a 7,000 foot peak.

If you are a climber, I hope you enjoy climbing one of these routes and are inspired to find new adventures and discoveries. You don't have to be strong to climb the routes. You should have experience placing natural protection and using natural anchors. Sometimes the only protection is a small bush you clip the rope to. If you depend on a GPS or technology to know where you are at, do not attempt these climbs. It's not irresponsible to leave a GPS or cell phone in the car - it's irresponsible to expect them to work or to believe you are safe because you have them. The false sense of security these devices give people leads them to do things they would not otherwise attempt.

This book is meant for those for which weather is not a factor. If you're the type that sees rain or snow clouds threatening and doesn't think twice about starting or continuing to climb - this book is for you. If you're the type who doesn't need a sleeping bag, and can make due with a sleeping pad cut to fit the size of your butt so you can pack light - this book is for you. If you're the type that considers an "alpine rack" three cams and six carabiners - this book is for you. If you the type that doesn't carry a bolt kit because you know you can get down anything without one, and you don't need bolts to "climb" - this book is for you. If you're the type that doesn't need gortex and are fine in the rain wearing an old pair of nylon pants - this book is for you. If you're idea of food is a loaf of bread, cheese, and few strips of jerky for several days - this book is for you. If you climb to escape vs. participate in a sport, this book is for you. You are a rare breed - you are what used to be considered a climber.

Beginning climbers: There's no harm in attempting to climb something you feel you might get over your head on. You can still have an adventure getting to the base of a peak, even if you fail to climb it. As you will read, my average success rate on a climb is about 30%. On average, it told me three attempts to figure a way up something. Much of the leg work for success involves figuring out the approach and getting your gear to a peak and back. Often it involves being able to find or carry water. Where there is no water, choosing the optimal season, i.e., early spring when there is snow to melt, is crucial.

The one thing I ask is that you don't place bolts on my routes. Climbing was never meant to be safe. In fact, one of the joys of reaching the top of a difficult climb is getting there by the skin of your teeth. It's a mental challenge. If you don't feel you are strong or brave enough to climb something without adding a bolt, please come down before you find yourself in a predicament where you feel must in order to get down safety. Barring this golden rule, I encourage you to go out and flounder. You'll learn something each time, and eventually find yourself with the skills to get up hard routes without placing bolts.

You're never to old. As I approached fifty, I thought I was getting old. Then I read stories in a book on the history of mountaineering and learned that in the late 1800s, husbands and wives routinely went climbing in the alps at the age of seventy and didn't skip a beat.

Postcards to the future: Someone suggested I wrote this book for myself - my future self. If I am dead, perhaps I left this as a roadmap. It's not just about climbing - it's about the connection to the land.

A backcountry permit, circa 1996. One-page, carbon copy paper.

PERMITS

A permit is not required to climb in Zion. A permit is, however, required to spend a night on a climb or to sleep anywhere in the backcountry. The reason is misunderstood. Permits are for monitoring environmental impact, to know what kind of activity, how many people are doing it, and where. Climbing permits are given to sleep on a climb - not at the bottom. If you need to camp on the approach or at the bottom of a climb, consult with backcountry rangers on where you are permitted to do so. In addition to a climbing permit, you may need a backpacking permit and a camping permit. A canyoneering permit is required to go down canyons.

RESCUE

Be self-sufficient. Most of the routes in this book are in locations where a rescue would be very difficult. Some are in areas where there is no reception for cellular or satellite-based devices. Your exact location based on a GPS may, therefore, not be accurate.

Having a permit does not mean the park service is checking on you to make sure you are OK. If you get into trouble, a search and rescue will not be initiated unless your Emergency Contact reports you overdue or injured. Always leave a detailed description of where you are going and when you plan to return with your emergency contact. Make sure the backcountry office has the correct phone number for your emergency contact.

If a law enforcement officer notices your car parked with a permit displayed that shows you are overdue, they *may* contact dispatch. The dispatch operator will then contact your emergency contact. They will not initiate a search and rescue (SAR) until they have confirmed with your emergency contact that you that you are in fact overdue. IT IS IMPERATIVE TO GIVE YOUR EMERGENCY CONTACT ACCURATE INFORMATION REGARDING WHEN YOU ARE LEAVING, WHERE YOU ARE GOING, AND WHEN YOU PLAN TO RETURN.

Do not relay on electronic devices. When I did the first ascent of Princess Spire, it was getting dark as I reached the top. I was supposed to be back at the car that evening. I decided to wait until morning to get down. That evening, I pressed the power button on my hand-held satellite communication device (Gramin inReach) to turn it on so that I could send a text message to friends that I was OK. It would not turn on. It was fully charged. I had charged and tested it before starting my climb. It had a software problem.

On one trip, my device turned itself on and then sent an SOS message. It has a safety switch that was supposed to prevent it from sending an accidental SOS. It was 10 pm. I didn't notice the "SOS IN PROGRESS" until after midnight. The International Emergency Response center in Texas had started planning. They were waiting for daylight. If I had not been able to reach a clear view of the sky that night and cancel the SOS, I would have caused a lot of people unnecessary trouble.

On several trips I noticed that my location was not being tagged with the text messages that I was sending. The device kept telling me to get a clear view of the sky in order for the GPS to know my location. It continued to tell me to get a clearer view of the sky when I was on top of a mountain. When I got home I called tech support who guided me through the process of rebooting the GPS subroutine in the operating system of the device, something not in its operating instructions. (This is a common satellite-based texting device sold at REI). If I had needed assistance, a search team would have had to rely on my text messages to find me.

On another trip, the device I was carrying stopped working when I was in the middle of my climb. I had been out two days and expected to be gone for two more. I worried that the sudden stop of communication between myself and my contacts would cause my emergency contact to panic. I abandoned my climb and came down.

I now carry a satellite-based device to use in case of emergencies. I charge it before I leave. I do not perform a software update or sync it before starting a trip. I carry the device, never turn it on. I use the old-fashioned way of being safe - I tell my emergency contact where I am going and when I expect to be out. I tell them not to expect text messages or GPS tags during my trip. No news is good news. Before I leave, I tell my emergency contact where I am going, what day I should be back, and if I become overdue they should send rescue troops, STAT.

ETHICS

Any trick is fair-game. The possibilities for fun and adventure are endless, when you find a way to get to the top without placing a bolt.

Leave No Trace. No means no. Leave nothing: no trash, no poop, no toilet paper, no anything.

Let it Be. In my opinion, there are two reasons for not placing bolts. The first is obvious: rock (sand) in Zion is soft. The second reason I share with Reinhold Messner. He made the first solo ascent of Mount Everest without using bottled oxygen, and was the first person to climb all of the 8,000 meter peaks in the Himalayan. Prior to that, he had been a rock climber, putting up hard routes, some which have still not been repeated. Messner has never placed a bolt. He said, "Placing a blot murders the impossible."

Today, climbing is viewed as a recreational sport. Climbers place bolts to ensure a greater sense of safety. I get that. If you want to be safe, don't climb outdoors. If you want to climb outside and needed to clip a bolt to feel safe, there are climbing areas that have bolts. Go there. Please leave the mountains in Zion as you find them.

To bolt or not to bolt is a debate no one can win. Who's to say how long or short a fall should be. The reason I choose to avoid placing bolts has nothing to do with being Dangerous Dan. If I can't climb something, I'd rather simply leave it for someone who is stronger and more capable, who *can climb* it. Sometimes I go back to these mountains when I am stronger and more confident. That makes reaching the summits all the more rewarding.

Resource Natural Areas (RNAs). These are off-limits. This means no climbing, no hiking, no going there. Some years ago, the park service was sued by an environmental group for not doing enough to enforce the charter when national parks were created. National parks were created for recreation *and* preservation. In the minds of some, preservation wasn't being considered as much. The park service was asked to designate certain areas of the park as hyper-wilderness, places no one can go. As a result, RNAs were established.

They chose places they thought no one could, or would want to go, places remote and hard to get to. You guessed it - RNAs can be places with high adventure. The good news is that only the summits of these mountains are RNAs. It is permissible to climb the sides of them up to the rim. It is not permissible to walk on top. Stop at the edge when you get there. If you make it that far, I'll respect it as an ascent. Respecting this ethic will ensure that the park does not close additional areas, i.e., those areas near the mountains, in

Sorting gear in preparation to climb.

addition to their summits.

LOGISTICS

Zion can be extremely hot or cold. Temperatures reach 110 F in summer and drop below freezing in winter. It can rain or snow any time. Water is the main factor for success on a climb. Having no water puts a stop to a climb quickly. In winter or early spring, you may find the rock wet or slippery. There is a sweet spot when the sun is out, the rock is dry, and a few spots of snow remain for making drinking water. There are some climbs for which snow is the only source of water. If you take a stove you can melt snow to make drinking water. These routes can only be climbed in early spring. Winter is usually too cold to be pleasant.

Too much of a good thing can be a bad one. Rain and snow lead to pools of water in canyons, pools which must be avoided unless you have a wet suit and are prepared to go swimming. Some of the routes in this book require crossing or descending canyons. This book is not a guidebook for and does not include information on the equipment and techniques required for entering, crossing, or descending canyons. If a route in this book enters or crosses a canyon, I would normally do it in the summer, and watch the weather for a window of five days with no rain. For some climbs, I waited until it had rained two or three days *prior* to starting my trip, so that I could expect to find pools to fill my water bottles, but not so much I'd have to swim.

There are places the rock holds water for weeks after it rains. In most places, however, the creek beds are sandy, and water soaks up and disappears within two or three days after a rain. You may find animal tracks at dry pools from critters that came to drink the last of the water you expected to find.

You get the idea. The optimal season depends. The optimal season to climb depends on where the climb is, how you will get to it, how long it will take to climb, and how you're getting back to civilization.

Bring a rain jacket. Afternoon thunderstorms are possible regardless of the forecast. The nature of the canyons and peaks make Zion a windy place. It can be uncomfortable without one. On alpine routes, those you expect to move fast and don't think you will need to spend the night - take a bivy bag or a space blanket (See Dangerous Dan Tips). The water in some areas contains clay and sediment that will clog a water filter after a few pumps. I carry water treatment tablets.

WHERE TO STAY

Expect the campgrounds to be full. Reservations are recommended for either hotels or campgrounds. If you don't make a reservation before you go, don't expect to be able to camp or stay in Springdale, the town next to Zion National Park.

It's difficult to stealth camp in Zion or Springdale. It's a small park with limited space. Like Yosemite, it's best to drive out of the park for the night if you need to camp. To the east is Kanab. To get there requires driving up switchbacks and waiting in line to go through a big tunnel. Except in dead winter when the park is quiet, it can be a long and frustrating wait at the entrance to the tunnel. I prefer going in the opposite direction, to the town of Hurricane. There's a four-lane, 60 MPH highway between Springdale and Hurricane. There are more hotels in Hurricane and St George, and more opportunities for camping.

GETTING TO THE CLIMBS

Because so many visit Zion National Park, there's not enough parking and blacktop for everyone's cars. The solution is a shuttle. There is a large parking lot at the Visitor Center, from which a shuttle transports people into the main canyon. The shuttle hours vary depending on the time of year. The hours and dates it operates change each year. In the summer, the shuttle starts as it gets light, reasonable for those wanting an early start. Be the first in line.

For some climbs you want to get an earlier start than the shuttle. The solution is to ride your bike. For some of the climbs in this book, I started at 1am or 2am, and rode my bicycle to the trail head. When I was finished with my climb, I was often too tired to ride my bike and took the shuttle back to town. Then I took the shuttle to get my bike. Since 2020 it's been legal to use motor-assisted bicycles. As that becomes popular, the road may get crowded. Fortunately, except for a few deer who have been up all night eating grass next to the road, few are out riding at the twilight hour you need to start.

SURVIVING HOT WEATHER

Weather is not a factor. I learned that in the Alps, sitting at a table in a hut in the middle of nowhere, preparing to go stir crazy. It was going to be several days before the weather cleared. The climbers sitting at the table next to me were preparing to go outside and climb. "You're going out in that?" I asked.

Without pausing, they replied, "Weather is not a factor." They said it as if it's that simple. Inspired, I vowed never to let weather stop me from climbing again. Ron and I did the first ascents of the Altar of Sacrifice and the big traverses when it was snowing or raining. The following are tips for climbing in hot weather:

Pack a speedo. I pack a bathing suit. I hike the trail wearing it, then change into a thick shirt and long pants before starting to climb.

Hike the approach in the dark. Hike at night when it is cooler. Plan your trip for when there is a full moon so you can see where you are going without a headlamp. It's easier to see the surrounding terrain when a headlamp is off.

Go slow. Take your time and don't get too hot. If you find yourself exerted, stop. Consider that when you stop, your body will stay at the temperature it is at for some time. When you find pools of water, bathe. That's what the swim suit is for. When I did the first ascent of Gregory Butte, the temperatures were in the 90s F. It was July, and I was out there for six days. I moved slower than a turtle. I took long breaks whenever I found shade, as I inched my way towards the mountain, taking mini-naps under each bush I came to.

Keep your feet dry. Take your boots off frequently to allow socks and feet to dry. This helps prevent blisters.

Wind is your friend. If you're lucky it will be windy. Up to 25 MPH wind is comfortable. 90 F heat with 25 MPH wind feels like 80 F. A wind advisory in the summer is your best friend. I have a string tied to my hat so sudden gusts of wind doesn't blow it away.

Drink. When you find water, rest while drinking all the water your stomach can hold. Re-fill your bottle before you leave the pool. Don't over eat.

When in doubt, turn around. On my first attempt to put a route up Death Point, is was only 85 F and I thought I could handle the heat. After I got to the climb (a ten-mile journey that required going up and down several canyons), I got the vibe something wasn't right. I turned around.

Carry water treatment tablets. I prefer treating water with tablets and not relying on a filter. The water in some areas contains clay and sediment. If a filter clogs, it's useless. I have drank untreated water when my filter clogged and I didn't have tablets, in a remote location where there was no livestock (no history of pooping). I recalled an experience I had with a solider in the United States Army, whose job is teaching survival skills to the troops. We had gotten separated on a big climb, on a big mountain. We had been successful climbing the mountain, and were on our way down when we got separated. At the bottom, I waited for him (it's best not to have two people looking for each other at the same time). I hadn't had anything to drink most of the day, when he found me, at midnight, sitting and waiting. He asked me why I had not drank water from a lake that was nearby. "Would that have been OK?" I said. "What if I got giardia (a parasite)?"

He laughed. "Hell yes it would have been OK! We can treat you for giardia. But if you can't walk because you're dehydrated, there's not much I can do for you."

Never drink water from the Virgin River, the river that runs from the Narrows through the town of Springdale. Never drink water from the creek in Hop Valley. It is most certainly contaminated from livestock grazing there.

On alpine routes and traverses, I cut off a piece of foam pad just big enough for my butt to sit.

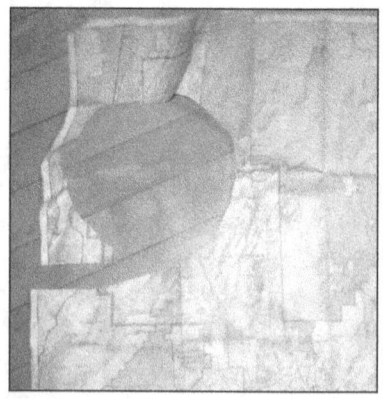

I once cut a portion of the map out so that I didn't have to carry the whole thing.

EXERCISE TO ELIMINATE EXCESS

Some kid's school backpacks are bigger than what you need to climb some of the peaks in this book. If you have a big pack, you will carry more. The weight will slow you down and make climbing more difficult. Try to go light.

One issue with taking less is that there will be nothing in your pack except gear that is critical for success. If you forget one important item you're in trouble. Therefore, I make lists. I'm confident if it's not on the list, I don't need it. After your next climbing trip, unpack your pack and take inventory. Make a list of what was in it. I have different types of lists: a list for one-day climbs, a list for climbs that take several, and lists for inclement weather, hot and cold. I keep boxes of gear sorted by the lists and potential type of adventure. I have crampons and gators in a cold box; a nylon bathing suit in the hot box. As I pack to get ready, I ruffle though the boxes to see if there's something I might take that's not on a list, especially if the weather has changed.

Carrying gear out after success on the Inclined Temple.

For this exercise, it would be interesting to see what you didn't need and might consider not bringing next time. Maybe you want to add something you didn't take that you wish you had. Maybe it's pepto-bismo for an upset stomach. That was in my box for some time. I carry just one pole, the lightest sold. REI said it was too light for what I do. I still have it. I use it not so much for the knees, as for balance when scrambling up steep terrain.

DANGEROUS DAN TIPS

I don't recall who coined my nickname, Dangerous Dan. It may have been while climbing at Mt Lemon in Tucson, when I was in college in Arizona. I was strong and could climb well, but not yet proficient at placing gear for protection. I had gotten strong by reading what John Bacher (a famous free-solo climber active in the 1980s and 90s) said about training. Bacher said if you could do ten sets of ten finger-tips pull-ups, you were ready to climb hard things. While I was held up in my apartment, studying to be an engineer, I took breaks to do finger-tip pull ups off the door trim over my bedroom closet.

Many times I'd hike out to the bottom of a climb with more experienced climbers. If a climb was minimally protected, we'd stand around at the bottom

Moonlight Buttress.

looking at a route, wondering if we should climb it. It came to be that if my mentors didn't want to go first, they would ask me if I wanted to. Without hesitating I said, "Yes." I assumed they would not have asked if it was unsafe. Sometimes the little gear I put in fell out as the rope dragged past it.

The first climber that gets to the top sets an anchor so he or she doesn't get pulled off the top as the next person climbs up. He or she pulls up the slack in the rope as the second person climbs. The person at the top is supposed to hold the rope tight if the climber follower falls. Some of the gear I placed to prevent myself from being pulled over the edge fell out or become loose. At the top of one climb, I tied the rope from me to a tree. I thought the tree was good until a fellow climber reached me at the top, grabbed the rope, yanked hard, and the tree branch snapped.

I learned from these experiences, and consider myself fortunate to have climbed with people who yelled at me for making mistakes and explained how to do things safer. I learned how to transform something dangerous into something safe. Today those who climb with me can't understand the moniker. They say I'm one of the safest climbers they know. As Donovan passed on chord progressions and a style of finger-picking on to John Lennon, I'm passing these tips on to you:

Tip #1: Don't fall. There are a lot of things that can go wrong. The gear you have may not fit inside a crack securely; the rock may be rotten; the direction gear is pulled when you fall may cause it to be pulled out. This is why Dangerous Dan has the rule:, never fall. If you don't fall, you don't have to worry about protection failing.

Tip #2: Don't hang on your gear. The protection you place should only be used if you fall. Never hang on gear unless you absolutely must. This includes at belays. Anchor yourself to the anchor; do not attach the device you use to belay, directly to the anchor. (Don't load the anchor as you belay). Aid climbing is the exception.

I was 100 feet from the top on a multi-pitch free-climb, when I stopped to rest. Sport climbers were climbing single-pitch routes on the bottom and rappelling back to the ground. I was climbing high above, out of sight, taking my time and being careful. My partner saw that I was getting tired, and yelled for me to rest by hanging on a cam I had just placed under a roof. I didn't want to hang on it. My partner began to freak out. He kept yelling at me to rest. I gave in. I had him pull the rope tight, as I gently put my weight on the cam. For a moment things were fine. Then kaboom! The of my weight on the cam caused a huge chunk of rock to break loose, sending me and the rock free-falling. In slow motion I watched myself falling. I was bear hugging the piece of rock, afraid to let go. It must have weighed 1,000 pounds. I knew I needed to separate from it before I stopped falling or it would crush my fingers when the rope came tight and we slammed into the mountain together.

A Space Blanket.

Tip #3: Don't stand at the bottom.
The people at the bottom were not as fortunate A climber was taking a break, eating lunch, his back against the wall. Rock fall seriously hurt him. A rescue was initiated to carry him out. Unless you are belaying, don't sit, stand, or hang out at the bottom. If you are belaying, wear a helmet, and stand tall so the chances of rock hitting you are lessened.

Tip #4: Take a space blanket. I've been stuck overnight on a mountain without a sleeping bag more times than I can count. Bill Paul gave me this advice. I wish I had taken it earlier and more often. A space blanket is a tiny, shinny, silver package that looks like a pack of kleenex. It weighs nothing and folds out into a silver tarp. You can wrap yourself in it. It reflects body heat. If the weather looks good and you are attempting a long route and not taking a sleeping bag, take a space blanket just in case it takes longer than you expect and you are forced to bivy.

Tip #5: Install two daisy chains on your harness. Permanently attach two daisy chains to your harness. Girth-hitch them to your harness. That way you can not accidentally unclip them from your harness. Use the daisy chains to clip into belay and rappel anchors by two points. Don't clip the daisy chains into the same piece of gear or bolt. Clip each chain into a different part of the anchor. That way, if you or your partner accidentally unclips one of your daisy chains, you will still be clipped into the anchor by the other.

Tip #6: Always stayed tied into the rope. Until you are at the top, stay tied in to the rope. This way, if you screw something up, as long as you and your partner are both tied into the rope, there's a good chance something or someone will catch you before you hit the ground.

Tip #7: Drink as much water as you can, the night before. It takes time to hydrate. Don't wait until you are thirsty. Twenty-four hours before you leave for a trip, cut coffee and soda, and start drinking as much water as you can. Don't chug in one sitting. Drink every 15 minutes for several hours. If you start a trip fully hydrated, you can expect to do well for at least a day or two, even if you can't find water.

Tip #8: Sing a song. Brandon Thomson taught me this. We were doing a difficult climb, one harder than either of us had done. It was a trad climb, meaning we had to place gear. There were no bolts. I was still learning. As I was preparing to start, I heard Brandon singing.

"What's that you are singing" I asked, knowing the answer.

"Jingle Bells."

He explained he chose to sing something silly to make him think of something other than the scary climb.

Tip #9: Get lost. This book is full of stories that would not have occurred if I not gotten lost. It seemed getting lost was imperative to me having an adventure. Perhaps I wasn't as lost as I thought. Maybe I just wanted to find unclimbed peaks, and following a map would have made me think everything had been climbed.

Turn your phone off. Leave tracking devices in your pack. If you worry about not being connected, understand that these days you are rarely alone. Consider what people used to do when they needed assistance - they found someone and asked for help. Sometimes they find you. My experience with Ben the Deer Sniffer (See Ivins Mountain) comes to mind. That's when the excitement of living begins. When the adventure is over, you wish you could hit rewind, erase memory of it, start over, and experience it for the first time.

Tip #10 Ask permission from the Guardians. If you don't receive it, turn around. If you receive it, give thanks and proceed. Right before I fell and broke my hip, I had told my partner that we'd picked up trash, have the best guardian angels, and nothing could go wrong. Six months later, still healing, a wise man I was telling my woes to offered me this advice:

"You were doing everything good, including picking up the trash. But that doesn't matter. It's how you connect with your heart. Your real energy is your divine connection, which is beyond ego. To say, 'I did good, therefore, I should be able to go,' is not going to work. You don't ask to pass safely because you don't litter. That's a prerequisite. You get to pass because you respect the power. Don't take it for granted. Don't make assumptions. Be grateful. Know who you are: a part of something bigger than you."

I didn't understand. Then I remembered - I had failed to recognize, had forgotten to ask for safe passage.

"The Guardians," he continued, "They guard the balance between light and dark. There are Landscape Angels. They are big. They are wonderful. We're surrounded by them. The mountains have them. They are anchoring the light, and part of the invisible hierarchy of how nature operates. There are also Black Shamans, thousands of years old, who are guardians. Maybe it's for you and others to discover: not the climbing routes, not the mountains, but your spirituality. Who you are. What you are."

After taking it in I asked, How should I tell people about this? "Is it OK to write my guidebook?"

"You'll have to learn about it. Go deep into your thoughts. Walk the paths in your imagination, and start to see what you did. Because you've been communicating with it all along. When you force your will as a climber, intent on going to these places and climbing these mountains, you will run into this. We have to be humble. You're in an interesting trajectory. Your soul school that you've created or are part of is good. But now you've been slowed down."

Attempting to free-climb the Beehive Wall.

"Why was I slowed down?"

"You made relationship with the Guardians, you made relationship with the mountains and with nature. However, there's something you didn't pay attention to in the same way. There was a moment when your will took over. My advice is wake up to the moment and stop trying, stop wooing yourself, to do something. For whom? To do something no man has done? Let go of that. One of the great mysteries is our own connection with all life, the source of creation, and why are we here. What are we here for. What are we here to share."

"So when I get better... is it OK if I go back and climb again?"

"Yes. Because you're a practitioner of sort. But now you know the danger."

Angles Landing, home of the infamous climbing route, Prodigal Sun. Above it, the white cap is Cathedral Mountain. My aid route on it, Iron Curtain, ascends its left skyline where the gray meets white.

We are Learning

The First Climbs I did in Zion and How I Learned to Aid Climb and Pack Light

PRODIGAL SUN

The first climb I did in Zion was Prodigal Sun. The name comes from the climb being in the shade most of the day. It was September, 1993. There was not yet a guide book or information about climbing on the internet. To get information about the climbs, one had to drive to Zion, go into the Visitor Center, and look at hand-draw sketches previous climbers had left. There were no photographs to accompany the drawings. After you left the Visitor Center, it took time and patience to find the routes, as you drove up and down the canyon road, armed with your hand-written copies.

A month earlier, I had meet Vince, my partner for Prodigal Sun, when I was in Yosemite. He was on his way back to Colorado, and like myself, had never climbed in Zion. We made plans to climb Prodigal Sun together. Vince stopped in Zion on his way home and did the legwork. He spent time in the Visitor Center and drove around the park to make sense of where the climbs were. When I arrived, he was familiar with the climbs and how to get to them. When I arrived, I was tired from driving. Instead of starting to climb, Vince played tour guide and took me to wade in the Narrows. I realized my shoes were not the best for climbing. I was always trying to save money, waiting to buy gear until past the time I needed it. After wading through the Narrows, we took half a day to shop for shoes. There were no stores in Springdale, the town next to the park. We drove an hour before considering there might not be a shoe store within one-hundred miles, and drove back to do our climb.

> Take your time and enjoy the space. Don't try to climb it as fast as you can. Allow faster people to pass. Really fast parties should have patience or consider doing a harder route, and leave this one for those doing their first wall.

The bottom of the Prodigal Sun is a stone's throw from the parking lot, except for a river. You have to cross a cold, swift river. It's a one-way street. When you get to the top, you can walk down the other side on a trail used by those hiking to the top of Angels Landing.

The Narrows, a popular, most-do.

We were pretty slow. On our first day, we fixed a rope to the anchor at the top of the first pitch, left it hanging on the mountain, and went to the campgrounds to sleep. At the end of our second day, Vince and I slept in our home made "portaledges" on the side of the mountain. The third night, we almost made it to the top, but didn't make it there before it got dark. We stopped at a spot called the Emergency Bivy. It was Vince's idea. He was always the smart one. In the morning when we able to see where we were supposed to go, and scrambled sideways, where we ran into the hiking trail at the top of Angels Landing.

Understanding that the rock in Zion can be loose, I rented a Roller Blade helmet from a skating rink.

A[...] [...]ace
Prodi[...]

First Ascent; [...]y, solo 9/81

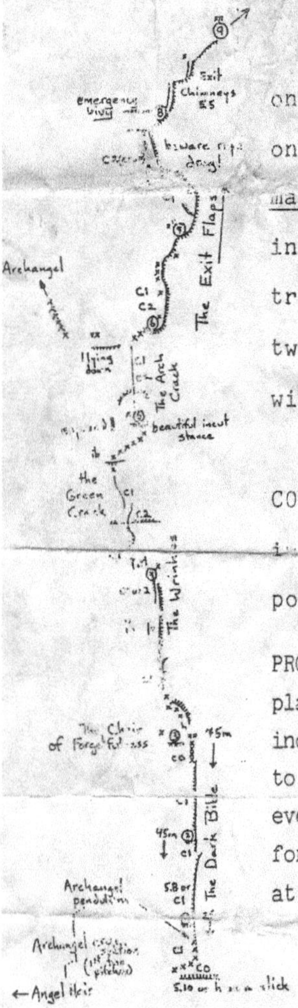

-Equipment- (Zion's lightest wall rack!)
one #6 tricam   one ⬨ hook   one tie-off loop
one each #½, [#1], #1½, #2, #2½, #3½ friend
many small n[uts] [...] up to 3cm- [th]at's about 1¼"-
including at least one set of ⬨ stoppers for
transverse taper placements)
two each ¼", 3/8" keyhole hangers (can substitute
wire hangers or [t]hinnest wire nuts with sliding heads
            -abbreviations-
C0 = fixed A1   C1 = clean A1   C2 = awkward or
insecure clean [...]   ib = intermediate belay
potential   Look!

PRODIGAL SUN is a clean aid route. There is a bomber nut
placement or a good fixed pin every 2 meters. C2 only
indicates awkward or insecure placements. Using a hammer
to "test" fixed pins only loosens otherwise good (and
even glued!) useful anchor points. Show some sensitivity
for the fragility of sandstone climbing, leave your hammer
at home and lighten your pack on the descent trail.

↑
Ball + Chain

8 AID PITCHES   PROBABLY GRADE Ⅵ
1 FREE PITC[H]   AT A MODERATE PACE

Topo annotations (left margin, top to bottom):
- emergency bivi
- Exit Chimneys 5.5
- beware rope drag!
- The Exit Flakes
- Archangel
- C1, C2
- The Arch Crack
- beautiful incut stance
- the Green Crack, C1, C2
- T.M.
- C1, C2
- The Wrinkles
- The Chair of Forgetfulness, C0, 45m
- 45m, C1
- 5.8 or C1, The Dark Bible
- Archangel pendulum
- Archangel aid option (1½" pitons)
- ← Angel Hair
- C1, C0, 5.10 or hook a slick

Vince, leading a pitch, high on the route.

Bivy on Prodigal Sun in my homemade portaledge. It cost $30 to build; Opposite page: the original topo for Prodigal Sun by Ron Olevesky.

SPACE SHOT

Space Shot was the next climb I did in Zion. At that time it was cloaked in mystery. It was hard to tell where it was. My friend Bill knew. He seemed to know everything. It was Halloween, 1993. We parked my truck on the side of the road, got out, and finished packing our gear. I heard it before I saw it. When I looked I saw a white cloud descending: rock fall, pounding down next to our climb.

We climbed up a few hundred feet to a large ledge where we slept the first night. The hardest part was hauling our bags that contained sleeping gear, food and water. Sleeping on the mountain was awesome. In the morning, Bill went first. He seemed to be doing fine. When he reached the anchor however, he came down and told me his wrist was hurting. His day job was nailing metal lath to stucco houses. He had hurt his wrist falling off scaffolding while swinging a hammer. This was before he became a full-time climbing and rafting guide in Jackson Hole. We went down. I'm glad he told me before we got higher.

Above: an avalanche or rock, falling on the descent for Space Shot. Top right: Bill on Space Shot. Right: Bill tending to his arm in the Grotto parking lot.

MOONLIGHT BUTTRESS

It was a cold Thanksgiving, 1993. Our permit came with a warning about cold weather. Vince seemed to be fine with bad weather. Perhaps it was the pilot in him. The cargo plane he flew had to get through, regardless of weather. A few cold days hanging from a strong, secure rope, didn't seem to scare him.

We parked at Angels Landing. There was plenty of room. No one was climbing. To get to the bottom, we crossed the cold river. It was tricky in bare feet carrying heavy bags. We tried wearing waders like fishermen, considering if we used them, we would have had to carry the wet waders in our packs to the top of the climb. We had only one pair. I went first, and found they weren't high enough to keep water out. The river was deep. On his bare feet, Vince slipped, fell, and reached dry ground just as he tumbled over.

We had two ropes, each two-hundred feet long. This allowed us to do what's called "fixing." We climbed the first day without bringing sleeping gear, and went back to the campground for the night. We left four-hundred feet of rope hanging on the mountain.

I thought it would be warmer in camp. But we didn't have a tent and I did-

Vince, sorting gear at the Big Bend parking lot in front of Angles Landing. Right: cold weather warning on our permit.

not have a warm sleeping bag. I had a cochin I brought from a lounge-chair next to the pool in Phoenix, and a tarp from landscaping. I put the lounge pad on the ground, got into my sleeping bag, and wrapped the tarp around myself like a burrito, trying to cover my head to keep the wind off.

The next day we drove back to Angels Landing, parked, and carried our bags across the river. Using what are called jumars, we went up the fixed ropes to our high point, a ledge 400 feet off the ground. It was a marvelous day. We appeared to be getting high up the wall and making progress, when what happened was a repeat of Space Shot. Having drove from Phoenix, gotten a permit, crossed the river, packed gear, and spent two days climbing, Vince told me the unfortunate news - his wrist hurt. He would not be able to continue. Pulling up on the fixed ropes had tweeted an injury he got playing roller hockey.

We had pleasant night on the wall before going down in the morning, as it started to snow. I slept in the ledge I made. It cost me $30 to build using a cot from Popular Outdoor (a now de-funk outdoor retailer). That made two failures for me in two trips to Zion. Not to worry, a plan was solidifying. I planned to come back and solo Moonlight. With Vince and Bill out of service,

Vince on Moonlight Buttress. Below: Me in my homemade portaledge.

my list of partners was getting short, and I was interested in finding out if I could solo. Mostly I just wanted to climb. The issue was gear. I didn't have enough gear to climb a big wall by myself. That problem solved itself when, without asking, Vince volunteered to loan me his entire rack. A big heart that Vince from Texas has. Even more helpful, he had the latest type of climbing gear, a type of cam called Aliens, made to fit securely in small cracks.

INTERLUDE

Baboquivari Peak, in the desert, southwest of Tucson, is where I leaned to aid climb using pitons. I knew how to aid climb using cams and free-climbing gear. I had climbed the Nose in Yosemite. But I had never pounded a piton. Pitons are pieces of metal a few inches long. They can be placed in rotten and loose rock where nothing else is secure, places nothing else will hold a fall. Being able to place them correctly is a key to doing some of the routes in this book. The person that taught me was Ron. He would become a long-time partner on many first ascents in Zion.

The first climb Ron and I did together was the Spring Route (V A4 5.9). It's one of the few peaks in Arizona that requires technical climbing to get to the summit. The guide book says: "A3 climb a tree in order to reach a crack and nail up for 75 feet." I wondered what "A3 climb a tree" meant. How hard can it be to climb a tree? (A3 means a difficulty of 3 on a scale 1 to 5 when rock climbing. The gear placements for A3 are not obvious and can pull out with body weight.)

I made it from the tree onto the rock, and climbed into a crack. As I climbed higher, I placed cams and nuts for protection, as I would when free-climbing. Then the rock became loose and rotten. As I tried to free-climb the A3 section, I fell.

I got back on the rock and placed another cam. As I put my weight on it, it pulled out, and I fell again. From below, Ron yelled up that I should place a piton. I refused. I thought pitons were damaging to the rock. And I didn't trust them. But did I really think I could free-climb rotten ,A3 rock?

After repeated falls, I took a break, hung on the rope, and listened, as Ron explained how to select the best size and type of piton for a crack. I picked one, placed it in the crack, pounded on it, and voila! It was an amazing feeling, better than sex. I could only imagine the places I could go, the climbs I could do, if I had pitons. But I wasn't yet good at placing them. After climbing ten feet higher I got stuck again. I came down to let Ron try.

Above: Baboquivari Peak; Below: Ron on the first pitch. Notice his hammer (a geologist might own something similar), ice-climbing boots, and foot ladders he made by sewing seat belts from cars together.

Ron didn't get much higher before he declared we could not finish in time to get back to work. We spent the evening at our camp, enjoying the view of Nogales. In the morning we hiked back to the truck, carrying our heavy packs across miles of the trailless, rugged, cactus terrain.

Pinnacle Peak in Scottsdale, Arizona was the next place Ron took me to continue my apprenticeship on aid climbing. On the west side of the main peak is a route called Brown Out, rated A4 on a scale A1-A5. Ron lead the climb first, to show me how it's done. When he got to the top, he came down and left his rope hanging. My first task was to go up the rope and remove the pitons he had placed. That way I could see how he had placed them.

When I got to the top, I came down and pulled the rope. It was my turn to try, baptism by fire. Placing pitons so fragile they will only hold your body

Leading A4 at Pinnacle Peak.

Walking the chain at Pinnacle Peak for balance practice.

weight is time consuming and mental. After you are comfortable you've placed the best piton you can, you stand on it. If it holds your weight, you clip a foot ladder into it, step as high as you can it, and reach for the next place the rock will accept a placement I got up it. Whew!

LEARNING TO PACK LIGHT

Our next outing together was an attempt to climb Mt. Sneffels, in the San Juan mountains in Colorado in the winter. We were planning on climbing the Northwest Couloir, a 45-50 degree ice climb. We drove from Phoenix to Ouray in Ron's two-wheel drive pick. It was late on a Friday. When we got to Durango, we were tired and slept in the back of his truck in a parking lot at a

> This is how we learned to climb without sleeping bags in cold conditions. The lesson was key to our success on several first ascents, including the Traverses of the Towers of the Virgin, and the Traverse of the Court of the Patriarchs.

shopping mall. In the morning we finished the drive, down steep, icy hills, into Telluride, where we stopped to buy sleds. Sleds, Ron explained, are used to pull gear behind you on the approach to base camp.

Telluride was quiet. The streets were empty. We were lucky to find a small hardware store open on main street. It did not have what we were looking for so we settled blow-up rafts, the kind used in swimming pools. We left Telluride and continued toward Ridgeway. The next difficulty was to find the correct road at which to turn off the highway to go to our climb. It was snowing and we could not see the mountain. We drove down a muddy dirt road as far as we could and parked when his pickup became stuck.

Using rope, we rigged a method of pulling the sleds behind us. The sleds were loaded with camping gear that included a tent, sleeping bags, climbing ropes, and so forth. Our plan was to haul the gear to the bottom of the mountain and set up camp. We planned to climb the mountain from a base camp.

We didn't have cross-country skis or the proper bindings. We had stopped in Flagstaff and rented normal skis. They didn't have "skins," a covering placed over the ski tips to provide traction when going up hill. The rafts kept tipping over. I kept sliding down the hills on my skis instead of getting up them. At the end of the day, as we started setting up the tent, Ron realized we forgot matches. We needed the stove to melt snow to drink water.

We skied back to the truck, still stuck in the mud on the side of the road. Back at the truck, we took a break and discussed another strategy. It seemed we were moving too slow. We brainstormed on what we could do to lighten our loads. The first thing that came to mind was to leave the tent. The next thing to go were our sleeping bags. Although it was winter n Colorado, we decided we would sleep in our clothes, inside bivy sacks.

It was still snowing. Following a compass, we proceeded in the direction in which we thought the mountain was. As it got dark, we set up a camp under trees where there was less snow, got into our plastic sacks, and said good night.

I woke in the middle of the night and had trouble feeling my toes. As the night wore on, I became cold everywhere in my body and started to shiver. We decided to get up. We gathered wet firewood. Ron unscrewed the cap to our bottle of white-gas, poured gas onto the wet pile of sticks we gathered, and started a fire. Saved!

MY FIRST SOLO

Moonlight Buttress was my first solo. I was still learning how to self-belay. Belay means to feed out the rope from the anchor. I estimated how difficult the next few feet would be, pulled up a few feet of rope, tied a knot, and clipped the knot to my harness. I took my time and carefully tied clove-hitch knots. If I fell while climbing I would only fall as far as that amount of rope. The difficult part was estimating how much rope to give myself. I didn't want

> **I have tried all the devices made for rope-soloing and self-belaying, and consider clove hitches with two locking carabiners and backup knots to be one of the best (safest and cheapest).**

to give too much. It makes the fall longer. If you don't give yourself enough slack, you may find you are in the middle of a difficult climbing move as the rope comes tight. When that happens, you feel like a dog on a leash, and are unable to move forward.

When climbing by yourself, you tie the rope to the anchor at the start. When you get to the end of it, you set up an a second anchor and tie the rope to it. Now you have a thread of rope between two points. You rappel to the bottom anchor, untie the rope connected to it, then go back up the rope. Back at the top, you pull the rope up and stack it in a pile so that it doesn't get tan-

Bivy on Moonlight Buttress during my solo. Cheap, homemade ledge. Priceless, wonderful experience.

My gear at the top of Moonlight Buttress. I carried it all down myself with a backpack (the purple bag on the left).

gled as you climb higher. And pull up the bag with your food, water, and sleeping gear. It's a lot of work. It can be demoralizing and cause you to think about giving up. It's easy to imagine how quickly you could be down and eating a cheese burger. You have to really want to climb something to be up there.

The weather was perfect. I had a thin nylon jacket in case it rained, one I found in my dad's garage in an old box of stuff. Instead of the type of haul bag climbers normally use, I carried a backpack (I didn't own a haul bag). When I got down I looked so dirty I didn't bother to hitch-hike. I hid the gear in tall grass next to the road, and walked. I had the time of my life.

MY SECOND SOLO

I was inspired by an article by Ron Olevsky in *Rock & Ice* magazine in 1987 and felt I was up to the challenge. I had climbed the bottom pitches of Space Shot with Bill, and was familiar with the route. I had the full rack of climbing gear Vince loaned me. In typical Dangerous Dan style, I dropped out of work at lunch on a Friday, and made the seven hour drive to Zion. My plan was to climb Space Shot on Saturday, in a day, and drive home on Sunday, so I could be back at work on Monday morning. There was the possibility I might not reach the top on Saturday, and have to sleep on the mountain overnight. You are supposed to register if you sleep overnight on a climb.

The first obstacle was the permit office didn't open until 8am. If I was

Bill leading the second pitch, before he came down.

going to have a chance of climbing the mountain in a day, I needed to start at the crack of dawn. If I got a permit, one I wasn't sure I needed, I would not start climbing until 10 am. In that case I'd not only have to sleep on the mountain, I might be stuck in the middle, in a location where sleeping isn't possible without hauling a portaledge. Later, the Park Service would tell me, with a straight face as if it's a no-brainer: Plan your trip better, i.e., arrive a day earlier. Some of us have day jobs that don't allow time to do that.

> The morals of the story are don't call the cops on yourself. They used the note I left at the Visitor Center as evidence. And when in doubt, talk to a ranger in the backcountry office. Ask if a permit is required for the activity you are planning. Make sure you follow all the rules. It's not worth the trouble not to.

I woke at 4am and stopped at the backcountry office on the way to the climb. I left a note under a rock at the front door. It had my name, license plate, where my truck would be parked, and what I was climbing. Although a permit is not required for day climbs, I thought it might be a good idea to let them know where I was climbing.

Things were going smooth until I climbed past where Bill and I had come down. Without Bill as a guide book, I took a wrong turn. There came a place where the crack split into two. I wasn't sure if I should climb the left crack or right crack. I choose left. At first things were not difficult, and I assumed I must be going the correct way. Hard is relative. I was strong and had just soloed Moonlight Buttress. As it became more difficult, I started thinking perhaps I was not as good a climber as I thought. Finally, I got higher up, craning my neck to see where the crack was leading, I realized I must have gone the wrong way.

Back at the belay, looking up at a pitch I had just lead on Space Shot, unaware that I was going the wrong way.

It was hot and sunny and I was roasting in the sun, exposed on the hot, desert rock. If I had a climbing partner, he or she would have lowered me, and I could I have easily swung over to the correct crack. Climbing by myself, there was no one to lower me. You learn by mistakes. I was learning a lot because I was making a lot of mistakes. As I was wondering how I was going to get back on the correct route, I looked down and saw someone standing next to my truck, looking inside it. It was a ranger giving me a ticket. It was 4 pm and still daylight.

It was midnight when I reached Earth Orbit Ledge, a ledge near the top, big enough for one person to lay on. I did not have a sleeping bag, was long out of water, and had no food. I laid down, closed my eyes and feel asleep. In the morning I climbed the last 100 feet to the top, then rappelled and down-climbed to my truck, parked next to the road at the bottom. The ticket didn't specify a fine. It said, "Mandatory appearance required."

I called the ranger and explained what had happened. He understood and apologized, but said there was nothing he could do since the ticket had already been issued.

HOW DO YOU PLEAD?

The summons came postal mail. I was required to see the Magistrate in Cedar City, Utah. It was the summer. I drove through Zion on the way but it was too hot to climb. I wasn't sure on how to approach the procedural part of a court appearance. Before I left I had called a few semi-famous climbers who had spent time in Zion and asked them for advice: Ron Olevsky and John Middendorf.

Olevsky was ecstatic. He didn't offer legal advice but he said he would be present as a witness in regard to the permit system. Ron had been an expert witness in a law suit brought against the Park Service regarding the deaths of a group of Boy Scouts. The Scouts were given a permit to hike down the Narrows, a slot canyon. They didn't need a permit to hike it - they needed it to camp. The park service gave them one. It rained, a flash flood occurred, and their leader and a few of the kids perished in a horrific way. Ron argued that by giving them a permit, the Park Service had implied that it was safe. His believes it should not be mandatory to appear before a Park representative to obtain a permit, but rather there should be a voluntary registration system,(if any at all), similar what's done in Yosemite.

True to his word, Ron was waiting for me on the steps to the court house. He was wearing a shirt and jacket. He cleans up good. The judge was not there. The doors to the court building were locked. No one was inside. I thanked Ron and drove back to Phoenix.

Back in Phoenix, I received a second letter in the mail from the court. It notified me that court had been postponed. It had the official seal from the judge and copies had been physically mailed to the prosecuting attorney, park service, and the others involved. It seemed a waste of taxpayer time and money.

I hereby acknowledge and certify that I have been advised of and that I understand the following facts and rights, and that I have had the assistance of counsel in reviewing, explaining and completing this form:

1. The nature of the charges against me have been explained. I have had an opportunity to discuss the nature of the charges with my attorney, and I understand the charges and the elements which the Government is required to prove.

2. I know that the maximum possible penalty provided by law for a violation of 36 C.F.R. §§ 2.10(b)(8) [FAILURE TO OBTAIN A (CLIMBING) PERMIT], as alleged in above referenced Notice of Violation is: SIX (6) MONTHS IMPRISONMENT; FIVE THOUSAND DOLLAR ($5,000.00) FINE; OR BOTH.

I know that if I am convicted of more than one count, the penalties may be concurrent or consecutive, and I have discussed that with my attorney.

I understand that a term of probation may be added to any prison sentence imposed on the Notice of Violation; that if the probation term is violated, I can be returned to prison for the remainder of my sentence.

I drove back to Cedar City the day court was rescheduled, another hot, summer day. This time, the judge was there.

The only other people present were two kids in trouble for skateboarding. The judge began by explaining that he could find us guilty and sentence us to a maximum of six months in jail and a $5,000 fine. This, it turns out, is the standard penalty for violating the general law (CFR regulation) the Park service uses when issuing any type of citation. I felt a surge of concern. Surely this was a mistake.

"Who wants to go first?" the judge said.

Neither me nor the two kids spoke.

"Mr. Stih," the judge said, "You have driven a long way. Why don't you go first. How do you plead?"

I didn't know what to say and began by stuttering. "Well you see your honor..."

The judge interrupted me. "At this time you must plead guilty or not guilty."

I thought if the judge understood he would dismiss my ticket or let me pay a fine, something more reasonable than sending me to jail. I began again, "I was still climbing when it got dark..."

The judge interrupted me again. "How do you plead?"

"Your Honor, I would like to explain. I didn't plan on sleeping on the mountain. I got off route, lost and..."

"At this time you must state how you plead. You must first tell me how you plead."

I fought for words, something that might trigger leniency. Before I could open my mouth to speak again, the judge, trying to be helpful, said, "I suggest you get a lawyer. I can recommend one for you. If you like, we can reschedule this hearing until after you have had time to speak to a lawyer."

"Yes," I said with gratitude. "I would like that."

The judge excused me. As I was leaving the courtroom the expressions on the kid's faces where of awe and fear. I don't think they could afford a lawyer. I'm sure they were found guilty.

Back home, I called another famous climber, John Middendorf. I wanted a shoulder to cry on, someone who might understand my position, and maybe had experience with this sort of thing. Like Olevsky, John lived in Hurricane, a small town near Zion National Park. His company, A5, was making outstanding technical gear for climbers at their headquarters in Flagstaff, Arizona. He gave me the name of his business attorney in Arizona.

I called her. She said she was licensed in Arizona and could not represent me in Utah. Having no one else to call, I called the lawyer the judge had recommended. He lived in the same town as the judge. Sound fishy? What else could I do. I drove to Cedar City to meet my attorney and to explain the facts.

My lawyer suggested I plead guilty and ask for a reduced sentence. That sounded insane. As part of the plea deal he said would request the park service adapt a voluntary registration system. That sounded great. I accepted. I drove back to Phoenix and waited for my next appearance.

Back in Arizona, I received a letter in the mail stating the new court date. I called my attorney. He didn't answer. Back then, we didn't have email or cell phones. I left a message for him to please call me to confirm the date. My attorney did not call back. I didn't want to drive back to Utah without confirmation. It was 110F, a ten-hour drive each way, and my truck was prone to

On Touchstone.

over-heating. When the day came, I didn't go.

My lawyer called me later that day and reprimanded me for being a no-show. He said he told the judge I must have had car trouble and that he saved me by negotiating a plea deal. All I had to do was pay a $500 fine and pay him $1,000. The park service did not instate a volunteer registration system.

TOUCHSTONE

Touchstone was the first wall in Zion that Ron and I climbed together. Being one of the easier routes in Zion, Touchstone can be crowded. There were two climbers in front of us. It may have been their first big climb. To their credit, they were having fun and not worried about how long it was taking. Two-hundred feet off the ground, we caught up to them. I decided to go down and wait on the ground. I rappelled, and left Ron on a ledge to wait for the climbers to get higher. I walked back to my truck, parked at Angels Landing and ate lunch. In the parking lot, I ran into Brad Jarrett. This was before he was famous as an ice climber in the yet to be invented X Games. Brad had a van and was hanging out inside it, eating lunch. He had just come down from a route on Angels Landing called The Swiss-American route. As we were chatting Ron came down and met us.

Ron and I decided to go back in the morning and climb it in a day. One of the hardest parts of climbing is getting up early when it's dark and cold. It was dark as we went up the ropes we had left hanging on the rock the previous day. The climbers that had been in front of us had bailed, gone down, and gone home. I don't know if they got scared, found the climbing too difficult, or had to be back at work. One thing is certain: They had fun while it lasted.

Left: the party we caught up with; Above: me on the last pitches of Touchstone, 5.9 free climbing. Can't beat the view. A fun climb with spectacular exposure.

In the late afternoon, it rained as Ron and I reached the top. I didn't have a rain jacket. Late summer is pretty mild in Zion. In desert fashion, the rain came hard and fast, then passed as quickly, leaving clear and beautiful skies. Water falls appeared out of nowhere. It was an awesome experience.

DAYS OF FUTURE

Days of No Future was the next climb Ron and I did in Zion. I was still learning to place pitons, and wearing goggles in case a piton came loose, flew out of the crack, and hit me in the eyes. I smiled because I couldn't believe the gear I was placed held my weight. We didn't get far for the usual reason - we ran out of time. We had to be back at work. The first hundred feet took us half a day, including time getting across the river and bush whacking to the bottom.

Ron looking for lines with his telescope.

Touchstone climbs the red rock at the top of the section of red dirt at Big Bend.

There was no guidebook. I think we started up the wrong climb. The important thing was I was smiling, having a good time, and didn't get hurt.

Ron preferred to spend time looking for new routes. He was better at spotting new lines than I. He would often got excited and call me to look at a "line" he found. When I looked through the telescope I didn't get it. "Where?" I asked. In my mind I didn't see something I could get my hands and feet into. Ron's telescope saw improbable cracks the width of a fingernail, ones he could *aid*.

One such line was on Angels Landing. I looked at it through the telescope and thought, why? To me the possible route seemed contrived. There were already a dozen routes on Angels Landing. *Why climb something new between two existing routes just to say you put up a new route.* We passed on it. Someone has since climbed it.

Another example of a route we passed on is located road side north of the

Weeping Rock pullout. It seemed logical and obvious and didn't look like it would need bolts. Ron feared a loose rock might bounce and land on a car passing by. Two years later someone decided it was worth the risk. Today the line is in the guidebook and popular.

THE LOWE ROUTE

In January, 1994, our British friend, Steve came to visit. It was Steve's first trip to America. He flew to New York, then took the train to meet me at my house in Tempe, Arizona. Being from Europe, he was used to taking trains. He didn't understand why I was surprised that he choose to take the train instead of flying. He said he enjoyed seeing everything.

I was renting a house on Mill Avenue, a popular destination for locals, tourists, and students at the nearby university. Steve and I walked from my house to get breakfast and sight-see. Ron had to work. I did too. After breakfast, I explained to Steve that I needed to make an "appearance" before we left to go climbing. He laughed and said, "Dan the company butt-Lick man."

I left Steve and went to work. All I needed to do to save face, to save taking vacation, was to walk slowly and deliberately down the isles in the office. I did this during prime time, when everyone was at their desk. I got there at 10 am, sat at my desk for thirty minutes, then created a tense, urgent energy, as if there was pressing business I was working on. We didn't have email yet. Inter-office correspondence was by paper mail. If you were on your computer, you were working. After furiously, fake-typing and looking at the screen on my computer, I switched to other fake work activities. The desks in our cubicles had a few file-cabinet drawers. I ruffled through them, removed items those watching might find interesting. Then, while making sure someone was watching, I put it all back, slammed the drawers shut, got up, and walked out. I had someplace urgent to be: my backyard, sorting climbing gear with Steve.

My house was an old, flat-roof duplex, in the backyard of my landlady's house. I parked in the alley, walked through the gate into the backyard, and stepped to my front door where there was a small brick patio with a table and two chairs. I found Steve sitting there, in the cool shade under a tree, reading a book. Steve wasn't shy about making himself at home. He had left home at an early age and wandered though Europe. He had an incredibly positive attitude and developed a skill for making the best of the moment, wherever he might be.

"Dan!" He said, with a big smile. He proceeded to tell me about his day. After I had left, he took a stroll down the avenue, shopping and making friends. With his worry-less smile and welcoming heart, he was like crocodile dundee, staying open to what came to him, whomever he met. He told me about places and things in my neighborhood I'd barely knew about.

Free-climbing the bottom pitches of the Lowe Route.

It was Thursday. The plan was to drive to Zion that evening and start climbing Friday morning. We would sleep on a large ledge, four rope lengths off the ground, and leave ropes hanging as we climbed, like a trail of breadcrumbs. Ron was going to drive up Friday night when he got off work, and join us.

Steve and I drove to Zion that night. In the morning, we got a climbing permit, parked at Angels Landing, crossed the river, and started climbing. We carried hundreds of feet of rope, sleeping bags, and rain gear. At the end of the day, we were snug as two bugs on a 10 x 8 ledge, 600 feet off the ground. It was January. We'd went from wearing shorts in Phoenix to thermal underwear and were in our sleeping bags at 8 p.m. Rain and snow were forecast. I outfitted Steve with a plastic bag to sleep. It wasn't breathable, but it would keep him dry. He came to love his plastic, orange shelter.

I was expecting Ron to meet us in the morning. Instead, at midnight, Steve and I were awakened, as Ron pulled himself flopped onto the ledge. I'm not sure how he found a place to cross the river and our ropes in the dark. Nothing seemed to scare Ron. He was carrying a heavy bag that contained his personal climbing gear, sleeping bag, and food.

I acknowledged Ron, then pulled the covers over my head and went back to sleep. I was expecting Ron would go to sleep too. It was cold.

"Put it out! Put it out!" Steve screamed.

What? I woke, poked my head out of my sleeping bag, and turned to see what the commotion was about. Ron was cooking dinner. Our gas stove needed to be primed. As Ron lite the stove, a ball of fire had shot into the air. Our ropes and gear were inches from being incinerated. There was nothing I

could do but watch. Steve seemed to be supervising so I laid my head down and went back to sleep. A deep sleep. I had a dream. I was climbing the Eiger... rock was falling...ouch! That hurt. I heard kaboom! I felt a thud on my head. What the....

I woke and came to understand. After eating dinner, Ron had started climbing. He thought he would get a head start for the morning. As he was climbing, he had fallen. His fall was caught by a piece of gear called a "nut", a wedge of metal he placed in the crack with a wire loop. After placing the nut, Ron had clipped his foot ladder into it to verify it would hold his weight. It did. So he stood on it. The nut placement was good. The rock was not. The pressure exerted by the force caused a large block of rock to break loose. The rock fell. So did Ron. He was 100 feet above us. As the rock fell, it bounced off the wall and broke into smaller pieces. One of the pieces hit Steve on his head. Fortunately, Steve had been smart enough to sleep with his helmet over his face. Ron came down and went to bed.

In the morning, we regrouped. The issue was not Ron's cooking or nut placements - it was time and weather. It had started to snow. I was not deterred. We had warm clothing. Snow is better than rain. Rain soaks, making it mushy and unsafe; Snow bounces off rock and can be brushed off where it sticks. I was sure we'd be fine.

Ron was not as sure. He decided it best if we went down. I looked at Steve for support. He agreed with Ron. I was out-voted.

"You can solo it." Ron suggested to me. "We'll leave you all the gear."

I thought about it.

"I guess that means you will give Steve a ride home, and when I get to the top, I'll carry everything down and drive home by myself." I was being sarcastic. "Come on! You guys!" I cried. "It's just a little snow," I challenged them in

a playful manner.

"We're going down," Ron announced, his mind made up.

I looked at Steve, non-verbally, to ask him to stay. It was no use. Steve seemed trust Ron more than I. Or he wasn't having fun. Steve is all smiles, no fear. The Brit in him doesn't back off easily. If Steve decides not to do something, it's because he's not having fun, not because he's scared. I knew there was no point arguing with them.

"That's OK," I said, "I'll go down with you guys."

We packed up the gear, rappelled to the ground, crossed the river, and walked back to our cars. Just as we reached the parking lot, the storm cleared, the sun came out, and the sky turned clear blue.

THE SEARCH FOR SOMETHING NEW

The next thing Ron and I tried to climb in Zion was something that had not been climbed. We named it the "Beehive Wall," a blank, smooth face below the south face of Meridian Tower. It was no picnic getting to the bottom. It was a struggle until we found a weakness in the cliffs that surround it, and scrambled up loose rock, past a water fall, wearing haul bags that weighed 80 pounds.

Ron had looked at the mountain with the telescope from the road, and there appeared to be a small crack that ran from top to bottom. Up close the crack was a groove the size of a finger nail, worn into the rock by water dripping. It appeared there might be a crack higher up. The bottom appeared blank.

To keep me from falling, and dragging Ron, to whom the rope was connected, down the mountain, Ron drilled a bolt at the start. He used his framing hammer. He preferred to use a heavier, bigger hammer than what climbers normally carry. After drilling it, he tied himself to it. I tied into the rope, clipped the rope into the bolt, and I began to "free-climb".

It was difficult. I only got twenty feet. To continue, I would have needed to place another bolt to keep me from hitting the ground. It seemed bad style to begin a climb by placing two bolts. My philosophy is if you can't do it without bolting, go home. Save it for someone else. The route still has not been

Jugging on the Lowe Route from our bivy up fixed lines to get a head start in the morning.

climbed. If you can climb 5.14, I saved this route for you. The top merges with the Meridian Tower. It will be a piece of cake to climb the remainder of the tower once you get to the top of the Beehive Wall (not to be confused with Beehive Peak that sits on top of the Streaked Wall).

SUN, TICKS, AND SNOW

On a weekend in 1996, I went to Zion to explore the possibility of climbing The Altar of Sacrifice. It sits in the large cirque called the Towers of the Virgin, behind the old Visitor Center (now the Museum). It may look close; it's a mile away and 3,000 feet tall. I bushwhacked uphill, a mile though loose rocks, cactus, and bushes. I wanted to get close enough to take pictures to plan a potential way to climb it.

On the way back I thought I'd take a short cut, and found myself struggling through thick, dead brush, in a gully overgrown with dead trees and their leaves. The gully smelled of wet dirt, must, and decay. I plowed forward.

As I got close to my truck, I started to notice an irritation, a biting in my arm pits. I held my underarm up to the rear view mirror and saw tiny round heads burrowing in my skin. I tried pulling them out with tweezers. They didn't budge. That seemed to make them dig deeper. Their eyes and face were buried. Their butts, too big to be swallowed by my skin pores, stuck out, ex-

Ron at the base of the Bee Hive Wall.

posed. I got a wooden match, lit it, blew it out, and placed it on the butt of a tick. That did not help. I needed help.

I was relived to find a medical clinic open in Kanab. It was good I had left the park. The next day it snowed eight inches and was zero degrees. An article I wrote on how to prevent and remove ticks, "Add it to your tick list," was published by Rock & Ice magazine. I was so excited when they sent me a check. It was the first time I had gotten paid to write.

When I got the film developed and showed the pictures to Ron.

"We can climb that! No problem. Alpine style - just a few cams, a few carabiners, and a dozen slings," he said.

I appreciated his enthusiasm, but didn't care to waste time trying to climb something without taking the gear required.

"It's not going to be that easy," I said.

We disagreed and made an alpine attempt. After failing, we spent the next two years making ten more attempts, each time with a different strategy, until we were successful.

The First Modern Climbing Fatality in Zion N.P.

A few days before New Year's Eve, 1996, I drove to Zion to meet my friend, Vince. We were planning on climbing the Lowe Route, the longest route on the mountain called Angels Landing in Zion National Park. I arrived a day early to fix rope at the start of the climb. Vince was bringing a friend from Russia, so I got a permit for three people. I parked in the empty parking lot in front of the mountain and began sorting the gear I would need. As I was packing, another climber parked next to me.

Bob was by himself and asked what I was up to. I explained I would be fixing rope to a big ledge on the mountain, and when my friends arrived, we would finish climbing to the top. Bob asked if he could join me. He understood that when my friends arrived he might not be able to finish the climb with us. He said he would rather get some climbing done than none, and I liked the idea of having a partner. We became friends and climbed to the top of the big ledge together. When we got to the ledge, we tied the ropes together and rappelled to the ground. As we reached the ground, Vince and Vladimir arrived.

Vince and Vladimir were OK with Bob joining the team. The next day, we crossed the river with food, sleeping bags, portaledges, and all the necessities to climb a big wall in the winter. It was foggy and overcast. Rain and snow were in the forecast.

On our third day of climbing, we noticed someone climbing Prodigal Sun, a route to the right of us. Prodigal Sun is shorter and easier, a route many climbers do their first time in Zion. Vince and I had climbed Prodigal Sun on our first trip to Zion in 1991. We took our time and slept on the side of the mountain — twice. On the second night we were close to the top but didn't make it. We stopped at a ledge called the Emergency Bivy. It was Vince's idea. He was always the smart one. Maybe that's why he made such a good pilot. In the morning, when we were able to see where we were going, we scrambled sideways to the trail and walked down the backside of the mountain to the parking lot.

The climber we saw was John Christensen. I took pictures of him as he climbed. I thought it would be nice to give them to him when he got down. His van was parked next to my truck.

Angels Landing. On the left is the Lowe Route we were climbing. On the right is Prodigal Sun, the route John Christensen was climbing. Circled and sideways, which here is shown under the emergency bivy, is the anchor John needed to swing to as he was rappelling from the Emergency Bivy.

John fixed two ropes that day, came down, and went to his van to sleep. He was planning on finishing the climb the next day, New Year's Eve. By fixing the two ropes, he had given himself a head start.

The next day, John hauled himself up his fixed ropes and proceeded to finish the climb. Late in the afternoon he slowed down. It's hard work climbing by yourself. After you climb up as far as the rope will reach, you secure it to an anchor, rappel down, untie the rope from the bottom anchor, and use the rope to hoist yourself back up. You hence climb the mountain twice.

The last picture I took of John was in the late afternoon of December 31st. He was high on the wall, looking confident and secure. At 9 p.m., as he used his headlamp to continue, I got into my sleeping bag and pulled the top over my head. It was cold.

In the morning there was no sight of John. I assumed he had finished the climb and hiked the trail down the backside of the mountain. Vince suspected otherwise. "Did you hear that scream in the middle of the night?" he said. "I'll bet you that was that climber on Prodigal Sun."

I shrugged his comment off. I didn't hear a scream and couldn't imagine that what he had heard was a climber falling to his death.

That same day, John's wife called the park service and reported him overdue. Rangers drove to the parking lot at Angels Landing and looked for him climbing. They didn't see him. They saw Bob, Vince, Vladimir, and myself. The river was flowing fast. They didn't want to cross it to look for John at the bottom of the climb. When they didn't see a climber on Prodigal Sun, they thought John might be climbing with us. My permit was for three people. I hadn't added Bob. The park rangers called John's wife and told her that they thought John might be climbing with us.

Two things should have raised doubts about the possibility that John could be climbing with us. When John started climbing, we were already halfway up the mountain. Our ropes could not have reached the ground for him to join us. His wife protested her disagreement with their idea. If John was going to climb a different and more difficult route, and climb it with strangers for several days, he would have told her.

We reached to the top that evening, soaked in the rain. After hauling our gear to the top, we walked down the trail and went to the campgrounds for the night. In the morning, I was woken by a tap-tap-tap on the window of my pickup. I was sleeping, curled in the front seat. My truck didn't have a shell, and it was raining, the ground soggy with puddles. I didn't have a tent. In my slumber, my first thought was that I was in trouble for not paying the camping fee. Then I remembered that my friends had paid it. I rolled the window down.

"Hi," the ranger said through the gap at the top of the window as he stood in the rain. "We're looking for a John Christensen, a climber that was sup-

Angels Landing, soaked in cold rain, just before it started to snow.

posed to be climbing Prodigal Sun. We thought he might be climbing with you guys."

I thought for a minute, half-asleep, still surprised I wasn't in trouble for something.

"No," I replied, "I don't know him. He's not with us."

"Don't leave. A special investigator is on the way. She'd like to speak with you."

I didn't understand what was happening. I got out of my truck, skipped across puddles of mud to Vince's van, and knocked on its back door. Vince knew exactly what was happening.

"You know who they're looking for," he said with the confidence of a pilot hitting turbulence, "that guy that was climbing Prodigal Sun."

At that point, the park service initiated a Search and Rescue (SAR) to look for John. They decided it was too dangerous to cross the river as we had done to get to the bottom of the climb. The team instead crossed a footbridge some distance down the river and hiked back along on other side, where they found John's body at the bottom. It was January 2nd.

The story run by the Associated Press was that a climber died when a botched rappel caused him to fall to his death. The news said there were no witnesses, and he got to the top but decided to rappel instead of walking the trail down. Rangers speculated that rock fall might have been a factor. Based on press reports, the author of the book *Death in Zion National Park: Stories of Accidents and Foolhardiness in Utah's Grand Circle* wrote, "It took searchers only a short time to find his body at the base of the peak." The SAR team reported that the cause of death was likely the climber had used ropes of different thickness causing the ropes to slip as he was rappelling. Readers were left

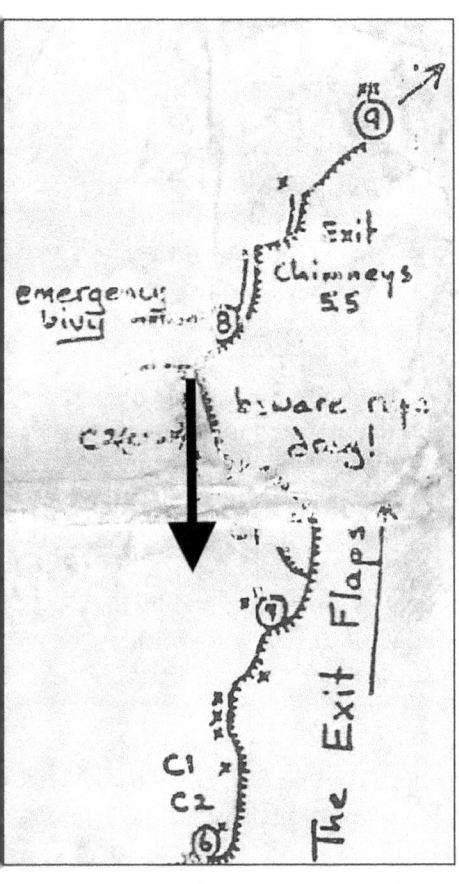

Excerpt from the map climbers use. The arrow indicates the direction John was coming down. Near the tip of the arrow he needed to go sideways to reach the spot marked "7", the 7th anchor. Instead, he kept going straight down, and in the dark, he didn't realize he had come to the end of his rope OR as he was going down, he realized he had passed the anchors, and fell as he tried to pull himself back up the rope with the perfect amount of slack required to swing over to the anchor.

to think that John was either too lazy to walk down from the top using the trail or didn't realize how ropes of different thickness may behave when you rappel on them.

Neither of these are true. John did not make it to the top, and the thickness of his ropes was not a factor in his death.

John did not make it to the top. He reached the emergency bivy, a flat spot 100 feet from the top. You don't want to stop there, but if it's dark, you are grateful for the opportunity to have a flat ledge to sleep on. The climb at that point does not go up. It goes sideways and looks impossible in the dark. If you get there in the dark, you are confused and find yourself stuck and unsure of how to continue. You sleep on the ledge and wait for morning.

Judging from where I took my last pictures of him, John likely reached to the emergency bivy early in the night. He may have waited some time before he decided to go down. He must have been very cold without camping gear. After midnight, he probably decided to go down by rappelling, most likely because he was freezing to death. I suspect he took a calculated risk. The longer he stayed on the ledge, the colder he would become. He decided to go down while he still had the mental and physical capacity that rappelling the ropes required.

To rappel a cliff taller than the length of your rope, you must stop on the way down at the same anchors you stopped at when you climbed up it. At each anchor, you pull the ropes and use them to go down to the next anchor. The process is repeated until you reach the ground.

Now consider what doing this would be like in the dark when you can't see the anchors below you until you are nearly at them. You can only see so far with a headlamp, and this was before the bright LED headlamps that are available today. In addition, the metal bolts used for the anchors are painted red to be camouflaged so they are not an eyesore to tourists in the daytime.

In the pitch black, John could not see the end of his rope as he searched for the next anchor. He didn't see the anchor because it was not below him: it was several feet to the side. The route between the emergency bivy and the anchor below is diagonal. He would have had to swing over to the anchor. John was looking down, when he passed the anchor and ran out of rope. It was then he went off the end of his ropes. The accident had nothing to do with equipment error or being too lazy to walk the trail down from the top.

The Associated Press said that coverage was limited to the statements made by investigator Dave Bucchello. Bucchello was not the investigator who spoke to us. The special investigator sent to question me and my climbing partners was a woman, someone without climbing experience, one without knowledge of the climbing routes.

I told her I had taken pictures of John and wanted his family to have them. I said I would mail her a set of prints and the negatives after I got the film developed. As we talked, the rain turned to snow. Puddles turned to ice. I called Ron, my normal climbing partner, to see if he wanted to meet me in Zion. We had tentative plans to climb something else.

"There's a big storm coming your way," he warned. "There's no way you're going to avoid it. Get out now." It seemed I needed to start driving home before treacherous weather made it dangerous in my two-wheel drive, so I left the park and drove home.

When I developed the film, I was surprised at how clear the images of John are considering the pictures were taken using a disposable camera in a cardboard box with a fixed lens. The park service would not release his family's contact information, so I sent a copy of the prints and negatives to the special investigator.

Exactly one year later, I received a call from John's wife. The park service had finally given her my contact information. She said the park service told her they lost the negatives. She was upset because his death certificate says January 2nd. Death certificates are dated at the time a body is recovered. She thought there must be more to the official story and asked me for clarity. I told her what I knew.

Rest in peace, John.

*What would life be
Without some of these
Don't tell me now
There's never be
Flowers
So many different ones
I like flowers
They're special
Everyone.*

- Daniel Isle Sky

Introduction to My Routes

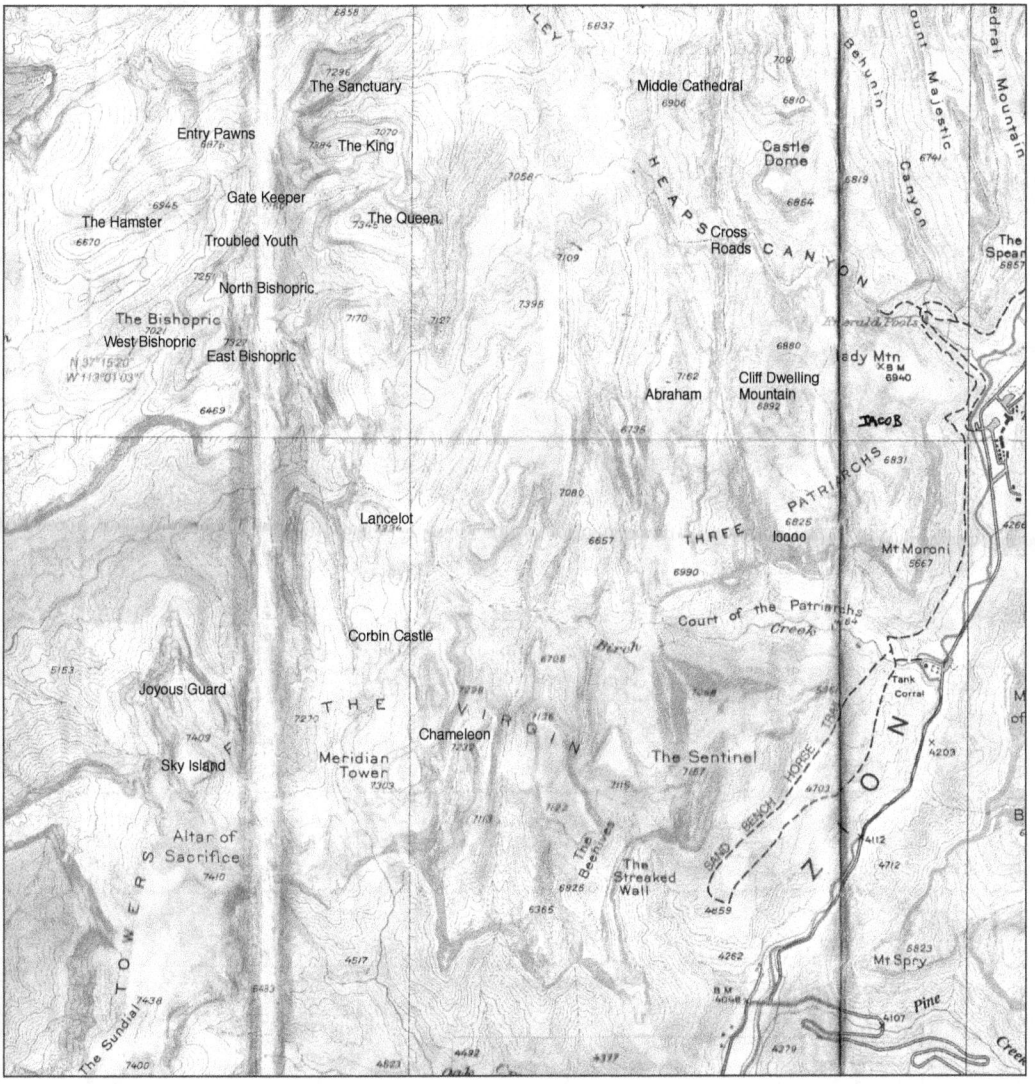

Opposite page: a unique view of Birch Creek as seen mid-way up the north face route on Big Red. Lancelot is at the head of the creek, top center.

RATINGS

I attempted to categorize my climbs based on the skill level required and the potential to have an epic. An epic is a miserable, I wanna go home experience. Some of these climbs were done when I was twenty, when I was able to do 100 pull-ups from my fingertips, and with a partner equally as fast and strong. Some may be under-rated, and more difficult than stated. Some climbs, on the other hand, I did years later when I was out of shape or soloing. Not having a partner makes things scary. Some of these climbs may be over-rated, meaning they are easier than stated. Given these factors, consider the ratings ballpark estimations.

MY FAVORITE ROUTES

I've had a unique and wonderful experience (and sometimes painful and scary) on each route. Every mountain has its own spirit and identify. Each gave me a unique moment. Each was a blessing. Each time, I cursed at the difficulties, and sometimes how hard it was to get down. Like a first kiss, however, I often wished I could repeat some and experience them for the first time all over again. On several occasions I had tears as I left a summit, wishing I could stay longer, before taking a deep breath and walking away.

Regardless of your climbing abilities, try to experience what it is like to climb something in a remote and beautiful location. Leave electronic devices at home or off unless absolutely required. Leave no trace and try not to place bolts. Threat the mountains with respect, and they will give you an experience you wont soon forget.

Star Rating	Route	Climbing Difficulty	Approach	Comments
****	Castle Dome	Fun	Easy	
****	The North Bishopric	Not hard (5.7-5.8)	Long	Required a few baby pitons. Small tricams or nuts may work instead.
*****	Traverse of the Three Bishoprics	Classic	Long	
	Death Point		Long	
**	Nice Line (Route at the Narrows)	A2+ 5.9+	Nada. Behind the restrooms at the parking lot for the Narrows	

Star Rating	Route	Climbing Difficulty	Approach	Comments
***	Abraham	5.10 R	Heaps Canyon	If doing a canyon descent and carrying a pair of rock shoes and gear to bivy, this is a stellar route on a coveted formation on the way.
**	Middle Cathedral	5.7	Heaps Canyon. Long	Mostly a scramble
***	Hammer and Sickle	A3, 5.10a	Steep	
****	Cable Mountain The North Face	A2, 5.8	Weeping Rock Trail	As easier, one-day route up Cable Mnt.
***	Ivins Mountain		Long	Could be free-climbed?
****	Center Pointe (Kolob Canyon)	Aid	Long. Dead tree climb on the approach.	
*****	The North Eye (Kolob Canyon)	Some aid. Mostly free	Long. Canyon descent required on approach.	
****	The Sentinel, North Face from Birch Creek	5.11 R	Approach by climbing the 1938 route and rappelling the north side to the bottom of the route.	Be prepared to descend Birch Creek if unable to climb back up to the summit.
*****	The Princess Spires (Next to Red Sentinel)	Aid and free	Long. Abraham Canyon	Three classic spires. Amazing summits, awesome location.
******	Triangle Peak, the East Face	5th class to the main summit. 5.9 to climb the red boulders on the summit	Climb the 1938 route on the Sentinel and Descend the NW face	A classic and not too dangerous adventure. A summit everyone sees from the road.
N/A	Altar of Sacrifice	High Adventure	Park at the end of maintenance road	The pitch, Couloir of Death says it all.
N/A	Traverse of Towers of the Virgin	Adventures of all kind. 5.10 R	Start by climbing the 1930's route on the West Temple	After rappelling the north face of the West Temple into the saddle between it and the Sun Dial, retreat and descent are difficult.
N/A	Traverse of the Court of the Patriarchs	High Adventure. The ascents of Abraham and the North Face of the Sentinel require climbing 5.10-5.11 unprotected face.	Start up the Old Lady Mountain Trail across from the Lodge. After climbing Jacob rappel from the saddle next to Lady Mountain into Isaac Canyon.	Likely more difficult than the traverse of the Towers of The Virgin. The descents of Cliff Dwelling Mnt and the east face of Abraham require bravery, commitment, and navigation skills.

First Ascents of Mountains Named on Maps

The Altar of Sacrifice

INTRODUCTION The Altar of Sacrifice is the biggest rock climb in the park. Although the West Temple is the highest in elevation, the West Temple is relatively easy to climb. The Altar of Sacrifice, on the other hand, has a 3,000 foot face, as tall as that of El Capitan in Yosemite. The Altar of Sacrifice sits in a cirque called the Towers of the Virgin. The best place to view it is on the back patio of what is currently the History Museum (the old Visitor Center). On the far left is the West Temple; on the far right is the Altar of Sacrifice. In between is a plateau, a flat land mass about 700 feet lower than the summits, on which the Sun Dial and several other peaks sit.

The bottom half of the Altar of Sacrifice is a broken, jagged mixture of cliffs, ledges, and bushes, that will make most climbers want to cry. The broken nature makes climbing easier. The issue is one cannot haul a bag of supplies. The bag will get stuck. A frustrated climber pulling hard enough will tear the bag or damage the rope. Some climbers have tried to go fast without hauling food or water. As the top half of the mountain becomes vertical, climbers find themselves wishing for a portaledge and water to continue.

HISTORY A plethora of strong climbers tried to climb the Altar of Sacrifice. In May, 1989, Royce Trapier and Rod Savage spent six day climbing a route on west side of the plateau. They reached the notch between the West Temple and Sun Dial. It appears they could not get across the east face of the Sun Dial to reach the Altar of Sacrifice. During the first ascent of the Sun Dial in 1997, Ron and I discovered a note tucked inside a pile of rocks in the saddle between the West Temple and Sun Dial. It said this:

> *The Grand Gateway to the Towers of the Virgin register. May 3, 1989.*
> *Six day exploration of access to the Sun Dial and the Altar through*
> *the lower slope of basin. Hampered by lack of water.*
> *- Royce Trapier, Springdale*
> *- Rod Savage, St. George*

During the second traverse of the Towers of the Virgin in 2021, Mike Dunn reports that the note is missing. It's likely time and weather took their toll.

In the 1990's, a Japanese team spent a month with a film crew trying to climb the Altar of Sacrifice. According to a ranger in the back country office at the time, they didn't get far.

Brad Quin, a prolific Zion local, put up steep aid route left of the Altar of Sacrifice, and reached the top of the plateau. It's unknown why he did not continue to the summit.

In 1995, John Middendorf and Carl Tobin climbed to the plateau, establishing the Mountaineer's Route (IV 5.10). This appears to be the third route to reach the top of the plateau. It's unknown why they did not continue to the summit. Based on evidence Ron and I found, it appears they might have been trying to go fast and light, and did not have enough time or water to continue. It appears they were planning on returning. We found discarded, empty water bottles, and a cup of bolts at the bottom of a beak ladder. Most modern climbers who climb the Altar do so by doing the Traverse, rappelling off the West Temple. Therefore it's likely no one has been to this spot since. Middendorf's supply stash may still be there.

In April, 1996, Ron made our first attempt on the Altar. We went alpine style. To go light we did not take sleeping bags and climbed using a small amount of gear. After two days, we were half-way up the main wall. We bailed because if we had continued we would have had to sleep hanging in our harnesses for at what seemed at least two days, and we didn't have a large rack of gear.

In November, 1996, Ron and I made several attempts, each leading to dead ends. On one attempt, we climbed 1,000 feet before the crack we were following ended at a blank face. I had to finish getting down by down-climbing after the bush I used as a rappel anchor pulled out.

In January, 1997, Ron and I attempted to climb the Altar of Sacrifice from Coalpits Wash. It rained the entire time. It was so muddy that the ranger said he was sorry to have to give us a permit. We were hampered by snow and mud, and found the climbing wet and more difficult than what we were looking for. I wasn't carrying a sleeping bag. We bivyed at the base of the ridge

Searching for a way to climb the Altar of Sacrifice from Coalpits Wash, winter, 1997. Note the original oil well ruins with charred wood compared to how the ruins look today after "restoration."

that jets out from the SW corner of the Altar massif.

In March, 1997, Ron and I returned to the east side. We realized that the only practical way to climb the mountain might be to fix ropes, the way Mt. Everest is climbed. We were successful, climbed to the top, establishing the Original Route. It includes a section of wide chimneys Ron named Couloir of Death.

In March, 1998, Ron and I re-climb the Altar of Sacrifice without using fixed

Top left: I believe the pillar with the corner in the shade to be Brad Quin's route. It's right of the gully we climbed on the bottom section. Bottom: half-way up, day two, April, 1996. We chose to bail vs. continue without a portaledge.

ropes. We carried a single, 9-millimeter, 150-foot dynamic rope, and a 200-foot, 7-millimeter static to supplement it for rappels. Over two days, we did a traverse from the West Temple and reclimbed the Sun Dial and all of the formations between it and the Altar of Sacrifice. When we reached the Altar, instead of climbing the Original Route, we put up a route on its West Face.

The Altar had been waiting for someone to put a direct line up its main face, one that does not touch the plateau. This amazing feat was accomplished by Mike Dunn and Ky Hart in December, 2021.

Summary of ascents: 1st: Stih and Raimonde, 1997 via Coulior of Death; 2nd: Stih and Raimonde, 1998 (West Face as part of "traverse"); 3rd: Dunn and Herlitzka, 2021 (West Face as part of "traverse"); 4th: Dunn and Hart, 2021 (new route on main face); 5th: Stih and Dunn, 2022 on "traverse"; 6th: Barrow and Baty, 2023 on "traverse".

FUTURE CLIMBING There are two cracks on the east face, on the far southern aspect of a shelf that runs along the base. This provides a lot of elevation gain (less climbing to reach the summit). The cracks are larger than they appear. The left crack appears to be include a chimney, potentially allowing free-climbing. Both appear to be two or three pitches.

Two potential new lines on the east face of the Altar of Sacrifice. They start on the plateau between the Altar of Sacrifice and Meridian Tower.

CLIMBING THE ALTAR OF SACRIFICE

WATER Do not expect to find water in summer or fall. Water from snow melting dries up by mid to late April, depending on how much it snows during the winter, The following are present during winter and early spring: **At the bottom of the Altar:** There is a spring on the far right side, at the bottom of a steep gully that comes down from the plateau on the east side of the Altar. (The plateau between the Altar and Meridian Tower.) **On the plateau:** In spring, there is run-off and pools on the south side of the Altar, and depending on snowfall during the winter, snow on the west side of the Altar in gullies that don't see sun. Notably, there is a large cleavage on the north side of the Sun Dial that captures snow, which may provide water as late as June in years with lots of snow. If there was little or no snowfall during the winter, water sources on the plateau may be limited or dry. In early season there may be snow on the summit of the Altar. It's nice to have snow to melt for water to drink.

SEASON Water is the main factor is successfully climbing the Altar of Sacrifice. Therefore, early spring (March to April) are recommended unless you haul water. Beginning late April to early May, water starts to disappear. It is possible to climb in winter. The disadvantage is the bulk and weight of warm clothing, days are shorter, and the rock might be wet.

---

1. THE ORIGINAL ROUTE A2, 5.10 *D Stih and R Raimonde, March 1997*

The first route established. It contains the Couloir of Death, a series of wide chimneys with loose rock.

EQUIPMENT REQUIRED: Full rack.

CAUTIONS / SPECIAL DIFFICULTIES: The Couloir of Death may have snow as late as March or early April. We didn't have an ice tool. Having one might be helpful.

TIME REQUIRED: Allow 3-4 days from the car plus a day for the descent.

STARTING POINT: Park at the Museum, and walk the service road to where it terminates. From a picnic table at the end of the road, hike a combination of hills and a drainage towards the mountain. The difficult part is near the start where it's necessary to get out of the drainage to avoid a dry fall. Staying high on the right is easiest.

THE ROUTE: Start by climbing a chimney at the bottom, on the right side of the large gully. Finish the pitch by traversing back left to a point above the gully. From there, traverse sideways before going back right. See the topo on the following pages.

---

2. THE WEST FACE *D Stih and R Raimonde, March 1998*

The second ascent of the Altar of Sacrifice, a moderate scramble, done during the first Traverse of the Towers of the Virgin.

EQUIPMENT: Slings.

CAUTION /SPECIAL DIFFICULTIES: In early season deep snow and wet rock may hinder getting started at the summit cap once at the bottom of the west side of the Altar.

CAMPING / TIME REQUIRED: It's one hour from the plateau to the summit.

STARTING POINTS: The top of the plateau, reached by one the following routes: A) Rappel off of the north side of West Temple as done for the Traverse of the Towers of the Virgin. B) From Oak Creek, behind the Museum, free-climb the bottom half of the Original Route, the Mountaineer's Route, or aid-climb Brad Quin's route.

Left: the chimney at the start (the first pitch) of the Original Route. Below: outline of the route we took to reach the plateau.

GETTING DOWN One of the cruxes to climbing the Altar of Sacrifice is getting down. This is high adventure and requires commitment. **The Gully on the West side of the Meridian Tower Descent:** This descent was established during our Traverse of the Towers of the Virgin and is the recommended descent. Rappel from the summit of the Altar into the notch between the Altar and Sky Island. From the notch, rappel to the plateau. Hike towards the Meridian Tower, The correct gully is on the immediate west side of the Meridian Tower. The gully is not obvious. Tall brush hides its start. At first is won't seem the way to go. It becomes ob-

The carin (pile of rocks) on the edge of the summit. Using a spotting scope, it may be visible from the back patio of the History Museum. I must have been scratching my head. We didn't have a phone. The white tube at the bottom of the pile contains a summit register.

vious as you start down it. The first rappel is not encountered until a long way down. The last rappel is over the edge into space before you reach the ground. **Alternate way:** From the bottom of Sky Island, on the way to the Meridian Tower you will pass by a canyon that goes down west to Coalpits wash. Although it looks steep, dark, and foreboding, it can be descended with one short rope. It's not recommended as it's a long hike out Coalpits wash to the highway. **Descending The Original Route**: This goes straight down the original ascent path, avoiding the traverse in the middle. This descent is not advised as we used two 300-foot ropes, there are no intermediate anchors, and the route is difficult to locate. From the bottom of the Couloir of Death, walk south to where progress is blocked by a canyon. Rappel 300 feet into the canyon and then scramble into a gully where you can comfortably sit. From there, rappel off trees. On one of the next rappels, look for big anchors on a wall 30 feet from the edge. This is another 300-foot rappel and overhangs, making it difficult to stop to drill an intermediate anchor. The rest is straight forward. Hike out to the service road and the old Visitor Center (now the History Museum).

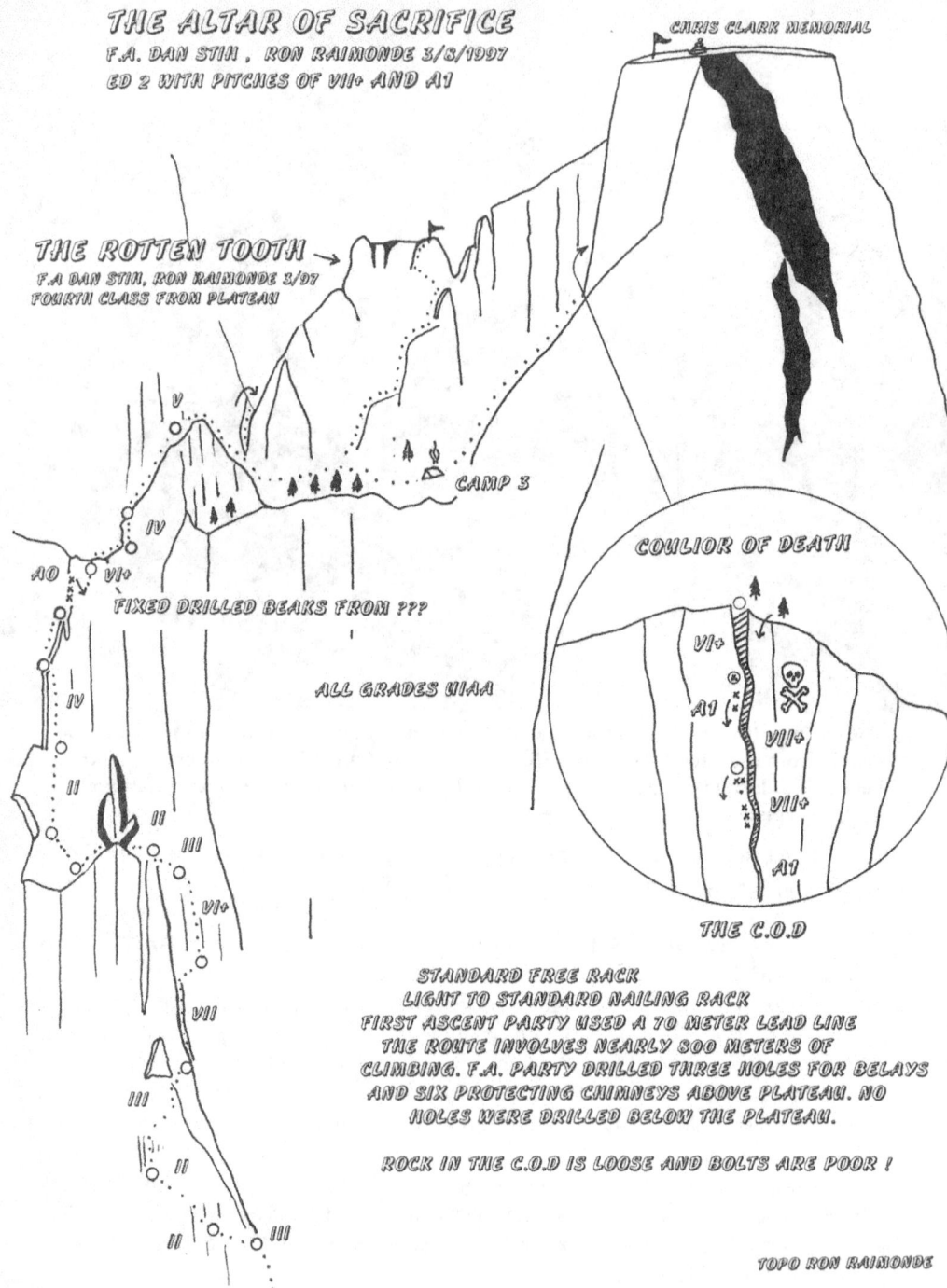

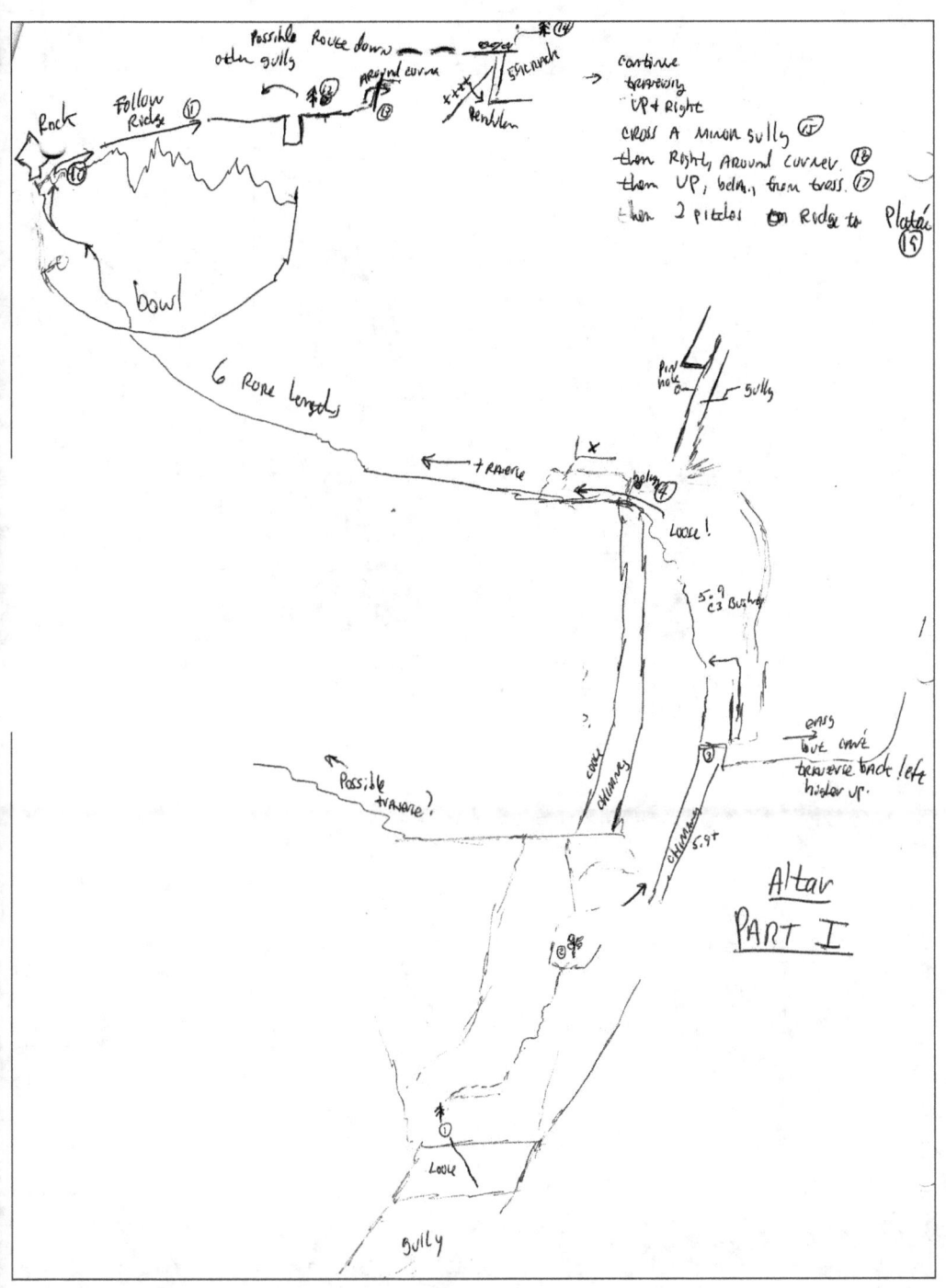

Part 1 of Dan's drawing of the route. The bottom section of The Original Route, from the ground up to the plateau.

Dan trying too hard. I came down from this stance, and at the suggestion of Ron, and we traversed sideways left (south).

Outline of the route showing the traverse left.

The top part of the Altar of Sacrifice, south face. Once on the plateau, the Original Route takes the left leaning crack (hidden), left of the center indentation.

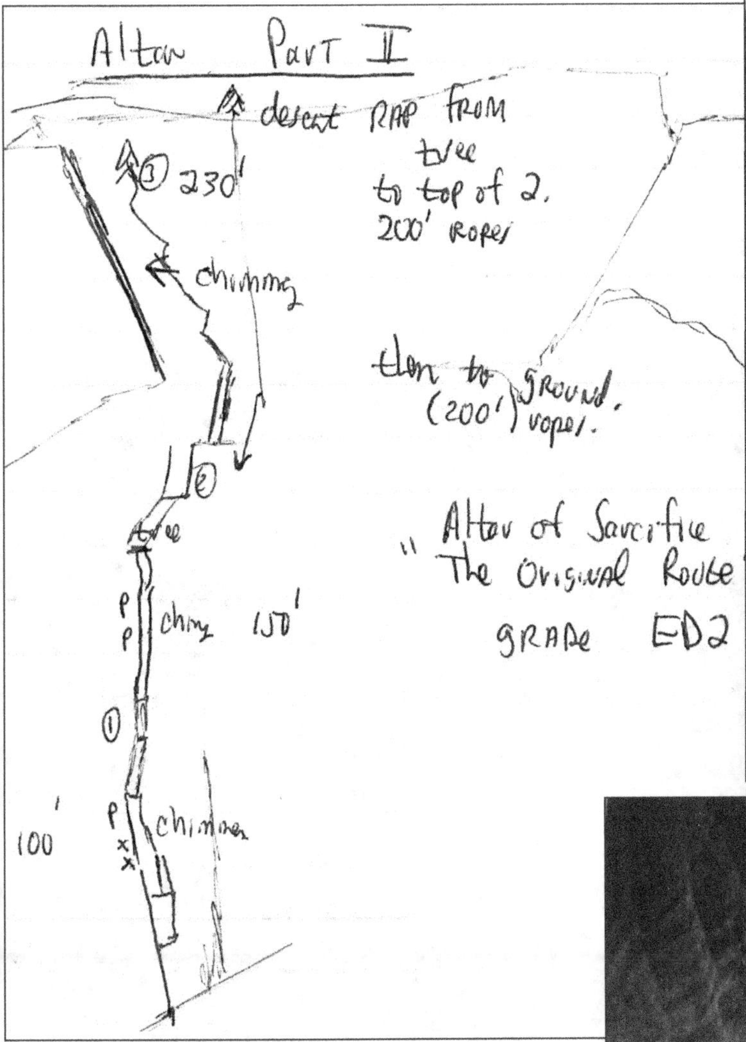

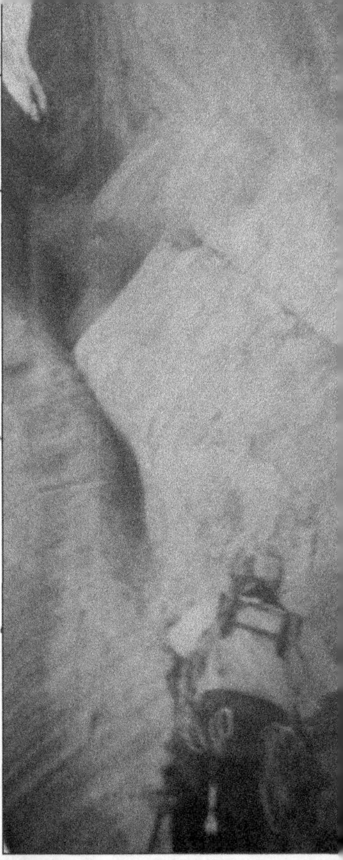

Above: Topo for the Original Route from the plateau to the summit via the Couloir of Death. Top right: Ron, at the start of the first of three pitches for Couloir of Death; Bottom right: Ron jugging to meet me at the top of the second pitch in the Couloir of Death. Below him and the snow is a vertical chimney with loose rock. Below: Aerial view showing the location of the Original Route [arrow]. The route on the west face used for the traverse goes up slopes on the left.

The Sun Dial

The Sun Dial has two proper summits. The NE summit was first climbed by Ron and Dan twice: once during the expedition of first ascent of the Altar of Sacrifice; the second during the Traverse; The third ascent of the NE summit was by Mike Dunn and Arthur Herlitzka in 2021; the 4th ascent of the NE summit, and first ascent of the SW summit, were done by Dan and Mike in 2022.

INTRODUCTION The Sun Dial is said to have got its name from citizens in the town of Grafton who regulated their clocks by the early morning sun hitting it. The Sun Dial sits on the plateau between the West Temple and the Altar of Sacrifice in the Towers of the Virgin. A good place to view the Sun Dial is on the back patio of the Museum. The Sun Dial can also be seen in Grafton, mid-way on the drive from Hurricane into Springdale.

As seen from behind the old Visitor Center (now the History Museum), left to right: the north end of the West Temple, Sun Dial, Witch Head, Broken Tooth, Rotten Tooth, Altar of Sacrifice.

HISTORY In May, 1989, starting from Coalpits Wash, Royce Trapier and Rod Savage spent six day climbing a route on the west side of the plateau between the Sun Dial and the West Temple. They reached the notch between the West Temple and Sun Dial. The Sun Dial can not be climbed (thus far, without drilling bolts) from the south side. In March 1997, Ron and I attempted to climb the south face. After several hundred feet the cracks ended and I couldn't climb higher. We retreated and put up a route on the north face.

In March, 1998, Ron and I did a traverse from the West Temple to the Altar of Sacrifice, and reclimbed the Sun Dial. There was so much snow, we were able to climb a direct route, kicking steps up the face next to the route we had previously established. The third ascent of the Sun Dial was done in March, 2021.

Ron, leaving a summit register on the Sun Dial, 1997. It's no longer there.

CLIMBING THE SUN DIAL

WATER Once on the plateau, snow and water from melting snow are the only sources. There is a large cleavage on the north side of the Sun Dial that captures an abundance of snow. In years with good snowfall, this may provide water as late as June. Do not expect water in summer or fall.
SEASON Early Spring (March - April) is recommended.

---

1. NW FACE *D Stih and R Raimonde, March 1997*
On his hand-drawn topo, using the international alpine rating system, Ron rated this adventure ED2 with pitches of VI (if starting from Oak Creek); D starting if from the plateau.
EQUIPMENT: An alpine rack with lots of slings. Ron's definition of an alpine rack is six carabiners and a half set of cams.
TIME REQUIRED: Based on my journal, it took Ron and I as long to climb the Sun Dial as all of the other formations on the plateau combined. Even though we had climbed it before, the second time it took five hours, round-trip from the plateau.
STARTING POINTS Start on the plateau on the north side of the Sun Dial. The plateau can be reached by one of the following routes: A) Rappel off of the West Temple as done for the Traverse of the Towers of the Virgin. From the saddle between the West Temple and Sun Dial, traverse across the east face of the Sun Dial, what looks improbable. Warning: there is no easy way to rappel into Oak Creek (to bail and go home) from between the Sun Dial and West Temple. The east face overhangs. The escape route would be down the west face, into Coalpits Wash, down a vertical wall, then hiking south in Coalpits Wash to the highway. B) Free-climb the bottom half of the Original Route for the Altar of Sacrifice or free-climb the Mountaineer's Route to the top of the plateau.
THE ROUTE: See the topo on the opposite page.
GETTING DOWN Continue by climbing the Altar of Sacrifice and the traverse OR if you reach the plateau by climbing the bottom half of the Original Route or Mountaineer's Route, and you are familiar with one of these routes, it might be best to descend the route you took.

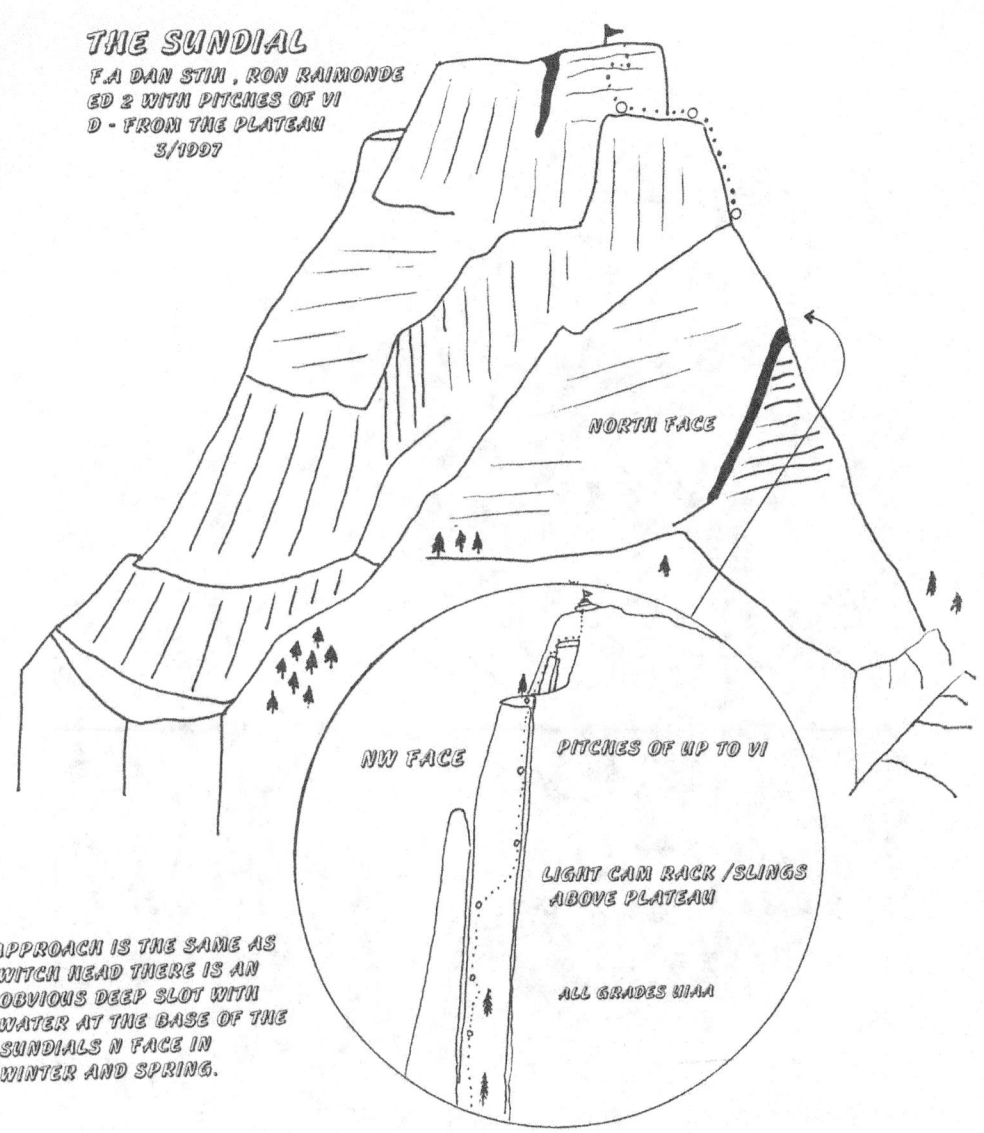

Abraham

INTRODUCTION Abraham is in an area of the park called the Court of the Patriarchs. The origin of the names of Abraham and the peaks in the court is indefinite. It is said Frederick Vining Fisher, an Ogden resident, named the peaks Abraham, Isaac, and Jacob, during a visit to Zion between 1914 and 1916. Fisher is said to have been accompanied by two locals: Rockville LDS Bishop David Hirschi, and his son, Claude Hirschi. Some say Fisher named it; others point to Claude Hirschi. A 1957 park brochure, Zion National Park Utah (Government Printing Office, 1957-O-434342) mentions "The Three Patriarchs" but does not mention or label Abraham. A 1929 map (Map of Zion National Park 1929) has "Three Patriarchs" marked on it, but not "Abraham".

HISTORY In 1990, John Middendorf and Walt Shipley established the Radiator (5.10+ A4) on the east buttress of Abraham's south face. They did not go to the summit. In *Mountain Review*, Middendorf wrote: "On the fourth day, we reached the top of the (east) buttress and drank the last of our water."

The highest point is on the far north side. I am reminded of when I climbed the Matterhorn in Switzerland. We reached the top in a blizzard. Under our feet, loose rocks moved under a layer of fresh snow and thin ice. It was dangerous to walk across the top to the true summit. My partner screamed as I started walking towards it, yelling to stop. I refused. It didn't seem to count unless we went to the highest point.

In November, 1997, Ron and I went to Zion with the intention of putting a new route on Abraham. We began close to the same spot John and Walt had, but instead of going left, we went up and right. After climbing several pitches, we had to drive back to Arizona to go to work. We left our ropes fixed at an anchor where I drilled two fixed pins. Ron didn't think I drilled good holes. To make it safer, after I went down, he placed my #5 Camelot in the crack next to the angles, tied the ropes to everything, and the rappelled to the ground.

Ron wasn't able to take time off from work for several weeks. When he had a free weekend, but not enough days to

Approximate line of the Radiator route.

finish the route with me, he went to Zion with his girlfriend. They hiked out into the Court of the Patriarchs where he showed her the route we were working on. The #5 Camelot was gone. Someone had gone up our ropes, taken the cam, finished the route, and reported the route to the *American Alpine Journal* as a first ascent.

The highest point on Abraham is the red cap on the north end, the far left.

Ron on the lower pitches of the route we started.

    I consider taking the Camelot theft. I can understand if the climbers thought we were not coming back. If their intent, however, had been to clean up and leave no trace, they should have removed our ropes. Ron had to go up the rope without the safety of the cam, and no way of knowing it was missing until he reached the anchor.

    Stealing a route is nothing new. Most people are familiar with Half Dome in Yosemite. Modern climbers consider Royal Robbins to be the first to climb the Direct Northwest route. He started the route after other climbers had fixed ropes on it. The other climbers were Ed Copper and Gallen Rowell. According to Rowell, he and Cooper left fixed ropes hanging on the mountain while Rowell headed back to college to take a final exam. Unknown to them, Robbins had seen them start the climb, and was trying to find a partner to finish the route before Copper and Rowell could return. As Alex Huber tells it in *Yosemite: Half a Century of Rock Climbing*, when he (Robbins) saw others start it (Half Dome) he sought Layton Kor to help him. Kor declined, feeling it would be wrong to intrude on other climbers. Robbins was able to persuade Dick McCraken, and Robbins and McCraken finished the route before Coper and Rowell could return. Cooper left Yosemite afterwards, discouraged. Robins sneakiness caused climbers to lose trust in each other.

    In his autobiography, *Spirit of the Age*, Robbins wrote that he felt he had "Saved the route from a fixed-rope and bolted-siege." Robins considered it bad style to leave a rope hanging and return after resting. He believed that you

At the tip of the white point is where Ron and started. We climbed straight up, with the intent of traversing right higher up. In marker is the Radiator route. Below: Looking down from top of the second pitch.

should start at the bottom and not come down until you reached the top. He also believed it was bad style to place bolts. But Robbins placed ten bolts and he wasn't going to college. If this sounds ridiculous and childish, it is. It's unfortunate when egos, personal beliefs, and competition contaminate the spirit of climbing.

Another example of stealing a route in Zion was during the first ascent of the Streaked Wall. Other climbers had fixed ropes on the Streaked Wall, when Conrad Anker and Mugs Stump swooped in and finished the route. It's possible the other climbers were contemplating where the route went. The top section is blank. In order to complete it, Anker and Stump had to drill hundreds of feet of bolts. The other climbers may have been pondering the ethics of drilling so many bolts just to reach "the top". Or perhaps they were in college and taking an exam.

Ironically, none (Ron, myself, those who climbed the Radiator, or finished the route Ron and I had started) may have been the first to climb the south face of Abraham. Jeff Lowe is said to have said, "What is properly called Abraham, which harbors the Radiator wall, was first climbed by George Lowe and me in 1972, via the huge corner system on the right side." Jeff appears not to have reported his ascent when he completed it. Either that, or it was reported in the 1974 AAJ under the peaked named Isaac instead of Abraham.

It can be difficult to discern who climbed what and when based on hearsay and what has been published. I would have preferred to ask Jeff. Unfortunately, in August, 2018, at the age of sixty-seven, he passed. He had been suffering from a neurological disease similar to ALS. Rest in peace Jeff. You were an inspiration. I still have gear manufactured by your company, Lowe Alpine.

I don't think it makes a difference who is first. The names of mountains on maps change each year. Perhaps the lesson Jeff left us is that no one but a small group of climbers will remember or care who climbed something. What matters is your character strength, and how you treat and inspire others while you are here.

A hero is an ordinary person
Who finds strength to persevere and endure
In spite of overwhelming obstacles.
- Tila, Bistra at Deep Creek Coffee, Springdale, Utah.

CLIMBING ABRAHAM

1. THE NORTH FACE 5.9+ R *D Stih and R Raimonde 1999*
EQUIPMENT REQUIRED: Slings and one cam between 3/8 to 1/2 inch.
CAUTIONS / SPECIAL DIFFICULTIES: Run out and difficult to protect. The decent requires careful route finding to avoid being stuck on the blank, west face.
WATER: Heaps Canyon on the way to the climb; Birch Creek on the descent.
THE ROUTE: Starting in Heaps Canyon, climbs the North-west face. From Heaps Canyon, scramble up white face on the NW corner. The crux is 100-degree 5.9+ face. You can't see above your head. The last piece of gear is a micro-cam, ten feet below your feet. After a few moves, the angle lessens, and scrambling and simul-climbing lead to the summit.

The North-west route starts on the left corner, the ridge-like feature where the sunlight meets shade.

GETTING DOWN: Option A: The normal climbing routes on Abraham use the east flank for descent, and exit using Isaac Canyon into the Court of the Patriarchs. According to Tom, this is a rarely traveled route. Near the end, Tom writes: Down-climb or rappel to "an airy perch, then rappel 280 feet to a spring." He notes that an old climbers rappel station can be seen halfway down the final rappel, but the anchors should be carefully checked. Middendorf reported it took him and Shipley fourteen long and tiresome rappels (to reach the canyon) plus three. To me Option B sounds betters.

When Lowe did the first descent in the 1970s it was unlikely he had 200-foot ropes. Climbers at that time only had 150-foot ropes. Therefore, it seems likely the descent can be done with a pair of 150-foot ropes. In July 2019, someone posted on a canyoneering blog: "The raps at the end are done easily in two stages with 130-140 foots lengths. The

The normal climbing routes on Abraham use the east flank for descent, and then goes down Isaac Canyon into the Court of the Patriarchs.

first anchors are getting water-worn and need replacement. The anchors down half way are in excellent condition. SMC hangers and 3/8 studs with nuts. Very little rust for 30 years and drum tight. Hangers didn't spin, and they were out of the watercourse."

It would make sense the bolts were drilled out of the water course. Modern canyoneers might be comfortable in water; climbers then preferred to avoid water. It's possible Lowe did not leave anchors at the top. He and his partner may have rappelled off bushes, trees, or down-climbed. Back then that's what climbers did. They didn't like taking the time to place bolts. If they started thinking about how dangerous something was, they would never have gotten anything done.

Option B: Ron and I pioneered a decent down the west face of Abraham into Abraham Canyon. We down climbed the west face until it was necessary to drill a rappel station, then hiked Abraham Canyon to Birch Creek. Avoid going down too close to the south face. From the top, starting at the south edge, backtrack north across the mesa to where it's possible to down-climb the west face as far as possible. Take the path of least resistance, zig-zagging down ramps with trees and bushes until it's not possible to continue without rappelling. At that point, rappel off a tree to the end of the rope and look for a set of drilled angles as a hanging belay before rappelling to the ground (Abraham Canyon). See The Traverse of the Court of the Patriarchs for details. From there I suggest using the Squirrel Route to rappel to the ground in the The Court of the Patriarchs. It hugs the SW corner of Abraham and is discussed in detail in later chapter in this book.

Alternate Descents: It might be possible to engineer a decent into Heaps Canyon from the north side of Abraham. The west side of the NW corner of Abraham appears to have trees and bushes that might be used to descend into a mini-canyon on the northwest side of Abraham, a canyon that comes down from Battleship Rock. From there, exit Heaps Canyon into Emerald Pools (a serious canyon route that requires two 300-foot ropes for the final big drop) or hike NW into Phantom Valley, past Church Mesa, then exit south via the approach used to reach to the Bishoprics from Terry Wash (epic and not recommended).

Cliff Dwelling Mountain

Circled is Cliff Dwelling Mnt. Front left is Isaac.

INTRODUCTION I'm not sure why early inhabitants named this mountain Cliff Dwelling Mountain. Steve Allen mentions Cliff Dwelling Mountain in his book, *Utah's Canyon Country Place Names*, but gives no details. I found no evidence of ancient civilizations on the summit. The summit is flat, dense with bushes, and without trees. It's possible ruins lay under the brush and may be revealed if there is a fire.

HISTORY It's possible the Anasazi or ancient culture lived on top of mountains in Zion. I don't think they needed to climb to get to their shelters. They may have had technology that enabled them to fly. The Anasazi are said to have suddenly disappeared. It may be that they left when they lost the technology or the entity that gave it took it away. When I did the second ascent (solo), I slept on top.

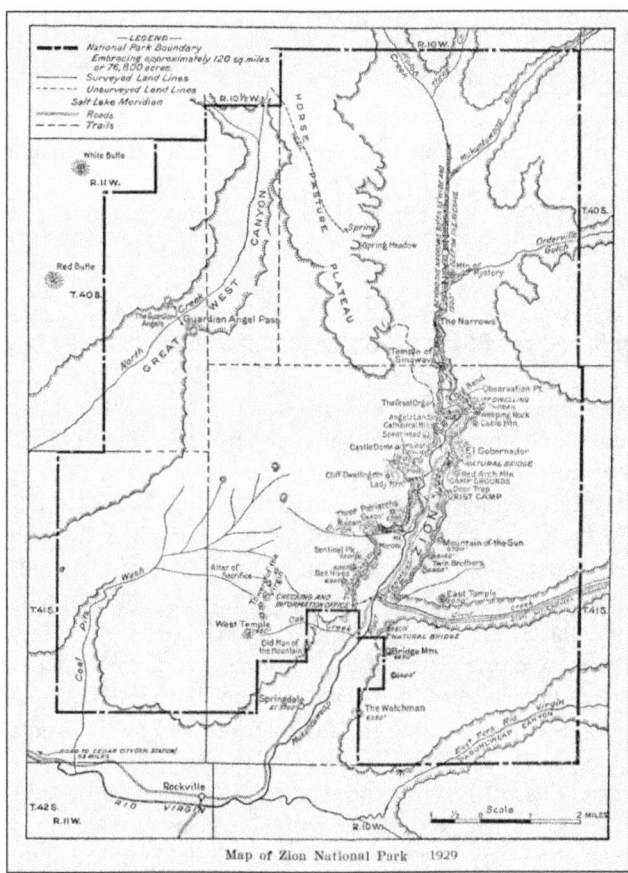

"Cliff Dwelling Mnt" is noted on this *Map of Zion National Park 1929*.

Looking over at the top of Cliff Dwelling Mnt, the flat, green mesa.

CLIMBING CLIFF DWELLING MOUNTAIN

SOMEWHERE ON THE NORTHEAST FACE 5.8+
D Stih and R Raimonde March 1999

The first route to the summit. Ron and I climbed it during our traverse of the Court of the Patriarchs.

EQUIPMENT REQUIRED: A light climbing rack of a few cams and long slings.
WATER SOURCES: Isaac Canyon.
SEASON: Spring.
STARTING POINT: Hike Lady Mountain Trail to the saddle between Lady Mnt and Jacob. Scramble down the other side until you reach a cliff. Look for a large tree to rappel from down to a hanging anchor (2 drilled angles). We did not leave slings, but subsequent parties may have. One more rappel (hanging bolt station) reaches the ground in Isaac Canyon. Scramble south down the canyon, then up to the bottom of the north face of Isaac. From the north face of Isaac, take the path of least resistance toward Cliff Dwelling Mnt, until it becomes necessary to rope up.
THE ROUTE: The crux is a 5.8+ awkward grunt up a loose, sandy corner, three-quarters up. I can not tell from photographs where the route is. It might be hidden. It might be there is a portal or invisible cloaking device shielding it. It's likely more difficult than I remember. It could be 5.10.

During our traverse of the Court of the Patriarchs, after we climbed Isaac, starting from the bottom of Isaac, I remember traversing north, then hiking sideways around the east side of the mountain, taking the easiest way, one I didn't need a belay. I recall traversing around a bowl. That suggests I would have gone north around a ledge at the top of a bowl on the east side of the mountain. At the apex, I stopped and waited for Ron, as it became too difficult to continue without a belay.

From there Ron and I did a few pitches of roped climbing. Some of the pitches were simul-climbing, but the pitch at the bottom to leave the bowl was the crux and hard to protect. There was a thin groove in a corner of a dihedral on the left. I was wearing a pack. Bushes right of the crack were in the way. I was turned around, facing outward, as if I might be to climb a chimney, but there wasn't a wall on one side. I wiggled my body and pressed my back against the face, while putting my feet in the corner on my other side. It was an ugly grunt, dirty and loose. After that the climbing eased. We came up to the summit, close to its south side.

GETTING DOWN: If you intended to do the traverse of the Court of the Patriarchs, walk across the summit towards the north-west corner. Avoid descending too early or you will end up on the blank side of the narrow and dark walls of Gunsight Canyon, and in deep water. Starting at the NW corner, most of the descent is down-climbing. Several rappels may be needed near the bottom. If you choose wisely, most of the descent will be down-climbing.

Alternatively, if you intend to only climb Cliff Dwelling Mnt, and have canyoneering skills, you could make camp the first night at the base of Isaac. Leave camping gear there, climb Cliff Dwelling Mtn, and return to camp. In the morning and go down Isaac Canyon into the Court of the Patriarchs.

2. NORTH RIDGE *D Stih August, 2017*

I soloed this during my traverse around the Emerald Pools. The climbing is easier than the ascent Ron and I did. Route finding may be as difficult.

EQUIPMENT REQUIRED: Light climbing rack. One of each cam.
WATER SOURCES: Heaps Canyon. There's always water there. Sometimes too much.
SEASON: Summer when there is not too much water in Heaps or the Gunsight.
STARTING POINT: The Cross Roads in Heaps Canyon.
THE ROUTE: From the Cross Roads, head south down the wickedly dark and narrow Gunsight Canyon. Never fear, you need not go far. Even in dry (August) conditions, you will soon be unable to avoid getting wet. At that point, backtrack, and look for a ditch coming down from Cliff Dwelling Mnt on your right. You won't be able to see the top of the mountain for bushes and trees. It's a jungle. Start walking up the ditch, yanking on bushes to pull yourself up. Keep following the ditch, taking the easiest path, sometimes going slightly up and left. Eventually, the jungle will clear and you will find yourself 1/4 way up the mountain. From there, take the easiest path up broken and steep red cliffs. Anything too difficult is not the way. In a few places I threw my pack up onto ledges to take the weight off, then French-Freed by leap-frogging pieces using my daisy chains. These were short sections, less than 10 feet. I didn't use the rope.

Cliff Dwelling Mnt is the big peak in the center. The west edge of Castle Dome is on the left, above which is the western edge of Lady Mountain. Lady of the Cliff is the small peak left of Cliff Dwelling Mnt.

On the summit of Cliff Dwelling Mnt. My pack and rope for my three-day traverse of the mountains around the Emerald Pools. I bived on top. Castle Dome is in the background.

GETTING DOWN: Rappel the east face of Cliff Dwelling Mtn into the saddle between it and Lady of the Cliff. (Lady of the Cliff is a sub-peak between Cliff Dwelling Mtn and Lady Mountain.) During my traverse around the Emerald Pools, I rappelled from the summit of Cliff Dwelling Mnt down its East face. I used two 200-foot ropes, and made two rappels off bushes and small trees. From the saddle, free climb (5.5?) up the other side to a large tree. There may be rappel slings around the tree from previous attempts to climb Cliff Dwelling Mnt from that side. From the summit of Lady of the Cliff, descend the other side. This might require a short rappel. Scramble up the NW ridge on Lady Mountain to its summit, then hike the Old Lady Mountain Trail down to the Zion Lodge for ice cream.

FUTURE CLIMBING: In "Tales from the Backcountry" in Zion National Park: Summit Routes, the author reports that the east face of Cliff Dwelling Mnt was attempted by Buzz Burrell and Jared Campbell. They were said to have been attempting to do a traverse of the Court of the Patriarchs starting with Mt. Moroni. They rappelled into the saddle between Lady Mnt and Cliff Dwelling Mnt and climbing two pitches of 5.8 on the east face of Cliff Dwelling before retreating. Future parties could finish the route. Approach from Lady Mountain, i.e., hiking the standard Old Lady Mountain Trail approach. Then climb the East face of Cliff Dwelling Mnt. To get down reverse course.

The Bishopric East

The Bishoprics (the three white peaks), as seen from Coalpits Wash. The East Bishopric is on the far right.

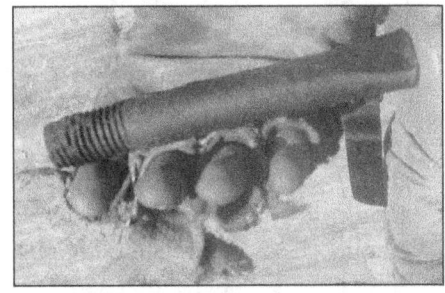

INTRODUCTION The area of the Bishoprics is one of the most beautiful and special in the park (not that there are places in Zion that are not beautiful). It's a remote and difficult to reach location. When I told Ron I had done the first ascent of the East Bishopric, he told me that in his opinion, I had climbed one of the last great mountaineering problems in Zion. He did not realize there is a way to get to the Bishoprics without climbing the red walls at the end of Coalpits Wash.

It's possible mine was the not the first ascent. I found old, rusty bailing wire that was used to make fences. At the saddle between the Hamster and

Above: the East Bishopric. The 5th class route ascends the left sky line. To the right are the Blob and Gate Keeper. On the far right is the western edge of Church Mesa.

Entry Paws, I found a rusted, three-inch bolt that may have been used to anchor fencing into the rock. The area was clearly used by earlier inhabitants to corral stock. By cutting off Inclined Pass, unless the stock were mountain goats, they would have been limited to staying in the area. The East Bishopric and West Bishoprics are mostly scrambles. It's likely ranchers and young and adventurous youth would have climbed them to keep an eye on stock or just for the view.

HISTORY In April, 2007, Dave Everett and I got lost (a Dangerous Dan tip) attempting to do the first ascent of the Meridian Tower. We went down a canyon on the east side of Inclined Temple and could not reverse course. We ran into pot holes filled with water. I had never seen pot holes, and was freaked out at the prospect of swimming. We climbed out of the canyon west of what would later be called the Hamster. I was afraid to tell Dave just how lost I had gotten us. It was our second night without sleeping bags, and it was cold and windy. The good news (to me) was we had inadvertently reached the Bishoprics, a place I never dreamed of getting to. I would have liked to have climbed all three of the Bishoprics. Dave was concerned about being lost. He an emergency device that sent a signal to a satellite, relayed to his wife, with a pre-programmed message we were OK. After the experience, I wondered if Dave would ever climb with me again. On our next outing, I asked him to attempt the Meridian Tower. We made it to the summit, but not before I got us lost, and we climbed another unclimbed mountain on the way. In March, 2017, I climbed a new route on the NW ridge of the East Bishopric.

AS DAVE TELLS IT...

Sunday, April 8. Our intent was to attempt a first accent on a backcountry spire Dan had been eyeing for some time. We filed for a backcountry overnight pass at the Visitors Center. After numerous warnings from the backcountry climbing ranger about their inability to perform any rescue in the area we were going, we were issued a three-night pass. He gave us some trail information, but said that he hadn't heard of anyone heading the way we were intending, so we were really on our own. He warned us: "Rescue would be impossible if we ran into trouble, so you WILL be on your own." A sobering thought.

Monday, April 9. Luckily, we didn't head out yesterday, because we had quite a storm blow in during the night. Lots of rain and strong winds. The forecast was clear with rain predicted Thursday. We had a clear 3-4 day window. We made a mistake in identifying the formation south of the Inclined Temple as Abraham, and headed into the wrong canyon. Unknown to us, we were heading west instead of our intended southerly direction. We ran into several cliffs that were only surpassed by breaking out the ropes and rappelling. It wasn't until we had gone all the way to the end of this canyon that we realized the terrain wasn't matching expectations. We decided that we needed to get to higher ground and breakout the map. As the sun set, we realized just how lost we really were. We didn't recognize any of the formations around us. We found a flat area where we could bivouac [After climbing two pitches of 5.8 to get out of the canyon] just as the dark of night enveloped us. It was a cold and windy night. The wind was blowing so much sand it sounded like it was pouring rain. Neither, Dan nor I got much sleep.

Once daylight came, Dan was able to orientate us. We were eight miles too far west. The area where we were at sits on top of 1000 - 2000 foot cliffs. Our plan was to make our way down to Coalpits Wash, follow the creek back to Highway 9, and hitchhike to town. We had to find a way down the cliff bands which ran for miles. We found ourselves at the base of a formation called the Bishopric. We decided to attempt to climb it.

The first 300 feet of climbing was easy. Protection was sparse; the rock rotten. The wind was horrific. A couple of times I thought it might blow me off the face and down the sheer 1000' cliff. After reaching the top and coming down, our next mission was to find a way home. We climbed onto a ridge to the south that promised the least resistance, and followed it until we had to start rappelling. The area of the cliff band we had chosen proved perfect. We reached the ground just as darkness surrounded us.

Wednesday, April 11. We took the path of least resistance until we hit the old mining equipment, where we picked up a trail that followed the creek and walked out onto Highway 9. We had to hitchhike. I was sure it was going to be a long time before someone picked us up because I'm sure we looked as ragged as we felt. God was smiling on us. The third car that passed turned around and gave us a ride all the way back to our cars in Springdale.

CLIMBING THE EAST BISHOPRIC

There are three Bishoprics. The West Bishopric is the easiest (5th class); the East Bishopric is the highest (also a scramble); the North Bishopric is the most difficult, and requires technical climbing. To get to any requires a long, steep hike without a trail. Those that have the tenacity are rewarded with solitude and beauty. Most hikers and scramblers will climb the East and West Bishoprics and the nearby Hamster. For those with time and skills, climbing all the Bishoprics in a day is adventure at a high (fun) level. The Traverse of the Bishoprics is covered in the chapter, Traverses.

WATER Water is almost always present in Terry Wash on the west side of the West Bishopric, at its south toe. In early season, water will be flowing in the valley between the East and West Bishoprics (Jennings Wash). The source is a snow bank on the east side of the North Bishopric at the notch between the North and East Bishoprics.

SEASON: Spring or fall.
STARTING POINTS:
I have always approached the Bishoprics from Phantom Valley, using the rappel anchors on the West Rim for the start to Heaps Canyon. I use the normal approach to exit: Follow Terry Wash (the creek by camp) SW to where it terminates at a big drop. From there traverse NW around hood doos before hiking straight down towards Cougar Mountain. Before getting to Cougar Mountain, go west down Trail Canyon (a hike) to where it meets the Right Fork of the Subway. The normal approach is the reverse. Dave and I exited the area by following the ridge on the SE side of the toe, south, scrambling to where it was not possible to continue, at which point we made a series of rappels off natural anchors to reach Coalpits Wash (not recommended)..
EQUIPMENT REQUIRED: Slings.

---

1. SOUTH TOE, 5TH CLASS *D Stih and D Everest 2007*
Start at the south toe. Take the easiest way up the white slabs. If it becomes too difficult, you are off route.

---

2. NW RIDGE, 5.5 *D Stih 2017*
A less glamorous way to get to the summit, this provides a full tour of the mountain. Bushwhack up the valley between the North and East Bishoprics to the notch at the north end of the canyon. From the notch, step right and scramble up the NW ridge to the summit. Descend by going down the South Toe route.

The south toe of the East Bishopric. The route goes up the low-angle white slopes.

Above and right: the NW Ridge route on the East Bishopric. It's just a scramble.

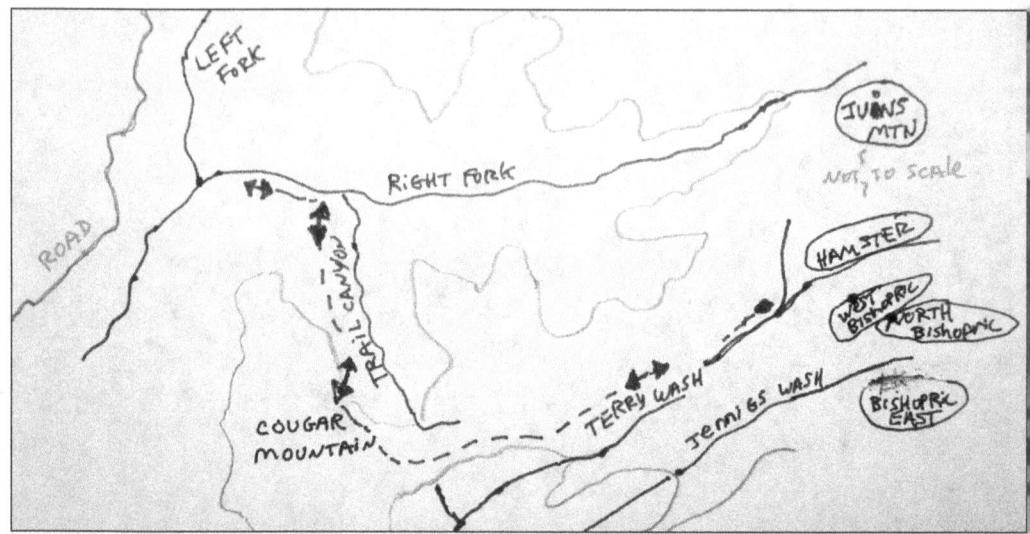

The normal approach to the Bishoprics starts at Kolob Terrace Road and used Trail Canyon to reach high ground and Terry Wash.

An alternative exit from the area of the Bishoprics for prepared canyoneers. The green arrows show the path from the bottom of the climbing route on the East Bishopric to the start of the canyon. The red arrow is a section that contains pot holes. The blue arrows show a canyon that has been descended from Ivins Mountain and the completion of the alternate descent.

FUTURE ADVENTURES: If you're a canyoneer and prepared to go down a narrow canyon with pot holes filled with water, you could exit the area of the Bishoprics by going down the canyon Dave and I climbed out of on our approach.

An itinerary would consist of getting to the Bishoprics by one of the previous described paths, climb the Bishopric, and then exit via this canyon. To enter the canyon, from camp near the creek on the west side of the West Bishopric, scramble up slabs to the east that lead to a high point south of the Hamster. Go down slabs on the other side and find the best way to descend into the valley on the NW side of the Hamster. Hike NW to reach the creek. Turn left and follow the creek west to where the canyon walls narrow and pot holes must be negotiated. You will exit the pot holes as the canyon meets drainage/canyon on the right that comes down from the south side of Ivins Mountains, a canyon CP reports has been descended. As you continue you will reach a big drop at an el blanco water fall, where I suspect that first descent party

Lost and not yet aware of it, Dave rappelling into the canyon from the south side of Inclined Temple. Below: Ivins Mountain (center), Inclined Temple (right) as viewed after climbing out of the canyon, just before reaching pot holes.

drilled anchors to finish getting down. From there, hike out. You will up in the Lower Right Fork of the Subway which requires a canyoneering permit. Obtain one before starting.

The North Bishopric

INTRODUCTION The last of the three Bishoprics to be climbed and the most difficult. In order to reach the north face, in the spring of 2016, Mike and Robbie attempted to climb up to a ridge up what later would become Nate's Tree Descent. In regard to the vertical, wide cracks that stopped them, Robbie later told me, "We were not aid climbers."

From October, 2016, through April, 2017, I spent eight outings attempting to climb the North Bishopric. On my first attempt, I carried a large rack of climbing gear, leaving only room for a single, 8-millimeter rope. I tried to climb the face to the right of Nate's Tree Descent and didn't get far. After coming down I walked around to explore the east side. As I tried to get a better look at a potential aid route on the east face, I put up a new route on the NW corner of the neighboring East Bishopric. I then attempted to climb to the North Bishopric from the ridge on its north side. I got as far as the Gate

Keeper and went down because I had only one rope.

In November, 2016, I returned with my Nephew. Only seventeen, Nathaniel Stih had never climbed or rappelled. We climbed to the Gate Keeper, continued along the ridge, and climbed The Blob. From its summit, we descended, rappelling off the ridge between the Blob and the North Bishopric, a descent we named, Nate's Tree Descent.

In March, 2017, I returned alone, re-climbed the north ridge past the Blob, and continued to the base of a choosy looking crack I named Vince's Groove. From the top of Vince's Groove, I scrambled to the summit.

6 Months, 6 Attempts, 11,000 Miles,

From October through April, I drove 11,000 miles and spent eight outings attempting to climb the North Bishopric. My first attempt was in October, 2016. I hiked up the West Rim Trail and rappelled into Phantom Valley carrying a large rack of gear. Due to the weight of my climbing and camping gear, I carried only a single eight-millimeter rope.

I attempted to climb the west face and got spanked. I thought it was because I was out of shape or scared. Later I learned that stronger climbers, those with a partner, had tried to climb the face and failed. I took a break, and explored the other peaks in the area, ones that had been climbed, are easy and fun. Other than the high winds, it was a lovely day and I was having a great time. I was walking back to camp when I saw a huge, dual-blade helicopter hovering. The military does training nearby. It seemed to be pausing to look at me, so I waved. I wanted to let them know was OK, and wondered why they found me so interesting.

Then I saw what they were looking at. The winds, in excess of 40 MPH, had blown everything in my camp away. Stuff was strewn on the ground and in the water like plane wreckage. Much had blown into the waterfall and the creek. I rushed to find everything and get it out of the water. Fortunately there was still a few hours of sun left. I spent the remainder of the day drying stuff out.

The next day I walked around the east side of the North Bishopric,

A potential route on the north-east corner of the North Bishopric. This is also the last rappel for the descent from the North Bishopric when doing a traverse of the three Bishoprics.

where I scouted two potential lines. Both would require aid. The issue was I only had one rope, and it was a thin one. From the bottom, I couldn't see if the cracks continued to the top. If I didn't reach the top I might not be able to get down with one rope. It crossed my mind to try anyhow. I let it pass.

In order to get a better view of the potential routes, I scrambled up the northwest corner of the neighboring peak, the East Bishopric. I kept climbing higher and higher and soon found myself on top of it. I came down the south side and went back to camp. That's when I noticed it. I was thinking there had to be another way to get to the top of the North Bishopric. I became aware of the ridge that winds down from its north side. The ridge looked long, with several obstacles that would need to be climbed before reaching the Bishopric. It seemed unlikely I could climb it in a day.

I started scrambling up it to explore how far I could get. On the way I soloed the first peak and named it the Gate Keeper. I thought it too dangerous to continue without a partner.

November, 2016. I returned with my Nephew, Nate. We explored further, and did the first ascent of the next formation on the ridge, the Blob. We continued toward the headwall on the North Bishopric. It was late in the day when we got there. We didn't have enough time to continue, and went down Nate's Tree Descent.

December, 2016. Each year, the *American Alpine Journal* (AAJ) publishes what it considers the most significant climbs of the previous year. The dead line for submissions is December 31. I wanted to submit the Blob so that Nate's name would be in print. I did not however, want to publish details without first having climbed the North Bishopric. I therefor returned and tried to finish climbing the North Bishopric before the end of the year. Although Nate and I had made progress on the ridge, I was not certain I could climb the North Bishopric that way by myself. It seemed the aid route would be fun, and have a greater chance of success. I packed extra knife-blades and lost arrows pitons, enough to do a big wall in Yosemite.

Unfortunately, the weather had

changed since Nate and I had been there. I was hampered by snow and ice. The creek at camp, typically a beautiful stream with a gentle water fall, was frozen inches thick. I had to pound on the ice and break the ice with my climbing hammer to collect water to drink. Because of the weight of the climbing gear, I was not carrying warm clothing or extra fuel for the stove. Night time temperatures were below 10 Fahrenheit. My feet froze. I had to keep a water bottle and my boots inside my sleeping bag at night to keep them from freezing. I had trouble finding the lighter for the stove. I found the matches packed as a backup in case the lighter stopped working. There was little fuel left. I thought if I could suffer through the cold, I could climb the aid route. Although there was snow on the ground, my aid route faced the sun.

In the morning I started climbing the aid route. I laid a tarp on the snow and placed my gear on it in preparation. Stepping as high as I could, I placed two pitons that rang to the hilt, a sign they were deep and solid. As soon as I stood on them, however, they pulled out with body weight. There was wet, caked sand on the ends. Apparently, sandstone is not rock - it's sand. It seemed it might be months before the "rock" was dry. I put the climbing gear in a trash bag to protect it from rain and snow, placed the package high up on the other side of the gully under a tree, and went home.

Back home, I couldn't let it go. I wanted to get the route done before the end of the year.

The following day I drove back to Zion. The highway was clear until I got to the east entrance of the park. I could have skied down Checkerboard Mesa. The shuttle wasn't running, so I was allowed to drive the main canyon road. I drove to the end of the road at the Narrows, got out of the car, and walked fifty feet. It was so cold I got back in and drove home.

When I got home I re-grouped and thought about what I could do to climb in winter conditions. I decided to take crampons, the kind I had used to climb the Eiger in Switzerland, and an ice axe - a short Stubi tool with a hammer head. My thought was if the cracks on Vince's Groove had ice, I'd use the ice axe. If the rock was icy, I'd put crampons on. Who knows, maybe that might be easier than rock climbing.

New Year's Eve, 2016. I drove back to Zion. It was warmer, 30F at night, but there was more snow. At the East Entrance, as I was paying the fee, I asked the ranger about the conditions. He said it had been crazy. A party of hikers had just been rescued by helicopter off the West Rim, when an avalanche buried the trail. I found that hard to believe. How could an avalanche trap hikers in Zion? I soon found out.

On New Year's Eve, I got a bivy permit and did my usual routine. I parked at Angels Landing at midnight and hiked up the West Rim Trail in the dark, with plans to rappel into Phantom Valley at first light. On the trail I found myself tired and frustrated as I post-holed knee-deep snow with a heavy haul bag. When I got to Little Siberia, the place the avalanche had occurred, I realized why the hikers had needed to be rescued. There was no trail. It was a mountain of ice and snow. Had I not been experienced with climbing ice and snow, I would have turned around. Instead, I continued a few miles and almost reached Camp 4 on the West Rim. There, I decided it was crazy to be doing what I was doing. I turned around and started down.

I had hiked a long way down the trail when I thought I heard voices. When you're alone, hearing other people returns a sense of safety and confidence. If they can make it, you think you can. I turned around and retraced my footsteps in the snow back to the top. Later I realized there were no people. My mind had been playing tricks on me.

Back at the top, at the end of my footprints, I could not see where the trail continued. I knew the trail did not follow the edge of the West Rim. Rather, it weaves back and forth, leaving the edge then coming back to it. I decided to go for it. The snow was at least three feet deep. I took a few steps past my tracks. Suddenly I was hit by a jolting pain in my right arm. It shocked me. It scared me. *What was this? What if it got worse when I was rappelling or climbing?* As I considered my condition, I also considered that I would not make camp that night, the place Nate and I had stashed sleeping bags. Dark clouds menaced, as if it might rain at night. At best I'd survive sleeping in my clothes. I decided to turn around. This time, I would wait for spring.

March, 2017. I abandoned the idea of doing the aid route, and concentrated on summiting the North Bishopric by what seemed the only practical way - the north ridge. Due to the heavy snow and rain that year, the normally brown, Mars-colored landscape now looked like the sod lawns in a rural neighborhood. The pass near the Inclined Temple was clear. There were patches of snow on the ridge and at the base of the Bishopric. That was good. I would be able to melt snow on the climb, saving me from carrying water.

On the trip with Nate, I had left my sleeping bag and gear wrapped in a tarp up the hill, about one hundred yards from camp. I found the gear. Mice had chewed holes through my sleeping bag and popped over everything,

Angels Landing, New Years Day, 2017. Bottom left: following my footprints at the top of the West Rim Trail. Bottom right: snow and ice on the West Rim Trail near Little Siberia.

making a huge mess (a reason not to leave stash kits in the backcountry). Thankfully, my sleeping bag didn't smell like mice. I took inventory, shook the mouse droppings off, and made two piles - stuff that was too stinky and damaged and would need to be thrown away, and what was left. I had a large trash bag. It was big and heavy when I was finished. I carried it out all the way back to the car.

My climbing gear was stashed on the other side of the mountain, where I had attempted the aid route. I hiked around to the other side to get it. There was still a lot of snow on that side of the mountain. The canyon between the North and East Bishoprics is sheltered from sun. The crack I had placed two pitons in on my last attempt was still under a ten-foot snow drift. When the snow melts, my pitons will be visible to those who may want to finish that route.

Luckily, I had left the gear high up on the side of the canyon. The snow accumulation nearly reached it, twenty feet up the side of the canyon. I took the gear back to camp and regrouped. I intended to pack my haul bag to the gills, scramble up to the base of the ridge, and take it with me as I climbed. At the bottom, I planned to leave the trash and stuff I did not need to climb, and come back for it. That included crampons, deer antlers, a frayed rope, and so forth. The haul bag weighed more than 80 pounds. Without someone to help me get it on, I had to perch it on a rock, slide my shoulders into the straps, and try to stand up.

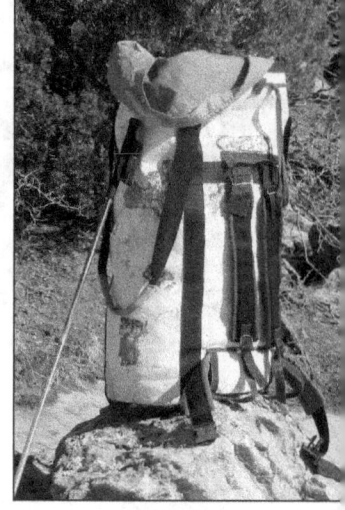

With the bag on a big rock, I slipped into the shoulder straps and stood. As I stood, I heard my knees twist, and a crackle-pop. I set the bag down, took a deep breath, paused for a moment. I hoped that I wasn't injured. After a few moments, I carefully moved my limbs to assess if they were functional. I was lucky. I put the haul bag back on, and proceed like a slow moving freight train, step by step, one foot in front of the other, up the valley towards the start of the climb. In my haul bag was bivy gear, a stove, pot, fuel to melt snow, a full rack of climbing gear, and two ropes. I intended nothing to stop me.

My first bivy was on the summit of the Gate Keeper. It was a spectacular place with 360 degree views. The stone outcroppings provide a cozy spot, protected from wind. It's as if the gods placed them there. It was so comfy I didn't need a pad. I fit perfectly between the stones. There is an area I call "The Kitchen" with a rock that looks like a kitchen sink. I was too tired to cook and enjoy what god had built. Although there were just enough blobs of snow to melt to cook with, I was too tired. I just went to sleep.

Bivy on top of Gatekeeper.

In the morning, I made two trips to port the gear down the other side of the Gatekeeper and across to the Blob. The haul bag was heavy and it would have been too dangerous to carry it in all in one trip.

Troubled Youth on the Blob is fairly easy climbing. When I had climbed it with Nate, I had him belay me (feed out rope as I climbed). Now, I free-soloed it, dragging a rope behind me. When I got to the top, I fixed the rope to a bush and went down to get the haul bag. From the summit, I walked across to the base of the North Bishopric. At the bottom was the potential crux that I considered might keep me from the summit - Vince's Groove.

I named the difficult section, a crack climb, after Vince Bert, an El Cap big wall climber from the 1990s. One afternoon at his condo in Solana Beach, California, he led me to his storage in the parking garage, and pulled out his haul bag. There, he gave me his haul bag and everything inside it, all of his climbing gear. He told me he had given up climbing to focus on other pursuits. For a while that included surfing. Then it was spending two years out of the country, riding his bike from San Diego to the tip of South America. In Patagonia, they told him he was a wussy if he flew home, so he rode it back to San Diego.

Melting snow to make water at the base of the Blob.

I felt confident I could climb Vince's Groove. It was the steep, broken, loose face above it that concerned me. I suspected it is what had deterred others from trying to climb the North Bishopric this route. Before I began, I took care business. At the base of Vince's Groove, I set up camp. Using small patches of snow, I refilled my water bottles and set out my sleeping bag to be ready should I get down when it was dark.

To my surprise and delight, I reached the top of

Vince's Groove.

The last part of the ridge leading up to the top of the North Bishopric.

the North Bishopric early in the day. Opposite to how it looks, there are numerous foot holds, and the face above the groove is not as steep as it appears. Vince's Groove was fun and classic.

At the top of the Groove, I untied, left the rope, and scrambled to the summit. I built a great cairn, a marker consisting of logs and stones. In the middle, inside a plastic bag, I left a water-proof notebook and pencil - a summit log. Someone had dropped it at the bus stop at the Angels Landing trail. I had picked it up as I got off the bus. It was blank and brand new, and I thank the person that left it.

I reported my success to T*he American Alpine Journal.* Unfortunately, the editor made an error, and omitted Nate's name in their publication. The editor wrote: "Alone or with various partners, Dan Stih..."

In my efforts to climb the mountain, I had only one partner: Nate. I had spent months responding to questions from the editor and submitted a photo of Nate climbing with an ice axe. No one carries an ice axe to climb in the desert. Nate was open to all possibilities. The editor responded to my suggestion to use the photo of Nate climbing the rock with an ice axe by saying they don't publish photos of climbers.

Really?

View from the top of the North Bishopric. The Inclined Temple is on the right.

Be sure to sign the summit register.

Joy on the summit.

CLIMBING THE NORTH BISHOPRIC

1. VINCE'S GROOVE 5.8+ A2 *D Stih 2017*
Mostly a free-climb. The A2 is based on protecting the start of Vince's Groove. I placed a few baby angles. I'm not sure if micro-cams or nuts will work. The fall would be bad. You'd land on the belay ledge and possibly tumble over the side of the ridge. The Groove is classic. It has face to fingers to wide stuff. After fifteen feet it takes protection exceptionally well, the rock is good, and the climbing fun.
EQUIPMENT REQUIRED: Except for Vince's Groove, slings are the only gear. At the groove the following: 1 of each # 3,4,5 camelots; 1 red alien (a cam approx. 3/4"); 4 baby angles (a mix of #1 and #2); 1 longer angle (3/4").

CAUTIONS / SPECIAL DIFFICULTIES: While this is a free-climb, a few small pitons may be helpful at the start of Vince's Groove to protect the face climbing required to get into the groove. Alternatively, I give permission to drill a bolt there. At the bottom of the groove, it may be tricky to protect the first ten feet. I suspect some talented and creative free-climber will find a way. Up high there is a hidden, chimney-like crack with incredibly good, big foot holds. It's a joy to climb. Make it to the wide part and you'll have no trouble getting to the summit.
WATER SOURCES: See East Bishopric. Water is next to camp on the west side of the West Bishopric's south toe. If approaching from Phantom Valley, fill up there. If it's early season (March) and there's snow, camp closer to the start of the ridge. There's an iceberg at the start of the route to climb the King (see map drawing). It melts fast. One week it's cold and snowy, two weeks later the water may be gone except for the creek on the west side of the West Bishopric.

Water flowing in early season between the West and East Bishoprics. Snow in early season (mid-March) on the east side, in the valley between the two. Below: The route.

SEASON: Spring (March 15 - May)
TIME REQUIRED: 3 days.
THE STARTING POINTS: See East Bishopric.
THE ROUTE: Climb the ridge on the north side of the North Bishopric. Start by climbing the Gatekeeper (see Gatekeeper and the Blob). A short rappel is required to reach the Blob. Continue down the other side of the Blob, along the ridge to Vince's Groove, a one-pitch classic free climb. From the top of Vince's Groove it's a scramble to the summit of the North Bishopric.
GETTING DOWN: A single rope rappel from a small pine tree at the top of Vince's

Groove gets you back to the ridge. From the ridge, rappel Nate's Tree Descent. There is also a decent on the NE corner of the North Bishopric used to link the Bishoprics during a traverse (see the Traverse of the Bishoprics). It requires courage. The exposure is great, and the rappel route is not obvious. Unless you are doing the traverse, Nate's Tree Descent is recommended.

Once back on the ground, exit via the normal approach. Mike and Robbie exited the area by rappelling down the

Nate's Tree Descent, the normal descent from the North Bishopric.

canyon that runs between the Sanctuary and the north side of the ridge leading up to the Gate Keeper, ending up in Coalpits Wash.

FUTURE CLIMBING The East Face of the North Bishopric has an aid route I started. There are two fixed pins at the bottom. I bailed after finding the rock too wet. The bottom does not get sun. In early season (Spring) snow melting off the top keeps it wet.

An unfinished aid route on the east face starts at the left-most crack that comes down from the top and curves right.

The Meridian Tower

INTRODUCTION Located on the 113th Meridian, east of the Altar of Sacrifice, it took me twenty years to climb this mountain. I was always planning and stewing on ideas, and trying to find a partner. If I had been successful on my first attempt, I would probably not have climbed so many other peaks in Zion. It was because I failed so many times and kept going, that along the way each time, I discovered other mountains that had not been climbed. Each time I learned a new trick, a new way of getting to things. Each time I found a new way of getting down when I got in over my head.

HISTORY Ron and I first tried to climb the Meridian Tower during our traverse of the Towers of the Virgin in March, 1998. We were unsuccessful. It was ten years before, in April of 2008, I returned with Dave Everett, and climbed to the summit of Meridian Tower's red cap. In March, 2016, I returned with Matt Mower and climbed the tower proper.

If at First You Don't Succeed....

In March, 1998, Ron Raimonde and I tried to climb the Meridian Tower during our traverse of the Towers of the Virgin. I was tired from climbing seven peaks in two days, but eager to climb the Meridian tower when we reached it. I didn't get my feet off the ground. The west face was too steep and blank. I should have kept looking but was too tired. Maybe it's due to me being anemic and having a low red blood cell count. I was secretly thankful. I hoped it meant we could go home. I waited, while Ron trudged up the canyon on the north-west side of the Meridian Tower to get a closer look. He came back and said, "It doesn't connect," referring to the gap between the main summit and the tower. We descended the gully south-west of the Meridian Tower into Oak Creek Canyon.

It was ten years before I attempted the Meridian Tower again. All the while I kept telling Ron I was worried someone might beat me to it. All the while

Ron kept smirking and replying, "No one wants to climb the Meridian Tower. Don't worry!" I was surprised Ron had no interest. It had been his idea to do the traverses. But he was more interested in finding thin cracks in Zion to aid climb. It was the same with Ron Olevsky, who when I called to see if he wanted to climb the tower with me, gave a swift and definite response: "You should have known you've got the wrong guy. I'm not interested in long approaches."

April, 2008. After the last epic I took him on (the East Bishopric) I was surprised when Dave said he would climb with me again. I wondered why, when I said I knew where I was going this time, he trusted me. Not to disappoint, I got us lost again. We were lucky we didn't have a more serious epic, and not stuck in a slot canyon filled with water. From the top of Church Mesa, I saw what I thought looked like the Meridian Tower. We descended Church Mesa too early. We came down into the crux of Birch Creek, a narrow passage filled with big pools.

We scrambled up Birch Creek, after which I took us up the wrong peak. To me Chameleon peak looked like the Meridian Tower. We climbed several pitches up it and bivied on it before I realized we were on the wrong peak. In the morning we descended, and continued up Birch Creek to the Meridian Tower. Progress was slow, blocked by steep water falls and deep pools. We didn't have wet suits, dry shoes, or a change of clothes.

After hauling our packs on a few pitches on the north face of the Meridian Tower, we found ourselves at a headwall wall that looked unclimbable. I was worried because Dave, assuming we had reached a dead end, was quick to start thinking about an exit plan. I let my brain go empty, to leave room for a solution to appear, as we decided to sleep on it.

In the morning, we decided to leave our packs to make climbing it easier. The risk was if we had to come back to get our packs, we might end up stuck in Birch Creek with no way home.

To get around the blank section, I climbed as high as I could, put in a piece, lowered on it, and swung around the corner. There was a huge amount of exposure, and I couldn't see if there was a way to climb

Dave and I rappelled down the canyon on the east side of the south face of Church Mesa into Birch Creek, the dark, tree-filled gully right of the red cap.

Birch Creek as viewed from the first pitch on Chameleon, the next peak down the creek from the Meridian Tower.

The North Face of the Meridian Tower. The obvious line of trees in the middle, slanting down towards the right, was Dave and my descent. At the top left of the tree line is the tension traverse.

up once I swung around the corner. Fortunately, when I got around the corner I saw there was a way to keep climbing to the top. It was loose, but I found I could tiptoe sideways, my hands hanging on loose rocks, to a more solid ridge. I ran out of rope before I could get there. Or at least I'm gonna say. I got scared and concerned about my position. I needed a break, and belayed Dave to meet me. He took the lead and got us to the top.

We were still not on what I considered to be *the* top. There is a large red cap in the middle of the summit. We climbed to the top of it - what I call the Red Cap. Then we argued about what to do next.

I told him we had not gotten to the true summit - the tower. To get to the tower would require lowering into a

Dan starting the A0 pitch that leads around the corner, climbing in his hiking boots. Bottom: Dave coming down the gully on the west side of the Meridian after rappelling from the summit. So much snow. So little water. We didn't have a stove.

chasm, and climbing up the other side. For years I had planned and dreamed about climbing the tower. Dave, however was not interested. He insisted we were on the summit and didn't need to climb the tower. The topographical map at the time seemed to agree with Dave. The map had "Meridian Tower" written across both the mountain we were standing on and the tower.

I walked towards the edge to get a better look at the tower. The brush was too thick to allow for a clear view. The idea of going into the chasm without being able to see what I was in for scared me. Dave quit arguing and offered to continue. Afraid, I took the opportunity to decline, and I said it was fine we just climbed the main summit.

We got down by rappelling to our packs at the headwall, then rappelling into the gully on the west side of the

Looking down at the notch and across at the tower from the red cap side of the Meridian Tower.

Climbing the tower.

The tree on the south edge of the red cap summit of the Meridian Tower, used as anchor to rappel into the notch.

Meridian Tower. The creek was dry. We had no water left. I was out of food. Dave offered me beef Jerky. It made me sick. My food the last two days had been one power bar. We'd been climbing for four days. We slept there, thinking there was not enough time to get down. It was a cold night. I got no sleep without a sleeping bag.

I haven't seen Dave since. He probably got fed up with my stubbornness. Those who have witnessed it can testify that when I get close to a summit I get crazy. I become possessed. No amount or reasoning can snap me out of doing anything to get to the summit.

My mom told me she had a dream. She said I was close to the top of a mountain with a tree on the edge, and everyone was rooting for me to make it to the top. I didn't let her know that we had not made it.

In March, 2016, Matt and I re-climbed the route as Dave and I had. We hiked across the summit and rappelled off a tree into the notch next to the tower. The park service knows the tree. A law enforcement officer told me they watched it burn after it got struck by lightning.

I collected a few pieces of charred wood from the tree. A shaman once gave me wood struck by lightning to rub on my heel to treat blisters. It didn't seem to work, but I thought it would make a nice gift for a friend who is a healer. To my surprise, when I gave it to her she said natives consider it bad luck. She threw it away.

I feel my mountains would never harm me. I always ask permission. Sometimes I get, "No." Sometimes I get pulled to take something I don't see the value or significance of, and don't want to carry. One time, I took a rock home, only to be told it wanted to go home - back to where I had picked it up. I made the journey and put it back.

After rappelling into the notch, I came face to face with the tower. Although the tower had looked blank from a distance, once we got to it, I found there to be good hand and foot holds. The rock was solid basalt, more secure than sandstone. It was an enjoyable, well-protected climb. The dream my mom had eight years ago perfectly described the scene, as I pulled myself up onto the top, next to a tree growing on the edge.

CLIMBING THE MERIDIAN TOWER

WATER: Birch Creek always has water. Depending on the season, there may or may not be water in the southern point of a creek on the west side of the Meridian Tower on the plateau. Water might also be found from snow melting on the plateau in a large pool far down the white slabs running down from the notch between the Altar and Sky Island. There usually is not water after May 1st. The exception is after a large rain storm in which water of poor quality (take a filter) might be found in the aforementioned pool.

THE MERIDIAN TOWER A0 5.8 *D Stih and D Everett, Main Red Cap, April, 2008; D Stih and M Mower, Main Red Cap and Tower (first ascent) March, 2016.*
EQUIPMENT REQUIRED: Standard rack of cams. In my journal I wrote the following were used when Dave and I climbed it: (1) each: #1, 2, 3 cams.
CAMPING / TIME REQUIRED: 3 days.
STARTING POINT: Birch Creek, on the north side of the Meridian Tower.
THE ROUTE: From Birch Creek, on the north side of the Meridian Tower, climb the easiest way possible (there are many) up broken face, sticking to cracks which take protection. It's about seven pitches of roped climbing. You will come to a flat section 3/4 up where, if needed, is a good place to bivy. You'll know when you are there because you won't be able to climb higher without going around the corner left. This is the A0 tension traverse across a slab below a headwall, where it's necessary to go left around a blank corner. Due to rope drag, belay as soon as you get around the corner. A long pitch or two of easier but steep climbing reaches the top. Wander around the red cap until you find the way up it. It's a scramble when you do.
ALTERNATE ROUTE: When Mike Dunn and Arthur Herlitzka did the second Traverse of the Towers of the Virgin in March, 2021, after descending the Altar of Sacrifice, they were low on water and chose to go to Birch Creek. They went up and down the gully that hugs the west face of the Meridian Tower to reach Birch Creek, then down the creek a short ways, then up a dirt gully that hugs the east side of the Meridian Tower,

between the Meridian Tower and Chameleon Peak. They report climbing to the larger summit of the Meridian Tower by traversing bushy ledges up its east face.

ALTERNATE ROUTE: I once attempted to climb directly up to the notch between the larger summit of the Meridian Tower and "tower", starting from the plateau on the west side. I found it terrifying and impractical. I was (rope) soloing without a belay device using clove hitches.

CLIMBING THE TOWER: From the summit with the red cap, rappel into the notch and climb the NE face of the tower. It's an enjoyable free-climb on good rock (basalt) that protects well with cams. It's one short pitch, 5.6- 5.8.

GETTING DOWN AND ALTERNATE EXITS:

Option A) Dave and I left our bivy gear on the large platform at the headwall before the tension traverse. From the summit we rappelled back to that ledge, then down a ramp with trees on the west side of the Meridian Tower. It required five double-rope rappels. I don't recommend this exit unless you leave bivy gear at that ledge. I recommended you take all your gear to the top. After the rappels we scrambled up and down the gully that hugs the west side of the Meridian Tower, to reach the plateau between the Meridian Tower and Altar of Sacrifice. From the plateau, the normal descent to civilization is the gully on the west side of the Meridian Tower. (See Canyon Descents).

Option B) If you have two ropes, you can fix a rope from the summit with the red cap down into the notch, climb the tower with the second rope, and go back up to the summit with the red cap to get your bivy gear and sleep on the summit. Or you could take your bivy gear with you and sleep on the tower. You don't need to go back to the top of the red summit. From the notch, it's possible to rappel down white slabs on the west face for a direct approach into the valley (plateau) between the Meridian Tower and the Altar of Sacrifice.

Rappelling off the tower summit back into the notch.

The Inclined Temple

The Inclined Temple (left) and Ivins Mountain (right) as seen from the West Rim.

INTRODUCTION It's called the Inclined Temple because of how the summit inclines on its south side. The south (inclined) side is not visible from Springdale. For early settlers to name it, they must have visited the area of the Bishoprics. Based on relics I found, it appears they used the area between the Inclined Temple (Incline Pass) and the Bishoprics to heard stock.

HISTORY I starting thinking about climbing the Inclined Temple when Dave and I got lost near it in 2007. In 2012, I did research, and asked locals if it had been climbed. There had been some activity from long-distance hikers, runners, and adventures of that kind, but none doing technical climbing in the area with the exception of an ascent of a neighboring peak named the Sanctuary in 2005. In March 2013, Michael Schasch, a local canyoneering guide, and I made an attempt. In September 2013, I attempted to solo it. In October 2013, I returned with Schasch. On Halloween, we bivied in Phantom Valley, and on November 1st, climbed to the top.

Rain Story

March, 2013. I had my eye on the Inclined Temple since Dave and I got lost near it in 2007. From the top of the Bishoprics, I tried to orientate the map to the peaks I knew. Looking at the Inclined Temple, I wasn't sure what it was. In 2012, I asked the locals if it had been climbed, and sent my agenda to Tom Jones, author of the *Zion Canyoneering*. I told him I needed a partner. He said he only goes down things these days, and hooked me up with Michael Schasch.

Mike was busy working, and only had the weekend off. We had two days to get to the temple, climb it, and hike out. The night before, I met him at his house. I arrived late, tired from a long drive, and nervous. I had not been climbing in a while, was out of shape, and worried I might not be able to keep up. Mike was younger and getting out on a regular basis for guiding work.

In the morning we had to stop at the Visitor Center to get a permit. They would not give us a "red pass," a type of permit that allows parking at the Grotto where the trail head for the West Rim is located. We therefore had to wait in line and take the shuttle. This put us way behind schedule. .

The hike was steep. My knees hurt. I was wearing heavy mountaineering boots, the ones I had used to climb in the Alps. I got the squirts. I got blisters. I was barely able to keep up with Mike. My hips hurt. With every step, I felt I needed a hip replacement. Finally, below the last approach slab to the saddle, I told Mike that I could go no further. Mike went ahead to get a glimpse of the backside of the mountain and the route. I waited for him at the pass. When he returned, out of breath, he said, "It's big..." he took another breath, "... and long." We started hiking home.

September, 2013. I returned with the idea of climbing the Inclined Temple by myself. I was in better shape and stronger. After hiking back and forth across the south face looking for the best way, I choose to start on the east corner. I scrambled up one hundred feet and got scared. I couldn't see what was above and didn't have the courage to make the moves by myself. I fixed my rope to a tree and went down.

The weather was nice, so thought I'd stay and enjoy it and hike out in the morning. I didn't have a sleeping bag. The forecast was all sun. I had no way

of knowing that after I had gotten into the canyon, the rangers had stopped issuing canyon permits for all of Zion National Park.

I woke in the middle of the night to the sound of rain. Since I didn't have a sleeping bag, I was wearing all of my clothes and a rain jacket to stay warm. Everything I was wearing was soon soaking wet. I had an orange sack that's supposed to be an emergency bivy bag. I was too tall to fit completely inside it. I put my legs and torso inside the bag, and used a space blanket, another type of emergency shelter, to cover my head.

In the middle of the night there was a break in the rain and I tried to start the stove to brew herbal tea to warm up. The stove was wet. I gave up as drops of rain started to come down again. I went back to suffering, curled in my orange bag, holding on to the space blanket wrapped over my head to keep it from blowing away in the strong winds. I was lucky it was summer. The low was in the high 40s. Had it been colder I might have had hypothermia.

The newspaper later reported: "Monday dawned as one more beautiful late-summer day. But clouds began to build by midday. Late in the afternoon, the rain started coming down. There was no way to know the region was in the first hours of what experts would ultimately call a 1,000-year rain." The same weather settled on Boulder, Colorado, killed eight people, and caused $2 billion in damage.

The rain washed out the road to the East entrance of the park. Left: the emergency shelter and the space blanket I used to cover my head. Neither kept me dry.

In the morning, in a break in the rain, I ran though Phantom Valley back to the West Rim. I was soggy. Everything I was wearing was soaked - shoes, pants, jacket. At the West Rim I had fixed a rope. As the rope went over the edge of the cliff it was being ground into wet sandstone, like a machine used to cut concrete with a steady stream of water. As I got close to the top, I found a spot where the rope as cut almost in two.

On the West Rim, I found the trail, and started hiking back to Lava Point where my Jeep was parked. There was break in the storm. I thought the rain would stop. Then, in the afternoon, it started again, at first softly, then dark and loud. I have never seen so much water on a trail. The last few miles of the trail slop uphill. As I hiked uphill, coming down at me was a torrent of water. The entire mesa around me was four inches deep. It was as walking in a lake, going uphill against a stream. If I stepped out of the flow, I would lose the trail and not be able to tell which way to go. When I got my Jeep, I threw everything inside, hit the gas, and tried to remember the proper way to steer through mud.

Halloween, 2013. I returned with Michael Schasch. On November 1st, we were successful and climbed to the top of the Inclined Temple. Other than it being a little chilly, the weather was perfect.

After climbing the Inclined Temple, I submitted a detailed report to the editor of the *American Alpine Journal* (AAJ). He asked me a ton of questions as he prepared it for publication. When the publication came out there was no mention of Mike and I climbing the Inclined Temple. The following year, I climbed Ivins Mountain, the mountain to the NW, and submitted a trip report, in which I referenced the Inclined Temple. That perked the ears of the editor who asked me, "Has the Inclined Temple been climbed?" I reminded him that our route on it was to have been published the previous year. The editor apologized for the oversight.

Mike, considering the options on the second pitch.

CLIMBING THE INCLINED TEMPLE

WATER Pots holes in Phantom Valley are one of the most reliable sources of water in Zion. In the spring there's water flowing from snow melt and seeps. In the fall, the pot holes hold water several weeks after it rains.
SEASON Spring or Fall.

---

1. THE SOUTH FACE 5.9 R *D Stih and Mike Schasch 2013*

EQUIPMENT REQUIRED: Standard free climbing rack.
CAMPING / TIME REQUIRED: Give yourself three days.
STARTING POINTS: There are several ways to approach the Inclined Temple as described in CP's *Zion National Park: Summit Routes*. Note: the summit of Inclined Temple is an RNA and off-limits. Consider a carry-over, starting on the West Rim, rappelling into Phantom Valley, climbing the Inclined Temple, then exiting via the approach normally used to get to the Bishoprics. The advantage of a carry-over is it's a sure way to get to Inclined Temple on the first day, and you can see the Inclined Temple as you approach it from the West Rim. You can climb it the second day, and spend the third finding your way home.

Start at the Grotto. Hike the West Rim trail to the rappel route for the start of Heaps Canyon. Rappel into Phantom Valley. Walk across Phantom Valley (there will be pools of water to fill drinking bottles) towards the pass between Inclined Temple and the Sanctuary (the formation on the left of Inclined Temple as viewed from the West Rim). As you get close to the Inclined Temple, scramble up a steep slab on the SE side of In-

The upper pitches. The large chimneys is avoided by climbing the crack left of it.

clined Temple. From the top of the saddle, bushwhack down the other side. The Inclined Temple will be on your immediate right. As you get towards the bottom, traverse hard right, toward the temple and the start of the route. The last reliable water is in Phantom Valley.

THE ROUTE: We climbed a total of seven pitches. In the middle, we simul-climbed 400 feet when we couldn't find good anchors. We began on the east side of the south face. I scrambled 100 feet straight up to a large tree, then sideways to grab some bushes, above which I could not see the route. Above the bushes we climbed back left. The second pitch is steep face with scant protection. From the top of it, traverse sideways left to the prominent crack that splits the middle of the south face. Once in main crack system, the climbing gets easier, and the protection better. We climbed it until just below the summit, where a large, overhanging chimney with a roof blocks progress. The chimney is visible from the ground. We tension traversed slightly (3M) left into the crack to the immediate left, then finished up the obvious weakness. On the last pitch Mike climbed a tree, then stemmed between the tree and the wall, before mantling sandy rock to get back onto the face. If you get nothing else out of this narrative, remember to aim for the obvious crack that runs down the center of the south face AND get to it by scrambling up and right from the bottom, before traversing back left.

GETTING DOWN: Rappel the route using natural anchor. Don't expect to find webbing. No bolts were drilled. Exit by hiking past the Bishoprics, per the description in *Zion National Park: Summit Routes*. It requires good map reading skills. The disadvantage of a carry-over is you'll be unfamiliar with that territory.

Ivins Mnt

The upper part of the route climbs the corner system where orange rock meets white. At the point where vegetation is visible, traverse right onto the main face.

INTRODUCTION Ivins Mountain is considered to be one the most remote mountains in Zion National Park. Be prepared to navigate deep into the backcountry. The climbing route requires a lot of gear. We had a rack similar to what is used to climb El Capitan in Yosemite. The first pitch is aid. After a pendulum and ten feet of difficult free-climbing, the remainder is fun and casual.

HISTORY I first attempted Ivins in April, 2014. I started down Wildcat Canyon from Lava Point, thinking I could scramble up to the base of the route. Wildcat Canyon turned out to be rugged, and I didn't get to the mountain. My next attempt was in October, 2015, with Matthew Mower. From Phantom Valley, we descended a gully on the North side of Inclined Temple. When we got into the canyon we almost couldn't climb out. Matt climbed a dead tree leaning against the massif. It took us six pitches of 5.9+ to get to the base. At that point, one of my legs was swollen from an infection, and we retreated. My third, and successful attempt, was in Easter, 2015.

FUTURE CLIMBING It's possible that the first pitch could be free-climbed. In that case, the route will go free. The leader might have to place pitons on lead or run it out. A free version will not require as much gear. We did not drill any bolts.

Ivins Mountain - Part 1

Ivins is another mountain I first noticed when I was lost. After we finished climbing the Inclined Temple, I looked at Ivins and suggested to my partner that we plan to try to climb it. The difficult part would be to be getting to it. "Maybe we should leave something for someone else," he said.

A generous thought. Unless Ivins was waiting for me. Six months later, I had still not found a partner, so I attempted to climb Ivins by myself. The ranger in the backcountry office suggested that to reach Ivins, I could hike down Wildcat Canyon. I asked if he had gotten to Ivins by going down Wildcat Canyon. He said he had, and that once I got to the end of Wildcat canyon, it would be "bloop de bloop de bloop," (easy to reach the start of where I planned to climb). I wondered. Later, I learned that I had gone down, and then climbed out of, The Upper Right Fork Direct to the Subway.

THE REST OF THE STORY...
Sometimes I'm touched by the mountains, and filled with awe by their beauty. On this trip, I was touched by the presence of a stranger. My journey began with wondering where to park. Understanding that I was climbing alone, the ranger said I could park at the trailhead for the West Rim Trail, even though the road was officially closed. There was a "Road Closed" sign on the gate. I checked the lock and found it unlocked. The gate was held closed by bailing wire. I untied the wire, opened the gate, and drove down to the trail head.

The road had been closed because of snow. The snow had melted, but downed trees lay in the middle or the road. I carefully drove around them and checked my permit. It said, "Park at the Lava Point trail head by campground." I finished driving to the trail head, dropped my pack off, and drove back up to where the gate was closed next to the campground.

The campground was closed. After a lot of internal worry and discussion, I decided to park at a picnic spot, a day-use area next to the campground, and walked a mile down the road to where I had left my pack.

I expected it to take two trips to carry my stuff to the bottom of Ivins. For

Deep in Wildcat Canyon, deciding which way to go.

the first, I planned to carry a lighter load, since it would be hike to find the way. Hopefully, it would be an easy way. I packed a sleeping bag, rain gear, a portion of climbing gear, and a rope.

After a short while hiking the trail, I came to the mouth of Wildcat Canyon, left the trail, and entered the canyon. The way the ranger had explained it, it should have been an easy hike. Instead I found myself bush-waking through thick brush and scrambling over an obstacle course of boulders. I had to be careful not to twist an ankle. There was no way I was going to be able to carry a heavier load next trip. I was getting tired and frustrated, and about to give up when I came to a flat clearing with a patch of grass. I stopped to rest.

As I sat down, I noticed something green other than the grass. Standing still and silent, was a man. He was dressed in green shirt, green pants, and wearing a green backpack. I'm so paranoid, the first thing out of my mouth was, "Are you a ranger?" Without waiting for a response, I added, "I have a permit."

He was not a ranger. He was a hiker, and planning on going past the Inclined Temple, the mountain next to the one I was trying to climb. He had just finished camping after thinking the route ahead was too difficult and that he must be off route. He had hiked down the canyon and came back to this spot. He was packing up and getting ready to go home. He didn't want to carry the water he had just filtered and was about to dump the rest out. He saw the look on my face and offered it. I took it with gratitude. Cool - a hiking partner with a water filter. I had tablets to treat water. I didn't have a filter.

His name was Ben. He insisted that we go up and out of the canyon, saying it was too difficult further down. I was certain we needed to go down the canyon, but gave my new friend the benefit. We hiked up the side of the canyon almost to the top of the West Rim before we stopped to think about what we were going and agreed we needed to go back into the canyon.

Wildcat Canyon was rugged and required lots of ups and downs to avoid pools of water. Ben was in good shape. It was mid-day before we took a break. I was pooped. I had not packed much food. I had intended this to be an easy hike and expected be back at the car quickly. I had already eaten the beef jerky, which was to have been my main meal. I eyed the bags of M&M and nuts Ben was eating. It was day one, and my only remaining ration was a Goo pack, something with sugar and caffeine.

"Do you want some?" Ben asked, pointing to the bag of M&Ms.

I took it, as he filled my water bottle again with the water he was filtering.

We camped in Wildcat Canyon and talked about splitting up the next day, when we came to the junction where I was supposed to go to my climb, and Ben was to go his way. He was headed in the direction of the Bishoprics and Cougar Mountain. I was sad and afraid of being alone. That was odd, since I'm no stranger to climbing by myself. In fact, I generally prefer solo trips. I hid the tears that came to my eyes when I thought of us splitting up.

That evening, Ben gave me a left over rice dish he cooked and a bag of beef jerky. Then he gave me his entire bag of M&Ms, nuts, a bag of dried apricots, and a few dried strips of banana he calls banana jerky. Somehow I had two head lamps, so I gave him one so that he could read the Mark Twain book he brought while resting inside his tent. Man, how does he carry that much and move so fast! To be fair I was carrying climbing gear and rope.

In the morning, we shared bagels with butter he toasted on his stove. His only vice was smoking pot. He seemed to do so precisely three times: breakfast, lunch, and dinner. Whereas most of the time I followed, after he smoked I tended to take the lead. Some say spirits are able to inhabit your body when you're drinking or stoned. Perhaps my guardian angel possessed him, and kept toking up in order to stay in a body.

I call Ben the "Deer Sniffer." Deer take the easiest way and create narrow paths though otherwise thick brush. When it was time to cross the canyon to the other side to avoid an obstacle or deep water, Ben had an uncanny talent for finding and following their paths. Just when I thought we had lost the trail, he would pick it up, following prints to a deer super-highway. Sometimes that was not best, since I was trying to get to a mountain the deer were not interested in climbing.

The next day went no better in progress. We keep switching sides of the canyon to avoid water. Smaller canyons converged into the main canyon from

At the start of the Black Pool.

each side. Eventually we found ourselves with nowhere to go unless we rappelled into water. I didn't know we were at the start of the Black Pool and the famous Subway canyoneering route . We both have the motto, "Never go down anything you can't climb out of." We didn't have wet-suits. Therefore, we went backwards. We climbed out of the canyon to higher ground, where we found ourselves on the opposite side of the canyon, and away from my climb.

There was still hope I could get to where I needed. The way Ben was intending to go, we would pass the east side of the Inclined Temple. On the north side, there is a canyon I thought I might be able to go down to get to Ivins. One plan was we would stick together until we came to that canyon. Then I would go down the canyon, drop my gear, drop down the other side of Ivins, and hook up with Ben. But I wasn't sure if I could get to the meeting point. I feared I might get stuck in the canyon or have to come back and try and catch up. I considered what I would do if I got lost, came back to the last spot I had seen him, and didn't know which way he went. I decided to abandon the idea of getting to my climb, and committed myself to staying with Ben.

Our next camp was past the Bishoprics, at the end of a creek as the creek turned to a water fall at a 1,000 drop. We were both going to be a day overdue on our permits. On my satellite phone, I texted my contact I was OK, and told them to call the park service to let them know we would out a day late.

The next day, the terrain continued to be rugged. Scrambling up and down cliffs, we came to flatter ground, this one with pleasant waterfalls. We followed along the side of the creek and came to a fork, as the creek widened and became a river. Instead of looking at the map to see where we might be, Ben plowed ahead. Miles downstream we finally stopped to check the map. We had been hiking parallel to a highway.

We needed to climb out and get to the road. Smooth basalt cliffs blocked the way. We found a weakness by following a cattle trail through the cliff bands. From the top, we walked a short distance and found ourselves at the highway. We dropped our packs and hid them behind a patch of rocks, then walked to the side of the road and put our thumbs out.

A few cars passed us before a van stopped. The driver was Mike, my climbing partner from Inclined Temple. He was guiding a group of clients. I was dirty, with long hair and a scraggly beard. I wondered what his clients thought of me. Mike was working, and driving the company van, so he couldn't give us a ride. He was headed in the wrong direction anyhow. After chatting he continued on.

Many cars passed us before we were picked up by two kids from Belgium in a rental car. They stopped in the middle of the road, turned the car off, and made room for us. There wasn't room for our packs. We left them hidden near the road. We reached Ben's car first. We stopped in the middle of the road and Ben jumped out. Suddenly, within a few moments, someone who had been my friend for what seemed like an eternity was gone.

The Belgiums wanted to go to Lava Point, which coincidentally, was where I had parked my car. When we got there, I found an orange sticker on my car window. It said I was over due with standard language regarding breaking the law and that my vehicle may be impounded and its tires booted. I panicked and looked for tire boots. I tried to use my cell phone. There was no coverage.

I got in my car and drove down the road until I came to the place where Ben and I had hid our packs, pulled over and stopped. Only a short time ago I was on a journey with a special friend. Now all that remained was wind blowing over the dry desert grass. I walked over to where my pack was hidden. As I went to pick it up, I noticed a cold beer stuffed in the top of it. I'm not a big drinker. But I pulled the tab and enjoyed, thinking of the times my friend Ben, the deer sniffer, had provide me food and water.

IVINS MOUNTAIN - PART 2

In an effort to get in better shape, (and get my head in shape) I went to do some normal climbing, what climbers call trad (traditional) climbing. What I had in mind were long, not difficult routes, in a place called the Needles, California, 165 miles north-east of Los Angeles. I was living in San Diego, and met Matt, a new partner, on-line. We climbed the South Face of Hermit Spire in the Needles, 5.8. It was summer and I wasn't wearing socks. I'd had the same pair of climbing shoes for ten years, got scared, and to get a better grip, tightened my shoes. By the time we finished I had oozing blisters the size of quarters.

The following day I felt bad throwing in the towel since we'd driven so far. Matt was anxious to climb something else, so we climbed an easy route called the Tree Route. Instead of wearing climbing shoes, I wore hiking shoes and padded the inside to soften contact with the blisters. Bad idea. The night I went to urgent care, where they prescribed antibiotics. My legs and feet were swollen and infected. Three weeks later I returned to urgent care. They didn't believe me when said my blisters were still infected. I begged for more antibiotics. It seemed I could lose my feet. They reluctantly gave me some. I kept my wounds covered and prayed. The blisters healed. Sort of.

October, 2014. Each night before going to bed I looked at the scabs on the back of my heels and tried to guess if they'd disappear before Matt and I were supposed to climb Ivins. When the time came, small, dime sized, crusty scabs covered what had been blisters. I decided to pad the scabs with moleskin and go for it. My feet weren't swollen. Things were looking good.

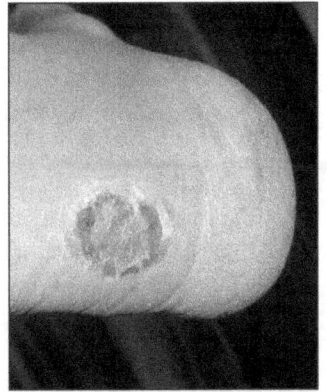

We got to Zion late. By the time we got our permit and drove to the trail head it was mid-day. Instead of going down Wildcat Canyon, we started at Lava Point and hiked along the West Rim. After several miles, we rappelled off the rim into Phantom Valley. We reached the ground as it got dark. Carrying heavy packs, it was a painful slog.

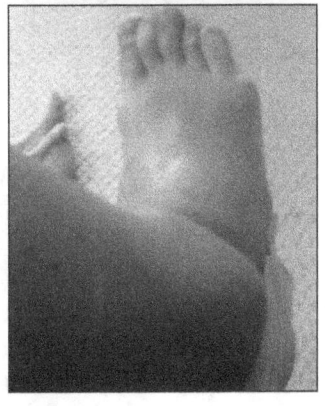

I had felt them soon as we started. But carrying the heavy bag, I had ignored the signal - my feet and blisters. We got into Phantom Valley after midnight. I had been there a few times and thought I could find our way in the dark. We started hiking across the valley, bushwhacking through thick, thorny bushes. We were not sure where we were going except to aim for a gully on the north side of Inclined Temple. I fell

Sorting and packing gear for an attempt with Matt.

over carrying an 80 pound bag. On the ground, in the dark, stuck in the thick bushes, I wanted to cry. I was tired, beat, and sick of bushwhacking. The bag was so heavy, I needed Matt's help to get back on my feet. When we reached the start of the gully, where we found a flat spot on a big rock. I insisted we camp. I did not want to go down the gully in the dark, and desperately wanted to rest.

In the morning I looked at my feet. They were in bad shape. Fortunately, Matt had a pocket knife. He cut holes in the backs of my hiking boots so there would be nothing in contact with the blisters.

Having found a way to walk, we continued down the gully. It was steep and loose. Carrying a haul bag in daylight was dangerous. When it was too difficult to down climb, we started rappelling. At the bottom we found ourselves in the same predicament Ben and I had been, and near Subway Canyon.

We walked through sand and water to where Ben and I had decided to climb out of the canyon. Matt and I, on the other hand, were intent on climbing Ivins. Without no other way out, Matt started climbing a dead tree leaning against the mountain. We couldn't climb the tree wearing the haul bags, so we left the bags in the canyon. We made it to the base of Ivins as it was getting dark.

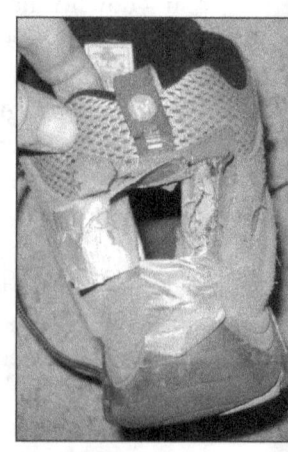

Matt wanted to fix rope off the edge of the canyon and go down and get the bags. I worried that it would be dark before we reached the bags. Cold air settles. It would be colder in the canyon. I would rather stay high and shiver vs. spend the night in a cold, dark canyon. I told Matt we should stay put. I found a place next to a tree with pine

Jugging the 8-mil static out of the canyon to get our bags up to Ivins.

needles. It helps to lay on needles and cover yourself with them to stay warm. I made a spot for Matt and rationed him needles. Matt refused to lay down. He spent the night pacing.

In the morning we tried our ropes to a tree on the edge and went down into the canyon to get our bags. The rope was only 8-millimeters thick, 300 feet long. It was not intended for hauling bags. After we got into the canyon, we got the bags and began the unpleasant task of pulling ourselves, and the bags, back up the rope. The cliff was so steep that the rope hung ten feet from the rock. Matt went first.

As he reached the top, he saw the rope being worn in two. The bobbing and hanging on the rope had caused the rope wear to the point of breaking. He

The last approach slab after traversing the west side of Inclined Temple. There should be water at the base of these slabs. Continue up the slabs to the right (east) and around the corner to the route.

cut out the damaged part, and told me to come up. I prayed, "Please God, don't let me die," as I went higher and higher, gingerly ascending. As I craned my head to look up and check the rope, my helmet fell off. I had forgotten to snap the chin strap. I made it to the top.

We were excited to be at the climb, but my feet were in bad shape. My feet had gotten wet in the canyon. Infected feet in cess water is not a good combination. I decided we should leave, considering we didn't know how long it would take to get home We couldn't go back the way we came. Before leaving, we hid the gear. I wrapped everything in a tarp and covered it with twigs, pine needles, and dead brush. We hide things so well I wondered if we would find them. Matt was surprised that I left my climbing shoes. Why would I need them. I suggested that rather than go back the way we came, we go in the opposite direction, around the back side of the Inclined Temple. We did, and found a ramp. We hiked sideways, and stayed out of a canyon. We got around the Inclined Temple in less than an hour. From there it was

Water at the base of the slabs

a bushwhack though Phantom Valley and a hike back to the truck. That night, I set to work saving my feet.

Over Easter, 2015, Matt and I returned for a successful climb. On the summit, I told Matt about another unclimbed mountain I wanted to do. I pointed to it, dreaming of another adventure. Matt wasn't so sure. He thought I was crazy. He could see it in my eyes and the smile on my face. I admit that I was.

Dan on the first pitch.

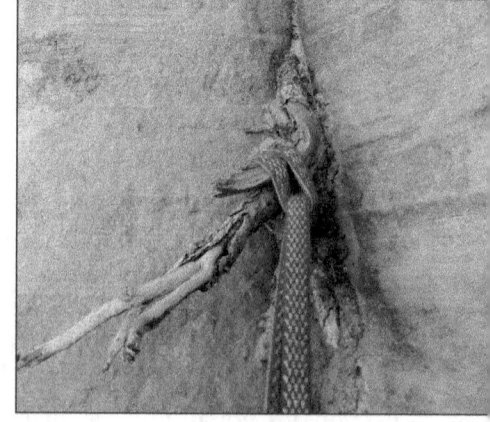

Above: Matt on the pendulum. Opposite page: using natural anchors i.e., tied-off bushes. Below: Matt on the last rappel.

CLIMBING IVINS MOUNTAIN

1. WEST FACE A2+, 5.9+ *D Stih and M Mower 2015*
Climbs the prominent corner system in the center of the east face. Six pitches, including a pendulum.
EQUIPMENT REQUIRED: KBs, bird beaks, tie-offs, and other pins. Three sets of cams to #3. (2) #4 cams. (1) #5 cam
WATER: Depending on the season, there is water in a pool at the start of the final approach slab on the south side of Ivins. After going across the shelf that runs along the west side of the Inclined Temple, you will come to a steep white slab. Look for the pool on the lower left before you head up the slabs to Ivins.
SEASON: The pool on the SW side of Ivins is likely to be dry in late season. Given the amount of gear you will carry, it's critical to find water there. March-April is best.
CAMPING / TIME REQUIRED: Consider doing a different route in the area to become familiar with the approach and water sources.
STARTING POINT: There is a 4th class shelf that runs along the west side of the Inclined Temple and provides access to Ivins. This is the only reasonable final approach.
THE ROUTE: On the first pitch I placed tied-off KBs, beaks, cams up to #3, two #4s, and a #5. From the top of the first pitch, a pendulum and slippery, sandy free climbing reaches a big ledge with a tree. From there enjoyable free climbing goes up the prominent crack/corner system. Near the top of the corner/crack system, traverse sideways right, onto the main face, then straight up.
GETTING DOWN: We descended using trees and bushes for rappel, and left no slings. We drilled no bolts. We left two pitons in a crack where there are no bushes. The last two rappels go down the face to the right of the first pitch and pendulum. The last rappel is long. Be creative. Two ropes are required and it may help if one is 300 feet.

Castle Dome

INTRODUCTION Castle Dome was one of the last mountains named on maps of Zion to be climbed. It's one of the easiest. I suspect its massive size and apparently blank white face caused the masses to assume it would be impossible. It's one of the few big peaks in Zion that can be climbed from the trailhead at the Grotto, round-trip, in a day.

HISTORY In doing my research, I was inspired by a post on Tom Jone's blog on Canyon Collective. Someone had asked, "Does anyone know if all the named towers and peaks in Zion have been climbed?" Tom's response was, "Ones that might not are Castle Dome, Ivins Mt, Inclined Temple."

A few weeks before I attempted to climb Castle Dome, I received an email from CP, author of, *Zion National Park: Summit Routes*. He asked, "In doing my research, I have a few questions. Do you know whether Castle Dome has been climbed?"

"Have you climbed Castle Dome?" I said.

"I have not. I think it could be one of the last two, unclimbed, named peaks in the park."

"Would you be interested in doing the first ascent with me?"

"It would depend on how epic of an adventure you're looking at. It's amazing that Castle Dome being unclimbed has been openly discussed for ten years. Hard men want to do big walls [Yosemite, El Capitan], people like me want to scramble obscure chose piles, canyoneers are consumed with slots, and the other 99% never leave the trails."

The circumvent route I took on my solo exploration. I rappelled into the chasm between Castle Dome and the finger leading out from the West Rim, then kept going down and around the SE face of Castle Dome, in search of a weakness.

On the summit of Castle Dome, looking over at the finger that jets out south from the West Rim and West Rim Trail.

Sand Castles Before Green Chili

Due to his schedule and wanting to bring a friend, CP could not meet me until November. It usually takes me two or three attempts to climb an unclimbed mountain. I thought that if we waited until November and failed, it might be too cold for another attempt that year. He wanted to bring a friend and told me that between the two of their schedules, they would have only two days off. I wasn't happy with a plan that only allowed two days to attempt to climb such a big peak. I therefore, planned to do a solo trip. If I failed, my outing with C.P. would be the second attempt.

The shortest way to the summit appeared to be climbing a crack on the north side that faces the West Rim. I hiked to the top of the West Rim, and hiked out a finger that leads towards Castle Dome. I left my sleeping gear on the edge, and rappelled 430 feet into the saddle next to Castle Dome. I spent the next two days exploring different sides of Castle Dome, looking for the easiest possible way to climb it. The north face looked like it could be climbed, but it didn't look that easy. In an effort to find the easiest way, I down-climbed to the NE, around the corner. I went down, down, and around. I continued until it became too steep to down-climb. At that point I rappelled, and left the rope fixed for my return. I found myself in a wide open space where I could easily walk. I had no idea I was on a hill just above Behunin Canyon.

I stayed high, hugging Castle Dome, and continued going around the corner. When I thought the face looked there might be good enough hand holds to climb it, I did the next thing explorers do - I went up and touched the

Near the top of Behunin Canyon where it meets the West Rim Trail.

mountain. I tried to climb the first twenty feet. I didn't find it climbable, so I continued, round, and round the corner. I could see the Zion Lodge below me, and wondered if people noticed me. I eventually reached a place it would be too dangerous to continue without a rope. I was out of rope. I was about 30 feet before the manzanita bush where the ledge petters out and things get sketchy. I couldn't see around the corner. I wanted a partner and a belay.

On my satellite phone, I texted my friend Matt in San Diego. I told him I would buy him a plane ticket to Las Vegas it he wanted to meet me to climb for the weekend. When he texted me back "Yes," I headed up my fixed ropes, hiked to town, and drove to Las Vegas to get him at the airport.

After picking Matt up at the airport we drove back to Zion. We had only a few hours of sleep that night. In the early morning we hiked back up the West Rim. Although the plan was to start climbing the next day, there was a lot of day light remaining when we got there. I decided to give Matt a tour.

We rappelled into the saddle where I had been exploring, to the spot I could not see around the corner. I decided that we had enough time to check it out. Matt fed me out rope as I inched my way around the corner, fortunate and lucky to find holds. After less than twenty feet, I could see the top of the mountain. Things got easier. I went to the end of my rope and reached a big tree. When Matt reached me at the tree, we simul-climbed to the summit. The rest of the way was easy. Loose, but not difficult. We made it to the top the same day we had started from the shuttle stop at the Grotto.

November, 2015.

I felt bad having climbed the mountain without CP. When, a few days later, he asked if I didn't mind re-climbing Castle Dome with him and his mystery partner, I said yes.

A few week later, they met me in the parking lot at Deep Creek Coffee in Springdale at 6 a.m. It was cold and dark. We were all wearing heavy jackets. I wondered who his mystery partner was. He was wearing a down jacket, his hands recessed in his jacket.

I reached to shake his hand.

"Other hand," he said.

"Ok." I shook his other hand. I thought that was weird.

The shuttle was closed, so we were allowed to park at the Grotto. As soon as we parked we were off and hiking. I was concerned because mystery friend kept asking questions. He asked what to bring and what the climbing would be like. What struck me was his tone. He was not worried, but clearly wanted to know as much as possible - like someone who wanting to know what time the bus came, but not worried if he missed it.

Half way up the trail, the path turned to snow and ice. Mystery partner joked, "Anyone have an ice tool?"

After not getting a response, he said, "I do!"

I didn't' get it. Not until when we reached the spot where the climb beings. He reached into his backpack and pulled out his arm. As he began to put it on, I said,

"Hey," I said, "Are you that guy who cut his arm off when he got stuck in a canyon?"

"Yep, that's me."

The sandstone on the upper part of Castle Dome is extremely loose. Matt and I had stayed roped up the entire time we were climbing. CP and Aron, on the other hand, didn't seem as concerned. As soon as we reached the big tree for the belay at the end of the traverse pitch, they said a few quick words and untied from the rope. I didn't have time to protest.

Exit the canyon here, just before the first rappel canyoneers must do when going down Behunin Canyon.

Left: the approach ramp; Below: the manzanita used as an anchor at the first belay.

I became scared out of my mind and sick to my stomach. CP was far ahead and moving fast. Aron was right behind. I kept eyes glued on Aron's feet. Wherever he put a foot, I put mine. Where he grabbed a handhold, I made sure I did the way. *Whose route was this?* I thought. Had I not just completed the first ascent weeks earlier?

A large foot hold Aron was standing on broke just as he shifted his weight off it. The rock crumbled into a powder that slide down the face of the mountain like a small avalanche. Aron didn't pause or slow down. It took a lot to compose myself and keep following.

When we got to the top, instead of rappelling, we retraced our steps, still unroped, and down-climbed to a tree above the first belay. There, we rappelled, and ended a few feet before the manzanita. We hiked back up Behunin Canyon to the West Rim Trail and down to the Grotto.

Back in town they bought me dinner, a chicken burrito. Half way though supper, I excused myself, went to the bathroom, locked the door, and hung my head over the toilet. I vomited hard. I stayed hunched over the toilet for several minutes, muscles cramping, squeezing and dry heaving. I attributed it having been scarred all day.

The next day, we set off to do another climb, one CP had tried but not gotten to the top of. I would redeem myself and go back to being Dangerous Dan. That story can be found in the chapter, Green Chili Left Over. The third ascent of Castle Dome was done by R Marsters, Sarah Marsters, and Dominic, a few weeks later.

CLIMBING CASTLE DOME

SOUTH FACE 5.3 *D Stih and M Mower October, 2015*
The consensus is this is 5th class, perhaps 5.3. I think they wore rock shoes. I climbed it in hiking boots and it seemed 5.6 to 5.7. The second ascent was done by myself, Courtney Purcell, and Aron Ralston, a month later. We approached by descending Behunin canyon from the West Rim Trail, what is now is considered the normal approach.
EQUIPMENT REQUIRED: About a dozen long slings for trees and bushes. Cams are not good. The rock is soft. Matt and I left a fixed piton or two on the second pitch. You'll come across these if you go right after the first belay (the big tree at the end of the traverse) instead of straight up.
CAUTIONS / SPECIAL DIFFICULTIES: Ice cleats starting in November if it's cold and snow on the trail.
WATER SOURCES: There's likely almost always some water in Behunin Canyon.
SEASON: I prefer fall, when the weather is cool and there's water in Behunin Canyon for drinking.
CAMPING / TIME REQUIRED: One full day. Twelve hours round trip from the Grotto. From the first belay, the climbing takes two hours to the summit. Round-trip from where one leaves Behunin canyon is about four hours for a party comfortable with simul-climbing and down-climbing exposed 5th class. Twelve hours round trip should be plenty for those who are slow and careful.
THE STARTING POINT: The Grotto. Hike the West Rim Trail to the top of Behunin Canyon. Leave the trail and hike down Behunin until just before the first rappel.
As you're coming down Behunin Canyon there is sharp, ninety-degree turn where the canyon widens. If you continue you will come to the first rappel for the Behunin Canyon Route. Backtrack and scrabble up the hill on the south towards Castle Dome. You will reach a high point that flattens out. Continue south, staying high. Aim for a ramp that hugs the otherwise blank, east face of Castle Dome.
THE ROUTE: Rope up where the ramp peters out. Set a belay at a tree 30 feet prior to reaching a manzanita bush where it's not possible to see around the corner. It's recommended to belay again at the manzanita to have as much rope as possible before starting the traverse around the corner. From the manzanita, traverse a long, straight way

Left: the ramp; Right: the first belay at the end of the ramp.

around the corner. Avoid the temptation to go up too soon. It's easier if you stay low and traverse most of a rope length sideways. Towards the end of the traverse you will come to a blocky section where it becomes easier. From there, climb straight up to a big tree, the end of the first pitch. The pitch may be 210 feet if you do not start from the manzanita.

From the big tree one can simul-climb up and left, or go right before coming back left to the same place. The more left you go (straight up from the tree), the easier it gets. If you go up and right, you will come across a fixed piton or two.

GETTING DOWN: Down-climb the route and head towards a cliff above the first belay. There are several trees to choose for a rappel that will put you back on the approach ramp just before the first belay. A rappel of 80 feet will reach the start of the traverse pitch just before the manzanita bush.

FUTURE CLIMBING Most who climb Castle Dome will finish by hiking back up Behunin Canyon to the West Rim Trail. Who will be first to finish by descending the rest of Behunin Canyon? There are also at least two possible future climbing lines. One is the North Face. Approach by hiking across the finger from the West Rim, and rappel into the saddle between it and Castle Dome. Climb the aerate that faces the finger. From the summit, rappel back to the saddle, then rappel toward Behunin, where you will find yourself on the approach to the normal route. From there you can hike up the canyon to the West Rim Trail, or finish by going down Behunin Canyon.

The other is a direct variation up the south face. After leaving Behunin Canyon on the normal approach, scramble up the hill to the main face of Castle Dome and look for a route before reaching the ramp for the normal route, before sketchy ledge.

Left: The north face of Castle Dome as seen from the finger leading toward it from the West Rim. Right: Another alternative is to climb a crack / dihedral before reaching the ramp used on the approach to Sketchy Ledge.

Gregory Butte

INTRODUCTION Gregory Butte was named for Herbert Gregory, a Yale geologist who did a survey of the Kolob. Gregory's recommendation led President Franklin D. Roosevelt to create a second Zion National Monument in 1937, one that included Kolob Canyons. This second Monument was incorporated with Zion National Park in 1956. The name Kolob comes from *Pearl of Great Price*, a book of scripture of the Church of Jesus Christ of Latter-day Saints. Kolob is a star said to be "Near the throne of God." The bottom of Gregory Butte sits on a plateau level with the top of Kolob Arch, the sixth longest natural arch in the world. Gregory Butte is a Resource Natural Area (RNA). It's summit is closed to recreation. Bolting is prohibited.
HISTORY My effort began in 2015, when CP asked me, "Now that you've climbed the Altar of Sacrifice, I suppose you are going to do Gregory Butte?" I

was not familiar with the mountain. I did an internet search. Gregory Butte in Lake Powell came up. I joked I would need a boat. Then I realized there is a Gregory Butte in Kolob Canyons. At first I thought I might pull a trick by climbing Timbertop Mountain and dropping a rope down the other side. Climbing Timbertop appeared to be a huge feat. With no more tricks up my sleeve, I attempted to climb Gregory Butte's southwest spur. After two days, I gave up. In my haste, I had started up an impossibly big route. I set out to find the gully (Arch Gully), as described by Ayres and Creswell. I eventually found it.

My first attempt to climb the gully was in May, 2016. The gully had water flowing down it. I played hopscotch to place my feet on dry holds but it was futile. I returned in 2016, a few days after the fourth of July, and over six was successful in climbing to the top of Gregory Butte.

Small Miracles, Hummingbirds and Blackberries

I left my house the day after the fourth of July, bored with city life and tired of firecrackers and parties. Even though water was not flowing and the gully was dry, the first two-hundred feet were covered in a healthy green moss that glowed florescent. The gully was slippery and dangerous. This was my first encounter with the hummingbird. It hovered near my face, wondering who I was and what I was doing. I used a knife blade piton to scrap thick moss off foot holds in the gully. It was like uncovering buried treasure. Hand holds were harder to come by. Ferns filled a crack in the back of the gully. They didn't take to pulling on and came out like plucking pedals off a flower as I used them for balance. There wasn't a crack in the gully that would take protection. I got one cam in at the bottom for a belay, and an angle piton half-way up. I panicked as everything was slippery and it seemed I might fall. I wasn't sure if I was in the right gully. Placing a bolt would not have worked. The rock was soft as mud. Near the top of the two-hundred foot pitch, the angle lessened, allowing me to scramble to a relatively flat spot. There I realized I was in the correct gully as the "great chock stone in the sky" became visible above.

The next two pitches were fun. It took time to belay myself. I squeezed through a hole in the canyon wall, crawled on my knees into a cave, and came out the other side. This is called the Cave Pitch. Exiting the cave was airy. This is where Ayres and Creswell had placed pitons for protection. I didn't find them. I later learned that someone removed the pitons and gave them to the history museum. I climbed up the wall and belly-flopped onto a flat section where there was a big tree. From there the gully widened, and I hiked though thick bushes to its end. There I was met with another steep wall I would have to climb. Before doing so I made three trips, back and forth, crawling through the cave, to bring my gear and water there. The last pitch up the gully was quite difficult, considering it was first climbed in 1954. Those guys were hard-men, true climbers. I scrambled to the top of the plateau where humming bird buzzed me.

Once on the plateau, I explored for a route that might be the best to get to the summit of Gregory Butte. The route I picked ascends the south face. It was a long hike from the gully. I made two trips to bring the gear there. It was slow going in the heat, and I didn't think I'd make the climb in time for the number of days on my permit. Small miracles. Although the route I picked looked discontinuous and no fun, it unlocked. I was able to climb what seemed over-hanging, dirty cracks. Hummingbird meet me on top. I scrambled east, across the ridge, until I was just below the summit. There, I ran into a vertical head wall thirty feet high. I didn't want to get back to get my rope so I free-soloed it. The Hummer hovered in my face trying to speak. I was on top.

Descent back to the arch trail took me a day and half. Because of the heat, I broke up the loads and made three carries back to the gully, then rappelled it three times. I went up and down to bring down the loads. Out of food, I noticed a crack at the bottom of the gully was chocked with blackberries. Humming bird watched as I picked the bushes clean. I took my time. Once out of the gully, I was back into the heat of direct sun. It was a hot slog back to the car.

Small miracles that my route unlocked itself and allowed me to climb to the summit, hummingbird to watch over me, and blackberries. Why wait for what you think it should be. Enjoy the space to get where you'll be.

CLIMBING GREGORY BUTTE

1. THE SOUTH FACE A2, 5.9 D Stih July 5-10, 2016, Solo
EQUIPMENT REQUIRED: Full rack. After the first pitch or so (may require a few small pins such as KBs and baby angles) most of the route is free climbing. Bolting is banned in Kolob Canyons. Leave the bolt kit at home.

WATER: Once on the plateau, I was lucky to find water in a single pot hole in a wash on the north side of Gregory Butte. It had rained a week earlier. In winter, the hanging valley between Gregory Butte and Timbertop Mesa is covered with snow. Snow stays on the north face of Gregory Butte into June 1st. This results in water dripping down the gully, and why historically, the gully was first climbed in July and August. I returned in 2024 and 2025 (re-climbing the gully, always finding it wet and a near death experience). Hiking the La Verkin trail, if the soil is damp near a wash due to recent rain, there will likely be water in pools along the north side of GB and where water goes over the edge between the Tree Route and Kolob Arch (see drawing on *The Cat Walk*). While you can't see it from the ground, snow on the north side of GB lasts till June 1st, keeping pools filled with fresh water (and frogs). Bringing a filter is helpful if pools are shallow. To

reach the pools, and avoid a manzanita bushwack, after finishing up the gully, skirt along the top of the rim in the direction of the arch.

SEASON: July - November.

CAMPING / TIME REQUIRED: I spent six days, car to car. Allocate one day for the hike in and finding the gully. Climb the gully and haul gear to the top of the plateau. This is laborious as the haul bag needs to be carried. The gully is in the shade and can be climbed in the middle of the day. It's a good place to stop and rest if it's hot. The third day may be spent porting gear to the base of the climb, searching for or hauling water, and fixing a pitch. The fourth day you should be able to finish climbing to the summit and get back to the ground (plateau).

STARTING POINT: From the parking lot and trail head at Lee Pass, hike to the junction for the Kolob Arch trail. Hike arch trail to where it terminates at the view point. From there, climb the "gully" to the top of the plateau. Hike over to Gregory Butte. My route ascends the south face, where it is the shortest distance from the plateau to the saddle between Gregory Butte and a ridge to the west. In the photo, it is where there is a patch of green trees making a point. The route may look improbable, discontinuous, and overhanging.

THE ROUTE: Start up a set of twin, thin cracks right of a roof. Direct aid may be required.

The start of the route to the summit once on the plateau.

At the top of this pitch things get easier. Higher there is a hidden chimney with incredible foot holds that makes it more of a scramble than a rock climb. A path will become clear, and what looked improbable from the ground will not be that difficult. From the top, walk east towards the summit. You will come to a wall blocking progress. A short section of 5.5 is required to gain the summit. It can be climbed (and down-climbed) without a rope.

GETTING DOWN: Rappel the route using trees and bushes. Two ropes are required. You should come down directly over the roof.

From the top of the plateau there are two options: I suggest walking back to the gully and descending it. In the gully, if you have two 300-foot ropes, you can rappel off a big tree at the top of the last rappel. Otherwise you may need to do a short rappel into the "cave," and then rappel off a bush with manky old webbing. Alternatively, you might go down Cats Tail Ridge (see *Cat's Tail Ridge*) which will take you to Camp 2 on the La Verkin Trail. The ridge requires continuous scrambling that might be cumbersome if you are carrying a large wall rack.

Rappelling the route back to the plateau.

ZION NATIONAL PARK
CLIMBING ROUTE DESCRIPTION

1. ROUTE NAME:

2. GRADE/RATING:

3. LOCATION OF CLIMB:

4. ASCENT PARTY (name, address, phone):
a.

b.

c.

d.

5. GENERAL ROUTE COMMENTS (i.e. special considerations, hazards, time spent, etc.):

6. DESCENT ROUTE:

7. RECOMMENDED PROTECTION:

8. FIXED ANCHORS (INCLUDING AT BELAYS):

9. TOPO ROUTE MAP, REFERENCED TO LANDMARKS AND KNOWN ROUTES, (ON BACK):

If you do a new route in Zion, I'm sure the rangers in the backcountry office would like to hear about it. If you want record of your ascent to be permanent, consider filling out a paper form such as this, and mailing or dropping it off at the backcountry office.

First *Climbing* Ascents of Mountains Named on Maps

Photos albums on my book shelf. There were no digital cameras or phones when I climbed many of the routes in this book.

1996

2018

1996

2018

Compare these photos taken in 1996 and 2018. Notice the wooden beam on the bottom front of the ruins, sticking out over the edge. Notice the cable hanging down the face of the mountain in the 1996 photo. I wonder how many other historical artifacts have been restored in the park without giving those who view them notice regarding restoration. I wonder where the original parts went.

Cable Mountain

INTRODUCTION Cable Mountain gets its name from the structure at the top that was used to lower lumber into the valley in the early 1900s. It is possible to hike to the top of Cable Mountain. The first climbing route, Hammer & Sickle, was established in 1996, a thin aid climb on the otherwise blank face.

HISTORY In 1888, 15-year-old David Flanagan got lost in the high country for several days while exploring. He wandered along the East Rim though the ponderosa and came to the edge of Cable Mountain. As he looked down at the canyon floor 1,800 feet below, it occurred to him that a cable could be used to lower lumber into the canyon. It had been the custom to haul lumber from Kaibab Mountain, a week away in Arizona.

In 1900, he obtained 50,000 feet of telegraph wire, and with three men, carried it to the top of Cable Mountain. The trail was not suitable for horses. They took turns carrying the spool on their backs. Three towers were built at the top, and two at the bottom. The wire, being soft and pliable, stretched further than expected. After three years of experiments, Flanagan perfected the device. From 1901 to 1926, millions of board feet of lumber were lowered from Cable Mountain to the floor in Zion Canyon. David sold the cable works in 1907. The new owners replaced the wire with a heavy twisted rope.

Ron Raimonde and I did the first climbing ascent of Cable Mountain in 1996. It was five years before climbers attempted to repeat our route, Hammer & Sickle. On November 25, 2001, climbers attempting the second ascent got within one-hundred feet from the top when they were stuck in snow, freezing rain, and high wind. They were prepared for bad weather. Ice stopped them. They could not free-climb the last pitch. Temperatures remained as low as 10F for several days, preventing the ice from thawing. They reported spending a night being blown back and forth and up and down in their portaledges before they asked to be rescued. I was in Zion at the time but didn't have a phone. When I got home there was a message on my answering machine from park rangers, asking for information about the route. I was impressed by their subsequent rescue. They broke trail through knee-deep snow, hiked to the top of Cable Mountain from the East Entrance, and lowered the stranded climbers rope. In October, 2018, I put up a new route, solo, on the North Face.

FUTURE CLIMBING A direct finish to Hammer & Sickle is possible. The route jogs left near the top. A future route could continue up and right, and possibly finish directly under the cable ruins. The issue is safety. During our ascent, Ron and I argued about the way. I wanted to go directly up , but Ron thought it unsafe due to the potential for rock fall to harm hikers on Weeping Rock Trail. Ron has good instincts. In August, 2019, heavy rains caused a substantial piece of rock to the right of the route to break off. The rockfall knocked down trees and showered visitors on the trail with rocks, branches, and a plume of dust and sand. Three visitors were injured and several people stranded. Hammer & Sickle is far left of where the rock fall occurred and was not affected.

NPS photo. August 24, 2019.

Bird Beaks.

CLIMBING CABLE MOUNTAIN

1. HAMMER & SICKLE A3 5.9+ *D Stih and R Raimonde 1996*
An excellent location and steep aid route. Seven pitches plus a few hundred feet of fourth class after the last pitch. This is a fun route to sleep in a portaledge. You can wear comfortable stiff mountain boots and aid climb most of the route. The only free climbing is on the last pitch. The free climbing there is mandatory and 5.9. Ron thinks someone creative could throw a rock with a rope tied to it and lasso a tree on the north face if they didn't want to climb the free pitch. I think that is wishful thinking. Starting with an attempt to do the second ascent, the route has had many bolts added. Climbers added bolts on the bottom pitch where I used bird-beaks, and in the middle where I lassoed flakes. They said they couldn't figure out what I did. To me, I wasn't doing anything too creative. I learned those tricks climbing routes on El Capitan in Yosemite.

Top: haul bags at the top of the first pitch of Hammer & Sickle.

EQUIPMENT REQUIRED: A 200-foot rope is mandatory for the first pitch. We used 20 KBs and 18 beaks. Due to the bolts added by climbers on later ascents, that number is lower now. Only a few angles are required, mostly to fill holes on the second to last pitch. Please do a community service and leave pins in the holes.
WATER SOURCES: None. Haul it from the parking lot.
THE STARTING POINTS: From Weeping Rock pullout, hike to the base of Cable Mountain. As the trail straightens out and starts to head into a canyon between Cable Mountain and Observation Point, leave the trail and scramble to bottom of the route.
CAUTIONS / SPECIAL DIFFICULTIES: Retreat after the first pitch is difficult. The route overhangs and traverses.
GETTING DOWN: Hike the Cable Mountain Trail several miles uphill to where it meets the East Rim Trail, then hike back down to the Weeping Rock parking lot.

Belaying, higher up the wall on Hammer & Sickle.

Ron placing lost arrows on the second pitch of Hammer & Sickle.

Dangerous Dan on the third pitch of Hammer & Sickle. In order to not bolt across the face, I lowered from a high piece and swung left to get into another crack. From there, I free-climbed until I was level with where I had started.

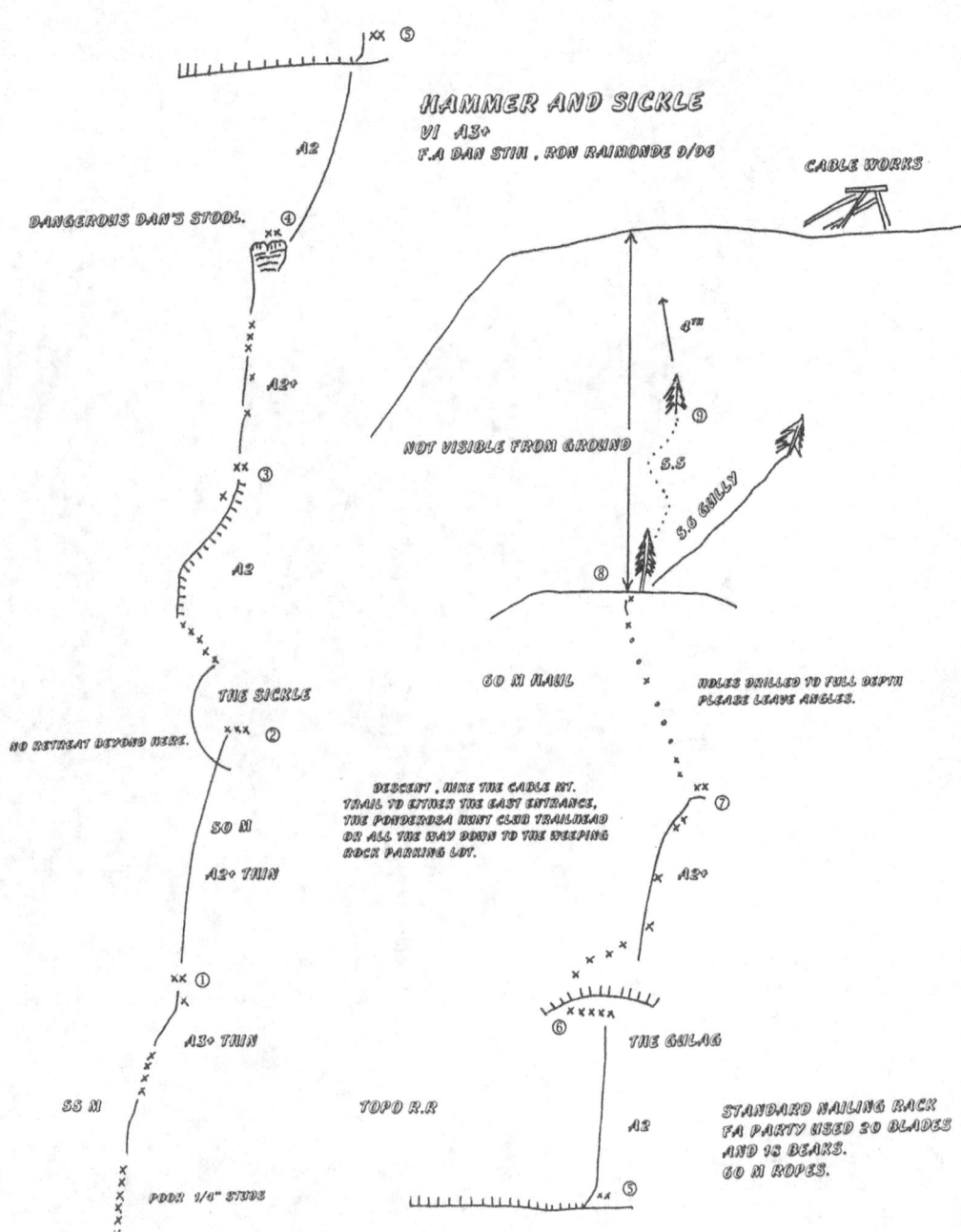

Ron's artistic topo for Hammer & Sickle

Aid climbing can be hazardous. During the first ascent of Hammer & Sickle, I accidentally hit my thumb with the hammer.

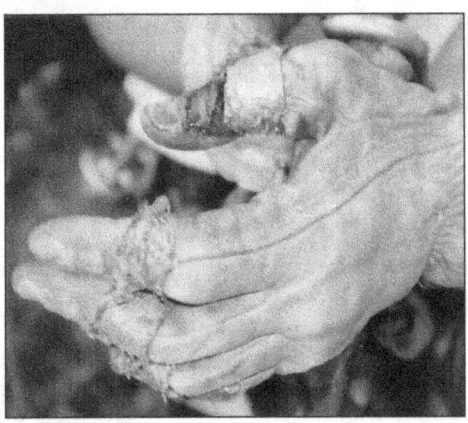

Going Back for Seconds

A mountain calls me when it's time. Out of the blue, it came into my consciousness: the North Face of Cable Mountain told me it was time to come. I searched for information to check if it had been climbed, and came across a post that was inspiring: "Anything new on the north face of Cable Mountain? There were no responses.

I had just started a project at the bottom of Gregory Butte. I drove to Zion, hiked out to the bottom of Gregory and flailed, a climber's jargon for a desperate and ineffective struggle (I was trying to climb Right Crack for the second time.) I gave up, packed my stuff, and carried the haul bag to the car. I wondered what I would do in the morning - drive home or climb Cable Mountain. I decided to wait and see what the morning brought.

I woke at 1am, sleeping in the back of my truck. I drove to Hurricane, a small town thirty minutes outside of Zion. I thought I was driving home. I got a donut and coffee, and sat in the parking lot thinking. When I started driving, I found myself driving back to Zion. Maybe I just wanted a donut. I told myself it wasn't a good idea. I was beat from my attempt on Gregory Butte. My legs, feet, arms, and poor body needed a rest day. The issue was rain. It was going to rain the following two days, and the rock would need a day to dry. If I was going to do a climb it had to be today.

I drove to the Visitor Center and got in line for the first shuttle. The first difficulties would be finding where to leave the hiking trail, getting cross a deep canyon, and hopping onto the bottom of Cable Mountain on the north side. There was only one spot I could cross over water in the canyon between Cable Mountain and Observation Point without getting wet or stuck. My pack was HEAVY. I found the spot. I scrambled up to the bottom of the north face.

My other concerns were time and weather. If it got too late to finish, it would do no good for me to try and get down. I would get stuck and lost in the lower section in the dark. I might inadvertently lower myself into a slot canyon filled with water, waiting to be flash-flooded if it rained. If it got dark before I reached the top, I would have to stay put, likely in the rain, and sleep hanging from on the rope without protection from the elements. I hoped I would not become a statistic.

When I reached the bottom of the north face, I looked for what I thought would be the easiest way to start climbing it. And what looked like the surest. There was not a continuous crack to the top. I would have to piece things together, connect the dots, and hope there were dots higher up. I could not see the upper part of the mountain.

I picked a place to start and climbed up twenty feet. There I got stuck, swung sideways to reach another crack, and climbed up to a ledge. I climbed

The main, west face of Cable Mountain, viewed on the approach to the north face.

another forty feet and stepped sideways again, then went around a corner onto a small ledge. The entire time I worried that I might get stuck in the dark or rain. I had a rain jacket but no rain pants. I was wearing cotton. It was hot. My pack was too heavy to carry anything else. If the pack had been too heavy I would not have been able to scramble the bottom section.

As I climbed, I wondered if I would need to be rescued in the rain. I was

Looking down on the first pitch, soloing the North Face route.

stressed the entire time. I have a belief that if I'm meant to climb something the mountain will help, that it will show you the way, make it possible. The start had been that way. I thought I was doing pretty good. But everything takes time, and I only had some much of it. In the middle of my climb, a bush pulled out as I stood on it, sending me falling ten feet.

   I began to worry. The cracks in the rock became too thin to hold pitons. I couldn't see a crack, just a fissure. The small cracks were filled with sand, dirt, and wet soil from rain two weeks ago. What seemed like good piton placements pulled with body weight. In vein, I pecked at the rock seam with a knife blade. The sun was going down. Clouds were building. The rope drag and climbing gear were so heavy I could barely move.

I took a chance and lightened the load. I decided to leave most of the climbing gear at the belay. I pulled up a bunch of slack and committed to "free" climb. It worked. I climbed across a blank section, climbed straight up, and reached a big tree. I was still worried. It looked like there was another difficult section, and retreat was impossible. God save me, I was able to scramble to the top, dragging the rope behind me. I got to the cable ruins just in time to watch the sun go down. The mountain had given me passage. I thanked her.

A bush that pulled out when I put weight on it. I took a short fall.

After enjoying the view, I began to hike back to the car. I had 90 minutes before it was pitch dark. Piece of cake. I thought.

The first hour was incredible. The threat of rain clouds had diminished. Yellow leaves of the fall season contrasted with evergreens and thick grasses. The moon rose early and highlighted dark purple and blue clouds. Orange clouds on the western horizon reflected light from a sliver of remaining sunlight. Deer ran across the trail in front of me.

When it got dark, the moon lit the way. The difficulties started again when I went into a section of thick forest in which I could not see the trail. I turned on my headlamp and prayed the batteries were not too old. I had forgotten to put new batteries in my head lamp before I started. When I navigated to an open space where the moon light permitted me to see again, I turned the headlamp off. Some of the tail was rocky and steep, treacherous where it cuts across the side of mountain. I was tired, but in zen fashion, I kept walking. The moment I started to daydream and think about something other than the trail I was walking on, I tripped. That's when I was reminded to stay in the now.

Approximate route. The top half of the large crack system in the center is the last pitch of Hammer & Sickle.

In some places I lost the trail, even with the headlamp on. The trail occasionally crosses slabs of rock where there are no footprints or visible trail. Whenever I lost the trail, my strategy was this: from the last place I knew the trail existed, I walked up and down perpendicular to where it might be. When I came to a big drop, I knew people couldn't go that way. Then I would walk up hill until I knew people couldn't climb that far. Up and down until I found the trail. Then I'd turn the head lamp off to save the batteries.

It was quiet. No birds or crickets were singing. There were no other people on the trail, no voices to chase for company. At some point I was so tired I didn't care if I slept on the trail and it rained on me. Then I came to my senses. I got up and kept going.

I reached the parking lot at Weeping Rock at 10:30 pm. I hid my pack in the bushes and started walking down the road to the Visitor Center. I walked the center line, in the middle of the road. There was no traffic. The moonlight lit the mountains and canyon walls around me. Animals were hunkered down, expecting rain. It should have been raining.

Just past the Zion Lodge, I stopped to sit on a rock on the side of the road. I could have gone to sleep sitting on it I was so tired. Then I saw a car coming. Hopeful, I held out my thumb and shined my headlamp on it to make my intention clear. The car moved slowly. The driver and passenger were discussing if they should pick me up.

The car, a mini-coper, stopped as it reached me. Inside were two climbers who had just gotten down from a big climb. The car was full of climbing gear. I had to get in through the hatch back and lay across their haul bags as they squeezed the hatch closed on top of me. They dropped me off at my Jeep at the Visitor Center just as it started to down pour a hard and cold rain.

The next day the heavy rain continued. Black sky, lightening, and thunderstorms. As I was sitting, drinking coffee in the lobby of the Cable Mountain Lodge, I noticed a large, high-resolution photo of Cable Mountain hanging behind the front desk. I became aware of how much the universe and my mountains love me. I felt lucky. It will always be OK, I thought. I'll be OK.

The moon was the key to my success and safety. I wasn't expecting that. As were the clouds staying away from the moon just enough so it could light the trail. As was the delay in the rain by twelve hours. As was being picked up hitchhiking just before it started to rain. Yes, I was a statistic. Not one of a rescue. One of living.

CLIMBING CABLE MOUNTAIN

2. NORTH FACE A1+ 5.5 *D Stih 2018, solo*
Climbs the western edge of the North side of Cable Mountain. Three short pitches. I soloed this in a day.
EQUIPMENT REQUIRED: 2 of each cams #1-3; (1) #4 cam; 1 each micro-cam; 2-3 small LAs (#1 and #2); 2-3 long LAs; 4 KBs (thicker bugaboos may be helpful).
WATER: Possibly in the canyon you must step over to get from the trail onto the north side of Cable Mountain. I suggest carrying water from the parking lot.
STARTING POINT: Hike the trail from Weeping Rock to the bottom of Cable Mountain. Continue around the corner and leave the trail shortly after passing through narrow canyon walls. Get onto the north aspect of Cable Mountain as soon as possible. If you hike too far up hill on the trail, backtrack and find a way across the canyon to get onto the north side of Cable Mountain. Once across the canyon, scramble up steep slabs to the west edge of the north face.

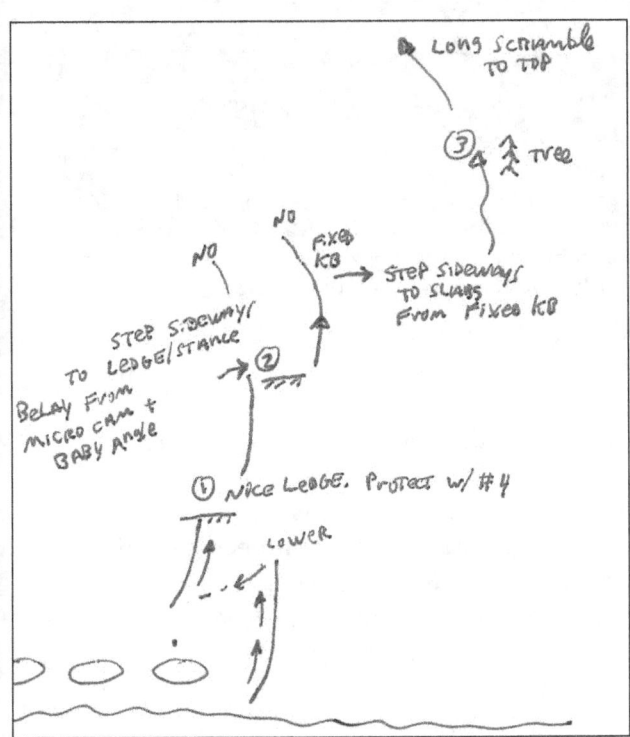

THE ROUTE: Start by free-climbing to gain a crack for the first placement. Continue on aid to where the crack stops, then lower and pendulum left to a another crack. Climb that crack to a ledge protected with a #4 cam. Continue up to another ledge. From that ledge, step sideways and climb up to a fixed KB on the last pitch. Please leave it. It marks the spot where you should traverse right. Step sideways right across slabs, then climb straight up to a big tree. From there it's a long scramble to the top. Do not climb straight up. Head up and left, diagonal.

Death Point

On the left is Death Point. My route climbs the rib that sticks out on the south corner. On the right is the series of peaks with Peak Inaccessible on the top right.

INTRODUCTION The point was said to have been named after hundreds of cattle perished in an unexpected snow storm. As late at the 1970s, it was possible to get to Death Point by a combination of four wheel drive roads and hiking. It was a long and difficult journey. In 1966, Desert Magazine wrote: "You must have a burning desire to explore the Kolob to take the ride to Death Point." The land along the east border of the Kolob Finger Canyons from which Death Point was previously accessed is private property and now closed to the public. The landowners are serious about keeping trespassers out. I recall being told by a ranger, "We don't go there. They know their rights."

FUTURE CLIMBING The faces on either side of the route are blank, broken or loose, making the potential for additional routes here unlikely.

My first attempt did not end well

I thought climbing Death Point would be easy, something I could kick off my list, as I waited for my climbing partner to get off from work to do something bigger. Maybe it's not a good idea to fill your plate too full. I got a permit for one night, thinking that's all I would need.

I started from Lee Pass hiking in the afternoon. Things began good. As I reached Le Verkin creek, I should have rested and drank water. It was a hot (90F) July day. Instead, swarms of white flies bite me as I stopped to drink water and it felt like I was in hell. (Rangers later told me the flies were unusual and due to heavy and late rainfall that year. They said many backpackers with permits to camp along La Verkin Creek retreated when they were not prepared with bug spray). It was painful to stop and drink water at the river. I needed one hand to drink from the bottle, a hand taken away from swatting at the flies. I was wearing a bathing suit. My sweaty, juicy thighs must have seemed like a thanksgiving feast.

As I hurried along the trail, I almost stepped on a rattle snake that slithered within four inches of my foot. Further down, I stopped to drink, as a pair of blue dragonflies kept the flies away.

Peak Inaccessible was my first stop. I thought I needed to climb it to get to Death Point. It was slow going as I carefully climbed while wearing a heavy bag of gear. I slept at the top of Peak Inaccessible. In the morning, I gave up climbing to the top of it, and went to look for an easier way to reach Death Point. I descended into a canyon to the south-east, and found a way to go up and down another canyon in order to get to the base of Death Point.

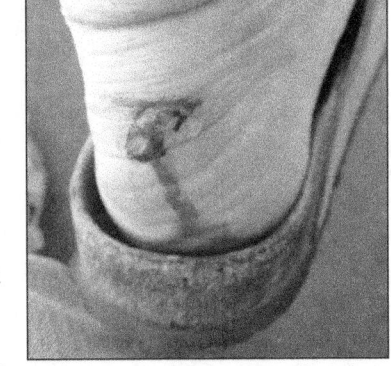

I got there. But I was feeling off. The heat had made me tired, almost exhausted. By 9 am I had only climbed 100 feet up the route on Death Point. Things slowed to a crawl as it became too steep to climb without a rope. At the rate I was moving I realized would never reach the top and get back to the car by dark. My permit was for one night, and I'd already used it to sleep on Peak Inaccessible. I considered that when I got to the top of Death Point, I would have to walk miles across the top of the mesa before rappelling a thousand feet. That would come at the tail end of the trip, when I would be exhausted and could make a mistake. I decided to retreat. I turned around.

It was not as easy to get back to the car. It was 100F and I had forgotten how I got to where I was. I knew that if I got to the trail at La Verkin Creek I would be safe. Then I discovered I had blisters on both of my heels. I stopped and covered the blisters with toilet paper and duck tape but it was painful to walk. With each step, I felt the back of my shoe rubbing on exposed raw flesh. There was not a cloud in the sky or the slowest breeze. The bugs had no mercy.

Back in town, I went to the Dairy Queen and drove to the city park to eat ice cream. As I sat eating ice cream, a praying mantis landed on my finger. I could see its small eyes. It was licking its feet. When it moved, it did so carefully and deliberate. It had perfect form. A symbol of stillness and patience When I was done with my ice cream, I held my finger out to a patch of grass. The mantis understood and hopped off of my finger and onto a blade of grass.

I've climbed in hotter weather, and wondered what else beside the temperate may have been a factor in why I felt so exhausted. I discovered that exactly when I had started my climb there was an increase in the level of radiation around the planet. I found a warning on the National Oceanic and

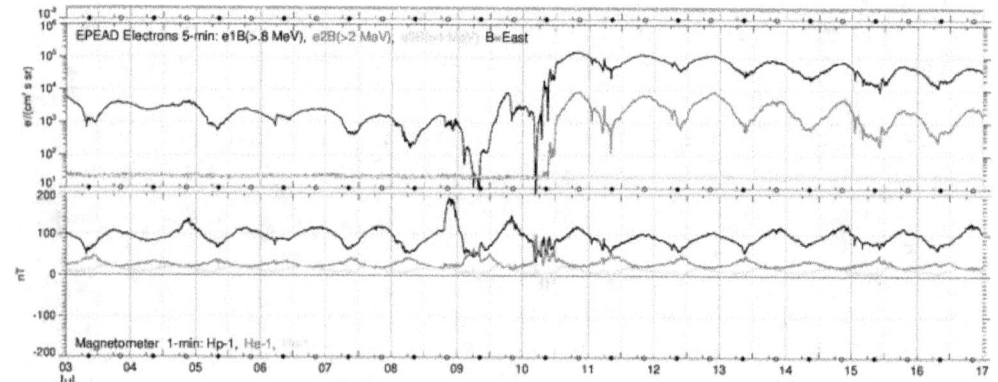

Atmospheric Administration (NOAA) website for space weather conditions which said an excess of electrons given off by the sun, induced by solar wind, had caused electrical charge to build up around the planet. I wondered how that might have affect people hiking and climbing on the surface. Maybe I'm just looking for excuses. I read what Louise Hay's *You Can Heal Your Life* says about blisters: "Resistance to life and not flowing with it." Me, resistant? I keep working my day job even though I'm burned out. I don't say no to anything.

I wore sandals for weeks and didn't

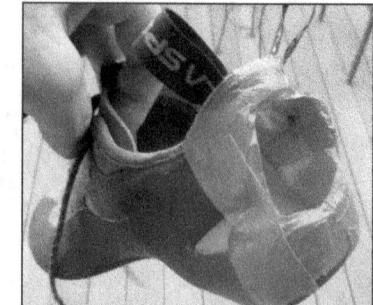

shower so my feet could heal. My right foot developed a brown patch of flesh I could not discern was a scar or a scab. My right foot was swollen. I started watching space weather for when it might be cool enough to go back and try again. I couldn't go anywhere until my blisters healed. I returned in the fall and was successful. (See Traverse of the Kolob Canyons.)

CLIMBING DEATH POINT

THE SOUTH FACE *D Stih 2019*
EQUIPMENT REQUIRED: A single rack of cams. Pitons (baby angles) are useful but not required depending on your comfort with run-outs. Mainly it's the first two pitches (400 feet). I was climbing by myself and being careful. There are bushes for protection. Bring at least a dozen slings. A single 200-foot rope is adequate, but it's highly recommended to have a second rope for the descent.
WATER SOURCES: In early season (Spring) there is plethora of water flowing in the area near the bottom of Death Point. The last remaining pool can be found in the last canyon crossed to reach the bottom of Death Point. In late Spring this water dries up. In the fall, carry all water from La Verkin Creek.

 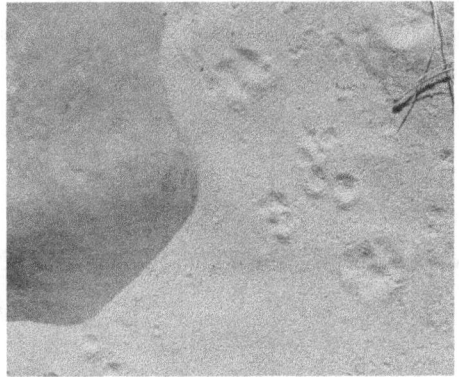

A pool in the last canyon crossed before hiking up to the bottom of Death Point in spring; Right: What to expect in late season.

SEASON: Spring is the optimal if you want to fill water bottles near the bottom of Death Point. Summer is too hot. In the fall bring extra bottles to carry water from La Verkin Creek.
CAMPING/TIME REQUIRED: The route can be climbed in a day. The approach and return take about 1/2 day each, making it necessary to bivy overnight somewhere. I recommend an early (3am) start from the Lee Pass trail head so that you reach the juncture to leave La Verkin Creek at first light. That will put you at the bottom of Death Point mid-day. Plan on biving on the route or camp at the bottom and climb it the next day. There are several spots on the route with flat spots for biving. (What Dangerous Dan considers flat.)
THE STARTING POINT: Start at Lee Pass. Hike the La Verkin Trail. Leave the trail just past the junction for Hop Valley, and do the approach to Peak Inaccessible as described in *Zion National Park: Summit Routes*. (Scramble up the gully to the cliff with the dead

View of the route after crossing the last canyon, heading up the approach slabs to the bottom of the route.

Looking up at the first pitch.

tree. Climb the tree to the top of plateau and start hiking towards Peak Inaccessible.) Just before Peak Inaccessible, descend into a canyon to the east. As soon as you get into that canyon, look for a way to climb out the other side. From the top of the other side, traverse south along the top, until it's possible to descend into another canyon, and up to the bottom of Death Point.

THE ROUTE: The route follows a ridge in the center of the south face. Take a look at the first pitch in the photo here. The best way to verify you're in the right place is this: when you think you are at the start, continue walking around the corner to the east. You will find the walls become steep and blank. Go back around the corner, and start. Look for a tree on a pedestal to the left of where the route begins. Don't start at the tree. The route goes up a crack system to the right of the tree. Take the easiest path straight up. It's about six pitches. The first two are the most difficult. After that it's a scramble.

GETTING DOWN: From the top of Death Point, I continued by hiking to the high point of Buck Pasture mountain and then across the mesa to Beatty Point. I rappelled and down-climbed Beatty Point to my car parked at Lee Pass. This is not necessarily the recommended descent, as I spent an entire day bushwhacking across the mesa, and a 1/2 day descending Beatty Point. The most straightforward descent is to rappel the route (about six rope lengths off bushes and trees) back to the bottom of Death Point, and reverse the approach. A trip itinerary of this nature would consist of getting to the bottom of Death Point the first day. Bivy at the bottom, climb the route the next day, and descend to the bottom for a second bivy. Return to the car on the third day.

First Ascents of Mountains Not Named on Maps

Colors in the fall.

The Witch Head

INTRODUCTION AND HISTORY In the 1990s, the park rangers in the backcountry office called this Batman. We did the first ascent when we had ropes fixed to the top of the plateau during our first ascent of the Altar of Sacrifice. We did second ascent the following year when we did a traverse of the Towers of the Virgin. The route is on the west side and is not visible from Springdale or the main canyon road in the park. In the topographical Ron drew, he graded it ED2 with pitches of VII+ using the UIAA alpine system. He rated it as such to factor in other variables, primarily, it's difficult to protect and has loose rock. I thought it 5.10. I must not tried to look for an easier way. The third ascent was done by local Mike Dunn and Arthur Herlitzka in March, 2021. Mike thought it was 5.0. They climbed it from the back (NW). From what I recall, Ron and I climbed the SW corner.

The Towers of the Virgin. Left to right: West Temple, Sun Dial, Witch Head, Broken Tooth, Rotten Tooth, Altar of Sacrifice.

CLIMBING THE WITCH HEAD

1. WEST FACE ED2 WITH PITCHES OF VII+ *D Stih and R Raimonde 1997*
EQUIPMENT REQUIRED: Alpine rack. Although Ron's topo says "Cam rack only above the plateau," a knife blade piton may be helpful to protect the crux at the start.
WATER SOURCES: Water from snow melting on the north side of the Sun Dial, and less likely depending on how late it is in the season, the south side of the Altar of Sacrifice on top of the plateau.
SEASON: Spring when there is water from snow melting.
THE STARTING POINTS: Climb to the plateau from one of two ways. One is to climb the Altar of Sacrifice; the other to rappel the West Temple as done for the traverse of the Towers of the Virgin, and traverse across the east face of the Sun Dial to reach the teeth.

On the summit of the West Temple, looking over at the Altar of Sacrifice in the morning light. The Witch Head is the wide and rounded mountain in front of the Altar of Sacrifice.

THE ROUTE: The route description is from the bottom of the climb after reaching the plateau. Start on the west side of the formation. The crux is about twenty feet off the ground. It's awkward face climbing in a flaring corner that provides some foot relief as you stem. Any gear you manage to get in will be small and suspect. After the crux, the route gets easier.

GETTING DOWN: Reverse the route. Rappel, using bushes as natural anchors.

Dangerous Dan on the summit of the Witch Head.

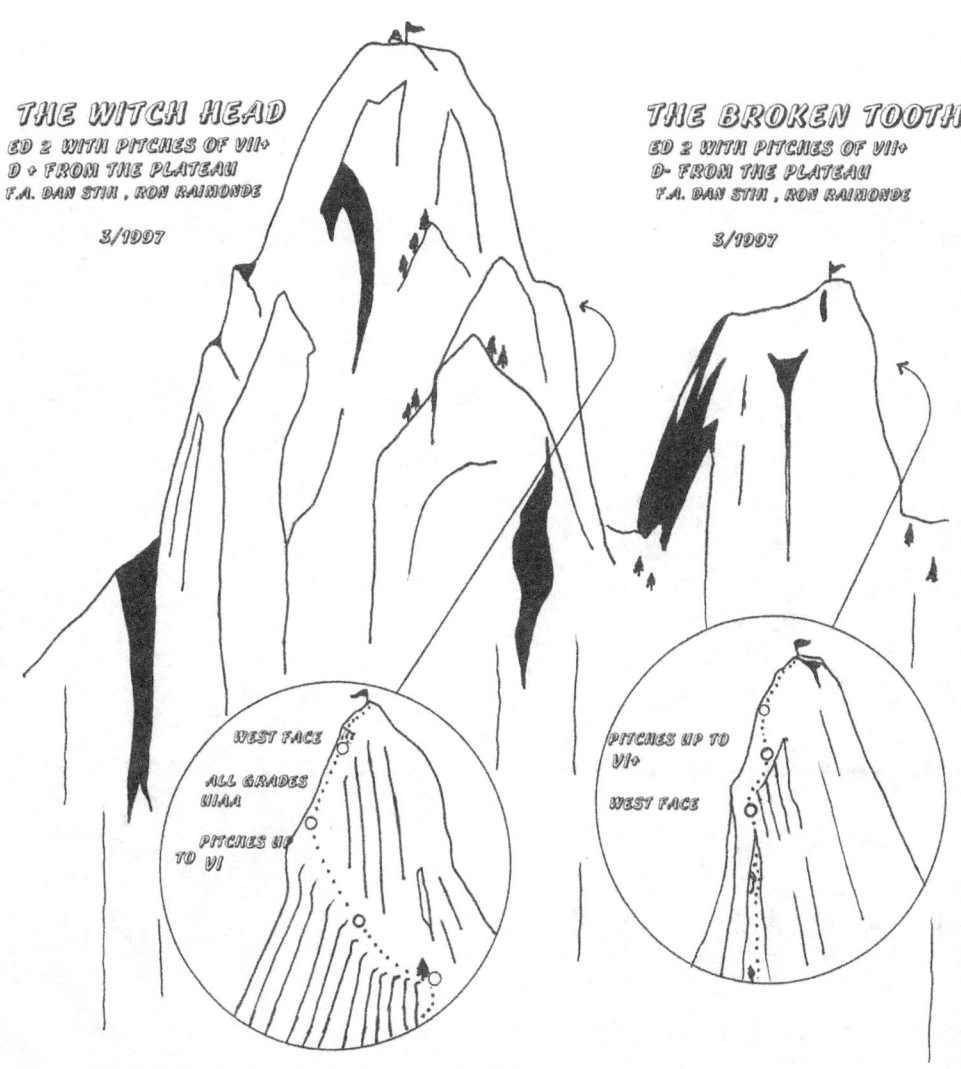

Broken Tooth & Rotten Tooth

Broken Tooth (left); Rotten Tooth (right) as seen from the east.

INTRODUCTION AND HISTORY These were first climbed in 1997, when Ron and I climbed the Altar of Sacrifice. When we were getting our permit, the ranger in the backcountry office told us that they call this "Broken Teeth." The second ascents were done the following year, when Ron and I did a traverse of the Towers of the Virgin. If you are going to climb them, chances are you are doing the traverse of the Towers of the Virgin. You will find climbing all the peaks on the plateau (Sun Dial, Witch Head, Broken Tooth, and Rotten Tooth) undertakings in unique ways. I didn't think Broken Tooth was as difficult as the Witch Head, the formation to the south. Rotten Tooth is easier and much easier than the Witch Head.

CLIMBING BROKEN TOOTH

1. WEST FACE ED2 WITH PITCHES OF VII+ *D Stih and R Raimonde 1997*
EQUIPMENT REQUIRED: Alpine rack. Lots of slings.
THE ROUTE: Start on the west side of the formation. The climbing route is on the west side of the formation, not visible from the main road in the park. The face is so broken it's a matter of finding the easiest way. Like other routes in this area, you will find there are not many ways to go. If you partner is one of those who likes to plow ahead, remind him or her to take the easiest way, even when it seems too easy. Doing so will prevent you from becoming stuck.
GETTING DOWN: Reverse the route. Take two ropes to rappel using bushes as natural anchors. 150-foot ropes are adequate.

Left to right: Rotten Tooth, Broken Tooth, and the Witch Head as seen from the west.

CLIMBING ROTTEN TOOTH

1. S/SE & SW FACES 5.5 *D Stih and R Raimonde 1997*
If you take the easiest route, it can be a scramble. As the name suggests, the rock is loose. This can be a fun route if the other climbs in the area are beyond your comfort level, you are camped on the plateau for a few days, and want to tag another summit.
EQUIPMENT REQUIRED: Alpine rack. Helmet.
THE ROUTE: A verbal description would be not be helpful. Begin on the west / SW side. Choose a way that appears to be the easiest. Don't take hand and foot holds for granted. It's not a good place to get hurt. From the summit, rappel using natural anchors.

Chameleon

INTRODUCTION I named this Chameleon because when viewed from Church Mesa, it looks like the back of the Meridian Tower. At least it did to me, which is why we climbed it by accident when we did the first ascent of the Meridian Tower.

HISTORY In April, 2008, Dave Everett and I descend a canyon on the east side of Church Mesa, in order to reach the Meridian Tower. We found ourselves in a difficult section of Birch Creek with pools of water. To avoid getting wet, we scrambled onto the south side of the canyon, and traversed high above the creek. (Difficult and not recommended.) We reached the NE corner of the toe of Chameleon, and climbed onto it. We were almost to the top when I realized we were not on the Meridian Tower. We bivied and went down in the morning. Getting down was easier. We scrambled down a loose gully on the west side of Chameleon (hugging the east side of the Meridian Tower), back into Birch Creek, then hiked a short way up the creek to the base of the Meridian Tower. In March, 2016, I returned and climbed Chameleon with Matt Mower on our way to do the second ascent of the Meridian Tower. From the west head of Birch Creek, we walked east down Birch Creek until we could go no further without getting wet. From there we climbed onto the center of the north face of Chameleon.

CLIMBING CHAMELEON

1. NE CORNER *D Stih and D Everett 2008*
2. THE NORTH FACE *D Stih and M Mower 2016*
CAUTIONS / SPECIAL DIFFICULTIES: Expect deep pools in Birch Creek on the approach.
STARTING POINT: As Church Mesa is an RNA, one way to get to Chameleon is the same as getting to the Meridian Tower: from the plateau between the Altar of Sacrifice and Meridian Tower, hike up a gully that hugs the west side of the Meridian Tower. Go down the gully on the other side to reach the head of Birch Creek.
THE ROUTE: From its west end, it's not difficult to go down Birch Creek to reach the north toe of Chameleon. Depending on the season (level of water), you will probably find it difficult to continue further. From that point, back track and look for a way up steep and unprotected face. After the initial difficulty, the angle lessens to low-angle slabs that lead to a rest area - a large open flat space on the middle of the mountain. From the rest spot, scramble up a ridge on the west side. The ridge traverses back left (east) to the summit.
GETTING DOWN AND ALTERNATE EXITS: Option 1. From the summit, continue south, down the other side (towards Springdale). If you're more into mountaineering than canyoneering (I don't like water), this is the easiest and logical decent. Go down the north face of Chameleon, to the saddle between the Point and Chameleon. Climb the Point, then head down into a valley between The Point and Big Red. From the valley between the Point and Big Red, you can choose one of the following to complete the descent:
A) The gully/canyon on the west side of the valley at the base of the red cliffs that needs to be negotiated to approach the Point from the valley. It's mostly a vertical drop (rappels) into Oak Creek canyon. If you're thirsty, there are pools before the drop.
B) The "Stinger", the canyon on the west side of the Beehives. To reach it, head east from the valley.

At the rest spot, half-way up the north side of Chameleon. The large peak in the background is Church Mesa. During my first attempt to climb the Meridian Tower, Dave and I descended the prominent, shaded gully to the right of the red streaks.

C) Advanced canyoneers that are prepared with wetsuits could descend the canyon between Chameleon and Big Red into Birch Creek. Go north from the valley to reach the mouth of a serious canyon that leads down to Birch Creek.

D) Another option would be to walk around Stinger Canyon, staying high. Pass under a big cave below the summit of Big Red, and climb up to the valley between the south face of Big Red and the north face of Beehive Peak. That will allow you to use the descent for the Streaked Wall. Climb up Beehive Peak and go down the other side.

Option 2. From the summit, reverse course, and start down the north side of Chameleon, going towards Birch Creek.

FUTURE CLIMBING : Climb the north face. Start the adventure by climbing up the descent used for the Streaked Wall. Climb up and over Beehive Peak, the traverse under Big Red into the valley between Big Red and the Point. Scramble up to the notch between the Point and the north face of Chameleon. Climb the north face of Chameleon.

From left to right: Big Red, Chameleon, The Meridian Tower (red cap). The ridge on Chameleon comes down the NW corner (right corner in this picture) to a flat rest spot before following trees (visible tree line on the lower left side of Meridian Tower) down a gully into Birch Creek.

The tree line on the upper ridge of the NE corner of Chameleon, as viewed from the Meridian Tower. Abraham is in the background.

Middle Cathedral

INTRODUCTION & HISTORY always ask a mountain what it would like to be called. This is what came to me. It points into the sky, and sticks out in the middle between Heaps and Gunsight canyons. I noticed Middle Cathedral when Mike and I were on our way to climb the Inclined Temple. As we were rappelling off the West Rim, I became aware of its massive, blank, west face and said to Mike, "What's that!" He wasn't sure. Years later, as I explored and climbed more peaks, I came to conclude it had not been climbed, and put together ideas as to how it might.

Middle Story

For years, I pondered what the logical way to climb the Middle Cathedral might be. The issue with any big peak in the backcountry of Zion is 1) getting to the mountain; 2) carrying enough gear so you can climb it when you get there; 3) carrying sleeping gear, because you are not getting back to the car the same day. One day I decided I was ready.

Starting at the Grotto, I hiked up the West Rim Trail and continued along the edge until it was time to leave the trail. I carried a haul bag. Inside were two normal climbing ropes, one thin 7-mil static rope, a rack of climbing gear, sleeping bag, dehydrated food, and a stove. I started bushwhacking through thick brush when I came to a finger sticking out towards Middle Cathedral. At the end of the finger I grappled with down-climbing a difficult section while wearing the bag, and set up a camp on the north edge of the rim. From the rim, I fixed two ropes down to the saddle between the West Rim and Cathedral Mountain. This might seem like cheating. It would be like fixing a rope down the Grand Canyon to climb a mountain on the other side. Consider that unclimbed peaks in the Alps such as the Dent du Géant, were attempted in the 1880s by shooting rockets with grappling hooks over their summits.

The crux on the final white cap section. I self-belayed using a 7-mil static rope and clipped a bush for protection.

After using two ropes to fix from the West Rim down to the bottom, I was left with only the 7-millimeter static to climb the mountain. I didn't find any water and couldn't cook. I had to eat dehydrated food dry. Once on the summit, I prayed that I could get down its north face with one rope. From the West Rim it had looked big and steep, as if there might be a drop longer than 100 feet. I got down. Then I went up the fixed ropes to the West Rim, and in the morning hiked the West Rim Trail back down to the Grotto.

CLIMBING MIDDLE CATHEDRAL

1. SOUTH FACE BUTTRESS (THE NORMAL ROUTE) 5.6+ D *Stih 2017*

EQUIPMENT REQUIRED: Slings to sling bushes. One 200-meter rope.

WATER: Don't expect water after rappelling from the West Rim unless you come the day after it rains. The sandy bottoms of the canyon on the west side of Middle Cathedral will be dry. It's out of the way to go down to Heaps Canyon to get water. There's always water in the Gunsight Canyon and at the Cross Roads.

SEASON: If you carry water, any season you've comfortable climbing. In winter, the West Rim Trail is icy and requires post-holing through deep snow.

CAMPING / TIME REQUIRED: 2-3 days if approaching on the West Rim Trail; If you're a canyoneer coming down Heaps, it's a 1/2 day round-trip from the Cross Roads to tag the summit and get back on your way down the canyon.

THE NORMAL ROUTE: From the saddle between Middle Cathedral and the West Rim, traverse SW, down, across and around the west face of Middle Cathedral to where a sucker canyon leads down towards the Cross Roads. Don't go down that canyon. Backtrack and scramble across the red face that is part of Cathedral Mountain. It's critical to find this spot. Avoid going across the red face too soon (too high) or passing this up. Once across this crux, take the easiest way up and across the red slabs. The target is a ramp that hugs the south face of the upper section of the Middle Cathedral. The ramp ends at a large chimney. I put rock shoes on when I got to the chimney, and short hauled my pack. Level ground and a rest spot are reached at the top. From there, climb the final head wall - the south white face. I went up and left. After a few slick moves it becomes a long and easy scramble.

GETTING DOWN: From the summit, on the east corner of the north face, I made several rappels off big trees using one 200-foot, 7-mil static. Be careful to study the descent from the West Rim before you start the climb. If you come down too far west, you may find yourself stuck on the north face. Once on the ground (the saddle between the north side of Middle Cathedral and the West Rim) climb up to the West Rim or exit using one of the other suggestions.

Middle Cathedral viewed from Heaps Canyon in Phantom Valley. Starting on the north (left) side, the normal route hugs and traverses the bottom until the far right.

FUTURE CLIMBING: THE CASTLE-CATHEDRAL TRAVERSE A cool traverse would be to hike the West Rim Trail to the finger that leads out to Castle Dome, and rappel into the saddle. From the saddle, climb the north face of Castle Dome. This has not been done. If you cannot climb the north face, to tag the summit of Castle Dome, down-climb around the corner to the south-east. At the end of the down-climb there's a short drop that requires a short rappel, where you'll find yourself on the approach to the regular route to Castle Dome. From the summit of Castle Dome, rappel down the north face back to the saddle.

From the saddle, go down Castle Dome canyon into Gunsight canyon. Two rappels are required. Be prepared, in the event you rappel in to water depending on the season. Walk Gunsight canyon south to the Cross Roads, and hop on to the east face of Middle Cathedral. Scramble up to meet the normal route, and finish climbing to the summit of Middle Cathedral. Rappel off the north side. Finish the traverse by climbing up to the West Rim. This would be a traverse of the formations around the Gunsight Start to Heaps Canyon. I'm sure you can think of a creative name.

Before starting this adventure, it would be prudent to hike out and look at the descent down the north face of Middle Cathedral and, as best possible, where you will climb up to the West Rim.

Expect to find water in Gunsight Canyon. If you don't want to have to worry about rappelling into water go in dead summer (August - September). In October, the days might be getting too short for a one-day attempt. It might be good to do in a warm season when a sleeping bag is not required.

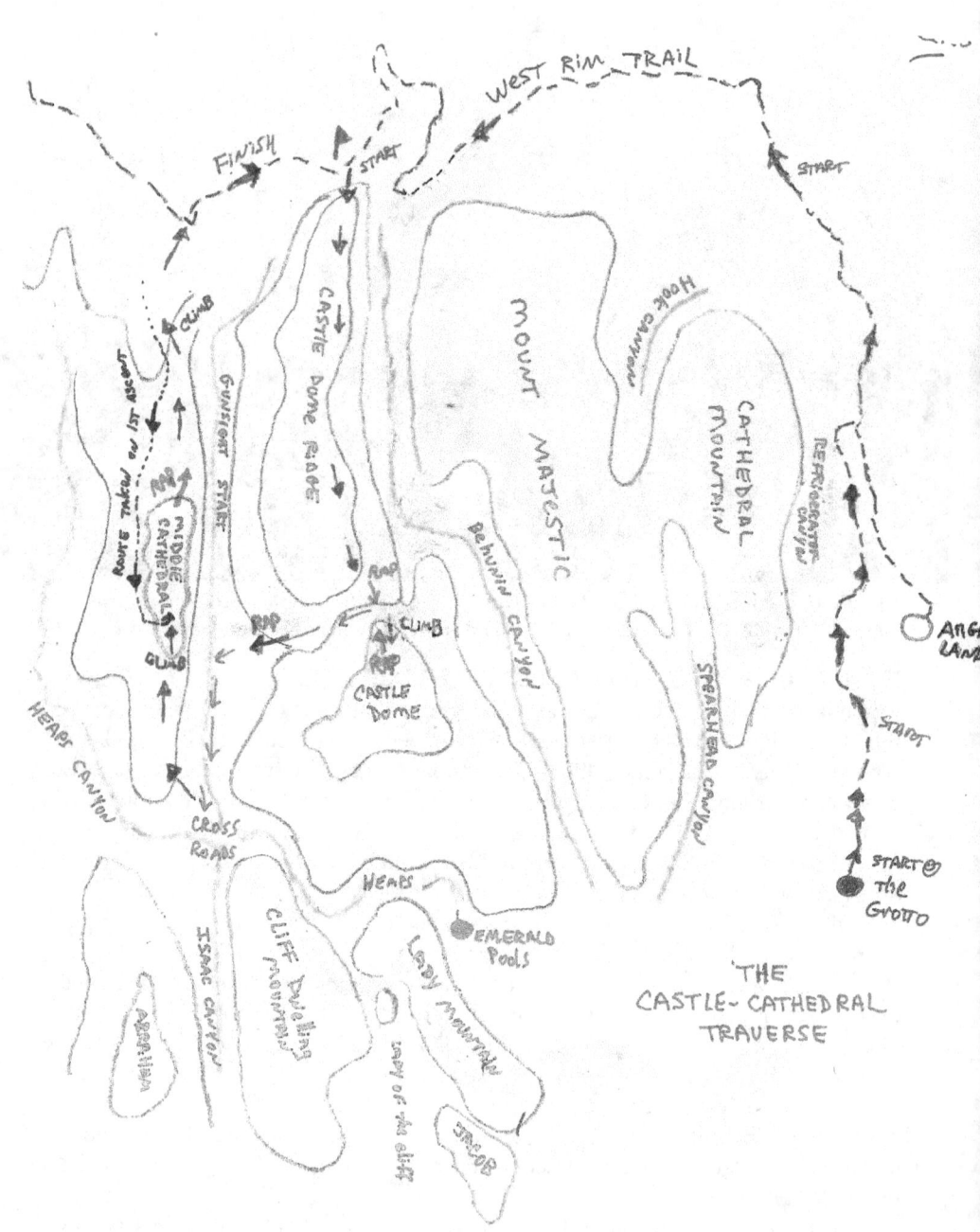

For a longer trip with more chance of success, camp on the West Rim on day one, do the traverse on day two, and hike down the West Rim Trail to the Grotto on the third day. Stock up on water when you reach the top of the West Rim at the spring. Reservations are suggested for the campsites on the West Rim. Often the lower campsites (1 and 2), those close to where the trail comes up to the top, are not as full. These might be a good choice, as they are closer to water, and there's no sense carrying all the gear further than necessary. Set up camp there the first day and hike up the trail to do a recon and become familiar with the approach across the finger to Castle Dome and the descent off the north face of Middle Cathedral.

If for some reason you can not climb up to the top of the West Rim after you climb Middle Cathedral, a wet suit and expert canyoneering skills will be required to continue down any of the canyons. The alternate exits are long and complex. Both have you going west through Phantom Valley, then south past the Bishoprics. To do the Cougar Mountain exit, from the west end of Phantom Valley, go south thru Inclined Pass (between the Sanctuary and Inclined Temple). Stay high and follow a deer trail that hugs the west face of the Sanctuary. You may lose the deer trails as you come to a section with white slick rock. Stay high and continue around the corner, going SW (around the Entry Pawns) then follow the valley (Terry Wash) south to its end. There's almost always water in Terry Wash where it meets the south end of the Bishopric. From there the navigation gets tricky, and scrambling west around hood doos is required to work your way south toward Cougar Mountain. As you get to Cougar Mountain, go west down Trail Canyon. That will lead you to the Right Fork which can be followed south to the highway.

The other alternative exit, perhaps shorter, more rugged, is Wildcat Canyon. Hike north-west to the end of Phantom Valley. Do not rappel or go down into Wildcat too soon. Hug the south face below the West Rim. Traverse under the West Rim until easier ground is reached and a more casual descent into Wildcat Canyon can be made. From there, navigate the canyon west to the trail (Wildcat Trail and Lava Point).

Summit of Middle Cathedral.

Side Roads: The South Toe of Middle Cathedral. The normal route comes up the west side (hidden) to meet the final white section of face near the top. On the right is the south part of Castle Dome. Between the two is the Gunsight start to Heaps Canyon. Following it to the bottom left, it meets the Cross Roads.

Side Exit: The ridge coming down from the West Rim that ends in a saddle on the north side of Middle Cathedral. It could probably be free-climbed at 5.7. The crux is near the bottom.

FUTURE CLIMBING: SIDE ROADS

I believe it would be possible to climb my route starting from the Cross Roads. It would make a fine detour for a canyoneer with the time. Start on the east side of Middle Cathedral at its south toe, where it touches the Cross Roads. Given its remote location and lack of bolts, if you think you're ready to climb Middle Cathedral from that position, you might also be capable of climbing up to the West Rim after climbing it via Side Exit. The section of climbing required to climb the south face of the West Rim is not vertical. The bottom appears 5.7. The top is a scramble. Gear would be required, a few small cams. As a backup, if you can't climb up to the West Rim (and you are not prepared to finish going down Heaps Canyon) you can call a friend and ask them to drop you a rope from the West Rim.

Cats Tail Ridge

View from La Verkin Creek. Below: view from the base of Cat's Crown.

INTRODUCTION Starting from the hanging valley between Gregory Butte and Timber Top Mountain, Mike Dunn and I climbed to the highest point on this ridge, The Tipping Point and then descended to Camp 2. I previously tried to climb the ridge from the bottom up and got scared. (I didn't have a rope). The grade is likely the same, up or down. To gain the summit from the Gregory Butte valley requires tenuous scrambling, climbing and rappelling. To gain it from the ground may require less work; to continue to Gregory Butte, however, may be as tenuous in regard to climbing and rappelling.

CLIMBING CATS TAIL

THE TIPPING POINT 5.8+
D Stih and M Dunn, 2025
EQUIPMENT REQUIRED: Alpine rack (one of each cam). One 60-meter rope.
STARTING POINT: See The Cat Walk: A traverse of the Gregory Butte Massif.

FUTURE CLIMBING: Climb it from the ground up, starting near Camp 2.

Cat's Tail Ridge as viewed from slabs at the bottom of the Cave Route on Cats Crown.

The Blob

INTRODUCTION The Blob is an excellent route if you want an adventure that does not require difficult climbing. It's in a spectacular location in terms of views and solitude. This is a good place to practice placing protection by slinging bushes. It's alpine climbing, as you might find in the Grand Tetons or Swiss Alps. Be careful. The rock is loose. When in doubt, rope up.

HISTORY In October of 2016, I had the sudden thought to return to the area of the Bishoprics. I had not been there since Dave Everett and I did the first ascent of the East Bishopric in 2007. I called my friend CP, author of one of the guidebooks to Zion, and an ear to what other climbers are doing, and asked him if he knew if the North Bishopric had been climbed. He responded, "Someone has been out there." I interpreted this as code for: "I can't tell you... I'm sworn to secrecy... someone might be trying to climb it... it has not been climbed yet." I didn't probe. I respect his position and often bounced ideas off him. He's good at keeping secrets.

Subsequently, I went out to try to climb it. I first tried climbing the west face. I failed. Then I started an aid route on the back side. The aid route was wet, so I went to look for a better way. That's when I noticed the ridge.

I climbed the ridge on the north side up to a formation I named the Gatekeeper. I wanted to keep going, but there was an obstacle in the way - the Blob. The rock

Nate, armed for bear, ice, and hiking in the dark.

too loose to get to it without making a short rappel. Since I only had one rope, no sleeping gear, and didn't know how difficult it might be, I turned around.

In November, I returned with my Nephew, Nate. He was seventeen, a city boy, and had never been climbing. After scrambling to the top of the Gatekeeper, we continued along the ridge and climbed the Blob. From the summit, we continued down the other side, towards the North Bishopric. It was late in the day when we reached the North Bishopric and we decided to go down. We established a rappel route on the west face of the ridge between the Blob and North Bishopric which we named "Nate's Tree Descent."

A few years later I spoke with the climbers who attempted the North Bishopric, the ones CP couldn't tell me about. They told me they attempted to reach the ridge by free-climbing *up* Nate's Tree Descent. They found it too difficult.

Success at Seventeen

Nate had never climbed or rappelled. In fact, he'd never been on a long hike and didn't own a pair of hiking boots. I dug through my closet to outfit him with the basic gear he needed: harness, helmet, and rappel device (for going down a rope). I dug out a rain jacket, down jacket (it would be cold), headlamp, sleeping bag, and so forth. I piled everything in a big heap on my living room floor. I didn't have climbing shoes that fit him, so he wore his Timberland (a brand of fancy, leather, street boots). He wore jeans and a Bern bicycling helmet. I told him to take whatever he wanted. It wasn't on the pile. He saw it in the corner in my living room — my Charlet Mosser ice axe. He thought it might be useful to climb steep rock. I didn't tell him that rock climbers don't use ice axes.

The plan was to try and climb what I and other good climbers had previously never attempted: the Blob. This might sound ridiculous considering better climbers had assumed it too difficult. But those climbers, including myself, had never tried. We had looked at the Blob and concluded that even if one climbed it, it would be impossible to get to the top of the North Bishopric from the other side. None of us had stood on top of the Blob, gone down the other side, and verified that. To me, it seemed the worst thing that could happen is that once we got there, we would find it to be too difficult and come down.

We started hiking in the late afternoon. At 10 p.m., Nate told me he thought a mountain lion was following us. In the dark he saw red eyes. Then he thought there might be bears following. I explained that animals are normally more scared of us than we are of them. Deer seemed to be following us. I didn't tell him that near our camp the following night, we would be close to Cougar Mountain, named so because of the large number of mountain lions.

We camped near the edge of a cliff overlooking a valley. In the morning, we rappelled using 400 feet of rope. We left the ropes hanging so that we could use them get back when we were finished. The Blob, was on the other side of the valley. There were no trails to get there. I explained that the easiest

Water in pot holes in Phantom Valley.

Slick rock on the south side between the West Bishopric and East Bishopric.

way could be found by following deer trails and droppings. Nate became an excellent deer trail finder.

The next day, I taught Nate the basics of how to hold the rope in case I fell. I tied one end of the rope to a tree and had Nate clip himself to the tree. Safely tied to the tree, he fed rope out to me as I climbed. When I got to the end of the rope, I set up an anchor, and he climbed up to meet me. We repeated the process as we made our way to the top of the Gatekeeper, the first peak on our way. We went down the other side and kept going, on virgin, unexplored territory. The Blob rose up from the ridge like a big obstacle between us and the North Bishopric.

We found the Blob to be easy to climb. We continued past the Blob and to the bottom of the North Bishopric. I wanted to climb the North Bishopric, but it was late in the day. We looked for a way to get down. We could not go back the way we had come. We wrapped the rope around a tree on the edge and threw both ends down the west face of the ridge. After we went down and were safe at another tree, we pulled the ropes to use them again. We repeated this, past six trees, naming it Nate's Tree Descent.

Today, when I stop by Nate's house, he's quick to let me know he has a college class to go to. I can't blame him for not wanting go climbing again. He probably thinks that's how climbing is supposed to be: a long and epic adventure. I returned the following spring, and climbed to the top of the North Bishopric.

Nate, using a Charlet Mosser ice axe to keep his balance on the approach slabs while carrying a haul bag and wearing Timberland street boots.

Looking down the face of the Blob.

CLIMBING THE BLOB

WATER There is a creek on the west side of the North Bishopric that likely flows year-round. This is the best place to camp, keeping in mind the minimum distance permitted for camping near a water source. Ask the rangers in the backcountry office. This area is destined to become popular, so please practice maximum leave-no-trace ethics. Pack out all trash and TP. Don't use the creek except for collecting water to drink.
SEASON Summer is hot. Winter is freezing. Late fall (October - November) is pleasant.

---

1. NORTH-WEST FACE 5.5 *Dan Stih and Nate Stih 2016*
EQUIPMENT REQUIRED: Slings and a few cams.
THE ROUTE: Start by gaining the ridge that comes down from the north side of the North Bishopric. There are two ways to get on the ridge. The shortest is to scramble up loose dirt and rock on the west face, just north of the Gate Keeper. Alternatively, you can start on the very north end of the ridge, as done for the traverse of the Bishoprics. This takes longer to get to from camp: hike north to the end of the valley between the Hamster (on the left/west) and Gatekeeper (on the right/east). Scramble up the white slabs on the north side of the Hamster, and walk NW clockwise around the corner (around the Entry Pawns). Once on the ridge from either route, scramble to the summit of the Gatekeeper, then walk down the other side towards the Blob. Just before the Blob a short rappel is needed to descend a loose cliff. Scramble up the NW corner of the Blob. It's one pitch.

The Gate Keeper

Onward, down the south side of Gate Keeper. Traversing across the ridge to get to the Blob

GETTING DOWN: From the summit of the Blob, continue south on the ridge towards the North Bishopric. Mid-way to the Bishopric, look for a tree descent on the west face of the ridge, a series of five, single rope-rappels. Avoid the temptation to down-climb the last rappel. It's harder than it looks, and you will find yourself in an awkward position, wishing you still were on rappel.

Nate, preparing to go down Nate's Tree Descent.

The King

INTRODUCTION I named this mountain the King, and the one to the east, the Queen, in sticking with the motif of other peaks in the area i.e., the Bishoprics, Sanctuary, and Church Mesa. There didn't seem to be an easy way to climb the King. The route I took was probably the shortest. It involved 200 feet of roped climbing, with a 5.9+ crux at a roof that had water flowing over it. I got soaked, but proceeded with the thought that if alpinists can climb through water dripping down the North Face of the Eiger, it should be possible in Zion. I was lucky to have survived and not die from hypothermia or fallen to my death. I climbed the King a second time during a traverse of it, the Queen, and the Sanctuary. This King is now an RNA.

The Sanctuary on the left; the King on the right. My route climbs a crack right of the center in this photo (left of the King), up to the ridge that connects the two.

An Epic Fit for a King

I explored the back side of the King and did not found an easy way to climb it. Therefore, I decided to give the wide crack on the west side a go. My route starts in chimney, and climbs up to a cave where a roof has to be turned. Above the roof is a shallow groove. Water was flowing down it from snow melting on the ridge. I climbed up to the cave and found myself exposed to cold water running over the lip of the roof. On a warm day, I was shivering and soaking wet even though I was wearing water-resistant pants and jacket. I focused on my breathing to monitor for hypothermia.

I had intended to aid the roof, knowing it was wet and probably too hard to free climb. When I got to the roof, however, I found there are no cracks. The rock was wet sand. I jammed hands into the groove, placing them into the cold running water. Anyone who has rope-soloed knows how difficult rope management is. The gear became wet and heavy, the rope reluctant to feed, my hands frozen.

I'm not sure how I made it over the roof. My feet should not have stuck to the face. I couldn't think clearly and didn't know if I should climb down or up. I was desperate, on the verge of freezing., and had stopped moving when, miraculously, I found my feet stepping up, holding onto invisible holds, held on the rock by an invisible force. It's as if my guardian angel and helpers held my feet in place.

I cleared the roof, my hands and feet in the water. At the top, I unroped and scrambled to the summit.

To get down I did a single rope rappel back to the cave, into running water. I picked up an extra rope I had left there, and I tied the two ropes together to rappel off a bush in the cave to reach the ground. The bush was like a post with the rope going around it. The knot was on one side of the post. When I got to the ground, I pulled on the end with the knot to pull both of the ropes down. Things were going well. Then, just as the knot came into view, and the other end of rope had left the ground, the knot got stuck. I had to climb back up to the cave to get the knot unstuck. Afterward I couldn't use the ropes to get down. I had to down-climb the wet chimney. Exhausted, I rushed to get the gear in the sun, hoping it would dry before dark. Rain was in the forecast that evening. The episode made me sick. Back home I spent two weeks in bed on antibiotics.

CLIMBING THE KING

1. WEST CRACK 5.9 *D Stih 2017*
Climbs the obvious wide crack on the west face, below a ridge that connects the Sanctuary to the King. From on top of the ridge, scramble to the summit. Descend by rappelling the route, using natural anchors.

Sorting gear on a bank of now at the bottom. Below: The route in dry conditions.

The Queen

The Queen. On the left side of the Queen, the bridge connecting it to the King is visible. In the background on the right is the southern-west part of Church Mesa. Photo taken from the North Bishopric.

Meeting the Queen

After doing the first ascent of the North Bishopric, I had half the day left and set out to explore two other, unclimbed mountains in the area - The King and Queen. I moved camp from the Bishoprics to be closer. Wearing the heavy haul bag, I started to go down the canyon on the north side of the Bishoprics. The head of the canyon was steep and loose. I found it difficult to manage wearing a haul bag, turned around, carried everything back up. I decided to start exploring first thing in the morning without taking sleeping gear.

Early in the morning, I descended the canyon, exiting it before it emptied

off a cliff into Coalpits Wash. I scrambled up the north side of the canyon onto flatter ground. It was peaceful. I enjoyed sounds of birds and the wind. I explored the back side of the King, and a part of the mountain that connects the King and Queen as if they are holding hands. None of these looked climbable. I continued hiking around the east side of the Queen. As I got close to Church Mesa, there was a huge drop. I scrambled up and down the face of the Queen on some potential routes as high as I could without a rope. I didn't find anything easy to climb, and continued so further around the corner, inching my way across a thin ledge, as one might tip toe sideways across a window ledge on a ten-story building.

As I came to the end of the ledge, I discovered a weakness: a steep chute of loose rocks and dirt. I started up the chute. Higher up it required some chimney climbing. Near the top, the angle lessened, and there were many ways to go. One lead me to the top. I explored the summit and found the "feet" God placed there humorous. After taking it all in, I made my way down.

CLIMBING THE QUEEN

1. EAST FACE 5.4 *D Stih 2017*

The practical way to climb the Queen is a chute its east face, the side that faces Church Mesa. The approach is from a canyon between The North Bishopric and The King. From the west head of this canyon, descend and exit a short way down it. Once out of the canyon, hike a long way around the southeast corner of the Queen. There's a huge drop on the east face of the Queen into a canyon between it and Church Mesa. Carefully steep sideways across the west face to reach the chute. The route is hidden until you get there. It's just a scramble. The Queen is currently an RNA. This route will allow you to tag the summit rim.

Lancelot as viewed from the canyon between the King and the north ridge that connects to the North Bishopric. Approach the Queen by hiking down this canyon.

2. THE NORTH FACE 5.6 *D Stih 2017*

I climbed the Queen a second time during my traverse of the peaks around it (The Sanctuary, King, and Queen). From the King, I descended a ridge on its south-east corner, a ridge that connects to the Queen. At the end of that ridge I climbed the NW face of the Queen. I rappelled from a tree on the lip of the summit, then descended by going down a canyon between the King and Queen, one that drains into a canyon on the west side of Church Mesa. Several rappels were required. The descent was thick with brush and loose rock. Early season snow added to the hazards.

Lancelot

INTRODUCTION I named Lancelot because of its color, prominence, and the way it stands tall and majestic - secluded, yet powerful, like the knight.

Lancelot (center) at the west head of Birch Creek, as viewed from a bivy 1,000 feet above Birch Creek, on my aid route on the north side of Big Red.

Blowing Off My Own Party

My family was planning my 50th birthday party. At the last minute, I told them I would be going climbing instead, by myself. They understood. They had a party without me, complete with birthday cake and a portfolio of my baby pictures. My feet were swollen right up to the day I started to climb. Miraculously, the swelling went down, and my feet were normal, when I got to Zion.

Constantly having swollen feet is not a good thing. I had gone to the doctor. There were blood tests, chest x-rays, EKGs, you name it. The results were fine. Nothing turned up in the blood test except a mild state of anemia, which I've had for twenty years. My previous first ascents in the area of the Towers of the Virgin and the Bishoprics were done without food and anemic. No wonder I get tired. According to Louise Hay, author of *You Can Heal Your Life*, feet represent our understanding of ourselves, life, and others. Swelling

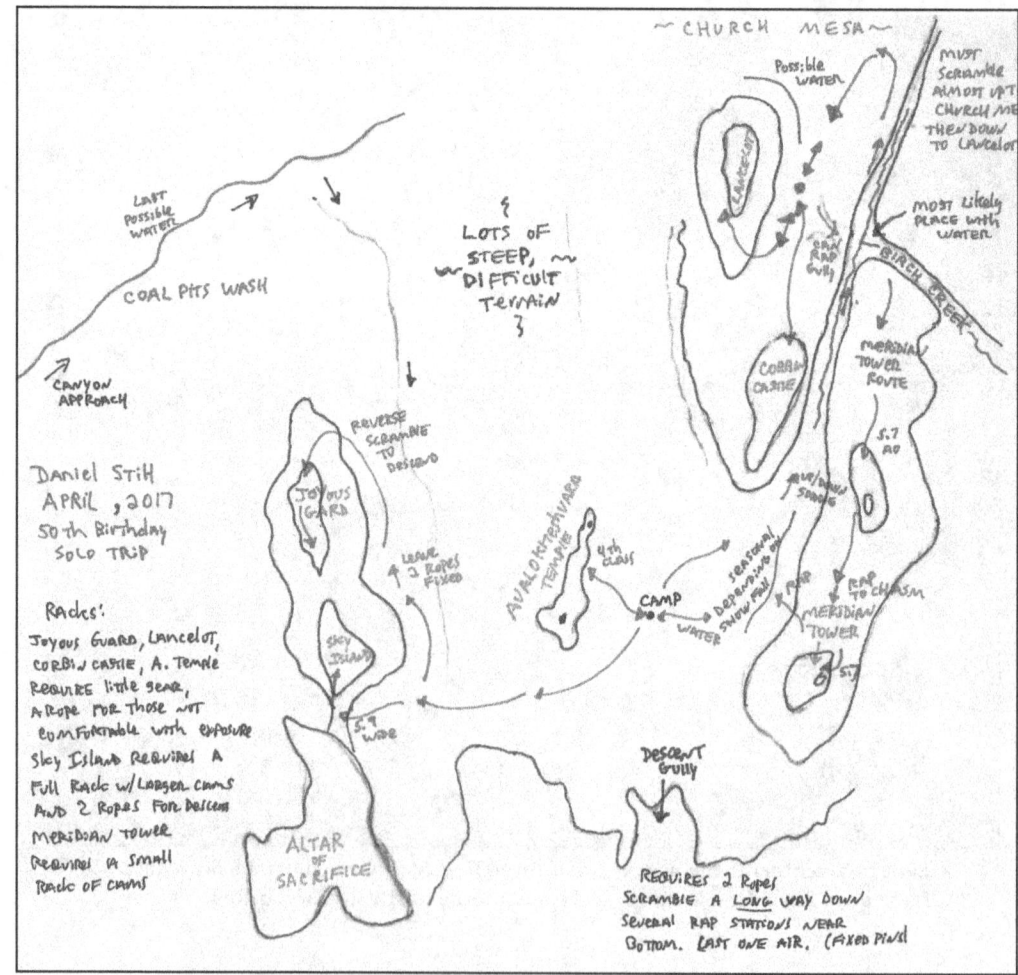

Topo map of the mountains I climbed on my 50th birthday, solo expedition.

is said to be due to being stuck in ideas and thoughts, and not letting things flow freely; being clogged instead of going with the flow. Her suggested positive affirmation is, "My understanding is clear. I am safe."

Going to the bottom of Lancelot with a heavy haul bag was not easy. I had to rappel in places I would normally have walked. Slow but sure, I reached the area near Lancelot, the first unclimbed mountain on my list. As usual, the issue was water - would there be any, if so, where? With all the ropes, climbing equipment, and sleeping gear, the bag weighed 65 pounds. There had been no room to carry water.

I dropped the bag on the east side of Lancelot, near the start of what would be my climb, and went to look for water. On a previous trip, from the top of another mountain, I had seen dark streaks on the north side of Lancelot that looked like water flowing. I hoped to find pools there. I got lucky. Not too far down around the corner, I found a shallow pool just deep enough to fill my bottles. I returned several times during the next two days to refill them. I was relieved and able to relax and not worry about hiking all the way back to get water. It meant I could use my stove to the eat the dehydrated food I brought.

Before starting the trip, I had checked to see if rain was in the forecast. My phone had displayed sun icons for a week. It didn't seem to match the forecast on my permit: 30% chance of snow, high of 40F, winds of 45 MPH. That evening, it snowed, my down jacket blew away, and hurricane-force winds make it too loud to sleep. I wished I had earplugs. I stuffed wads of duct tape in my ears but that didn't help. I only fell asleep as I was so tired. Wind is an inherent part of the land around Zion. The strong seasonal winds is how the nearby town of Hurricane choose its name. The following day, the wind died, the sun came out, and I made it to the summit.

CLIMBING LANCELOT

WATER The north side of Lancelot is a reservoir for water that soaks into rock from snow melting. There is a spring on the NE corner responsible for water draining into Coalpits Wash, and dark streaks visible when the water dries up. Hike north down the canyon on the east side of Lancelot to its NE corner. In early season you will find pools there, just deep enough to fill water bottles. As the season get late, it may be required to go further down the canyon to find water. Don't expect water after the end of April or early May.

SEASON Late March (depending on weather) through the end of April.

TIME REQUIRED At least three days. Allocate one or 1 1/2 days for the approach, a 1/2 day to climb Lancelot, and one day to exit. Give yourself extra time to enjoy the location and scramble other peaks in the area.

STARTING POINT This is a remote location that takes a lot of effort to reach. As Church Mesa is an RNA, the only permitted approach is from the valley between the Meridian Tower and Altar of Sacrifice. To get there, hike up Coalpits Wash to a wash on the north side of Joyous Gard. Hike up this wash to a flat, open clearing at which a spring coming out of the side of Joyous Gard provides fresh water year-round. From there it becomes a steep gully. Climb up the gully to the plateau between the Altar of Sacrifice and Meridian Tower. The most difficult scrambling and climbing is in the upper half of the gully. A rope is required. The gully is treacherous in early season and when

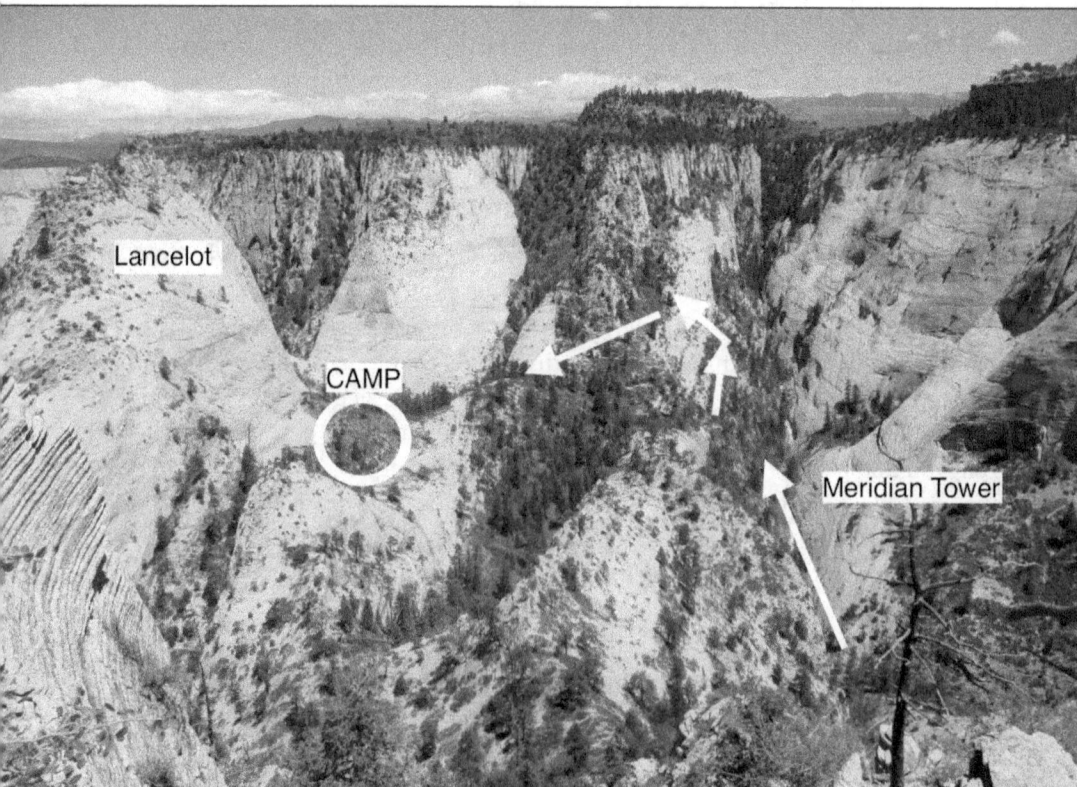

The approach from the valley between the Altar of Sacrifice and Meridian Tower

The south side of Lancelot as viewed from Corbin Castle. My route takes the tree line up to a section of steep white stone on the left skyline. In the background on left is the East Bishopric. The normal route on it ascends the ridge on its left skyline. On the right is Church Mesa.

The north face of Lancelot viewed from the North Bishopric.

it's wet. It has snow through March. Once on the plateau, hike over to the Meridian Tower and up the steep hill that hugs its west face. Go down the other side, a steep gully. Continue north, past Birch Creek, then get out of the canyon (a creek), staying on the left (west) wall on the side of the creek. Don't try and climb straight up to get out of the canyon. Head up diagonally. As you reach the top of the canyon, scramble back left towards Lancelot.

SOUTH FACE 5.2 *D Stih 2017*
The obvious (not ridiculously steep) route is on the south side. From the green valley on the east side of Lancelot, walk around to the south face and scramble easy slabs to the summit. A rope is not required for those comfortable scrambling exposed 5th class.

FUTURE CLIMBING The North face looks wild and steep.

Corbin Castle

INTRODUCTION Corbenic is the town where the castle with the Grail was kept. During King Arthur's reign, the overlord of this elusive place was Pelles, one of the Fisher Kings, and lord of Corbenic. His name, derived from peller, means a wise man or wizard. He was custodian of the Grail and host to several Grail seekers. This is the Grail Castle. The path is fraught with danger. The ridge to the summit is crumbling. I hope you find what you are looking for.

View from the north.

CLIMBING CORBIN CASTLE

1. THE SOUTH RIDGE *D Stih April 2017*
STARTING POINT: I approached Corbin Castle from a camp on the east side of Lancelot.
THE ROUTE: I initially attempted what looks to be an easy scrambling route, across a big ledge with trees on its west face. The ramp terminated at a dead-end, hundreds of feet below the summit. The only practical route is the north ridge. To get to it, I climbed the crux, a 5.7 hand and fist crack. Up high, the ridge narrows to less than two feet, and turns rotten, making a rope useless. From the top, I downclimbed the route, something more precarious. While Lancelot was enjoyable, I wouldn't recommend the castle to any but the most dedicated Grail seekers.
DESCENT FROM CAMP When you are done climbing Lancelot, the other formation in this area, you could descend a gully on the north side of Corbin Castle and go down into the canyon on the west side of The Meridian

The route on Corbin Castle.

Tower and the head of Birch Creek. In early season there will be water in this gully (as well as Birch Creek), another possibility if you don't find water near Lancelot. At the end of the gully, on the north side of Corbin Castle, you will come to a cliff. Rappel off a big tree at the edge. One rappel using two 200-foot ropes reaches the bottom. You won't be able to see if the ropes are on the ground or, more importantly, if there is water in the canyon, until you have started rappelling. I landed in a dry spot. If you plan to come this way check the water on your approach from the west side of the Meridian Tower. Just before you get to Birch Creek, look up the wall on your left.

Once in the valley between the Meridian Tower and the Altar of Sacrifice, depending on how much time you have, and if you find water, consider taking a rest day and climbing the various peaks there, including Avalokiteshvaram, a name given by CP during his ascent in 2015. These are easy scrambles and do not require a rope. They may have been climbed by unknown parties in the 1990s or earlier.

Other peaks in the area.

Joyous Gard

Joyous Gard, as seen from the East Bishopric. Note the impressive shield-like face. The route climbs the obvious ridge towards the green summits. The green summit caps to the right are Sky Island and The Altar of Sacrifice.

INTRODUCTION When Lancelot saved Guinevere from the stake at Carlisle, he brought her to Joyous Gard, his castle. Arthur subsequently besieged it, and Lancelot was persuaded to release her. The conflict was the beginning of the demise of them both. Lancelot's body was taken to the castle for burial.

Guarded Island

The day after I climbed Corbin Castle, I was uncertain and stressed. I moved camp from Lancelot to the valley between the Meridian Tower and Altar of Sacrifice. It was slow hiking. I wobbled as I carried the eighty-pound haul bag and carefully descended the gully on the north side of Corbin Castle. I had to step around pools of water and large boulders. If my feet slipped, I'd had fallen in.

At the end of the gully, I found myself at the edge of a cliff. I got out the ropes and set them around a tree to rappel into a canyon. As I went over the edge, I wasn't sure if the ropes reached the ground. I blindly rappelled, hoping I didn't rappel into water. Luckily the water level was low. I landed in mud. If I had come down ten feet to the left or right, I would have gotten wet.

I found myself in a familiar place - the north side of the Meridian Tower, a place where with a partner, we had started our climb on the Meridian Tower. I found the helmet I had accidentally left there a few years earlier.

I continued up the canyon next to the Meridian Tower, to the valley on the other side. I ran into obstacles, some difficult to overcome carrying a heavy bag. There were water falls I needed to climb up and around. I duct-taped the crouch of my new Gramici pants when I ripped them sliding with the haul bag. After tearing a large hole in my pants, I accidentally sat on a cactus. Thereafter I decided to try eat cactus, something I found easy when you don't care about of a few needles in your hand or butt.

I was happy when I made it to the top of the saddle, where I started descending into the valley. I worried I would not find water on the other side. I got excited when I found a wet, sandy stream bed on the SW side of the Meridian Tower. I worried when the wet sand didn't materialize into water. Finally, just when I feared the worst, I found it - running water in a creek. And the perfect camp - flat ground, fifty feet from the creek. Camp and was next to a tall monolith of stacked boulders that served as a land mark. I was so happy to have water. I'd end up drinking gallons and using all my purification tablets before the trip was over. The next day was my 50th birthday.

I had wanted to climb the "other summit" of the Altar of Sacrifice (Sky Island) since doing the first ascent of the Altar of Sacrifice in the 90s. It was one of those peaks you wonder *will that ever get climbed*? My first day, I thought I was being clever. There appeared to be a ridge on the NW side. I traversed (hiked sideways) across the base of the massif as far as I could, and came to a big drop where I fixed both of my 200-foot ropes down a chimney, and rappelled. This allowed me to gain the other side, level ground on which I could continue scrambling.

I was excited to be on the other side of the obstacle, and scrambled easy ground up the ridge. Unfortunately, when I was at the top, I found that the ridge does not connect with the summit (Sky Island). There is a gap. One-

Climbing, and porting loads up the canyon on the north-west side of the Meridian Tower after leaving the head of Birch Creek.

hundred feet below where I stood on the top, there is a small bridge of rock that connected the two summits. If I could get down to it, I thought, maybe I can climb up the other side. Without a rope. I was driven and thought about it. *Try or go home.* I thought about it. *If you fall, you will die.* I thought about it. *The rock is loose and unpredictable, you don't know where you are going, and if you get to the top, you won't have a rope to get down. You're likely to have an accident getting down, putting your foot on a loose rock as you lower yourself by your fingertips.*

The chimney I rappelled to reach Joyous Gard on the first ascent. It required leaving two ropes (425 feet) so I could get back. To fix the ropes required scrambling two pitches of dicey, hard to protect climbing. On the second ascent, another solo in 2025, I found a way to scramble up ledges on the north side of Joyous Gard out of the gully that leads up to the saddle between the Altar and Meridian Tower. As a result, the entire climb was "just a scramble." This is now the recommended path.

    I wasn't sure what to do. Then it happened: I started to climb down into the gap, as if I was going to climb up the other side without a rope. I watched my body move, as if not being able to stop it from eating an entire bag of potato chips. Then, just as unexpected, something inside me decided to stop. As if in mediation, I watched myself slowly turn around and reverse course. I went down the ridge, back the way I had come, and to where I had left ropes fixed. I jumared (pulled myself) up the ropes and went to look for another way. I would have to find another way to climb Sky Island.

CLIMBING JOYOUS GARD

1. NW RIDGE *FA: Daniel Stih April 2017 (fixing ropes to get there). Second ascent: D Stih, Feb 2025 (scrambling across ledges in the gully to gain access). 3rd ascent: D Stih and Raphael Tansen, November 2025.*

The original route to Joyous Gard from the base of the Altar of Sacrifice and Sky Island was done fixing ropes after climbing the east buttress of Sky Island (a three pitch route). The second time I found a way to scramble out of the approach gully from Coal Pits, through a rock wall, to step onto the white slabs of the Gard (Arrow at bottom of photo).

EQUIPMENT REQUIRED: Alpine rack. Single Rope. There's a fixed rope (45 feet) half-way up the gully for which an ascender is useful.

CAMPING / TIME REQUIRED: From camp in the meadow, a long day, up and down.

THE ROUTE: Start at the Guacamole Trail head at the end of Doulton Wash Road. Descend into, then hike up Coal Pits Wash to where the gully/canyon on the north side of Joyous Gard meets Coal Pits Wash. Hike up the gully to a meadow at which there is a spring that runs year-round. Camp there. (Appox. 7.2 miles from the trailhead.) To climb the route, finish going up the gully, passing a fixed rope. Just before the top of the gully, traverse a dirt ledge on the right. (About 1,500 feet of elevation gain from camp). An easy way to find this is: go past it to the top of the gully (only a short distance longer). Then start down it, and as you are coming down from the saddle, this is the first big ledge system on the left. Head up and right (SW) towards Joyous Gard. Find and scramble through a weakness in the rock cliffs. Once through, continue to where it's possible to cross over, onto the white slabs of the Gard. Scramble up the ridge to the summit.

GETTING DOWN: Reverse the route.

FUTURE CLIMBING:. There are potential long free routes on the west face of Joyous Gard that start directly out of Coal Pits Wash. None yet reach the summit.

Joyous Gard, as viewed from the Queen. The red cap in the top center is the West Temple. Coalpits Wash is in the lower far right.

The route up the ridge once onto the white slabs.

Sky Island
(The North Altar of Sacrifice)

The Altar of Sacrifice (Left), The Finger (Center), Sky Island (Right).

INTRODUCTION I had wanted to climb this "other summit" of the Altar of Sacrifice since doing the first ascent of the Altar of Sacrifice in the 1990s. It was one of those peaks you look at on a map and wonder if it will ever get climbed. It took me two attempts over three days by three routes to find a way.

HISTORY There are two major crack systems on the west face. In April, 2017, I climbed half way up Right Crack before considering it too steep and coming down. I decided to give the chimney (Left Crack) a go, and made it to the summit. In 2022, I returned and climbed Right Crack. The 3rd ascent was done a week later, 4/18/22, by Mike Dunn and I after we did the Traverse of the Time Machine. From the summit of the Altar of Sacrifice, we rappelled into the notch between the Altar and Sky Island. From there, we climbed the last pitch of my original route on Sky Island, Left Crack. Where I had scrambled and down-climbed the final red cliff bands that block the summit, we used a rope to climb it and to rappel back to the base of the red cliff bands. From there we descended the drainage for the Left Crack route, the most straightforward descent. The 4th ascent of Sky Island was done by James Barrow and partner during their attempt to do a complete traverse of the Towers of the Virgin, rappelling off the summit of the Altar into the notch and repeating the last pitch of Left Crack from the notch. They report there are now finger pockets where I placed pitons on the first ascent and they felt that pitch is one of the hardest on the traverse, 5.9+. I thought that was the easiest pitch. To date, the first two pitches of Left Crack, the hardest and most desperate, have not been repeated. Right Crack has also not been repeated.

Skyward Bound

Having failed to reach the top of the sister summit of the Altar when I climbed Joyous Gard, I attempted to climb it head on, real climbing, no scrambling about it. There are two major crack systems on the west face. They both start at the saddle that connects the main summit of the Altar with Sky Island. From the ground, the larger crack looked like a chimney. I expected at the top, I could climb onto a ridge that connected to the summit.

I left my gear and ropes at the bottom of the chimney and retreated to camp for the night. Camp was further than I thought. The territory is broken with

Left Crack and Right Crack with the Finger in between. The Altar of Sacrifice is on the left; Sky Island is on the right.

lots of canyons. If you are not careful to stay high and avoid going down too soon, you'll find yourself stuck in a mini-canyon. As I got closer to camp, I looked for the big stone sticking up, the marker.

Back at camp, using the large plastic coke bottle I had lugged around since leaving the car, I went to do the first chore - I went to the stream and re-filled the water bottles. I needed to keep drinking, including in the middle of the night. Whenever I woke up in the night, I would reach over and take a chug. I wanted to be ready to go first thing in the morning. I didn't have anything left to eat for breakfast, but I wanted to have a water bottle full and ready to take with me in the morning. I had not planned on being out this long and was out of food. The last two days my food ration each day had been two Goo packs and two packs of Starbucks instant coffee - a total of 200 calories.

The next day, I climbed the chimney crack. I found I could not climb the back of it, where the crack is not wide to place protection. I had to stay out front to keep my balance, and "chimney" the wide part. It was awkward, wide, sandy, and long.

At the top of the saddle I was disappointed. Instead of finding an easy scramble, a steep, broken, loose face loomed, with no sign of the summit. I abandoned tying backup knots in my self-belay system, as the rope drag kept pulling me down. The backup knot would come tight just as I was in the middle of a difficult move. That put me at risk while I stopped and, using one hand, united the backup knot. I didn't have a drill or bolt kit. If I got stuck or found the climbing too difficult, I would have to down-climb.

At the end of the third pitch (600 feet up) I found a small tree I could rappel from if I got stuck. It was getting late. I

A #3 cam in a sandy crack. Think it would hold a fall?

High on the third pitch, working my way around loose rock, hoping to find an way to the top, praying it wasn't leading to a dead end.

expected I might not get down before dark. I had brought a space blanket to wrap myself in if I got stuck. Even if I got to the ground, the way back to camp involved navigating a long and complex sequence of canyons. I would probably not find camp in the dark. I didn't care. The summit was on my mind. I didn't want to have to come back on another trip with more gear. *Please, let me get to the summit.*

When I got to the top of the forth pitch, things leveled off, and I saw the final, red cliff band. I also saw there was a gap between the cliff band and myself, and feared the worse. It reminded me of the gap between the mountain I climbed the previous day (Joyous Gard), one I couldn't get across.

Fortunately, this gap was small. I scrambled over it. The rest of the way looked easy. I left the rope, and simul-climbed the last twenty feet, using daisy chains. Daisy chains are long slings of webbing you attach to your harness. You can reach high, place a piece of protection, and clip the protection to the chain. If you fall, the chain catches you. I left the pieces in place, with long slings so I could reach down and clip into them as I down-climbed on the descent. A day with two goo packs and one Starbucks. I was on the summit.

As I walked toward the highest point, the harsh wind turned calm, and I smelled fragrant flowers. Instead of thorny manzanita bushes, I was greeted by gentle grasses and flowers. Instead of loose rock, a flat path of paver stones welcomed, beckoned me.

I sat on a log at the top and enjoyed the peaceful beauty of a place. I soaked in the vibes. I wasn't in a hurry. I wasn't going to cut my experience short. The way I figured it, there was no way I was getting down before dark. I'd be sleeping in the cold somewhere. Why not up there. I sat and looked out at the horizon, and soaked it in.

Looking over at the top of the Altar of Sacrifice from the summit of Sky Island. Circled is a mountain goat. In the background (upper right) is the red cap summit of the West Temple.

When I felt complete, I put it in high gear. I made several rappels from trees and bushes and made it to camp just as it got dark. Dinner was a cup of instant coffee. Tomorrow it would be time to go home. At least I had plenty of water.

I had done the descent from this area before: a large gully next to the Meridian Tower that you can walk down most of the way. The steep gully is full of loose rocks. With a heavy bag it is difficult and requires careful movement to avoid twisting an ankle. The gully turns to a blank, steep wall, six-hundred feet before the ground. A few rappels are required. Then you find yourself at the top of a maze of cliff bands with no trees to use for rappel. The descent was brutal and took a lot of energy.

When I reached the ground, I hiked back and forth to look for a break in the cliffs. I talked, argued, and put up with the whining and complaining inside my head, chatter with my shadow self, the part of the mind that talks negatively, incessantly. I tossed the haul bag down when I needed to down-climb. The bag started to blow apart. I held it together by wrapping my aiders (foot ladders) around it and the last of my duck tape. I was so tired and intent on making it down I thought I could fly. When needed, I threw the bag down and jumped. I wasn't worried about falling.

As I reached the service road, I became worried I might get stopped by rangers. I had to pass by their headquarters. There are large windows in their offices. I was a day over-due on my permit. I was pleasantly surprised that no one came out to greet me. I reached the main road and kept walking. When I thought no one was looking, I hid the haul bag in the grass next to the road, and took the shuttle bus to get my bike locked at the Grotto, the place I had started.

After getting my bike, I rode down the highway towards the Visitor Center where my jeep was parked. It was while riding my bike that it came on sudden and unexpected. I had not had a bowl movement the entire time I was climbing - seven days. It was not for lack of water. I used all fifty tablets for water treatment and drank six gallons.

I was stopped to get a view of the Towers of the Virgin. I was looking at them, chatting with tourists, when I realized I had to go. I told them I was going into the bushes to pee, and excused myself. Before I could relive myself, I peed in my shorts. *No problem*, I thought. *I can hide that.* Then an uncontrollable spasm came over me, and I pooped in my pants. I thought I could hide that too. Then I heard it. A sloppy pile of brown goop hit the ground next to my boot. I looked to see thick, brown smudge on the side of my leg.

I rode my bike to the VC, went into the restroom, cleaned myself up, enjoyed the rest of the sunset, and started driving to Phoenix, Arizona. Although my family had a party without me, cake and presents were still waiting. The swelling in my feet returned on the drive home. Happy feet when climbing, back to swollen when not.

Some birthday party. If you had visited me during my recovery you'd have thought I had too much to drink. As runners understand, I felt like I had a ran a marathon. It was all I could do to roll off the couch. It took me a week to recover. I had sucked every juice from the mitochondria of my cells. My glands were swollen, perhaps from being stuck with cactus needles. My recovery was long and mysterious. Something inside me was used up and had to grow back. It took time.

CLIMBING SKY ISLAND

1. LEFT CRACK TO SOUTH FACE *5.9+R D Stih, April 2017*
EQUIPMENT REQUIRED: Full free-climbing rack with extra wide stuff. No need to get too wide. Two #4s and one #5 cam. Two ropes.
WATER: Until all the snow that collects along the bottom of the east face of the Altar melts, there is a large pool far down the slabs on the east /NE face. Water also collects in this pool within a few days of a significant rain storm. The water quality from snow melt is good; poor from rain. Bring a filter for rain water. Water might also be found next to the Meridian Tower, subject to snowfall. In early spring (March - April) a creek flows out of the NW face of the Meridian Tower from water that soaks into the mountain during winter. It magically seeps out of the side of the mountain in seasons with high snowfall. There is a small chance this creek is running, depending on the amount of snow that winter. At best, expect the flow to last through the end of April.

Location of a seasonal pool (from snow melting) on the south-east side of the Altar.

Above: Looking over at the last pitch on Left Crack from the top of the Altar; Right: Mike Dunn on the last pitch of Left Crack, before the Finger is reached during the third ascent of Sky Island.

SEASON: Spring (Mid-March through May 1st)
THE ROUTE: Climb two pitches up the wide crack at the saddle. At the top of the saddle, belay at a large tree. From the tree, climb up and right, on steep, broken, face. The summit will not be visible. At top of the forth pitch, things level off, and the final, red cliff band come into view. Hop over the gap and scramble the red cliff band to the summit.
GETTING DOWN: Decent is down Right Crack. From the summit, scramble down a loose gully in between the Finger and Sky Island until you get close to the edge of a drop where you'll find slings around a bush. Rappel to another bush with slings and then to the ground. The last rappel (two ropes required) requires down-scrambling the gully as you pull the ropes in order to reach the ground.

2. RIGHT CRACK 5.9 A2+ *D Stih, April 2022*

The second ascent of the island and the first summit I reached after recovering from a broken hip. Porting gear out Coal Pits Wash and up the approach gully was physical therapy. Slow as a turtle, I made several carries over a few months, my tendons healing after each.

EQUIPMENT: Requires some aid gear such as a few beaks and small angles. (This may take cams now that the pin scars have washed out into finger pockets.)
THE ROUTE: The free climbing traverse under and around the roof is cool. The fun is spoiled by a tenaciously blank section near the top that requires some aid, and tunneling through bushes to reach the upper drainage from which it's a scramble.

Altar of Sacrifice (Left), The Finger (Center), Sky Island (Right).

CLIMBING THE FINGER

WEST FACE 5.5 *D Stih and M Dunn, April 2022*
EQUIPMENT REQUIRED: Very little.
STARTING POINT: Most get there by climbing the last two pitches of Left Crack while doing a traverse of the Towers of the Virgin. From the top of Left Crack, my original ascent for Sky Island, you will walk past the base of the Finger on the way to climb the red cliff band, the final bit that bars the summit of Sky Island. Alternatively, climb Right Crack to reach the base of the Finger.
THE ROUTE: One short and easy pitch. Start at the face on the northwest side. Climb into the obvious wide section and chimney to the summit.
GETTING DOWN: Rappel back to the base of the Finger, then descend to the ground (the plateau) via the ascent line for Right Crack on Sky Island.

Center Pointe

The back, north face of Center Pointe, as viewed on my hike from the summit of Death Point to Beatty Point.

INTRODUCTION I named this peak Center Pointe as it's literally in the center of the action, surrounded by big peaks and canyons, in the center of Kolob Canyons.

Donuts, a Car, and a Song

It's the waiting that's a problem. A rock star can tell you they enjoy being on stage. But from the moment they finish a concert, until the moment they are back on stage, the time in between is a killer. Climbing in Zion is a waiting game - watching the weather when it's not too hot or too cold, and for rain and snow.

My first attempt was on New Year's day, 2018. There was a break in the cold weather and it was extremely warm, 57 F degrees. No one was in Kolob Canyon. Camp sites are usually reserved months in advance. I could stay at any camp I wanted to. I stayed at several, including Camp 10, near my climb, and Camp 4 on the hike out.

Because it was warm, the river was flowing heavily. When I got to the approach gully, the river covered the trail. I had to hike up the side next to the canyon, through thick bushes and cactus with a full haul bag, two ropes, a rack of iron for an aid wall, and sleeping gear. Climbing the dead tree

The dead tree that must be used to climb a cliff on the approach.

to reach the top of the plateau was a nightmare.

I tied one end of the rope to the bottom of the tree, gave myself slack, and tied the other to my harness. Now if I fell I would not fall down the gully. I climbed the tree looking for foot holds on branches that were not rotten. The rope got wrapped around the tree, and the friction caused it to get stuck. As I went higher, the rope would not move. I had to pull up slack and drop a clean bit to the ground, go down, undo the other end, and start over. I wondered if the tree, leaning precociously against the cliff, was going to slid off the mountain and take me with it. Since my rope was wrapped around it, I didn't see how I wouldn't be taken for a ride.

I untangled the rope, and got my gear to the top of the cliff. When I got there, I was tired from the ordeal. After resting, I started carrying the bag toward Peak Inaccessible. I decided there was no way I could carry all the gear up Peak Inaccessible, and down the other side to get to Center Pointe. Add to that I would need to come back with water. I put the haul bag down and went on a recon.

I scrambled to the top of Peak Inaccessible. From the top I saw I didn't need to climb it to get to the bottom of Center Pointe. In fact, it could be reached by walking sideways where I had come up at the top of the leaning tree. I was beat. I decided to bail. I made two trips up and down the gully to get my gear back to Camp 10 at La Verkin Creek.

The next day I decided not to give up. I went back, carrying (yet again) a rope to re-climb the tree. (I've climbed the tree and cliff too many times to remember). The recon went well. But snow and colder weather were coming, so I decided to go home. As I hiked back to the car it became cold (20F) and cloudy with a chance of snow. My water bottle froze that night. The river was already frozen. Back to the waiting game.

Looking south on top of the plateau after climbing the dead tree.

I missed an opportunity go back the first week of February because I chose to keep an appointment for a TV interview for my day job. I could have re-scheduled, but the host couldn't find a replacement and I admit, I did not want to miss an opportunity to be on television. I thought I could go after the show. Then the weather changed. Literally the day after the show, it started to snow. I can't tell you how many times I packed and unpacked my jeep. I need to remember my priority: climbing.

It remained cold, as February should be. My gear remained ready to go, taking over the bathtub in my apartment. When a window of good weather appeared, I went for it. On a Monday I drove to Farmington, New Mexico for work, seven hours round-trip. When I got home, I looked around, felt the vibe and thought, if you're here tomorrow you will wish you had

Peak Inaccessible (left of center), Center Pointe (right of center). In the background is Hop Valley and the Hop Valley Trail.

gone. I packed my jeep. I was gone by 6 pm.

On the way, I was stuck in traffic on the interstate. After waiting for an hour, I saw people turning around and driving backwards, something I though insane until I looked in my rear view mirror and saw a police officer talking to the people in the car behind me. I followed that car. We drove backwards, and exited the freeway by driving up the on-ramp, what's normally the wrong side of the road. The police cleared the road behind us. The highway ahead was closed due to an accident. *Was that a sign not to go climbing?* I drove on. From 10 pm to 2am, I slept in my car in the familiar place, a Love's gas station. In the morning finished the drive to the Visitor Center in Kolob Canyons.

I was cold just getting out of the car, in the low 40s. I wondered what I was doing. It was cloudy with snow on the peaks. The ranger warned me that hikers had turned around a short way down the trail because of mud. *Did I really want to do this?* I considered that I prefer spring or summer when the warm wind is blowing, birds are singing, and the grass is green. *Don't be a winnie, Dan.* The snow-covered icy peaks didn't vibe with me. *Let mother sleep.* I put my worries aside and got started.

I felt good on the trail, even as I carried a heavy bag. The mud was not so bad. I found if I hit the muck head-on instead of trying to step around it, I didn't slip.

When I reached the intersection of the river and Hop Valley Trail, I stopped to check the time on my inReach satellite device. My heart sank when the inReach would not turn on. I had charged it the day before I left and sent myself a test message. The only notice I have given my brother I was going climbing was a text as I was leaving the parking lot at the trailhead. It said "Going climbing for a few days. Out Sunday." Which would be fine, except my family would expect some text messages during my climb, and would worry if they didn't receive any.

I decided to continue, then heard some hikers and waited to intercept them. They said they didn't have a

A fixed piton placed at the beginning of the climb to protect free-climbing.

phone, but would call my family when they got to their car. I left the trail, and started hiking up the gully towards the tree leaning against the cliff. There was a constant chatter with myself. The slippery conditions scared me. I had slipped on snow on the approach to Castle Dome and almost slid off the mountain. I was being vibed out. I thought of the positive. Snow is good for having water to drink. *What is it that's bothering me?* The hikers would let family know. That's a sign, right? I would not have run into them if it were not meant to be. In a short time it would be dark. I had a decision to make.

I made the decision to go down. I hiked out in the dark, fourteen miles round-trip. As harsh as this sounds, I was happy that I had left home. If I had stayed home, I would have regretted it. I felt as if I'd done 1,000 sit ups. I can't say what really spooked me. Maybe it was the rock on the climb would have been wet. I remember when I did the first ascent of the Bishopric. Two weeks after the snow was gone the rock was mud two inches beneath the surface. Back home, I went back to watching the weather. Snow was in the forecast.

A few weeks later, I spoke at a conference in San Diego on business. I almost bailed. It seemed I spent most of my time checking the weather to go climbing. I had a thought that perhaps universe was getting tired of giving me chances - chances to climb, not pick and choose what I want to do, and when I think I should go climbing. After speaking, I went for a walk on the beach. That's when my heart began beating fast. *What if I blew it?* As I walked up and down the beach bare foot, the old Plantar fasciitis started up. I had gotten fasciitis taking a leap off the top of a mountain to get down after a climb. I landed hard, wearing rock climbing shoes, on flat rock. Nothing was broken, but I was on crutches for six weeks.

Bottom pitch.

The weather suddenly improved. I started packing. I wondered if I should find a partner. I remembered that it's not a race or something I need to do to prove anything. I enjoy being out there. I feel that's where I belonged. It's as if the fork in the right place in the drawer and not in the spot for spoons.

When the time came to go climbing, I had in two weeks, driven 3,000 miles for work. I was tired. I got a few more calls to work. I drove to El Paso for work, through snow and rain. When I finished, I drove home and packed to go climbing. I had a job on the way to Zion. My plan was to pack a ladder and equipment needed to work, drive to work, then drive to Zion that same evening. I got to Zion and slept in my jeep outside the park.

In the morning I hiked to the tree and Peak Inaccessible. On the way my foot started to throb from the plantar. I wondered if I should stop a hiker, one that looked like a boy scout, and ask for some Ibuprofen. I didn't.

Climbing unclimbed peaks is usually a religious experience. States alter between heaven, hell, and in-between. You might have sore feet, be scared, cold, thirsty, hungry, or all the above. The scenery, seclusion, and peace make it worth it. The first day I was so tired that I wished I was somewhere else. I longed to be home, drinking a glass of wine, watching the sun set from the comfort of my living room.

I climbed the tree by leap-frogging my aiders around it like a log jammer. The tree started to move as I reached the top. The bottom is stuck in loose dirt, a foot away from the edge of a cliff. The tree would fall over if not for a small bush and a pile of rocks onto which it is leaning. I pulled myself up, relieved to have gotten to the top safely, walked over to a living tree, put the rope around it, and rappelled back to the ground to get my haul bag. Then I jugged back up the rope and hauled the bag behind me. This is when the first of several things occurred that would later contribute to saving my life.

I had used the same rope to haul the bag that I would use to climb with. When I got the bag to the top of the cliff, I noticed the rope had a spot worn from being dragged up it. The protective sheathing was cut, exposing strands of rope. I made a mental note that when I used the rope to climb, to tie into the other end.

There was still time left in the day to start climbing. I hiked to the base of the mountain and climbed fifty feet. It was getting late, so I lowered, left the rope and hiked back to camp.

The next day I hiked back to the bottom, went up the rope, and started climbing higher. When I was only one-hundred feet up, I felt I needed to go down and rest. I was already tired. It didn't seem like I was that high. One end of the rope was tied from me to the anchor at the bottom. I put some strap around the bush to use it as an anchor, and secured what I thought was the middle of the rope to it. I got ready to rappel the other, lose end, to the ground.

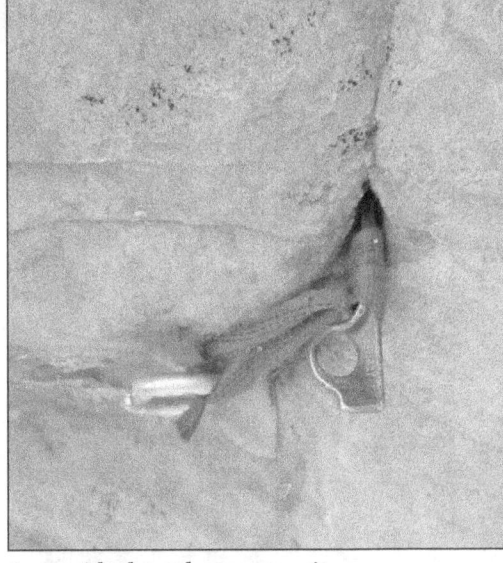

An upside down lost arrow piton placement in a shallow crack. The red nylon webbing is used to put the force close to the rock to reduce leverage from torque. Doing this can make the difference between a piton pulling out or not.

To be safe when rappelling, I use what's called an auto-block. It's a method of wrapping a cord around the rope, and clipping it to your harness such that if you were to accidentally let go of the rope with your break hand, the cord will lock onto the rope as you rappel, and stop you. Thinner cord grips better than thick cord. But the heat generated by friction can cause it to melt. It's good practice to periodically replace the cord. I had just bought a new cord. The new one was thicker too. I looked on my harness and couldn't find it. Instead, clipped to my harness was the older, thin cord. I would have to use it.

I started rappelling, looking up to make sure the rope wasn't running over any loose rocks that might fall on my head. Suddenly, the auto-bock cord would not slide. Still looking up, I tugged on the cord with my brake hand to make it slide. I needed twenty more feet to swing around the corner and reach the ground, where the plateau meets the mountain at the bottom of the climb. Directly below was a drop of 700 feet into a dark canyon.

Looking down and across at the route. The bush in the center was a belay.

I was frustrated, stuck, hanging on the rope. I tried to pull rope up and feed it through my rappel device. Nothing budged. I began to curse. Finally, I looked at my brake hand to see what was stopping things. The cord was locked on the rope, stuck on the sticker the manufacturer places on the rope, three inches from the end. The rope would have pulled through my rappel device, and I would have fallen to my death, except the cord was biting so good it had gotten caught on the sticker.

With one hand and all my strength, I grabbed the rope above my head. On big climbs, I rappel with a jumar (clamp) attached to my harness by a cord called a daisy chain, so that I'm ready to clamp on to the rope should I need to. With my other hand I placed it on the rope. Saved!

As I hung on the rope, I asked why. *Why was I still here*? The list came quickly. I'm OK with simple things. The first: bring the staff where I get my mail, donuts. The second - buy my nephew a car. He was almost eighteen and had been putting off getting his license because he didn't have a car. Third - record Home is Here, a song I wrote with friends. Three things. Three things had to have occurred for me to live.

You might think such an incident would have caused me to go home and stop climbing. Instead, after taking a break, I decided the only way to continue was to sleep on the mountain. I took a minimum amount of gear. I packed a sleeping bag, water, and two power bars. Instead of hauling the bag, I attached it to my harness, and carried it as I cleaned the pitches. The bivy was awesome. A spectacular location where I found a ledge big enough the sleep. The scenery and peace are the reasons I climb. From the bivy there was a pitch of face climbing, then a scramble to the top.

You might ask what the third (or forth) thing was that had to have occurred for me not to have died. When I was on the way out, and back at the top of the tree climb, I noticed what looked like piece of strap laying on the slabs below the edge of the cliff. I thought it was trash. When I got closer, I found it was the new, thick auto-block cord I had brought. If I had used it I might not be alive. Did I drop it? More likely my capital G, guardian angel took it off my harness when I wasn't looking. For a moment I thought of a higher power. Ass I was thinking that, a tiny toad hopped across my path.

CLIMBING CENTER POINTE

PRACTICE YOUR SCALES A2+, 5.8 D *Stih 2018*
Difficult to protect except for bushes and tied-off pitons. It requires skillful route finding and the gumption to go up what appears to be improbable. There is a lot of free climbing.
EQUIPMENT REQUIRED: The cracks are shallow grooves. Most placements are tied-off knife blades and other pitons. Only a few cams are required: one set from 0.5 - 2; (5) knife blades, (2-3) long angles, several baby angles; Leeper pins may be useful for stacking in shallow grooves; long slings for natural features.
CAUTIONS / SPECIAL DIFFICULTIES: The approach requires climbing a dead tree leaning against a cliff. It appears to be held in place by a second dead tree. The bottom sits on a stump as if chewed through by a beaver. Regardless of how precarious it looks, the tree seems to be stable. At the top, the trees lean against a dead log and a bush which are not stable. The dirt is getting washed out from under the log at the top of the cliff. Don't pull on it.
WATER: The last reliable water is in La Verkin Creek. Fill up there. There is no water on the plateau above the gully. Once you leave La Verkin Creek, the clock is ticking on your water supply.
SEASON: Because water is not a factor (there is no water near the climb) heat becomes the factor. Summer is miserable and will consume water quickly. Winter can be brutally cold, but if you like winter conditions, you will find snow on the plateau which you can melt for water. In those conditions take ice cleats and be careful on the approach.
CAMPING / TIME REQUIRED: 3-4 days. Give yourself a full day for the approach, 1 - 1 1/2 days to climb, and 1 day to hike out. For a leisurely trip, reserve a camp site close to the Hop Valley Trial junction the first night. I prefer sites near the Kolob Arch junction and not those past the Hop Valley junction. It's pleasant to have a camp site on the last night. You can bring your gear down, relax, and hike out in the morning. This is especially nice in hot weather. You can hike out in the morning when it's cool. That also allows you to experience the creek in addition to your climb. If it's extremely cold (Jan-Feb) there may be few people, and you can pick and choose camp sites.
STARTING POINT: Park at Lee Pass up the road from the Kolob Canyons Visitor Center. Hike the La Verkin Creek Trail past the junction to Kolob Arch. Continue to the junction with Hop Valley Trail (you can also approach by hiking the Hop Valley Trail, but that

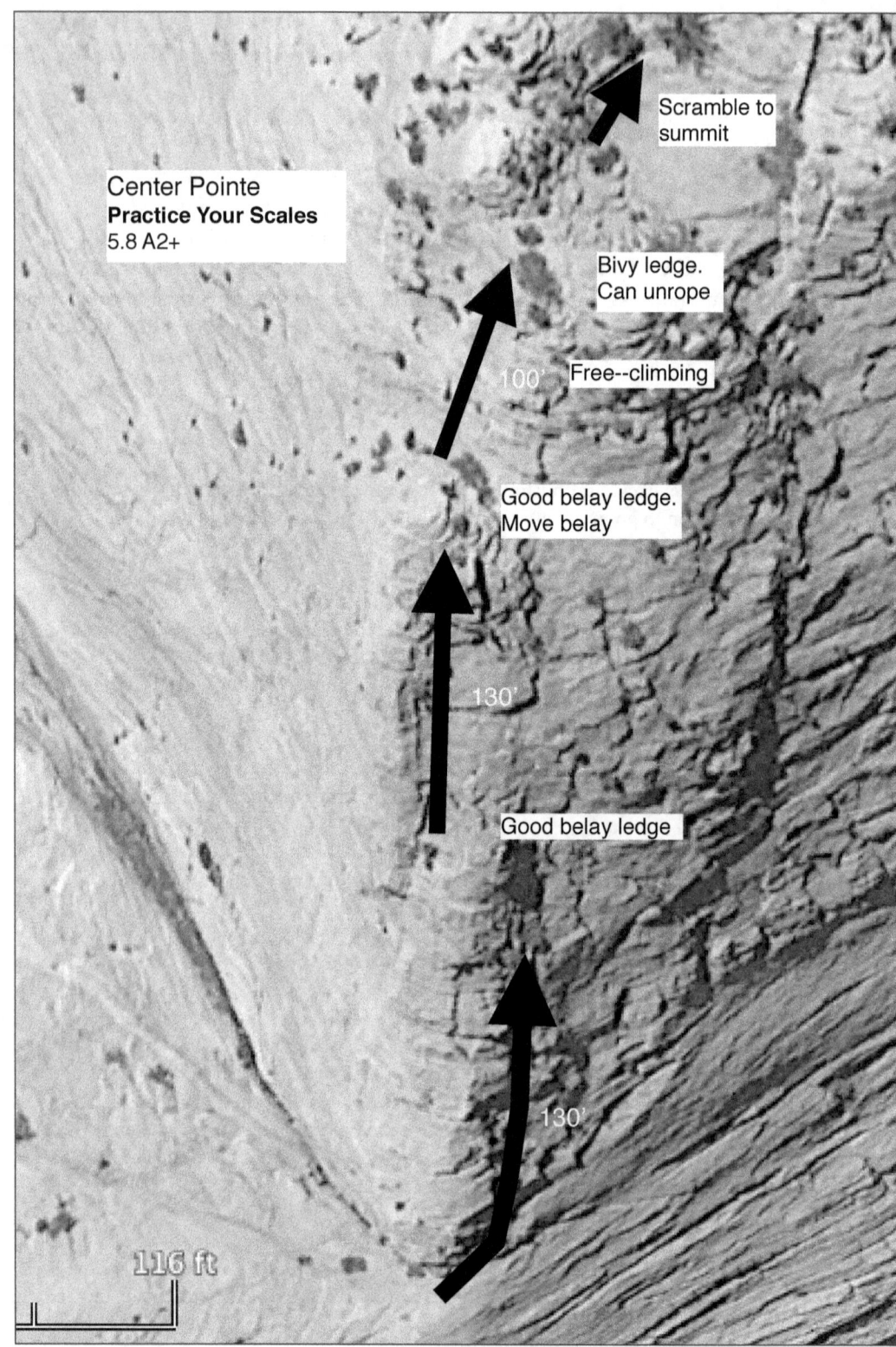

trail is sandy and harder to follow in the dark). At the junction, stay on the left side of the creek, and walk a short way. If there's a lot of water (early season) the trail might be underwater here or not readily visible. Go up dirt talus on the left and make you way around the corner to get into the gully. Go up the gully to a saddle, encountering obstacles that can be surmounted either on the left or right side of the drainage. Both are bushwhacks interspaced with bouldering and scrambling. When you reach the top of the gully you will come to a saddle and see a tree leaning against the west face of a cliff. The tree appears solid. The upper part may move as you climb it. Be ginger. There is a crack next to the tree that takes protection. Take a few medium sized cams as you climb the tree (one of each 0.75, 1, and # 2). When you get to the top of the tree and onto the plateau, there is a rappel sling around a big tree to the right (south). It's best to fix a rope to the tree and haul from there. Hike north towards Center Pointe. Staying low for the first half is easier than going high. Head for the right skyline of Center Pointe.

THE ROUTE: Start on the SE corner. Carefully scramble up a few feet, and stand on the last good stance you will get before committing. A fixed piton, is a few feet up. From there, careful route finding is required to piece together a series of flakes. I bivied on a big, flat ledge, 3/4 way up the route.

GETTING DOWN: I rappelled the route, using natural anchors (bushes). It's my policy to not leave slings but I may have done so in a few places. As I was climbing, I put pink ribbons around the bushes at the belays so that I would have a guide on the way down. As you come down, you need to go sideways, south. If you rappel straight down you will end up on a blank face, 700 feet above the canyon below, and unable to swing over to the start of the climb.

FUTURE CLIMBING A new line could go up the south face. I scrambled up the bottom section. The issue is protection. Bolts (or drilled angle pitons) may be required, depending on your mental frame and faith in slinging bushes. The crux appears to be 3/4 up the wall, where it gets possibly too steep to free-climb. If the upper section is too steep to free-climb, try to traverse left and zig-zag to finish. It will either be fun and a moderate free-climb, or unclimbable. On the positive side, not much of a rack will be required.

The south face of Center Point with the approach plateau visible on the right. My route is around the corner from the right skyline. A potential new route, a free-climbing route, would start right of the overhang in the middle-center, and go diagonal left under the overhang section.

The North Eye

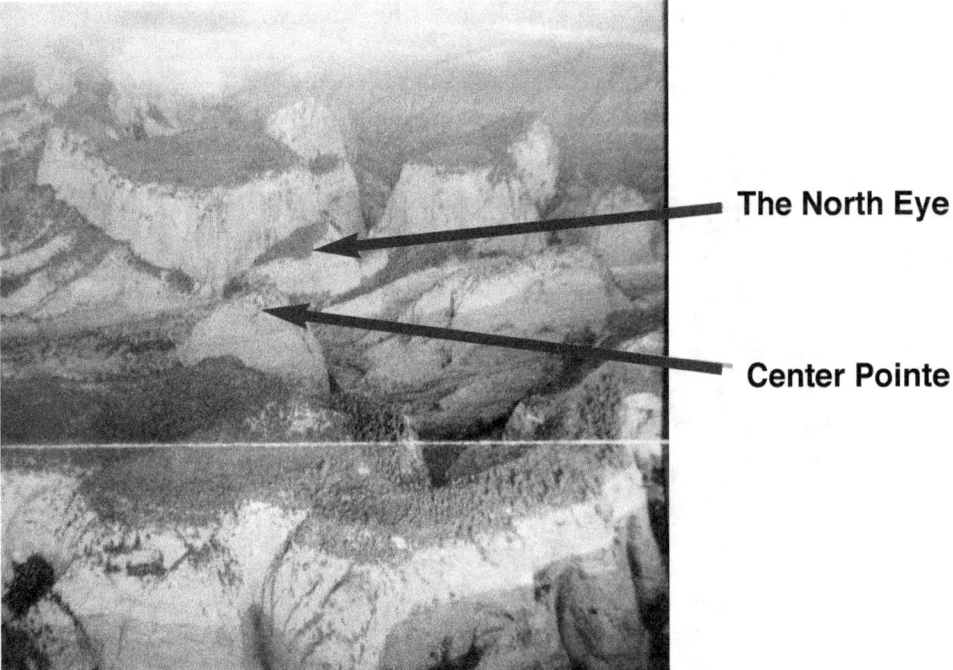

- The North Eye
- Center Pointe

INTRODUCTION The mountain is visible in a photo inside the brochure given to visitors. It is in a remote location, and difficult to reach carrying a haul bag with climbing and bivouac gear.

I'm Back

From a camp site next to La Verkin Creek, I filled my haul bag with ropes and climbing gear. I didn't pack sleeping gear. The bag would have been too heavy. I went out for the day.

It seemed the best way to get to the North Eye was to go down the canyon on the east side of Center Pointe, a canyon I would have fallen to my death in when I almost rappelled off the end of my rope climbing Center Pointe.

I found the gully to be steep, loose, and choked with thorny bushes. Going down it, it seemed if I lost my balance, I would get hurt. Whenever I came to a drop, I threw the bag down and down-climbed. Copious thorny plants in the canyon clung to my pants and shirt. They didn't bite me until I tried to break free. I discovered it worked well if I trampled and whacked them with my pole. In some sections it was too steep, and I had no choice but to grab heaps of them with my bare hands to keep from falling.

The North Eye is surrounded by narrow canyons. I was able to step around pools and relieved I didn't need to swim. The pools allowed me to fill water bottles. This was wonderful, as the alternative would have been to go back up the gully to the plateau with Peak Inaccessible, go down the cliff with the dead tree, and then hike down to the La Verkin Creek and back.

As I walked further down, the canyon narrowed and it became impossible to step around the water. Worse, there did not appear to be a way to climb

Opposite page left: The pass leading to the south side of the North Eye and, if you continued, Ice Box Canyon. Opposite right: In the canyon. It seems water might be gone in summer or late fall unless it rains before the trip. Above: the large cave that's a marker. It's full of rodent poop and would be an unpleasant place to sleep. Scramble to the bottom of it before traversing straight right sideways (east) to surprisingly secure scrambling up to access the climbing route.

out of the canyon to get the climb.

    I turned around and backtracked, looking for a way to start climbing up the steep face of the canyon wall in order to get to the climb. I figured I'd do whatever it took to climb the mountain. Then I found it - a narrow passage where the canyon walls leaned inward, overhanging. The water was low, and I walked through it, to where it opened into another canyon. I kept walking until it started to look like there might be a big drop. At that point I spotted what looked like a place I could climb out of the canyon. I walked up slabs a few hundred feet towards a large cave. I could not see the climbing route above me. It was high above and out of sight.

    I took the gear into the cave. This at first appeared to be a spot where I could sleep when I came back with the camping gear. I soon realized, however, that it was a place I did not want to camp. As I used my boots to flatten a spot for a camp, I noticed, the deeper I dug, the more poop I unearthed. It's a given in Zion, a place that's millions of years old - there are going to be mouse droppings, termites, or other bugs under every rock.

I set the bag down, got the rope out, and prepared to climb around the side of the cave, taking just enough gear to self-belay. After a bit of scrambling and carefully looking for the easiest route, I found myself above the cave, where there were flat spots to sleep. I looked at the mountain, now in plain view, for options on how I might climb it.

I decided on the shortest way. The start was a blank face, sandy, slippery, and without cracks to place protection. I put my rock shoes on. In a dirt filled crevasse, small enough for a few blades of grass, I pounded a knife-blade piton. Remember the tip not to hang on your gear. If it pulled out I might have fallen testing it. I used it as a belay. I carefully climbed fifty feet up to a large bush, fixed the rope to the bush, came down, and went back to get the rest of the gear I had left on the plateau, at the top of the gully next to Center Point and Peak Inaccessible. I slept there.

In the morning, I went back to the climb, carrying the rest of the gear. For the next two nights I slept at the climb. I found the top section to be easier than expected. There is a large crack in which I was able to squeeze my body and wiggle up. Unlike the slippery face below, up high it was good, solid rock. I was inspired. I was almost to the top when I became stuck by a large roof. I couldn't climb over it. There were two ways to go under the roof - left or right. I couldn't see what was around the corner.

I found a crack in the roof to place a good cam. As it was above my head, it would shorten a fall. I choose left, and blindly traversed around the corner, under the blocky roof. What I found was a blessing - solid rock with good hand and foot holds. The issue was protection. I was loaded with gear, and the rope was heavy and dragging. I decided to leave most the gear and gave myself a bunch of slack. It lengthened the distance I would fall, but made sure my rope didn't get stuck as I was climbing. I made it to the top. He ya. I tied the rope around a tree and walked to the true summit on the far north side of the mountain top.

I had half a day left when I got back to my camp at the bottom. I was so tired I decided to camp there another night. The next day I did what I thought would be impossible - I carried all the camping and climbing gear up the gully in one trip. In places I hung on precariously, grabbing thorny bushes for help. When I reached La Verkin Creek, I took a long rest, got the stove out, and made supper. At the last minute I got the vibe to go. I got back to the car two hours after dark, hiking without using a headlamp, as a full moon lit the way.

On the summit of The North Eye, looking at Nagunt Mesa (left) and Peak 7410 (right). Naga is Paiute for bighorn sheep. The canyon between Nagunt Mesa and Peak 7410 may not have seen a descent, as technical climbing is required to reach it. The approach would be to climb Peak 7410 and walk down its south-west ridge. The Slickrock Pass Route canyoneers use to get to Icebox Canyon pass is on the far right (just out of sight).

CLIMBING THE NORTH EYE

1. EYE LINER 5.9 A2 D *Stih 2018*
EQUIPMENT REQUIRED: Baby (#1 and #2) angles; a few long angles; a single set of cams with doubles in the 0.5 - 1 range for the crack on pitch two; a mix of a few other pitons including a KB.
WATER: Before leaving La Verkin Creek on the approach, fill up with enough water for rest of the day, what is needed to get to the mountain. In the spring, plenty of water will be found in the canyon at the base of the route. In the fall there may not be water near the route unless it has rained recently, in which case all water will have to be carried from La Verkin Creek, a miserable task.
SEASON: Spring is probably best. April or May. There's water in the canyon for drinking, and it's not too cold or hot. Fall would be pleasant, but it might have to rain a few days before the trip for there to be water in the canyon at the bottom of the climb.
CAMPING / TIME REQUIRED: Starting from the bottom of the mountain, the route can be climbed in a half-day. Give yourself a day to approach, longer if not familiar with the area or getting a late start. Allow a day to get back to the car.
GETTING THERE: Gain the plateau for the approach to Peak Inaccessible as described in *Zion National Park: Summit Routes*. Traverse north along the edge of the cliff far below Peak Inaccessible, then head up NE towards a gully on the north side of Peak Inaccessible. The gully is uphill (backtrack south) from the start of the route on Center Pointe. Descend the gully. At the bottom, hike through the canyon until you reach a fork on the left. Pay attention. The canyon opening on the left is small. Take the left, and go towards Ice Box canyon. As the canyon opens, slabs become evident on the right that allow an exit and a scramble to the bottom of The North Eye. Head straight up the slabs to an obvious cave. From the cave, scramble in a straight line east, staying as high as possible. As you approach the east rib, a weakness will be revealed that allows a scramble up to easy ground, a bivy spot, and the climbing route.

The lower arrow is part of the approach; the upper two arrows the route.

THE ROUTE: Much of the route can be free-climbed. The rating is based on piton placements required for protection. It's difficult to set a belay for the first pitch. The first pitch climbs slippery face to gain bushes. The drama eases after gaining the bushes. There's a good ledge at the top of pitch one from where the next crux, a wide steep crack, looms. The rock in this crack is good and takes cams well. Follow it to another good ledge. The last pitch looks impossible. Take the easy way up to a roof where there is a choice to go left or right under the roof. Good cams can be placed under the middle of the roof in otherwise rotten territory. From under the roof, step left and blind around the corner. Easy face climbing becomes apparent once around the left side. From there it's a long scramble to the summit. The true summit, the highest point, is on the far north.

GETTING DOWN: From the summit, make your way back to the top of the route. You may want to leave cairns in order to get back to the top of the route. It's a long and vegetated summit. It would be easy to get lost and come down too far south-west, which would put you on the wrong side of the mountain. Rappel from natural anchors on the route (bushes). From camp, go back up the gully next to Center Point, across the plateau, down the dead tree, and to La Verkin Creek.

Looking up at the start of the first pitch (at the tip of the 2nd arrow). Until the bushes are reached, it's difficult to protect.

Magic Rabbit Peak

INTRODUCTION The summit is the highest of a cluster of peaks at the SE tail of the Court of the Patriarchs, north-east of the Sentinel. The last pitch is the crux. Similar to the Mace on Cathedral Spire in Sedona, Arizona, there is a chasm between you and the summit. It is 5.8X. The summit is similar to Ancient Art in the Fisher Towers - only one person can stand on it at a time. The views are spectacular.

Green Chili Leftovers

The previous day I had been scared out of my mind. I had taken CP and Aron to do the second ascent of Castle Dome. I had done the first ascent a week earlier. Whereas I had stayed roped up the entire time, CP and Aron untied from the rope after we got above the difficult section. Aron coiled it and put in on his back. CP was in the lead, moving fast. Aron was twenty feet behind him. I kept my eyes glued on Aron's feet. Where ever he put his foot, I put mine. Where he grabbed a handhold, I made sure to do the same. *Who's route was this*, I thought. My head exploded with fear. It took a lot to compose myself.

That evening, CP and Aron bought me dinner, a chicken burrito. Half way though supper I excused myself and went to the bathroom. I hung my head over the toilet and vomited. I kept my head over the toilet a few minutes, as my muscles cramped and I dry-heaved. I attributed it being scarred all day.

The following day, we set off to do Magic Rabbit Peak. CP was our guide. It was a peak he had attempted before and failed on. We hiked out to Court of the Patriarchs to where the scrambling begins. CP and Aron went first, scrambling up the cliff. I gave them space and tried to not let on that I was still sick. When I thought they were far enough ahead, I went into the bushes and puked. I leaned over, opened my mouth, and a gush of green goop poured out. I wanted to get it all out and kept my mouth open, dry-heaving the last bit onto the sand, a green goobery, smelly mess. I was successful. Except Aron and CP heard me puking.

"Are you OK Dan?" They asked from above.

"Yes" I replied. "I'm fine now. All I have to do is not eat or drink anything and I will be good."

"Dan!" Aron shot back. "I'm concerned about your caloric intake and not drinking any water."

I found that humorous.

"Compared to a guy that went for days without food or water before cutting his arm off, I think I can manage!" I yelled back.

We carried on. Aron lead one of the bottom pitches using the tool on his arm. We were nearly at the top when we reached an obstacle less than one-hundred feet from the summit: a gap. A deep chasm we would have to step over. On the other side was a blank wall. There was nothing to catch me, the leader, if I fell into the chasm while attempting to climb the rock face on the other side. If I fell it would be serious. Standing on the edge of the chasm, I leaned over to take a closer look at the rock face. I placed my hands on the other side and checked for handholds. At the same time, both CP and Aron yelled at me to step back from the edge.

Really? Are these the same guys who unroped yesterday on the face of a mountain more than a thousand feet off the ground. They are concerned?

I realized they were serious. The instant I saw obstacle, I knew I could climb it. I also knew their concerns, as they persisted, would start to crack my confidence. My experience is that if you listen long enough to those who worry, you start to worry. That can cause you to get scared and make mistakes, as your mind focuses on the worry instead of the task at hand.

Previous page: CP belaying on the NE corner before we reached the belay for the crux. Above: Dan, leaning across the chasm at the crux.

"I've got this!" I yelled back, keeping my toes on the edge, leaning over the gap, feeling the face for hand holds. The issue was protection. I couldn't find any. I placed a piton near my head, three feet to the side of where I planned to climb the face. It was pointed downward and would probably not hold a fall. It was the only protection I could find. Before they could talk me out of it, I choose a hand hold on the face, aimed for a foot hold on the other side of the chasm, and committed myself. I shifted my weight off the edge of the cliff and onto the foot hold. I stuck. Knowing my fate if I were to fall, I quickly climbed to the top.

Although Aron climbs quite well using the tool on the end of his arm, this was a face climb. The hook on his arm was not going to be able to grab the holds. I pulled up the other end of the rope and made a rope ladder with loops, into which he could insert his tool. It took two or three attempts for me to adjust the distance between the loops, after which he quickly climbed the rope ladder up to meet me, and said, "It wasn't that hard."

The tippy top was still a few feet away: a six-foot spire just large for one person to stand. We took turns belaying so each could have a turn standing on the summit.

CLIMBING MAGIC RABBIT PEAK

PORK GREEN CHILE 5.8+ X *D Stih, CP, A Ralston, November, 2015*
EQUIPMENT REQUIRED: Standard free-climbing rack plus a few pitons to select from as you try and protect the crux near the summit.
FUTURE CLIMBING The R rating is due to the only protection being a tied off, downward facing piton, where a fall would send you tumbling into a chasm. I have no quarrels about someone placing a bolt there. If a bolt is added, it could be one of the funnest climbs in the area. This route combines the elements of a fun adventure: bushwhacking, route finding, scrambling, getting high off the ground, technical rock climbing, and a spectacular summit. The best part is when you are done you can go back to town and have a nice dinner. It's not an epic like many of the climbs in this book.
CAMPING / TIME REQUIRED: A day climb.
THE STARTING POINTS: Take the shuttle or park at the Court of the Patriarchs. Start hiking the Sand Bench Trail, going left (south) at the junction across the bridge. Leave the trail after a short way into the Court of the Patriarchs, cross the meadow, heading NW, and hike up a steep hill on the north side of the cliffs east of the Red Sentinel.
THE ROUTE: From the bottom on the north side, scramble up, belaying as needed, taking the easiest way. Work over onto the south side, where exposed scrambling across ledges leading towards the east leads to the final difficulties. As you reach the SE edge of the peak, start climbing straight up. You will come to a big, flat ledge. Step across the chasm, and climb the face on the other side (the crux). Take turns standing on the summit block.

Birthday Cake

INTRODUCTION This peak is on the west side of the Inclined Temple. Mine is likely not a first ascent as it's an easy scramble. In 2019, I emailed CP, "I saw in your guide book you named the peak between the Sanctuary and Inclined Temple, 'peak at the saddle' Has anyone you know climbed it?" CP replied he was unaware of anyone who had, saying, "I was alone on my half-hearted attempt. I turned back at a committing spot, more or less thinking, I'm a long way from an ambulance if this doesn't go well." I wish I had tried climbing it during my other explorations to the area, i.e. Inclined Temple, Bishoprics, and Ivins Mountain. It's a long approach. In 2022 I decided to make the trip just to climb it. I wasn't certain how difficult it might be and carried a rope and a rack. I didn't use any of it. It turned out it was just a scramble. The crux is the hike while carrying the gear. I climbed (scrambled) it on my 55th birthday.

CLIMBING BIRTHDAY CAKE

1. PIECE OF PIE 5.5 *D Stih, April 2022*
EQUIPMENT REQUIRED: A rope is not required. Take one if you're uncomfortable with exposure and loose rock.
THE ROUTE: Scramble up the north skyline, the obvious weakness with vegetation.
GETTING DOWN: Go back the way you came.

Lucky Charm

CP, leading the 2nd pitch, a traverse after the crux pitch at the start.

INTRODUCTION Lucky Charm (peak 6680) peak sits to the immediate north of Sneak Peak, east of the two sneak routes (alternate starts) to the Imlay Canyon canyoneering route.

Third Time's a Charm

CP scouted this peak. He had tried it before. He turned around on his first attempt because it didn't look like "just a scramble." On his second attempt, he tried it with me. We were hampered by snow and ice. When we got to Zion and saw the conditions, I went to the canyoneering store and rented a pair of crampons. We gave it our best shot. It was miserable. There was snow, ice, and water in the canyon. No matter how we tried, our hands and feet got wet. We trudged onward, neither of us wanting to quit. I wasn't having fun and was a low on motivation as well as energy. The main concern wasn't snow. We were taking too long to get there. We might have reached the top, but would have had to sleep there without a tent or sleeping bags in the snow.

Before we gave up, we came to a steep slab in the canyon that, in dry conditions, would have been just a scramble. We stood in the snow looking at it. The slab was icy. We decided to rope up. I put on our only pair of crampons. The plan was I would climb up, find a tree at the top, tie myself to it, and try to pull CP up. He would slip and slide like a two-wheel drive car on an icy highway, but I believed I would be able to get him up it. I wondered about the absurdity of the idea. As I thought about it, the branches on the tree I was standing under dropped a pile of snow on my head. I took that as a sign. I think my guardian angel shook the branches. We turned around.

October, 2016. We got past where we were turned around by snow on the previous trip, and reached the start of the climb. We had almost not brought cams for protection, thinking it would be "just a scramble". It was good we had. I used them to sew up the wide crack at the start, the first pitch.

CP asked me what we should name the peak. A song I wrote, Lucky the Unicorn, came to mind. A playful, gentle summit that seemed to require luck.

The hike back down the West Rim Trail was pleasant. I felt re-energized. I had thought perhaps it was time to take a break from climbing. When I got home I meditated on it. There's a saying, "When you choose the path in your heart, a path will open." For a long time I had been trying to find another path. I thought it was work, hoped it was music, but if I looked back at my life, I keep forgetting - I chose climbing. And I'd been on that path for a long time. The one thing constant in my life has been climbing. Part of me feels that it is selfish to go climbing, that there is something more important and community service orientated I should be doing. I felt lucky not to have found it.

CLIMBING LUCKY CHARM

An attempt in snowy conditions.

1. LUCKY CHARM 5.6 *D Stih and CP 2017*
EQUIPMENT REQUIRED: Standard free-climbing rack, a few cams, and long slings.
WATER SOURCES: Carry water from the Grotto. You may, depending on the season, find water in the canyon on the approach. Don't count on it.
CAMPING / TIME REQUIRED: A long day route, round-trip from the Grotto.
THE STARTING POINT: Approach via the Sneak Route for Imlay Canyon. Hike up the West Rim Trail, past Scout Lookout, to where the trail traverses the north side of Cathedral Mountain. After passing the wooden foot bridge, leave the trail and head north. Soon after leaving the trail, descend into and cross a canyon. After crossing the canyon, a trail used by canyon folks approaching Sneak Route is found high on the east side of the drainage that runs due north towards the peak.
THE ROUTE: We climbed the northwest ridge to where it ceases to be practical, then climbed a chimney/hand-crack to gain the northwest face. Once on the face, we traversed left before going straight up.
GETTING DOWN: Down-climb and rappel the route using natural anchors. The rock on the last rappels is loose. It may be wise to lower a lesser

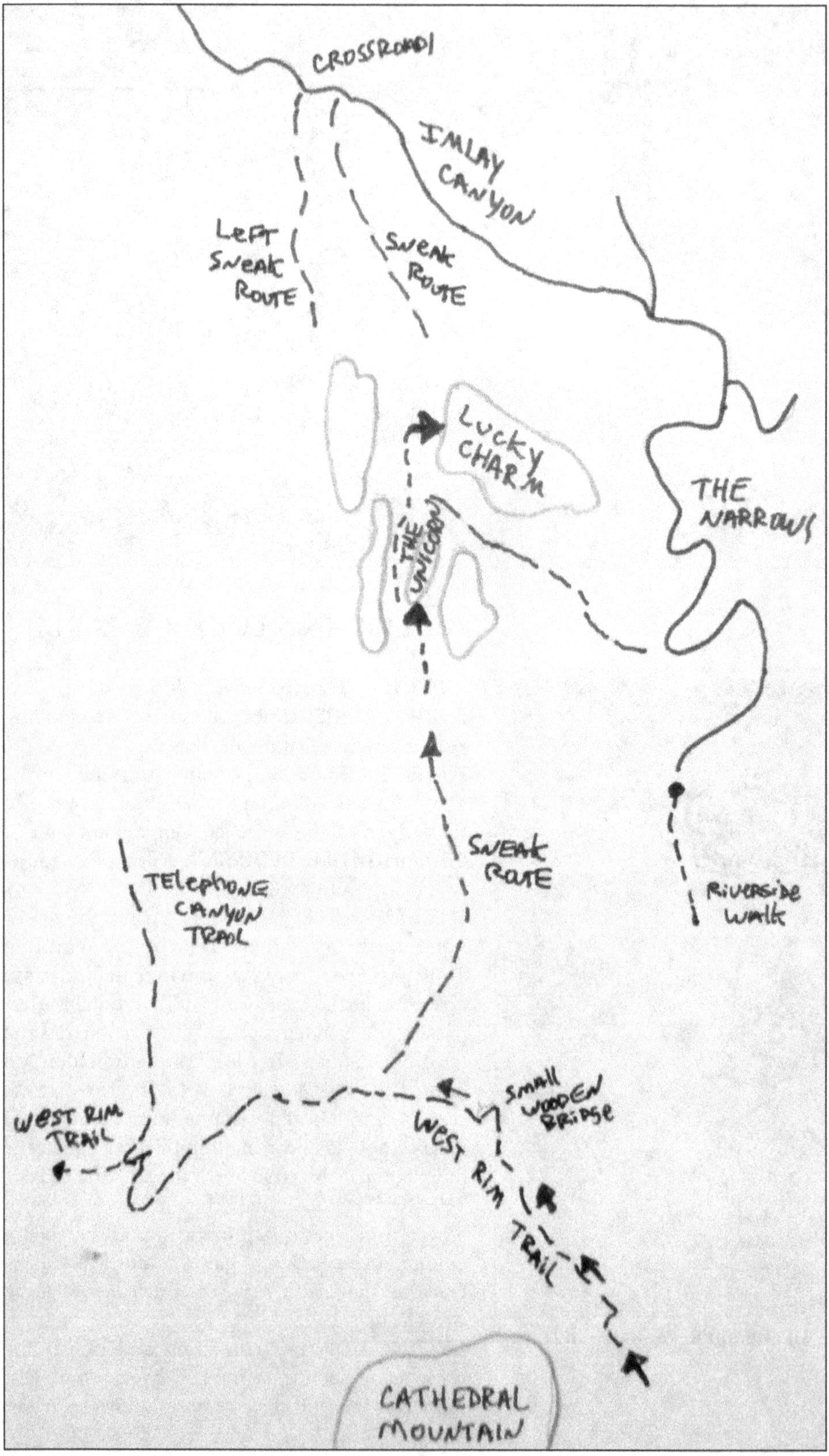
CROSSROAD!
IMLAY CANYON
LEFT SNEAK ROUTE
SNEAK ROUTE
LUCKY CHARM
THE UNICORN
THE NARROWS
SNEAK ROUTE
TELEPHONE CANYON TRAIL
RIVERSIDE WALK
SMALL WOODEN BRIDGE
WEST RIM TRAIL
WEST RIM TRAIL
CATHEDRAL MOUNTAIN

The Unicorn

INTRODUCTION A picture of this peak is on posters made by Steffan Gregory to promote the first public meeting of the Zion Climbing Coalition. Steffan was also the editor between climbers doing new routes in Zion and the American Alpine Journal. I had submitted that photo with a trip report for doing the first ascent of Lucky Charm with CP. At the time I didn't realize I was mistaken: we had hiked around the Unicorn in order to access Lucky Charm. We had not climbed the Unicorn. When I saw the poster, I didn't tell Steffan the peak had not been climbed. I was waiting until I had climbed it. In the meantime, those who saw the poster were unknowingly looking at a peak in the park that had not yet been climbed.

I twice carried gear to the base of the Unicorn thinking I might rope-solo it. Finding the bottom improbable, I considered scrambling up the peak to the east, dropping 600 feet of rope down its west face, rappelling into the notch between it and the Unicorn, and getting to the summit of the Unicorn by free-climbing the remainder of its east face from the notch. I considered either attempt would be epic, and decided to wait for a partner.

CLIMBING THE UNICORN

1. WHITE MAGIC A2+ 5.9- *D Stih and M Dunn, April 2022*
EQUIPMENT REQUIRED: Some aid gear such as large Black Diamond beaks.
TIME REQUIRED/THE STARTING POINT: A long day, round-trip from the Grotto. See Lucky Charm and the map on the previous page for information on the approach.
CAUTIONS / SPECIAL DIFFICULTIES: Loose rock after the first belay.
THE ROUTE: 4 pitches. Aid the first pitch up to a fixed pin used to pendulum left to a belay stance on the right side of the obvious chasm. Note: before surrendering the lead to Mike and his suggestion that he could aid climb the line to the right, I tried to free-climb the wide, bomb-bay chimney that appears a logical line. I don't recommend it. Expecting the peak to be a free-climb, Mike back-cleaned a lot and was VERY low on gear when he reached the belay. If you have ample gear, instead of penduluming left near the end of the first pitch, consider continuing straight up for a direct and new route. If you pendulum to the belay, the next pitches are free climbing.
GETTING DOWN: While it should be possible to descend the route, a cleaner descent with less lose rock, is made by down-scrambling SE from the summit to where one is in direct line with the first aid pitch. Two ropes are required. Rappel from tress and bushes. If you didn't do the alternate new route, you will preview this potential line on the way down.

The Little Bishop (Peak 6020)

INTRODUCTION Peak 6020, aka, the Little Bishopric, lies a few miles due east of Checkerboard Mesa, just outside the Zion National Park boundary. We named it due to its resemblance to the (big) Bishopric on the west side of the park. There are two short pitches of roped climbing, 5.4-5.6 in difficulty. Much of the difficulty has to do with placing protection.

HISTORY I published a trip report on-line. Upon reading it, Walt, one of the climbers on the ascent, wrote to me: "Do you generally write when you think you've made a first ascent? How do you know? I feel like I've made some, but have no clue how to tell for sure."

I wrote back:

Climbing 25 years in Zion
Talking to local climbers
Asking the authors of guidebooks
Looking for records in the Visitor Center
Talking to park rangers in the backcountry offices
In the end it's possible ours was not the first ascent
That's always the case.

It's possible early explorers, settlers, or natives, climbed some of the peaks we think we are the first to climb. Just because we need a rope and climbing gear to get to the top of them, does not mean others did. People, climbers, used to have more courage, and believed risk was part of adventure.

CLIMBING THE LITTLE BISHOP (PEAK 6020)

1. NORTH FACE 5.6 *D Stih, CP, Walt Hutton 2015*
EQUIPMENT REQUIRED: One or two baby angle pitons in addition to an alpine rack.
WATER: Carry water from the car. In early spring there will be snow on the east side of Checkerboard Mesa. If it has rained recently, there might be water in pot holes on the approach.
SEASON: We climbed it in March when the weather was cool. Doing so made the approach a pleasant hike.
TIME REQUIRED: A long day, round-trip from the parking lot in front of Checkerboard Mesa.
STARTING POINT: Little Bishopric is approached by a longish overland route via the pass between Checkerboard Mesa and Crazy Quilt Mesa. Park at the parking lot for Checkerboard Mesa. Look at a topographical map.
THE ROUTE: From the base of the peak's south ridge, scramble several hundred feet of slabs to a shallow corner on the crest. The 15-foot crux is marginally protectable. Continue scrambling along the crest, making a few delicate moves across an exposed tower. Shortly beyond, more scrambling leads to a headwall below the summit, where twenty feet of easy climbing leads to the top.
GETTING DOWN: Using natural anchors, we rappelled the north side. We wanted to explore the peak in its entirety.

Red Tooth

INTRODUCTION Red Tooth is NE of Bridge Mountain, on the edge of the cliffs above the tunnel road. Access is the same as Bridge Mountain. If you climb Bridge Mountain, on the approach you will hike up a couloir. Bridge Mountain will be on your left; Red Tooth is on the right. A picture of Red Tooth is on page 33 of the (out of print) *Exploring the Backcountry of Zion National Park: Off-Trail Routes* by Thomas Brereton and James Dunaway, a book affectionately called the Green Book, published by the Zion Natural History Association in 1988.

HISTORY According to some, the first known ascent of Bridge Mountain

CP at the bottom of Red Tooth.

was in 1965. Given that Bridge Mountain has been climbed countless times, one might ask why it took so long for someone to climb Red Tooth. There are likely two reasons. The first is that Bridge Mountain is a class 4 route, for which a rope is suggested, but only slings are required for protection. To climb Red Tooth requires a rack of climbing gear. The second reason is lack of protection. The bottom of Red Tooth is a smooth slab. The crux comes close to the ground, in a precarious position. I had to compose myself while finding a place to place a thin knife-blade piton in a shallow seam. I did not want to trust it to hold my weight.

FUTURE CLIMBING A fast party could link Red Tooth with an ascent of Bridge Mountain and do a traverse of some kind.

CLIMBING RED TOOTH

SOUTH FACE 5.8+ R *D Stih and CP 2015*

EQUIPMENT REQUIRED: A light free-climbing with one set of cams and a few knife blade pitons.

WATER: Carry water from the car. There may be seeps in washes, depending on the season or if it rained recently. These dry quick and are not reliable. Any water found should be filtered.

SEASON: Spring or Fall. We climbed it in November when the cool weather made for a pleasant hike.

CAMPING / TIME REQUIRED: This is a day trip, roundtrip from the parking lot. It's approximately 8 miles and 10 hours roundtrip to Bridge Mountain. Red Tooth is slightly shorter to reach, but more difficult to climb.

THE STARTING POINT: Park at the east entrance to the East Tunnel at the Canyon Overlook Trail. The approach is via Gifford Canyon and Hepworth Wash. See *Exploring the Backcountry of Zion National Park: Off-Trail Routes* by Thomas Brereton and James Dunaway and *Zion National Parks: Summit Routes* by Courtney Purcell for directions to Bridge Mountain.

THE ROUTE: We climbed four roped pitches with two cruxes of 5.8+ to 5.9R. The first crux is a mantle up smooth rock without hand holds. The second crux is an unprotected boulder move above the belay. There are four summits. The route climbs the face on the south side to the first summit. The highest summit is reached by traversing north across the top, in the direction of the East Temple as the crow flies.

GETTING DOWN: Scramble down and rappel the route using natural anchors.

Battleship Rock

INTRODUCTION Battleship Rock is the peak on the west side of Abraham. It's reached from Phantom Valley. From the summit, a descent may be made going down Abraham Canyon and rappelling Birch Creek into the Court of the Patriarchs.

Battle on the Battleship

I climbed Battleship Rock on my journey to find a way to get to the Princess Spire. I rappelled off the West Rim using the anchors to start Heaps Canyon. After passing across Phantom Valley, I reached an unclimbed formation on the west side of Abraham (Battleship Rock). I considered if I should climb it. The factors were the possibility of rain and the short autumn day. I didn't have bivy gear. I decided to have a look.

I was so confident, I left my rope and pack at the bottom. I scrambled up the bottom half, and came to a steep section of loose dirt covered with pine needles. I set my hiking pole down and charged forward. I climbed to what seemed like less than one-hundred feet from the top. Then it got difficult. I found it too dangerous to continue without a rope. I decided to go down, and to continue on my journey without climbing the peak.

When I got to the bottom and my pack I thought, *Where's my trekking pole?* I had left if where I set it down as I climbed across the loose spot, and forgotten to grab it on the way down.

OK, I thought, *If I have to go back to get it, I'm taking a rope and climbing the mountain.*

I ran back up to my high point and quickly found myself in a dangerous spot. The trouble with climbing by yourself is that if you need a rope, speed comes to a grinding halt. There's no one to feed the rope out. I tied one end of the rope around a large tree, pulled up ten feet of slack, tied a knot in the rope, and clipped it into my harness. I grabbed a bush above my head. There's an art to pulling on bushes. There can be dead branches and green ones. You look for green to make sure the thing is alive. Often you have to pull on dead stuff. That's OK if the roots are good and you don't pull too hard.

I grabbed a bush and walked my feet up. A moment later I heard something crack, just as I got a bird's eye view of the bush. Although it was green, the bush had snapped in half, and was ready to snap free.

After a struggle, I reached to the top, and walked to the true summit on the opposite end of the mountain. I took pictures, then hurried down. I was afraid it might rain. Clouds were dark and menacing. I calculated what would happen if it rained. I had a big trash bag. I thought could put my down jacket in it, put my rain jacket on, and suffer the

The approach slabs on the west side of Abraham after leaving Phantom Valley.

storm. When the storm passed, I would have a dry down jacket to spend the night in.

I began a descent into the canyon on the west side of the Battleship. It was a dense jungle of dead leaves, and a tangled mess of rotten debris. I plowed down, cursing at the thickness, and found myself in Abraham Canyon. It didn't seem like it should be that far or take long, to get down to civilization. My destination was Birch Creek. It would take longer than imagined and turn into a frightful epic.

Water on the approach, Phantom Valley.

CLIMBING BATTLESHIP ROCK

1. NORTH RIDGE *D Stih 2018*
EQUIPMENT REQUIRED: Slings and a few cams
WATER SOURCES: There's always water in the canyons between Phantom Valley and Battleship Rock. There's always water in Birch Creek.
SEASON: Fall is best. Spring will have more water in the canyons and the water fall will be flowing at Birch Creek, making a wet suit required to go down it.
CAMPING / TIME REQUIRED: 1 - 3 days depending on chosen approach and exit.
THE STARTING POINTS: Get to Phantom Valley either from the West Rim using the rappel for Heaps Canyon OR from the Bishoprics, hiking up Terry Wash. Once in Phantom Valley, head towards Abraham. Avoid hugging the immediate west side of Abraham. Take the easiest route between Abraham and the east side of Church Mesa.
THE ROUTE: From the saddle between Battleship Rock and Church Mesa, climb the NW ridge of Battleship Rock. At first it will be a scramble. As it becomes steep and loose, there's a crack that can be used for protection and bushes to sling. The summit is on the far south end.
GETTING DOWN : One could go down Abraham Canyon to Birch Creek, and rappel Birch Creek into the Court of the Patriarchs. Done this way it could be a long day trip if you started hiking the West Rim Trail in the dark, such that you get to the anchors for the rappels for Heaps Canyon at first light.

Alternatively, you could reverse course, and go out Phantom Valley, turn south and go past the Bishoprics, and exit towards Cougar Mountain. This would be a long trip and require 2 to 3 days.

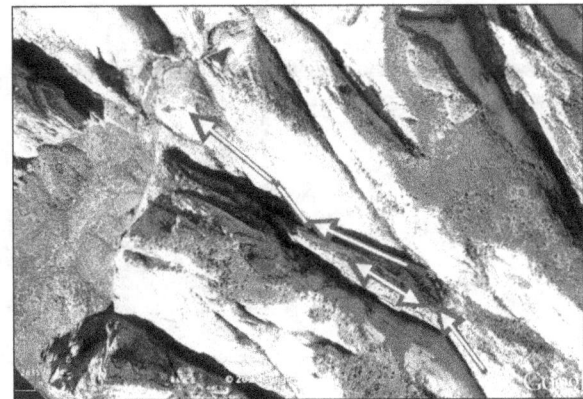

My route from Phantom Valley, up and down Battleship Rock. From the summit of Battleship Rock, I rappelled to the bottom of the route, went down into Abraham Canyon, and then climbed out of it and up to the summit of Nipples Peak (two summits) before rappelling Birch Creek into the Court of the Patriarchs.

Nipples Peak

INTRODUCTION & HISTORY Nipples Peak sits between Church Mesa and Abraham. There are two summits. They are best approached by traversing onto the east face of the upper nipple peak after starting down into Abraham Canyon from Battleship Rock. They can also be climbed from the bottom from Birch Creek, a path that would require careful route finding to avoid more difficult climbing. I climbed the Nipples Peaks twice during my attempts to reach Birch Creek to climb the Princess Spire.

A Dangerous Dan Epic

I packed a small backpack with 800 feet of 8.0-millimeter static rope, considered to be very thin rope. The pack was heavy, and I was tired going on long, solo epics. I had waited all year for Fall, a season when the weather is cool enough to climb, but not too cold. At one time I thought I'd take the entire months of November and October off to climb. Now, I found myself tired of epics, driving, and being scared. It's not so much that I am scared while climbing. I just noticed and became aware of the dangerous situations I find myself. It's more like gosh, not again. I've got to quit this.

I wondered, *why*? I don't climb for the challenge. If that were the case it would be easy to quit. It's because if I am lucky and in the right place at the right time. If I'm disconnected from technology, possibly lost, definitely hungry, and maybe low on water. Then I get a glimpse. It's a feeling, one I've been searching for.

I slept in my truck at Canyon Junction, the closest I could park to the trail . I would start by riding my bike up a highway that's closed to traffic except for a shuttle in daylight hours. Before going to sleep, I filled the tires on my old bicycle so it would be ready to go in the morning. I slept in climbing pants.

At 1:30 am, I woke and wasted no time. I started the truck and drove to the Grotto. I left the truck running, got out and hid off my pack behind a tree. This way I didn't need to wear the pack while riding my bicycle. I hoped a ranger didn't see me. A sign warns visitors the road is closed except to shuttles. I drove back to Canyon Junction, parked, and got on my bike. It was 2:00 am. I rode the bike uphill, back to the Grotto. Although it was only a few miles, I was out of breath when I got to there. I've had the bike since 1990. The gears rattle, stick, and don't shift completely. I locked the bike and hid the pump under a log in the grass. The tires were old and would be flat when I returned.

I rode my bike because the shuttle does not start operating until 7am. That would have gotten me to the trailhead at 7:30 am. I needed all the daylight I could get. I wasn't carrying a sleeping bag or warm clothes to spend a night out. It was below freezing. I hiked past Angels Landing to the West Rim, in the dark. At the top of the West Rim, I left the trail, and went to find the rappel anchors that canyoneers use to get into Heaps Canyon. I had turned off my headlamp to enjoy the moon-lit scene while I was hiking. I turned it on to find my way. Rain had washed out foot prints from canyoneers. I began to think it might be light before I found the anchor. I found the way by getting out of my head and letting my feet do the walking. It was 7:30am when I found them. I had gained five extra hours of daylight compared to if I had taken the shuttle.

As I started to rappel, the black of night transitioned to orange clouds. Yes-

The route from Battleship Rock, out of Abraham Canyon, across Nipples Peak to its upper summit, and then down to the lower nipple. Left to right: Triangle Peak, Big Red, Chameleon. On the far right, parts of the Meridian Tower and Church Mesa.

terday morning, the sky had been clear. Although rain was not in the forecast, my grandmother had a saying, "Morning warning, afternoon delight." I told myself to quit thinking about it and not waste time. There are only twelve hours of light the first week of November. I didn't know where I was going and what getting there would be like. I needed to break the journey down into steps. If I thought about the overall amount of work ahead it was overwhelming.

Getting to Abraham required constant route finding. Sometimes it was easier to walk through canyons than cross-country across them. It had rained a few days ago, and some pools were full. In places the canyon walls narrowed such that progress was not possible without swimming. If I went down a canyon and was confronted with swimming, I back-tracked and found a way out of it. I carefully thought of which side of a canyon I should be on. If I climbed out the wrong side I could get stuck.

As I reached Abraham, I left the canyons and started scrambling up smooth slabs on its west side. I should have filled my single water bottle before leaving the canyons. I was expecting things to be easier. I thought I would reach Birch Creek sooner. The risk of rain also propelled me to keep moving and not rest.

As I came to the top of the slabs, I came to an unclimbed mountain on the

Summit of the Upper Nipple.

west side of Abraham. After climbing it (see Battleship Rock), I descended into Abraham canyon, a narrow passage on the west side of the Battleship. It was a thick, dense, messy jungle. I thought the difficulties would be over and became discouraged. Frustration turned to alarm, as I came to a drop with a pool at the bottom. It would be possible to step around the pool. But it was too steep to down-climb, and the rock was covered with moss. I would need to rappel. I considered if I was presented with another pool further down the canyon I would be stuck. I decided to climb out of the canyon and to higher ground.

I back-tracked, and scrambled up a cliff on the west side of the canyon. It was not so steep I

The summit of the lower nipple, characterized by red rock at the lower elevation.

In the Court of the Patriarchs, looking up at the 8-millimeter ropes I fixed down from the top of the waterfall at Birch Creek.

needed the rope. It was steep enough that if one sandy foot hold made me slip, or a bush pulled out when I yanked on it, I would fall to my death. More than a few times a near miss occurred. A branch I pulled on broke. I stood on the side of the mountain, still and balanced. Several times my feet slipped, but the branches and bushes I grabbed didn't rip from their roots. I climbed to the top of the mountain and named it Nipples Peak.

From the summit, it took me several rappels to get to Birch Creek. I went as fast as I could, keeping in mind I did not have warm clothing or sleeping gear. When I saw the ground in the Court of the Patriarchs, I thought, *piece of cake. I can get there in time.* I did not know the epic that was to about to follow, one that would make me question my reason for climbing and almost walk away from climbing forever. My intention had been to fix the ropes I was carrying to a tree at the top of the water fall for Birch Creek, and leave them hanging to the ground. I planned to use them to come back and climb everything around Birch Creek. What I had not realized was how far it was to the ground, and how steep the cliff was.

I was dead tired. I was thinking about the shuttle, getting a hamburger, and where I would sleep. I gently reminded myself to keep it together. *Not now,* I told myself when I'd start thinking of something other than what I was doing.

The back of the Court of the Patriarchs. From left to right: The descent for Birch Creek (first major black streak with obvious trees), Abraham Canyon (black streaks at top), and the Squirrel Route (a crack-like corner that hugs the south face of Abraham) named after the squirrels I met climbing up it as I was going down it on a later trip.

The 800 feet of rope I had was comprised of several pieces left over from previous climbs, some cut into pieces. I had only one rope 300 feet. I looked over the edge and saw a tree on a ledge below. It was less than 150 feet, so I choose one of the smaller ropes. I rappelled to the ledge.

For the next rappel I choose to use the 300-foot rope. I wasn't sure how far it would be until I touched another ledge. I tied one end of the rope to a big tree, threw the other over the edge, and began rappelling. As soon as I went over the edge I found myself handing in space, terrified. I counted the moments until my feet landed on another ledge.

Suddenly, my rappelling device locked onto the rope and would not feed. My auto-bock, a sliding knot that keeps you from sliding down the rope if you lose control of your break hand, had locked onto the rope. The knot used to tie it had gotten stuck under the sliding portion. To get it unstuck, I would need to take my weight off the auto-block, while hanging on the rope. Twenty feet from the rock, gently spinning in a circle, I put a jumar (a clamp) on the rope above my head, and put all of my weight on it. I continued to spin as I tried to get the knot on the auto-block to move. I wondered how much spinning I could take, and what would happen if I got sick or dizzy.

Normal climbing ropes are between 9 and 11-millimeters thick. The one I was hanging on was 8-mil. Thin ropes are prone to abrasion. I worried that the spinning and bouncing might wear the rope to the breaking point. I got the knot unstuck and reached the ledge below in gratitude.

I hoped that was the end of my terror. The ground looked close. Others had been this way, a long time ago. Tied to a heap of bushes for the next anchor was webbing that had rotted in the sun, and a rusted metal ring to feed the rope though. Instead of using it, I used a tree. Not to waste rope, I tied what was left over from the rappel I had just completed to a piece of shorter rope I dug out of my pack. Together, I expected they would reach the ground.

When I went over the edge, I once again I found myself hanging in space. I was scared and I couldn't tell if the rope was on the ground. When I reached the knot that tied the two pieces of rope together it was difficult to pass. I had to take my rappel device off the rope and put it on the other side of the knot. This is done by placing a clamp (jumar) on the rope above you, and hanging from it. You then remove the rope from your rappel device completely, and put the rope on the other side of the knot through your rappel device. Then you have to take your weight off the clamp you're hanging on, as you shift your weight off of the clamp, and back onto your rappel device. There is no room for a mistake. Hanging in space on an 8-millimeter rope, looking at the rocks below, I felt like being on a cliff by the ocean, looking at sharp rocks below. I told myself to stay focused and swallowed fear.

After passing the knot, I thought I might be going home to the ground. Then I saw the rope was still not on the ground. I stopped, allowing my auto block to catch, hoping I had enough scraps of rope left in my pack. Auto blocks are made with small diameter rope. There's friction. The heat generated can melt the rope. If it melted, the auto-block would fall apart, and I would go sliding off the end of the rope to my death. Putting this fear aside, I performed the unpleasant task of passing a knot again, this time knowing for sure the rope was on the ground. I made it to the ground. Mission accomplished. Sort of.

Safe on the ground, I would became too scared to go back up the thin ropes. I came up with a solution. I went and bought 600 feet of thicker rope (9.2-mil in diameter). The following day, I repeated the journey. I woke up a 2am, rode my bike up the road, hiked the trail in the dark, climbed up and over Nipples Peak, and down to Birch Creek. I dropped the new ropes down next to the firs set. All this so I could return to climb the mountains there. Even with the thicker ropes, I wondered if I would I have the courage to up them, and if not, how I would get the ropes down.

CLIMBING NIPPLES PEAK

1. THE UPPER AND LOWER NIPPLES D *Stih 2018*

EQUIPMENT REQUIRED: Slings. A rope in case you take a more difficult path or need to rappel.

STARTING POINTS: *From Battleship Rock:* From the saddle between Battleship Rock and Church Mesa, head down into Abraham Canyon. A short way down it, and before the first drop, backtrack and find a way to scramble onto the mountain on the west side of the canyon. Once on the white slabs, avoid the temptation to traverse sideways. Head straight up and diagonal towards the summit. After tagging the upper nipple, backtrack and look for the easiest way down the east face, a ramp/gully-like ledge system that angles down and right. If you find the easiest way, you won't have to rappel.

From a flat rest area where the peaks meet, hike across a bridge that connects the upper and lower peaks. Tag the summit of the second nipple. From there it's an easy scramble down. Go down the south side, what might seem out of the way, considering the target is the water fall at the end of Birch Creek. Going down in the direction of Abraham Canyon might look shorter, but it's more difficult and may put you in water.

From Birch Creek: This approach is for canyoneers who are doing a descent of Birch Creek and have time and energy. I can't imagine I'd want to do that given the serious nature of the descent down the waterfall at the end of Birch Creek that awaits. Start up the red slabs on the SE side of the lower nipple. Tag the summit of the lower nipple. To continue, look for a ramp going up and right diagonal to the summit of the upper nipple. If you find *the* ramp, it should be a scramble up a gully-like ledge that goes up and diagonal to the north. If you miss it (or try to take a short cut by climbing straight up) you'll find the climbing more difficult. Tag the upper nipple.

DESCENT: If you got this far I'm going to bet you have an exit strategy. Perhaps it's Birch Creek (at the waterfall which may be flowing in Spring). Maybe it's directly down Abraham Canyon, the top of which is smooth and overhanging. I wouldn't have thought someone went down that. Steffan reports seeing bolts on its face, half-way down, while looking for me in a helicopter on my first attempt to climb Princess Spire. There are four ways to go down: Birch Creek, Abraham Creek, Sentinel Canyon, and a descent I established called the Chipmunk Cliff. I recommend Chipmunk Cliff. It's at the south side of Abraham. From the bottom of the Nipple Peak, hike towards Abraham, crossing Abraham Canyon (a water course that will be wet or dry depending on the season). The nice thing about this descent is that except for a few spots, it's not overhanging, is the shortest way to the ground and is always dry. The pitfall is loose rock. The loosest section is the last 300 feet. For route details see the chapter Chipmunk Cliff in the section Canyon Descents. No canyoneering is involved other than rappelling.

The Subdial

INTRODUCTION When the Sun Dial massif is viewed on the drive from Hurricane into Zion National Park, the Subdial appears as a formidable, impressive shield of white rock that is part of the Sun Dial. During my explorations, I realized it's a separate peak. I had already climbed the Sun Dial several times, and did not want to repeat the traverse of the Towers of the Virgin to climb the Subdial. I considered an easier way: climb the West Temple, fix a rope down its west face, climb the Subdial, go up the fixed rope, and descend the normal route on the West Temple back into Springdale. I got the idea from Steffan who suggested it as a way to climb the Sun Dials if you don't want to do the traverse.

HISTORY I pitched my idea to Mike Dunn who also had noticed the Subdial had been overlooked. Mike preferred to attempt to climb it over several days by a new route on its west face, starting from Coalpits Wash. I convinced him my way was more practical and surer. We went the day before Halloween and did it in a day. We climbed the West Temple carrying a single 320-foot static rope. As we reached the red cap, instead of hiking up the final chute of scree to the summit, we traversed left under the red cap to a point where it is

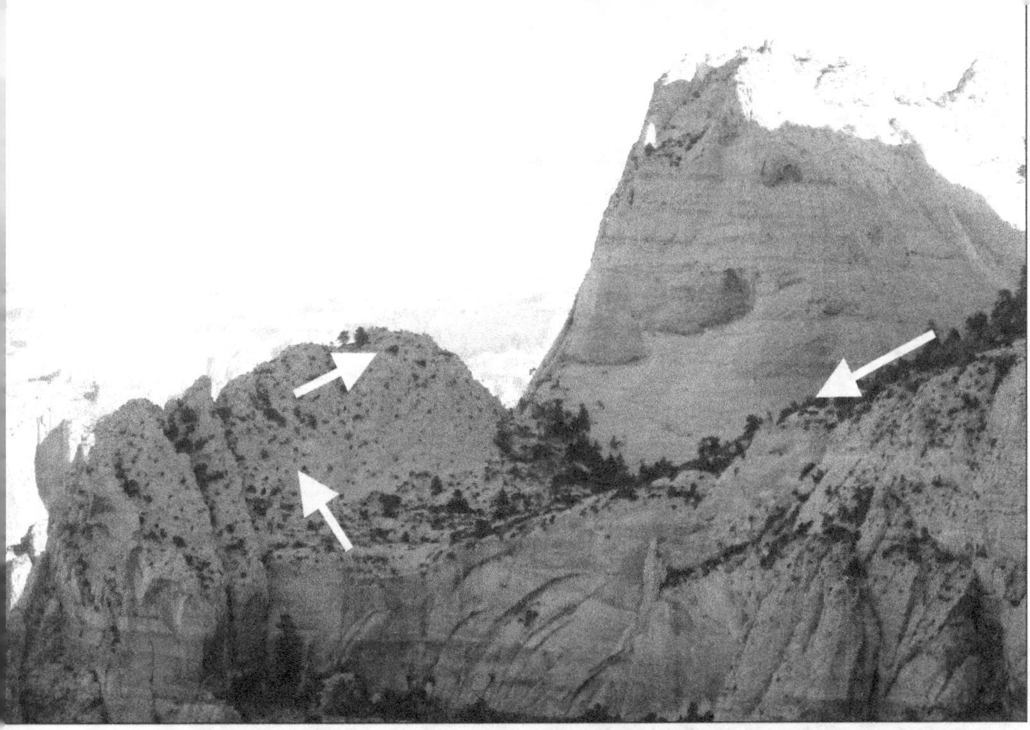

The route up the south face of the Sub Dial. The Sun Dial is on the right. Below: the location we fixed a rope off the west side of the West Temple to access the Subdial.

the shortest distance to the ground. From there we fixed the rope on a bush. The 320 feet did not quite reach the ground. From the end of the rope, we tired our etriers together to provide security as we down-climbed. Fortunately we didn't need a rope to scramble the south face of the Subdial. I wonder if Royce Trapier and Rod Savage climbed the Subdial when they spent six days climbing a route from Coalpits Wash to the area between the Sun Dial and West Temple. Unlike the carin and note they left, which Ron and I found on the traverse, Mike and I found no evidence of a previous ascent.

CLIMBING THE SUBDIAL

1. SOUTH FACE *D Stih and M Dunn, 2022*
EQUIPMENT REQUIRED: It's just a scramble up the south face.
STARTING POINTS: *The West Temple:* This peak is best done as part of the Traverse of the Towers of the Virgin. After rappelling off the north side of the West Temple, from the bottom of the last rappel, scramble due west, up and down slabs and the canyon between the Sun Dial massif and West Temple to reach the Subdial. As a rope is not required to climb the south face, leave your gear at the bottom of the rappel and come back to it to continue the traverse.

The Subdial as seen from the Sun Dial massif on the Traverse of the Time Machine.

The Princess Spire

Looking into the Court of the Patriarchs from the shuttle stop. Princess Spire is in the upper left. Just right of the center of the back, the prominent black streaks are from water flowing down Birch Creek and Abraham Canyon.

INTRODUCTION I named it Princes Spire after finding a fallen balloon near it with the word, "Princess". The spire is on the south side of the back of Court of the Patriarchs. The summit is actually composed of three towers. The spire is not be climbed from the Court of the Patriarchs.

HISTORY On Thanksgiving in 2000, Ron Raimonde and I tried to climb the spire from the ground in the Court of the Patriarchs. We started up a line with big chimneys. We bailed because Ron wasn't having fun. He was hoping to find an aid climb. The climbing was 5.10+ free-climbing. Although he would have continued if I wanted to, I took the opportunity to vote to bail. It was a smart move. The chimney leads to nowhere.

In November 2018, I soloed the Princess Spire towers that make up its summit. I reached the spire by traversing across a ledge from the Birch Creek.

Above: Dan on the second pitch on an attempt with Ron in 2000. Bottom: our bags (circled) at the bottom of the first chimney tower. The arrow points to the summit of Princess Spire. Opposite page: Preparing to sleep on the mountain for a few nights, wearing the shorts I had on when I left Phoenix, Arizona.

The Bags at Top of Pitch 3

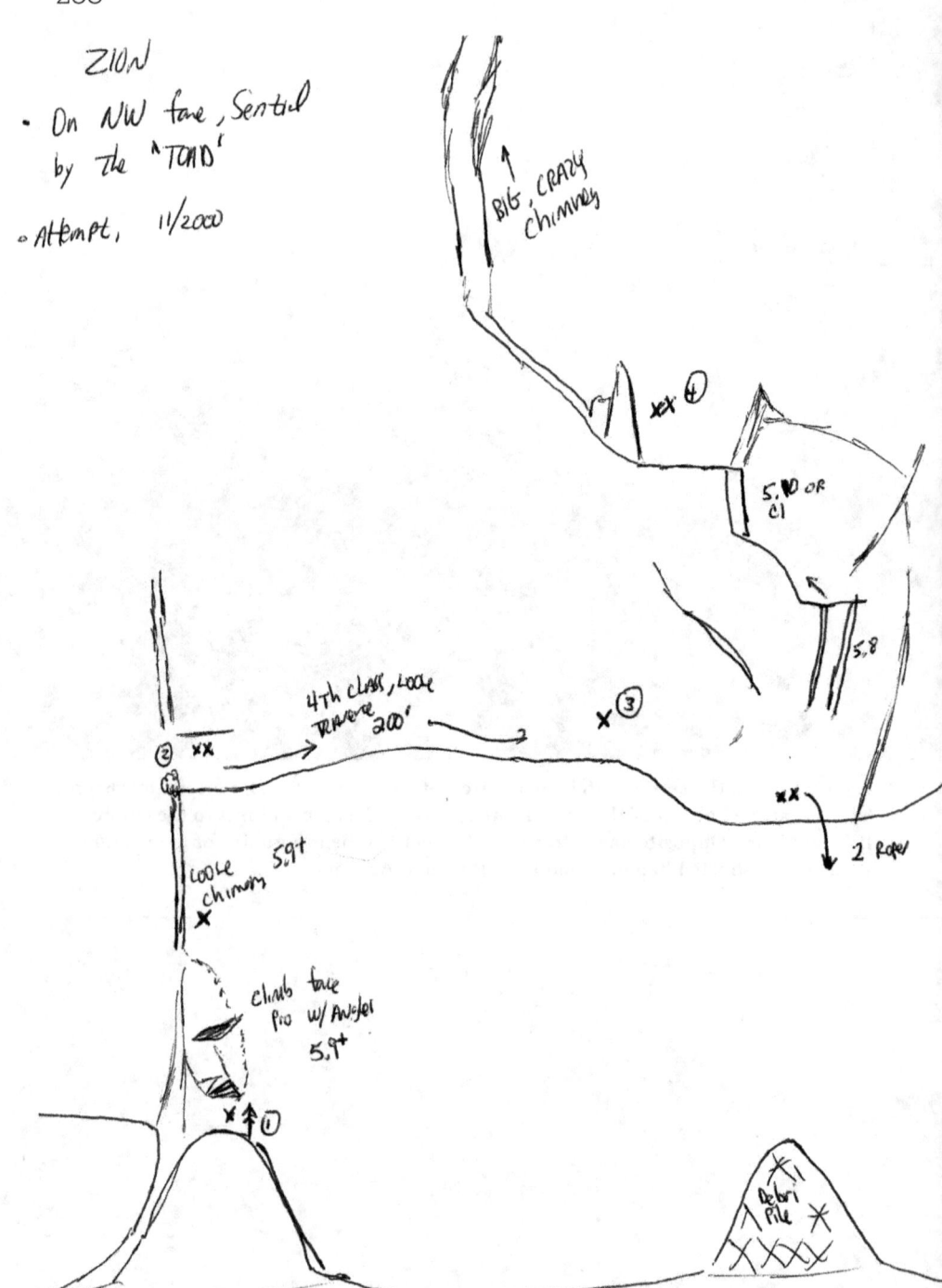

A sketch I made soon after our attempt to climb the spire from the ground, starting in the back of the Court of the Patriarchs. Someone could finish climbing this up to the top of the chimney towers.

Thanks at Thanksgiving

I was driven by two things: a work colleague had recently passed. He wasn't old. It was health complications. Here today, gone tomorrow. Although I'm a musician, it was my climbing that he mentioned when we last spoke. He knew where my heart was. I had to remember to keep my priorities. I rescheduled work so I could climb while it was warm, in the 60s.

The day after I arrived in Zion, I got up at 5 am and caught the first shuttle to the Court of the Patriarchs. It was dark and cold. I hiked to the back of the Court to where I had left fixed ropes, and put my ascenders on the ropes. (See Nipples Peak for how I fixed ropes down the waterfall in the back of the Court of the Patriarchs). I got five feet off the ground and stopped. I was scared. Going up the ropes, hanging in the air was spooky. I asked myself, *why do something you don't want to do? Why do something you don't need to?"* I waited for a response. After hanging for a few minutes, I found my body moving. It was coming down.

The idea of going up 800 feet of 8-millimeter (thin) rope didn't vibe with me. I went back into town and had a pizza. At 4 pm, I thought I'd had enough hanging out in Zion. I had planned to meet a group of friends in Sedona before Thanksgiving. I thought I would surprise them by getting there early. I started driving to Sedona.

At 10 pm, sixty miles north of Flagstaff, I returned to my normal state. The fear of going up the fixed ropes had passed. Suddenly, I found myself pulling over. I watched as I found myself turning around. I was going back. I suspected I'd get scared again, waste a ton of gas, and drive an extra seven hours for nothing. I was back in Zion at 1am.

In the morning, I took my time and went for pancakes. I knew I couldn't take *too* long. The waiter asked what I was up to. I told him my state - I was there to climb, but I'd probably get scared again. I realized I was wasting time, left the restaurant, drove to Canyon Junction, where I parked, not sure what I was going to do. I was packing my gear, going through the motions, when tourists parked next to me - Trish and Alton.

They asked if I knew of a good hike. I told them if they wanted something off the beaten path, they could follow me out to my ropes. They had street shoes. I didn't expect they'd make it that far. They made it. They hiked with me all the way to my fixed ropes. Alton held the end of the rope so I didn't spin in a circle as I went up. I didn't look down. I didn't look up. I tried to remain calm.

Each rope was secured to trees growing out of the side of the cliff. I had to stop at each to haul my bag with the climbing and sleeping gear. I was grateful the bag didn't get stuck. The drop was too big for a single rope, and I had tied several ropes together. A knot will not pass through a pulley. The rope has to be removed from the pulley and the knot placed on the other side of

Going up my free-hanging fixed ropes in the back of the Court of the Patriarchs, scared to death.

The gear I carried while climbing.

the wheel. This was technical because of how heavy the bag was. It took all day to get myself and my bag to the top of the cliff. Before going to sleep, I turned on my inReach satellite phone to let my friends know I would not be meeting them in Sedona, and to tell my brother I would not be arriving for Thanksgiving until the last minute. The device would not power on. My heart sank.

The next day I started climbing the Princess Spire. I didn't get to the top.

I left my rope fixed to my high point and went back to camp. On the way I found a balloon on the ground that said "Princess."

It was still daylight when I got back to camp, so I used the time to coil the ropes I would use to get down when I had finished climbing. I moved a pile of ropes and stacked them next to Abraham, the place I planned to go down.

The next day, I almost reached the top of the spire when I heard a helicopter. The pilot and passenger saw my camp: a sleeping bag and ground tarp. They couldn't see me climbing on the back side of the spire.

It was getting late in the day, when I considered that I would have to figure out how to get down, once I reached the top. I decided to wait to finish climbing to the top until the morning. I left my ropes fixed on the spire and went back to camp.

Back at camp I felt a sense of peace, as if where I was is where I belonged. It seemed there was order in the Universe. Whereas before I had been scared and concerned, I knew now why I climbed. I knew my place in the order of things. I also knew I that according to my permit, I was supposed to be on the ground the following day. I thought if I could finish and get down tomorrow, I could call my friends before someone reported me overdue.

The next day it took me longer to finish climbing the spire than expected. I reached the top. But by the time I got back to camp, I decided it better to wait until the morning to go down. The in Reach satellite device would still not turn on. I was later told by technical support that it needed a software re-boot, something not in the instructions.

The three towers of the Princess Spire, as seen from Sentinel Canyon.

I woke when there was barely enough light enough to see, and raced to where my ropes were laying in a pile at the edge of the cliff. I threw the pile of ropes over the edge and started rappelling. None had gone down the way I was going. I hoped it would not be too loose or dangerous. I hoped I could get down the way I was going. I heard it before I saw it. The high-performance helicopter flew over the main canyon road, turned into the Court of the Patriarch, and headed towards me. As it reached the cliff, it stopped and hovered,

293

The towers that make up the three summits of Princess Spire, as viewed from the plateau on the north side of the Sentinel. The search party in the helicopter was unable to see me as I was climbing the side of the spire seen here in the shade.

one-hundred feet in front of me. I didn't yet know it was the second day they had been searching for me, and that at this point they were carrying disposable gloves and a body bag, fearing the worst.

I was tied to a bush on the side of the mountain, looking down, assessing the best way to finish getting down. My ropes were in a tangled mess at my feet. I didn't know what else to do, except to give the pilot a thumbs up sign and smile. I hoped he understood. I was afraid that smiling too much might undercut the seriousness of the situation. When a simple hand signal didn't work, I smiled bigger, then went back to sorting the ropes to demonstrate I had things under control. The passenger got the idea, and the bird flew away. A few minutes later, the copter returned, just to be sure. I waved again. I wondered how much trouble I had put people in. First thing first - get down safe.

When I got to the ground, I started hiking to the road. There wasn't a trail. As I got close to the road I thought, *this is either going to go really good or I'm in big trouble. Hope for the best. There's nothing else you can do, nothing you can do different.* Across from the shuttle stop at the Court of the Patriarchs, there is a service road that goes back to a water tower and a small parking lot. As I reached it I saw them waiting for me: two law enforcement officers stood outside a patrol car. A paramedic stood next to the back doors of an ambulance.

"Are you Daniel?" one of the officers asked.

"Yes," I said.

"Are you OK?" the paramedic asked.

"I'm OK," I said, "Just thirsty. I dumped my water out before coming down. Do you have any water?"

"We don't have water. Do you want a ride to your car to get some?"

"That would be nice," I said.

The driver opened the back door of the ambulance and put my bag inside.

"Do I have to pay for that helicopter?" I asked the officers, trying to keep a

The overhanging cliff at the end of Birch Creek where it drops into the Court of the Patriarchs. On the right is the blank face of Abraham. I had just started down it when I was greeted by the helicopter searching for me.

positive attitude.

"We ordered for you."

The officers let that hang for a few moments before, seeing how concerned I was, and that I didn't understand, added, "No, you don't have to pay for it."

I got into of the ambulance, shotgun. The driver drove me to my truck parked at the junction on the side of the road. As we got close to it, I was a bit casual, as if getting a ride from a friend. I was too tired to think clearly.

"That's it there," I said. "You can drop me here."

"We have lights," the driver said. Although it was a busy holiday weekend and the road is a single lane in each direction, the ambulance stopped in the road. We got out. She got my haul bag out of the back and set it near my truck. The officers pulled up and parked next to my truck.

As I unlocked my truck to get some water, the ambulance left. The officers stuck around. They were waiting for me to finish drinking some water. On the hood of a car parked next to my truck, they laid out a laminated map, marked with where I might have been climbing. They produced a notebook they found that contained notes on the gear that might be required, and descriptions I had made about other mountains I had climbed. They had found them when they searched my truck for clues. Somehow they had contacted Steffan, a local climber and friend of mine. Steffan had been in the helicopter. Steffan did not, however, know which of three potential mountains on my list I might have chosen to climb. I had chosen the Princes Spire at the last moment, when I got up there and realized it might be the safest to climb by myself.

The rangers asked me how hard the climb was.

"Hard to say," I replied. "Loose sandstone that rubs off on your fingers. Upside-down piton placements. Could be A2". (On a difficulty scale of 1 to 5).

"In granite," one of the ranger suggested. He understood that granite is more solid, and that the same level of climbing on sandstone can be twice as difficult.

Satisfied, the other ranger, said. "You know we don't want to do this… We have to."

"I understand," I said.

"Have you ever received a ticket in the park before?"

My heart sank and I became seriously worried. I had received a ticket years ago when I started climbing in Zion. I had been forced to make a mandatory appearance before a magistrate and have since tried to stay out of trouble. I remembered to keep my responses short and simple. Things are what they are.

"Yes sir," I said.

I had not realized why they were asking. The officer was holding the ticket in his hand, upside-down. I tried to read it. I couldn't believe what I was seeing.

"You can contest it or mail it in."

I was relieved. At the bottom he had hand-written $100. For whatever reason, everything was turning out well. Perhaps the episode could be viewed as an exercise for when someone really needs a rescue in that area. I was climbing in an area that is hard to get to, one a rescue had not before been attempted. (In 2021 I did need a rescue there, as told in Sentinel Canyon).

The officers got into their vehicle and drove away. I got into my truck. After making calls to family and friends, I started driving to Phoenix for Thanksgiving. When I had started this trip, I was feeling scared. Now I was feeling good about coming back. But I would never not be scared. Every time I went back to climb in that area, it felt as if some spirit in the canyons made contact with me. For good or bad, my life the following year was not the same. Part of my spirit was stuck in Zion. I've heard it said that this spot is a power spot for me. It's the same place I would need to be short-hauled underneath a helicopter to safety when I had an accident descending Sentinel Canyon a few years later. Powerful, yes. The question I have for the spirits there is: Are you a good witch or a bad one?

The Chipmunk Descent, a new decent route I pioneered on my trip to climb Princess Spire.

CLIMBING PRINCESS SPIRE

SEASON: Fall is best. In spring, water is flowing at the waterfall. Winter is cold and icy. The climbing routes on Princes Spire are on the north side of the spire, and face into a canyon that does not get sun. In early season, the bottom will be green with moss, wet, and slippery. If it has rained or snowed recently, the rock may be wet, even when conditions on the ground are dry. Summer is hot, but if you can make it there without overheating, the creek provides a wonderful recluse to cool off and water for drinking. Most of the routes are in the shade. The top the spire see sun in the afternoon. If climbing in winter, know that camp near Birch Creek does not see sun until 11am, and the warmth only lasts one hour before the sun goes behind the Sentinel.

CAMPING / TIME REQUIRED: Four days? All three towers can be climbed in two days, once in Sentinel Canyon. Allocate at a day to get there and a day to get down. A fast party should be able to climb at least one tower each day. The shorter tower is just one pitch.

EQUIPMENT REQUIRED: Full Rack. Baby angels (#1, #2), a few long angles, and a few knife blades in addition to a normal rack of cams up to #4.

WATER SOURCES: Water can be found in Birch Creek year-round. In dry conditions look for pools further up the creek.

FUTURE CLIMBING: Try and free-climb the two biggest towers.

THE STARTING POINT: From the waterfall at the top of Birch Creek, traverse a tree covered ledge towards the spire. Cross over Sentinel Canyon. It's an easy hike to cross the canyon and scramble up to the bottom of the SW side of the spire. The first part of the back side of the spire is a scramble, 5.5 up a crack in a corner to a hole that is crawled through. Come out the other side of the hole, and you will be halfway up the spire, at the junction at which three towers meet. Scramble up to a tree between the two largest towers. Use it as a belay when climbing the two tallest towers. When climbing the short tower, belay on a nice spot to sit, as soon as you exit the hole.

The tree covered ledge that is traversed to get from Birch Creek, across Sentinel Canyon, to the base of the Princess Spires.

---

1. PRINCESS SPIRE A2+ 5.8 *D Stih 2018*

The tallest tower, and the one seen from the ground at the shuttle stop. From the tree between the two tallest towers, climb a crack (A2 or free) up to a ledge with a loose block. I set a belay with a #4 cam behind the block. The second pitch climbs face past two bolts (fixed angles) to a belay at a ledge with a bush. The bush is also used to rappel the route. The last pitch can be climbed either by going left up a crack above the bush, or walking sideways right on a ramp.

The approach pitch, 200-300 feet up to the "hole."

The hole crawled through to access climbing routes for each of the towers.

After coming through the hole. Belay at the tree for the routes on the main and west towers.

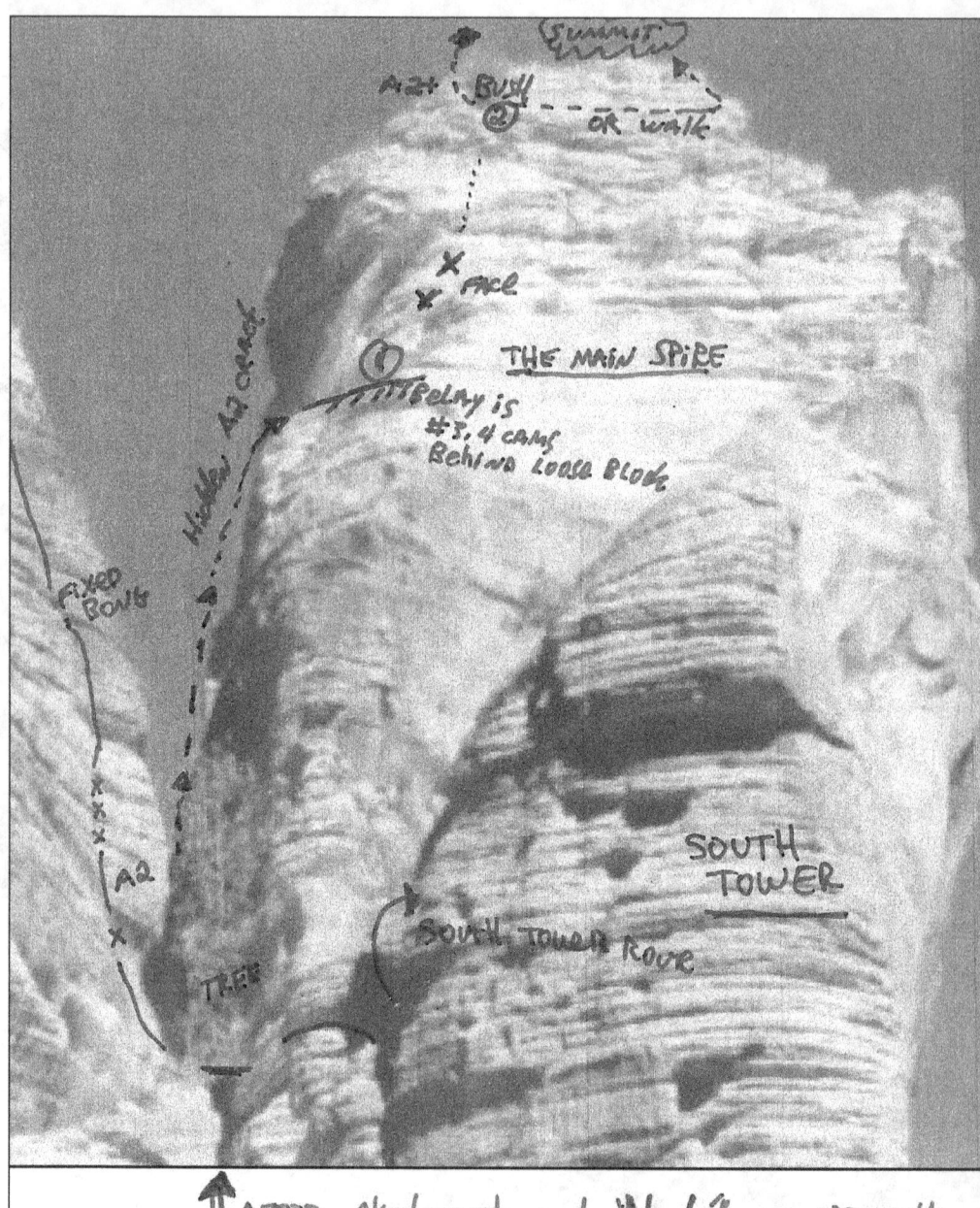

2. THE WEST TOWER A2+ 5.8 *D Stih 2018*
Start on a ledge on the left side of the tree between the two tall towers. Climb a crack to a bolt (fixed angle) visible a few feet up. A2 or free past a blank section to a fixed bong (please leave it.) Continue up the crack to a nice ledge and a bush. The bush is used to rappel the route. Scramble to the summit.

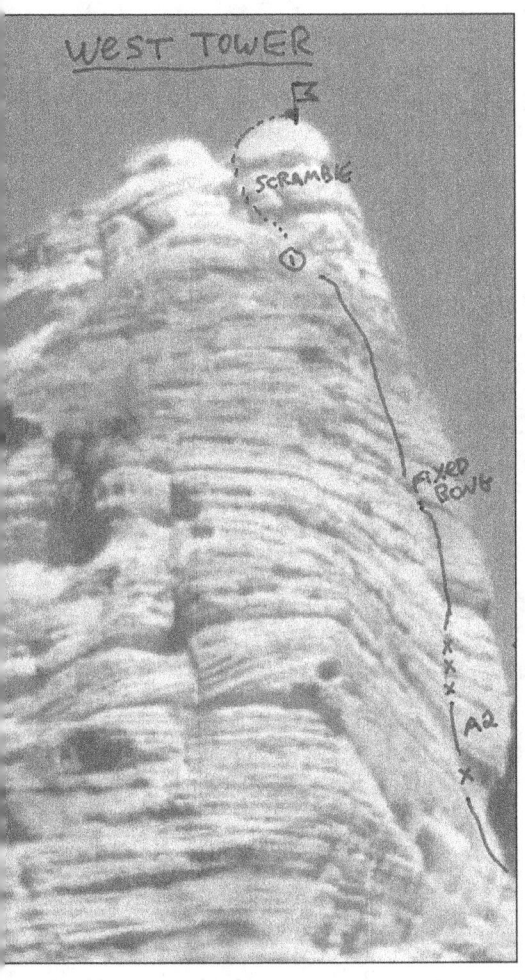

Left and above: The West Tower, second tallest of the three summit towers.

3. THE SOUTH TOWER 5.7 *D Stih 2018*
Set a belay on the other end of the hole that is crawled through on the approach. From the belay, crawl east across a ledge and around the corner. A cam can be used to protect the crawl. Around the corner, stand up and clip a fixed pin. Climb to the top of a ledge. Standing on the ledge, wrap aiders or slings around a stack of loose blocks above your head and mantel. Walk a few feet to the summit. There's a fixed pin on the summit to use for rappelling back to the belay. The rope may get stuck if you try to pull it. It might be easier to lower and down-climb to the belay.

The South Tower.

FUTURE CLIMBING: THE RED SENTINEL NORTH FACE CHIMNEYS

This will make a good free-climbing route for those who have a fetish for extreme chimneys. Climb the two chimney towers and lower off. Alternatively, from the top of the second tower, step right, and continue up what may be the Big Easy (VI 5.10 R A3, Denise-Hammond, 2000). The *2017 American Alpine Journal* has a picture annotated by Brian Smoot in which The Big Easy is shown to climb the first two pitches of our route, then continue straight up, climbing the left side of the second chimney tower.

TIME REQUIRED: Spend the first day on a recon. Hike the approach to find the easiest way to the climb. Consider fixing ropes to the top of pitch four. On the third day go for it and climb the chimneys.

EQUIPMENT REQUIRED: Full climbing rack. Big stuff. Possibly a selection of pitons to protect free climbing on the first pitch. (This can be avoided by climbing the first pitches of the Big Easy but that is an aid route that might require more gear.

THE STARTING POINT: Shuttle stop for the Court of the Patriarchs. Walk the service road across from the shuttle stop. Near the end of the road look for a faint trail on the right that leads across a foot bridge to the Sand Bench Trail. Walk the trail as far as possible before heading back into the Court. The route is on the far south-west side, near Princes Spire. Expect difficult bushwhacking to get to the bottom of the route.

THE ROUTE: Climb to our high point. (See topo and pictures in chapter Princess Spire.) Start by taking the high ground (a mound). Scramble up to a tree. Belay at the tree. The next pitch climbs a face with a discontinuous crack. It's 5.10, runout, going up and diagonal left. The second half of that pitch grunts up a loose, wide crack in a corner to a nice ledge. To the right, two bolts provide an anchor at the end of the pitch. Alternatively, you could climb the first pitches of Big Easy. What's important is to 4th-class 200 feet sideways west, at this point, to another bolt for a belay in the middle of a big traverse. Continue traversing, then start climbing up, taking the easiest way. The face is broken. The anchors at the top of pitch 4 provide a good place to re-group and look at the first chimney tower. Another pitch is required to get to the bottom of the chimney. The top of the first chimney has a big ledge. At the top of the second chimney tower, you may find anchors for Big Easy. It appears to climb the left side of the second chimney tower (perhaps not a chimney on that side). Although it continues to the top of the Red Sentinel, once at the top of the second chimney tower, I would say your work is done. Rappel the route. It's your route. Name it!

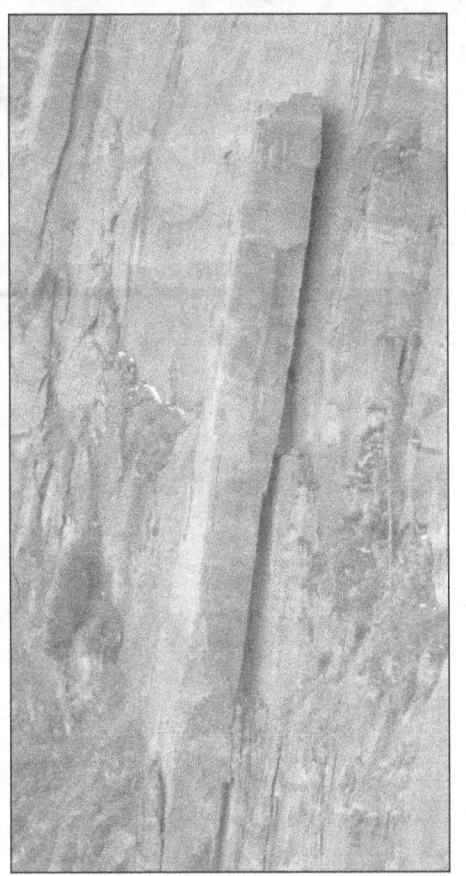

Close up of the 2nd Chimney tower.
Top: first chimney tower. Right:
second pitch from the ground.

Big Red

View from Springdale, as you enter the park on the west side. Left to right: the Meridian Tower, The Point, Big Red (arrow), Beehive Peak, the Sentinel.

INTRODUCTION Big Red is the mountain at the north top of the Streaked Wall. Of all the mountains I have climbed in Zion, if anywhere I saw what might be ruins, it was on the top of Big Red. I saw places where rocks appeared stacked in formation in patterns which may have once been walls. The entire summit was seeping in water. There is a spring on top that forms a creek that drains at a water fall on the NE side, into the canyon between Big Red and Triangle Peak. It's odd there are no ruins in the big cave under the south rim of Big Red, a cave visible from Springdale and in post cards and aerial photos. Locals report the top of Big Red caught fire a few years ago. The south side is a scramble once in the valley on the north side of Beehive Peak. The highest point on the mountain is on the far north side.

As seen from the east entrance after exiting the big tunnel. Left to right: Beehive Peak, the Streaked Wall, Big Red (white from this elevation), Triangle Peak, the Sentinel (red cap formation).

Red Rodeo

It was hot and I took frequent breaks. Half way up, stopped to rest on a large flat spot and took my boots off to air them out. As I set my water bottle down, it lost its balance, and started rolling down a slab. I watched as the object of my desire rolled away from me. I thought I could grab before it rolled off the edge. It teased me, almost coming to stop, then bounced and vaulted over the edge.

I went to look for a place to set up camp. What I found was an oasis. There was an ice-berg melting against the base of the mountain. I wished I could put some of the ice in a freezer to preserve it to ensure a supply of water. Before I began to climb the top part, I had to go down and get my camping gear. The following day called for rain. I decided to go down into town instead. I wanted to be nice to myself and to sleep in a hotel. It was my 52nd birthday.

As predicted, it rained and got cold. By late evening there was a power outage, blowing wind, flash flooding, and thunder. An unbelievable amount of water flowed in the Virgin river. On a scale of low to high, the flow was marked "!%*&!", well past "Dangerous". Then it started to snow. I was glad I had came down. I stayed in the hotel in Zion a few days as it poured buckets of water into an already wet sand box.

After it stopped snowing and raining, and after two days of full sun, I got a permit for six days, and went back. As I went back up the fixed ropes, I told myself, *double check everything. Pay attention.* I tried to ignore the voice that complains about how strenuous it is, how you wish you had better sunglasses and more food. I told myself, *focus on what you are doing.* Take care not to let your attention wander to something that has nothing to do with getting up the fixed ropes safely. No thinking about work, missed phone calls, money, and the bills that might not get paid because you've dropped out to go climbing.

It seems it's just me, yet I talk as if "we" are doing something. I wonder,

The route from Birch Creek to high camp and the upper section. A seen from Nipples Peak. The top of Big Red (upper left).

who is here. The voice that chatters can't belong the same as the one who hears the chatter. I couldn't win the fight or ignore the chatter. The constant bickering with myself was as challenging as the climb.

I wish I had brought binoculars. I can't read street signs without glasses when I'm driving, yet I was confident I could determine the best way to climb the top part of the mountain by looking at it from the bottom, a 1,000 feet away.

I studied the mountain carefully, looking for a route on which I would not have to drill bolts. In mountaineering, the classic routes are often found on ridges, low-angle corners on the edges of mountains. I saw shorter routes to the top of Big Red, but if I couldn't climb them without drilling bolts they would be dead ends. The ridge provided options. The downside was it made the amount of climbing I had to do twice as long.

I started climbing the ridge. It was hard to protect. Under a layer of dry sand, the rock was wet chalk. The roots of mosses and grasses grew deep into cracks and kept the dirt wet. I doubted the gear I placed in the rock would hold a fall. I was scared and holding on tighter than normal. When I had only climbed 100 feet, my legs and arms felt like I'd spent the day at the gym. My hands were dirty and cut. I climbed another 100 feet, fixed the rope, and came down. I washed my hands in a tickle of water from snow melting, hoping bugs or bacteria wouldn't infect them.

I spent the next two days inching my way up the ridge. I was so far out from civilization that I felt as if I had gone to the moon. To get to my camp, I had 700 feet of rope fixed at the Birch Creek waterfall in the back of the Court of the Patriarchs, and another 1,000 feet on the lower section of Big Red that was reached after hiking up Birch Creek. I wondered if I got injured how would someone find me.

That night I was bitten by a spider on my back: four bites in a perfect square. I read that the number 4 is an angel number, a reminder that your

The upper section of the north face of Big Red, reached after scrambling 1,000 feet up out of Birch Creek.

guardian angel is there.

On the firth day, I got within 100 feet of the top and decided it was too risky to continue. The rock was mush, still wet. The white-cap sandstone, like dust on a good day, saturated with water, crumbled in my hands. The bushes were too small and fragile to pull on. It was hot. My legs and arms were tired. I was out of water.

I tied a piece of strap around the root of a tree sticking out of the mountain where the sand around it had eroded. It seemed like it might hold body weight. I lowered myself and swung over to a bigger tree, one safer to rappel from, then went down to camp. It was too late in the day to go down into town.

In the evening, I watched thunder clouds build. White billowy clouds moved in from the south. They stalled as they were meet by dark clouds from the north. The two battled it out. Thunder rung as each side announced its intention. Reinforcements arrived for each side. A tie was reached as the clouds merged into one big rain storm. I should have been preparing for the rain instead of watching the show. I didn't have a tent. At the last minute, I laid my sleeping bag on the ground, placed a tarp over it, and placed rocks around the edges of the tarp to keep it from blowing away in the strong wind. I carefully slipped under the tarp. The 6x8 tarp was just long enough to cover my head. The rain passed, as a windy colored light show entertained me. It would have been fun, if I were not worried about getting soaked.

In the morning I packed everything up and started heading down. As I came walking down Birch Creek, I saw the water bottle I had dropped two weeks earlier. It was a like a fisherman's bobber in the water, still half-filled with water, as it had been when I dropped it.

I got to town at noon. By 3 pm there was a calamity as a rain storm hit town. If I had stayed on the mountain I would have gotten wet. It was going to rain for a week. I needed someplace cheap to stay. I remembered that when I was on the mountain and scared, I promised to take care of myself. I remembered that I shouldn't worry about spending money. A week in a hotel just seemed like a long time. I started to look for a hotel, got tired of looking for a less expensive place to stay, and went to Flanagan's, one of the nicest. As I walked up to front desk the assistant manager saw me. "Give Dan one of the suites at the normal rate," she instructed the clerk.

On my second day at the hotel, still waiting out the rain, I got call to do a job in Texas. *It's time to go*, I thought. Time to make hay. It was a smart move. It rained in Zion for a month. I got home to find an inch of snow on my patio. I opened the front door, stood in the doorway, and assessed how I felt. Nothing seemed to matter. There were nice things in my house, but I didn't need them. It felt nice to be able to sleep in my own bed. But I didn't miss it either.

I felt better in the morning, no longer depressed or worried. Everything seemed OK. My hands healed. No blisters. No infections. I went back to watching the forecast. I downloaded pictures taken with my camera, and blew up the images to examine the last 100 feet of climbing. No matter how much I looked, there did not seem an easy way to get to the top. To be able to climb it, I would need to let go of my fear of falling, and my concern about the possibility of getting hurt in a place I dared not dream of a rescue.

Since I had not taken binoculars, I had not seen the arrow the mountain had drawn for me. It pointed to where I might have started climbing. *That's the way I should go*, I thought. *Maybe I should start over, and try the route with an arrow.* If I got there and it was not possible I'll laugh hard. It would be the most time I've spent trying to climb a mountain.

It rained and snowed for two more weeks. I waited at home, eating all the time, and started to notice flabby skin, as if my body had shrunk. During the last two climbing trips I had been out six days at a time on a diet of less than 1,000 calories a day. I was regaining fat, not muscle. To which, I did something I had not done in a long time - I went to the gym.

June, 2019. It's as how it feels when you're in love - nothing else matters. I felt an immense peace, just driving through the park entrance. When I got back to my high point on the mountain, I trudged through the bushes to look at the route with the arrow. I stood still and asked for help deciding what to do. Remnants of the arrow, washed out in white, were still visible from a certain angle - the side of the mountain I had gotten within 100 feet from the top.

Option 1: Me and My Arrow. The arrow points to a small seam which might link the larger, obvious two cracks.

I took this to mean to go the way I had been going, and not to start over.

The snow was gone. Only a puddle of stagnant, orange water remained. An oily film was on top of the puddle. Pine needles and organic materials supported algae and mold growth. I filled half a bottle before my filter clogged.

I went up the ropes to my high point, climbed almost to the top of the mountain, and came eye-to-eye with red dirt. There was nothing to grab onto except loose rocks. It was like a house of cards. If I pulled on the wrong rock, the top three feet of the mountain might come tumbling down. I spent an hour, hanging a foot from the top, carefully moving one stone at a time to one side. Finally, I belly flopped onto the summit, got up and walked a few feet to a good bush, and tied my rope to it. The sand on top of the mountain was still wet.

It's amazing how one moment you're struggling and holding on for dear life, the next you're in a lush oasis on a summit. I really dug the summit and felt at peace on it. I felt nurtured and loved. Maybe the reason Cliff Dwelling Mnt was taken off the map after 1929 was that they didn't want people to know where it was. Maybe the ruins are actually on top of Big Red, and they put "Cliff Dwelling Mnt" on another mountain as a distraction.

The next mountain I wanted to climb was Triangle Peak. I planned to climb it using a Dangerous Dan trick: there is a saddle between the top of Big Red and Triangle Peak, a chasm of 600 feet. Rather than climbing Triangle Peak from the bottom, I thought I would tie 600 feet of rope around a tree on the east edge of Big Red, go down to the saddle, and climb the last 600 feet of Triangle Peak. I went to have a look.

When I looked, I was downtrodden. The top 600-feet of Triangle Peak looked difficult. Blocks of white sandstone appeared loose and ready to fall. I considered if I got hurt or something went wrong, I'd have to go back up 600 feet of rope to the top of Big Red, carry it across the top, throw it down the other side, rappel 1,000 feet, and then go down to Birch Creek. I decided to go down.

Summit selfie.

I went back to Flanagan's to see if my room was still available. It was, but only for one night. I took that as a sign that I should go back to climbing the next day. It would be a rest of 24 hours.

I stayed the night, got up early, packed and ready to go. I went back up to the top of Big Red, and threw ropes over the edge, into the saddle between Big Red and Triangle Peak. Even though the rock looked loose and impossible, I wanted to get a closer look. That's what explorers do.

The first 300 feet of rappelling was not scary. Then I went over an edge, and found myself hanging in space, twirling from an 8.3-millimeter rope. I got over my fear and finished rappelling to the ground.

Once in the saddle, I walked over to where I thought would be the way to

Creek on the summit of Big Red.

climb Triangle Peak. The bottom was overhanging and wet. Water seeped out of the rock. It didn't look fun. I could climb it. I didn't want to. It occurred to me that I didn't want to climb the peak as bad as I had thought. I decided to let it go. *Why do something you don't feel like doing*? I reversed course and went home. When I got home, I opened the door and felt a relief. Comfort. I was tired of climbing.

The good feeling only lasted a week. I became anxious, angry, and blue. What was negative about my life? To me, I was lucky. I considered there might be more to the story of Dangerous Dan and his obsession with Zion than just climbing. Maybe I used to live as cliff dweller or a Paiute. At the end of the ice age, 100,000 ago, there was a wet period that carved the canyons in Zion. Prior, the area may have been underwater, as in Atlantis. The Anasazi lived in Zion from 500AD to 1300 AD. Where'd they go? Maybe the Anasazi are related to the Anunnaki, a race who built the pyramids. Certainly they would have had the technology required to live on the sides of cliffs.

An expedition in 1776 by Fathers Dominguez and Escalante is the first recorded visit to Zion by Euro-Americans (Anglos). The purpose was to locate a route from Santa Fe, New Mexico, to Montgomery, California. It also became the ground-work for the Spanish Trail.

Rappelling down Big Red from where the spring flows over the east edge into the saddle between Big Red and Triangle Peak.

The original Spanish Trail passed through my backyard in Santa Fe. The Sandias, the mountains to the south, are one of my favorite places to be. Coincidence? Since my first outing in Birch Creek things have been weird. I get scared each time I go into the Court of the Patriarchs. I feel as if spirits attach to me. I take them home where I think they get cleared.

CLIMBING BIG RED

1. NW FACE, 5.9 A3 *D Stih 2019*
EQUIPMENT REQUIRED: Full rack.
WATER SOURCES: There's always water in Birch Creek. But it's a lot of work to haul it. In early spring, if there's been a lot of snow, there may be water and snow on the plateau near the bottom of the upper section. In very wet seasons there may be water on the summit, from a spring in the middle of the mountain.
SEASON: Spring when there's hope of finding water from snow melting on the plateau at the bottom of the upper section. The final pitch is loose, and not recommended during early season, when it is likely to be damp from snow melting and water running off the top. May is probably best. Fall is pleasant but would require multiple trips to stock camp with water from Birch Creek.
CAMPING / TIME REQUIRED: I suggest four six days: two climbing the bottom section and hauling gear to a high camp on a flat section below the top half; two climbing the upper part and getting everything back to Birch Creek. It took me longer to climb something big in the backcountry, solo. The location and adventure are worth it.
THE STARTING POINT: From the top of the water falls that empty into the Court of the Patriarchs, walk up Birch Creek a ways. From the south side of Birch Creek, scramble 1,000 feet up slabs, mostly 4th-5th class with 400 feet of roped climbing in sections that contain 5.6-5.7 moves depending on the route taken.
THE ROUTE: Once at the bottom of the upper half, there is 1,000 feet of 5.9 A2+, with a break of 5th class in the middle where there is a ramp with big trees.
GETTING DOWN: Go back down to Birch Creek and exit via one of the Birch Creek descents. Alternatively, carry-over Big Red and use the descent for the Streaked Wall.

FUTURE CLIMBING Option 1) A possible new line would be an aid route on the north face I call "Me and My Arrow." Once at the bottom of the upper part, the back (north) side, climb the crack in the photo. I almost tried to climb this route instead of the one I took. I was not sure if the area near the arrow might require bolts to link a seam at a potential blank section. I wanted to put up a route without bolts. The arrow may have washed away.

Option 1: Me and My Arrow.

Option 2. The crack that might be free-climbed or aided on the SW corner of Big Red, left of the big cave.

Option 2.

Option 2) From the valley between the Point and Big Red, scramble up to the SW corner of Big Red. Aid or free the crack on the SW corner. It's about 300 feet, I suspect 5.11. The crack is on the left side of a ridge that comes down the SW side of Big Red. A big cave is on the right (east) side of this ridge.

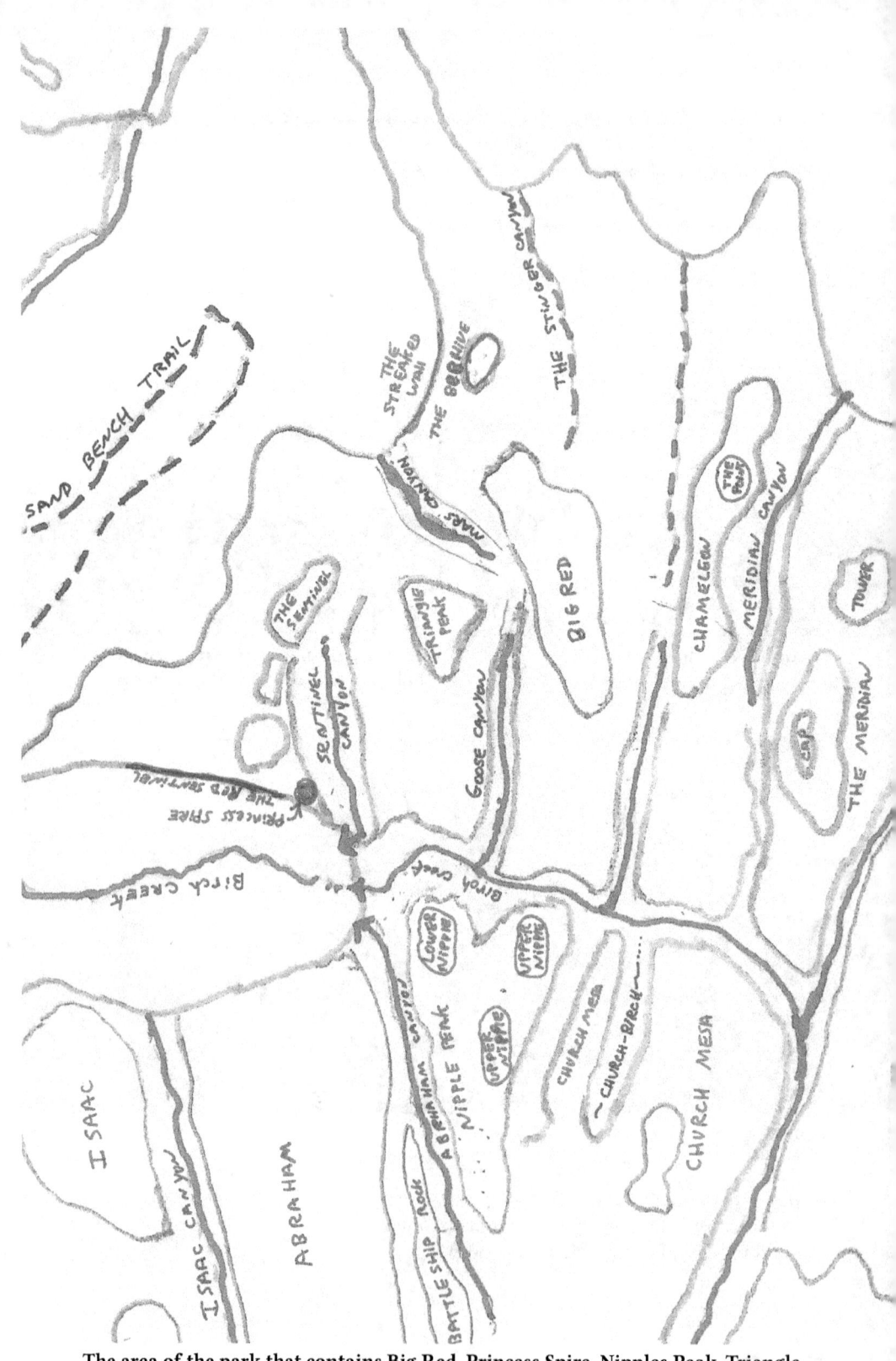

The area of the park that contains Big Red, Princess Spire, Nipples Peak, Triangle Peak, Chameleon, The Point, The Meridian Tower, and others.

Rosebud Peak

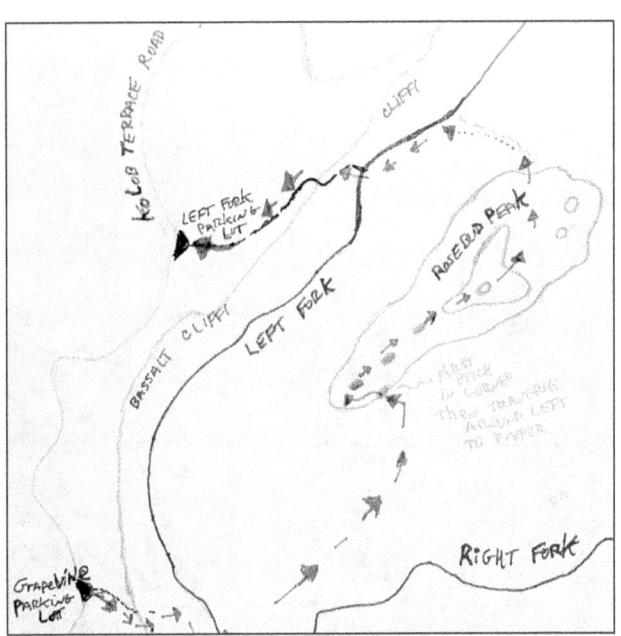

INTRODUCTION I climbed this peak with Mike Dunn on Easter Sunday. We left Springdale well after noon, after I had breakfast with friends. One gave me a gift: a chocolate covered peanut butter egg. I ate the entire thing. Subsequently, I felt nausea the entire time I was climbing, naming the route, PB Jesus. This is a fabulous day adventure which includes hiking, river crossings, and climbing at an easy grade.

HISTORY C.P. named this peak, after scrambling up the northeast slope, our descent route.

CLIMBING ROSEBUD

1. SW RIDGE (PBJ) 5.7 OR 5.8 *D Stih and M Dunn, Easter 2023.*
SEASON: Summer is hot. In early Spring a tenuous river crossing is required.
TIME REQUIRED: 1/2 - 3/4 day
EQUIPMENT REQUIRED: Light rack of cams, single rope, climbing shoes are optional.
THE STARTING POINT: Park at the Grapevine parking lot. Hike a dirt path down through cliffs to the water and find a way to cross the river. Head up steep slopes around the NE corner of the south face. There are fairly steep routes on the main south face. After hiking around the corner NW, you will see two potential easier was to start. Choose the one furthest left as you look at the peak from the east side - a corner composed of good rock with a crack. This is the first route around the corner from the steep and blank stuff.
THE ROUTE: A short pitch (the crux) leads to easy ground. Walk SW around the corner to the proper SW ridge. From there, pick the easiest way. Various short boulder problems and easy pitches lead to the first summit. Tag it, then continue across the ridge, tagging each of the summits. The tallest summit is on the far north edge.
GETTING DOWN: Walk north/NW (a short down-climb is required) into a drainage that heads west down into the Left Fork. Cross the river and pick up the trail on the other side. DO NOT MISS this point - the trail exit. Hike up the trail through cliff bands to the Left Fork parking lot. Walk Kolob Terrace Road down to your vehicle at the Grapevine trail head parking lot.

The Point

The Point, as seen from Springdale. It lies between the Meridian Tower and Big Red.

HISTORY In 2019, I climbed Big Red. On the summit, as I looked over at Chameleon Peak, I realized there was another peak in front of it: The Point. I fixed a rope off the top of Big Red into the valley between the Point and Big Red, and went to explore the valley and to climb it.

A Dangerous Dan Moment

From the top of Big Red, I walked to the edge across from The Point, and threw 300 feet of rope down. It was just enough to reach the ground. I packed light. Instead of a normal climbing rope, I brought a 7-mil static to climb with. Since I had gotten an early start, I was back to top of Big Red by 1pm. As I looked over at what I had climbed, thinking I had I gotten to the top of the Point, I realized I had not. I had confused it with the steep white faces of other peaks. My legs and arms arched. I needed a rest day.

The next day, at my high camp on the north face of Big Red, I slept in. I buried my head in my sleeping bag to shut out the light past 10 am. During the day, I sat in the shade, filtered water, clogged my new water filter, and

View of the Point from the Top of Big Red. In the background is the West Temple.

spent the afternoon taking it apart to unclog it. I had nothing else to do.

The next day I went back up to the top of Big Red, dropped the rope over the edge, and rappelled into the valley. Upon reaching the ground, I realized I had forgotten my pack with the climbing rope and other gear. I had set it down next to the tree I was using as an anchor as I was preparing to rappel. I jugged back up the 300 feet of overhanging rope, got the pack, and came back down. It started to get warm. I had taken my time in the morning, brewed coffee, and now gone up and down the fixed rope twice. Oh well. I got to the summit this time. The proper one.

CLIMBING THE POINT

1. NW FACE *D Stih 2019*
EQUIPMENT REQUIRED: Slings. It's just a scramble, once in the valley between it and Big Red.
WATER SOURCES: There is water in a big pool down the canyon in front of the red cliffs on the east side of the Point. There should be water there into late May or possibly later if it rains before your trip.
STARTING POINT AND THE ROUTE: I climbed Big Red, then rappelled 320 feet off its SW corner into a hanging valley. From the bottom of the rappel, I scrambled down white slabs towards the Point and found a weakness in the red cliffs that attempt to block access to the Point. I scrambled up the lower half of the massif to a flat section on its south side. From there I walked around west, and scrambled up the north-west face to the summit.
Alternate Route #1: The other way to get there would be to descend the south tip of Chameleon Peak to the saddle between Chameleon and The Point. Climb up the north

Top: the rappel route off of Big Red. Above: The approach to The Point after rappelling off the SW corner of Big Red. In spring time there are pools for drinking water in these shallow canyons.

face of the Point from the saddle. Mike Dunn and Arthur Herlitzka did this in March 2021 on the traverse.

Alternate Route #2: Climb up the descent for the Streaked Wall to the top of Beehive Peak. Scramble down the north side of Beehive Peak into the valley between Big Red and Beehive Peak. Stay close the Big Red, and traverse around the mouth of Stinger Canyon, the canyon on the west side of Beehive Peak. Once around Stinger Canyon, climb up into the valley between Big Red and the Point, and climb the Point as previously described. Starting from the old visitor center, James Barrow reports rope-soling this adventure, round-trip, in a day in 2022.

Triangle Peak

INTRODUCTION Triangle Peak sits between Big Red and the Sentinel. It's visible when driving down the switchbacks from the big, east entrance tunnel. I named it Triangle Peak because of how it looks on a topographical map: the summit is triangle-shaped. Also, when seen from the top of the waterfall at the end of Birch Creek, it has a triangular profile like that of the Matterhorn in Switzerland. Over several months in 2019, I attempted to get to the top by three different routes. Success came climbing the easiest way, what I believe is classic.

FUTURE CLIMBING The NW face of the Sentinel is an alternative way to get to and from Triangle Peak. Climb the 1938 route and descend the NW face. If you come down the NW face of Sentinel and are unable to climb back up it, there are alternative exits.

The Three Corners of a Triangle

The east face of Triangle Peak in early morning light.

I thought I'd go back and get the ropes down from my route on Big Red, and use them to climb Triangle Peak. I decided not to do the canyons surrounding Big Red and Triangle Peak (I've since done them). I'd been sick for a month. Two weeks after finishing antibiotics, I still felt stuff in my sinus. Going down a canyon in wet suit didn't seem like a good idea. The only reason to do them would be to say I had explored everything in the area. It felt like my ego talking instead of my heart.

The ranger warned me about the wind. But I thought wind would be great. Wind makes things cooler. And it did. Although it was almost 90F, the wind almost made it too cool. I went up the fixed ropes.

At the top of the waterfall I took off my boots to let my feet dry. That's when I noticed the back of my heel where the scar from a blister was red and flamed, soggy from sweat. I was on the verge of having another blister. Using a pocket knife, I cut a hole out in the back of my boot. The issue was I would not be able to risk putting climbing shoes on. I decided to try and climb without wearing climbing shoes.

Before I could try to climb Triangle Peak, I needed to bring down all the fixed ropes I had left on Big Red, a daunting task that would take two days. I decided to sleep on the top first. I was sad. Just normal depression I guess. I noticed the flowers were gone. They can only last so long. I saw them in June. Now it was the end of September.

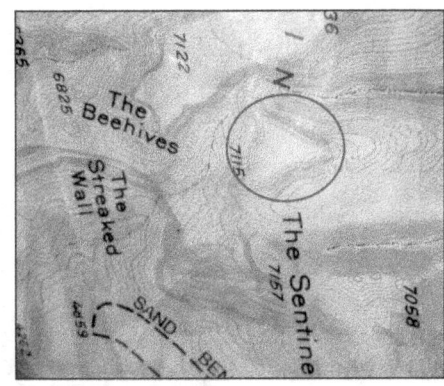

Trails Illustrated **topo map, 1988.**

I took a light weight sleeping bag and a 1/2 gallon of water. On the summit, I took my time to explore each of the beehives on Big Red. I finished exploring early, and spent the rest of the day on top in Zen fashion, sitting and moving around a tree that provided shade. As I sat, a honey bee buzzed me. Bees? I'd never seen one on a summit in Zion. Perhaps I just hadn't noticed. Now, as I sat and let other thoughts not clutter my mind, I noticed things. It was a long night staring at the starry sky, and then what was left of the full moon.

I spent the next day, rappelling the route, pulling ropes down, and hiking up and down to port all the ropes and gear down to Birch Creek. I was blown tired when I was finished moving all the gear to a camp where Birch Creek meets Goose Canyon. I wasn't sure what I was going to do next. My choices were to go to town or trying to climb Triangle Peak. I reminded myself I didn't need to climb Triangle Peak. I decided to let my body decide. The first task was to get more water.

The only water nearby was a near empty pool in Goose Canyon. It was convenient. And green. There were frogs in it. Tadpoles with tails like an airplane rudder, and two front feet, desperately trying to climb out of the pool. They wiggled their tails to propel them, clawing the rock with their front feet,

Above: traversing under a steep section on the second pitch of the approach ridge up to high camp. Below: high camp at the base of the "triangle".

held back by having a tail instead of feet on their back ends.

Because my water filter had clogged, the only method I had for treating water was iodine tablets. Normally, I'm OK with that. But the water in the frog pound was stagnant and green. I wondered, *would it be safe?* My choices were limited to drinking it, abandoning my climb, or going to look for another pool. I remembered how environmentalist use frogs as a way of assessing how polluted water is. *If it's good enough for frogs, it's good enough for me.* I filled the bottles and apologized to the frogs for taking a few gallons of their home. I promised I'd pray for rain after I was gone. (It rained the first night after I finished my climb.)

Stocked with water, I began an effort. I feared it would be a difficult free-climb, one that would have been good to have a partner. I started on the far edge, the ridge of the mountain, where there was some slope. I told myself to not step on anything insecure. No iffy holds. No risk taking. I wasn't wearing climbing shoes. I carefully worked my way up. When I got to the end of my ropes I had to go down and get more. (I was fixing the ropes.) By the end of the day I was up the difficult part. The climbing was getting easier. The issue was loose rocks on the side of the cliff on loose red dirt. I had to make sure I didn't knock rocks off. Sure, there was no one below. But if a rock landed on my ropes it could damage them.

At the end of the second day, I reached a flat, white rib. It was an amazing place. I felt good. I was in the zone finally, enjoying what I was doing. I was "happy" again, and I felt loved. I constantly thanked my Guardian Angel, the universe, and the mountain for my safety.

The third day on Triangle Peak, I went up to the spot I planned to make a new camp. I thought it might take me at two days to climb the final "triangle." I had only two days remaining on my permit. If for some reason, it took longer, I didn't want to get in trouble. I stocked the camp with climbing gear and two gallons of frog water. In the morning I went down and drove to Phoenix to visit my nephews.

October, 2019. After a week of visiting family, I headed back to Zion. What a difference a week can make. A week ago it had been so hot that I had to leave in the early morning and take breaks in the shade. Now it was cold (37F). I laughed because my suitcase was packed with shorts. It took all day to get into the groove, as I jumared up the 700 feet of rope fixed in the back of the Court of the Patriarchs. I wondered what was different. Then I remembered - I had forgotten to thank Nick, my guardian angel, his helpers, and other angels. I had forgot to thank the mountain for safe passage.

It was a long, scary way to go up the ropes. Instead of complaining and thinking how far I had to go, I imagined sitting safely at the top. Vision, imagination, and positive thinking. When I got to my camp I found the frog pond low on water. I thought it might have gotten a re-fill when it rained. I hope the frogs had survived. Perhaps their tails had turned to legs, and they had left to find a bigger pond. Later, I learned that frogs are able to burrow in the sand and hibernate through drought. Maybe they were taking a siesta.

The second day, I jumared up the fixed ropes I left on the ridge, carrying all the camping gear with me, including a stove and food for five days. The only thing lacking, something to monitor, was water - I had 1.5 gallons of frog water. I had only two ropes with which to finish the climb. One of the ropes was an 8.3-mil dynamic to lead on (what was I thinking!); the other a 300-foot 8-mil static.

I began an effort to climb a route on the Triangle's north face. Standing on a small ledge, the wall above blank, I swung around a corner to look for a crack. I wasn't encouraged. There was no crack, just loose blocks hanging onto the mountain. Since I had planned on taking it easy and slow, I went back to camp to consider things.

In the morning, I decided to go for it. I packed the haul bag with a sleeping bag and the remaining water. I left the stove and dehydrated food at camp. I took the turkey jerky and power bars. I wasn't sure where I'd sleep. There is a tree growing on the side in the middle of the route. I thought if I could make it to the tree, I could wrap my legs around it and tuck my sleeping bag over my feet up to my chest. It would be just one night.

I went back up to my high point, lowered, and swung my way around the corner. I attempted to climb what I thought was a crack. After several A5 placements in dirt, I realized it was an illusion, created by shadows of loose blocks. To continue, I would need give myself slack and free-climb. I wondered what I should do. I wasn't scared. I was being in the moment, pretending to be Dangerous Dan. Which meant I had skills. I just had to stay in the moment and not get distracted by a voice in my head that can take me into a downward spiral of negative thinking.

The answer came. And it was No. I felt no. As much as I wanted to climb Triangle Peak, it felt nice to get "No", not because it meant I could go down and not worrying about sleeping with my legs wrapped around a bush or tree; not because I could plan on eating a hamburger sooner than later. Rather, it's part of the reason I climb. It felt good to be in the state where knowing what to do comes with ease. I decided to leave the mountain for someone else to climb, someone with a partner or bolder than I. I lowered myself, pulled the ropes, and carried my bag back to camp.

On the way, out of the corner of my eye, I noticed the NW face of the Sentinel, the face Ron and I climbed in the 1990s, as part of our traverse of the Court of the Patriarchs. I thought it would be nice to have some pictures of that area, and went to get a closer look. I set the bag down and started walking around the corner. I didn't think I'd get far, as the steep sandstone looked like it might drop off.

Looking across at the mesa that is an extension of the ridge coming down from the NW corner of the Sentinel. Ron and I climbed up the left edge of this during our traverse of the Court of the Patriarchs. An alternate, easier, descent from this area is to go down the canyon in front. Abraham is visible in the background on the left.

Left to right: Red Sentinel, The Sentinel, Triangle Peak. From a high up on Triangle Peak, I traversed left across the white face and around the corner to reach the gap on the right side of the Sentinel. A tree is visible in the gap.

Looking up a the east face of Triangle Peak. The route goes up to the right side of the hood doo, then, as seen in the photo on the opposite page, up the notch.

I was surprised. As I got around the corner, I saw another way to climb Triangle Peak. Whereas a moments ago I thought the trip had been a wasted effort, I was blessed. It was the start of a new adventure. I didn't have a rope and the day was half-over. I went back to camp.

In the morning I went back, armed for bear. There was a chance I'd run out of daylight on my one-day attempt, and end up sleeping on the mountain without a sleeping bag. I needed to go light to be able to climb without wearing climbing shoes. That meant no thermal jacket or pants. I left camp with a half-liter of water, one power-bar, and a wind breaker, at the first sign of dawn, when it was 37F. It was extremely windy, and got windier as I moved onto the exposed east face of Triangle Peak.

At the bottom, I left the water, jacket, and non-essentials. I started climbing at the easiest place. Instead of heading straight up, I zig-zaged, going away from my destination, then back towards it. To keep my load light, I dragged the rope. It wasn't clipped into anything. There wasn't a place on the rock to place protection. I reached a ledge that was a resting point, pulled the rope up, and tied one end of it to a tree. The next section looked harder. Little of the gear was useful. The cracks were shallow water grooves, the depth of carbon left from drawing a mark with a pencil. I became concerned I might not find a way.

I climbed straight up on good foot holds to where it looked improbable and

overhanging below a beehive on the SE corner. There, I couldn't believe my eyes. A ramp with reasonably sized foot holds went sideways to the saddle between the hive and main summit. There were not great holds, but if I took my time and was careful placing my feet I could do it. I made it to the top. Then, to ensure I reached the highest point, I climbed the red boulders on top. I was back at the resting tree at the bottom by noon.

With time to spare, I explored the canyon that comes down between the Streaked Wall and Triangle Peak. I stopped in the cave that Ron and I had slept in to get out of the rain and snow when we did the first ascent of the NW face of the Sentinel. It seemed a powerful spot. I spent another night at my high camp, then began the huge task of getting everything down to Birch Creek.

It seemed warmer at camp at Birch Creek, probably because it was 1,000 feet lower. I ported three trips, with a heavy bag, to the head of Birch Creek. It was hot. The only place with shade (and cool air) was a dry part of the canyon, normally under six feet of flowing water, in which I found a feather from a hawk. I seemed to be receiving a blessing. A good-bye, tidings from another long adventure. Farewell beloved mountains and friends, seen and unseen.

On my last day, as I was porting loads from Goose Canyon to camp at a flat spot on the rock near the waterfall, I found a hot air balloon in the bushes.

This one said "Hello Kitty." Not sure if I will name a climb Kitty. The next day I went down to the ground, the haul bag packed with as much gear as I could muster. The following morning, I went back up the fixed ropes in the Court of the Patriarchs with an empty haul bag. At the top, I filled the bag with gear and went down again. The next day I went up again, this time to begin the task of removing the ropes. I took the first shuttle, in the cold and dark at 7am. It took all day. After going down the first set of ropes, I tried to pull them down they got stuck. I went back up and down four times to get them to move. Perhaps my mountain didn't want me to leave.

The next day I got up at 6m and took the shuttle. I made four punishing trips. Each time I packed the bag as heavy as I could without hurting my knees. Because I had cut holes in the backs of the socks to avoid rubbing the blisters, a lot of dirt and cactus got into my shoes. I finished at 5pm.

I had started with a swollen right foot, cause unknown, and a weird pain and weakness in my knee. All had been good on the mountain. When I got back from my last trip of bringing the ropes down and carrying them to the car, after I took my boots off, I felt pain in my right foot.

The following day, I went back to where it all began. A few days before Thanksgiving, the year before, I had been sitting in the restaurant, looking out the window, eating pancakes, wondering what I should do. I had been wondering if I should even climb. Now I was wondering what I could do next, and I knew what it should be: a day off! It was one of the coldest mornings in some time, 27F, perfect for taking a break.

CLIMBING TRIANGLE PEAK

1. EAST FACE *FKA D Stih, 2019* (It's probable this peak was first climbed in the 60s or 70s when the first descent of Goose Canyon was likely done.) The East Face is classic in beauty, location, and exposure. It's a scramble, once you get the bottom of the triangle. Getting to it and back home are the cruxes. High adventure.

Triangle Peak in early spring after a snowfall. The normal route ascends the left skyline. The North Face route would ascend the right skyline.

EQUIPMENT REQUIRED: (from the base of the triangle) Slings. One 200-foot rope. The bottom is a scramble. A belay can be set at a tree on the north-west side if desired. A purple Camelot (cam) provides a solid placement half-way up the steepest pitch.

WATER SOURCES: There is a drainage between the Sentinel and Triangle Peak with pools that have water in the spring. In late season (Summer and Fall) there will not be water except in Birch Creek. In winter, snow accumulates in the saddle between Triangle Peak and Big Red and, being in the shade, does not melt until late spring (May) depending on the amount of snowfall.

STARTING POINTS (possible routes to the base of the triangle):
Climb the 1938 Route on the Sentinel: This is a logical approach, and the most difficult. Climb the Sentinel and descend (rappel and down-climb) the NW Face. At the bottom, turn east (left), and scramble through a notch between the Sentinel and Triangle Peak. Pass through the notch, go down the other side, and look for the easiest way to scramble up white slabs on the right, the NE side of Triangle Peak.

Left to right: Triangle Peak, Goose Canyon, Big Red. The approach From Birch Creek climbs 1,000 feet up a tree covered ridge to a rest and bivy below the Triangle.

The North Face of Triangle Peak. A high camp with lots of flat spots is mid-way up. In early season there may be snow to melt for water. If climbing the North Face route, continue straight up. To climb the standard route, traverse left around the corner.

Birch Creek: From Birch Creek, climb the west face of a ridge that comes down from the north side of Triangle Peak into Birch Creek. The logical and legal way to get to Birch Creek is though Phantom Valley. Cross Phantom Valley and head towards the west side of Abraham. Scramble up, past Battle Ship Rock, onto the highest point of Nipples Peak. Descend to the lower Nipple, then to Birch Creek.

Hike up Birch Creek towards Goose Canyon. The ridge to climb is on the east side of Goose Canyon. From Birch Creek to the top of the ridge is 1,000 feet of climbing, 800 feet of which is 4th or 5th class. From the top of the ridge, scramble up white slabs toward the north face of the triangle. Don't go all the way to the triangle. Rather, look for a way to traverse left, sideways, around Triangle Peak towards the Sentinel. Once around the corner, scramble to the notch between the Sentinel and Triangle Peak. Pass through the notch, go down the other side, and look for the easiest way to start climbing up white slabs on the NE side of Triangle Peak.

Triangle Peak sits between Big Red (left) and the Sentinel (smaller area on right).

THE ROUTE ON THE TRIANGLE: Scramble up white slabs on the N/ NE face of Triangle Peak, heading up and right for a tree on the east face. From the tree, scramble straight up to the notch between a beehive on the east (left) and the main summit to the north. Another short pitch of scrambling reaches the end of roped climbing (if roped up). Walk to the summit. To stand on the highest point, find the tallest of the red boulders that liter the summit. It's on the left (west) just after reaching the summit. A boulder problem. A spot is recommended.

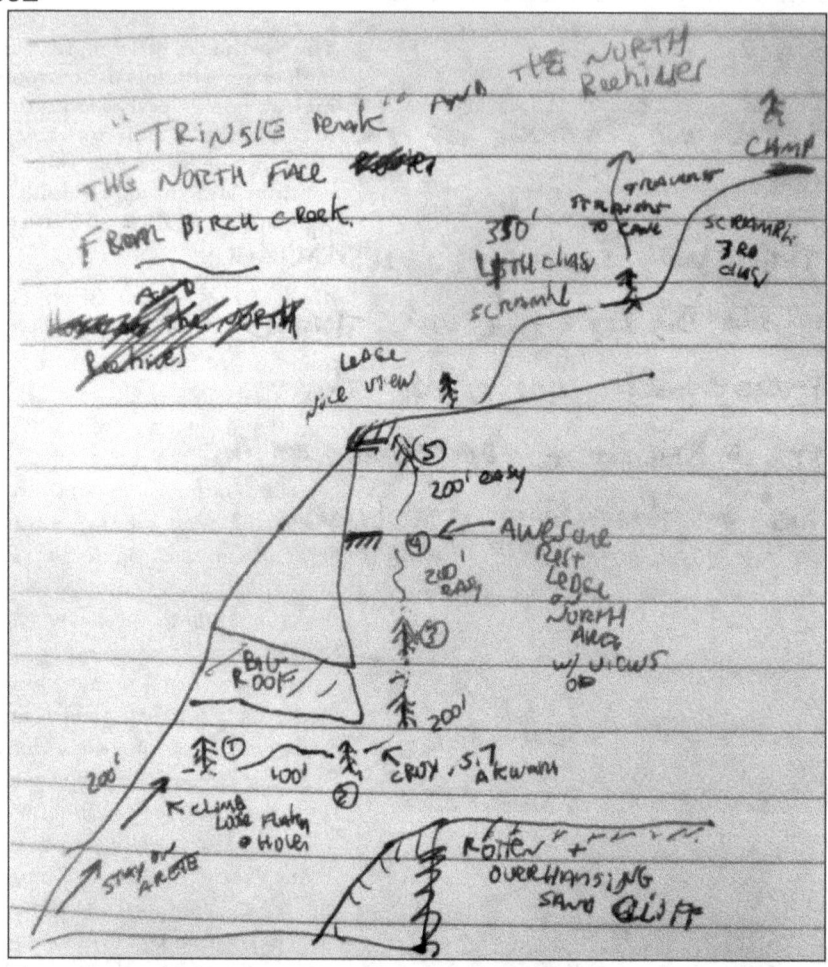

The route to a high camp on the north side of Triangle Peak, starting from Birch Creek, where Goose Canyon meets Birch Creek. It climbs the ridge on the left (east) side of Goose Creek.

GETTING DOWN (possible descent routes):

Climb up the NW Face of the Sentinel: The fastest way to exit may be to climb the NW face of the Sentinel and descend the 1938 route to the Sand Bench Trail. This is a difficult route that requires 5.11 runout face climbing. The crux is near the top. Only a few slings are required for protection, tied around small bushes. Make sure you are familiar with the descent, the 1938 Route. Climb and descend it on a pre-trip recon.

Descend to Birch Creek: If you started in Birch Creek and climbed the ridge leading up to Triangle Peak, descend that. If you have not climbed this ridge, and want to exit via Birch Creek, consider rappelling the drainage between the Sentinel and Triangle Peak. Stay in the drainage. Avoid going high on the ridge to the east which is a continuation of a ridge that comes down from the Sentinel, one that requires copious amounts of down-climbing and rappelling. Once in Birch Creek, hike to where it becomes a waterfall. Depending on your preference and if it's flowing, continue down the waterfall (it has big drops, the last in excess of 300 feet) or descend the Chipmunk Cliff route, which starts by hugging the south face of the SW corner of Abraham.

FUTURE CLIMBING Potential new routes to be climbed on Triangle Peak are as follows:

#1 The Saddle Route: Climb the NW corner of Triangle Peak from the saddle between Triangle Peak and Big Red. Get there by rappelling from the summit of Big Red. Rappel where the drainage on the east face of Big Red drains into the saddle OR by climbing Triangle Peak and descending (rappelling) the route. From the saddle, the first pitch appears gross, overhanging, undesirable. The first twenty feet may require aid. Higher, the main issue is loose rock. Consider leaving gear you don't need to climb (bivy gear) at the saddle, and returning to the saddle to descend Goose Canyon into Birch Creek when you are finished. Done this way, it's a classic and proper adventure.

#2 The North Face: Finish the route I started on the North Face. To get there, descend the NW Face of the Sentinel and traverse west, across slabs to the north side of Triangle Peak OR start in Birch Creek and climb up the ridge that runs north from Triangle Peak down into Birch Creek. From the bottom of the north face of the triangle, the first pitch is 100 feet up to a tree. From the tree, tip-toe left to a stance on a flake, then tension traverse around the corner. Around the corner it becomes loose and uncertain.

 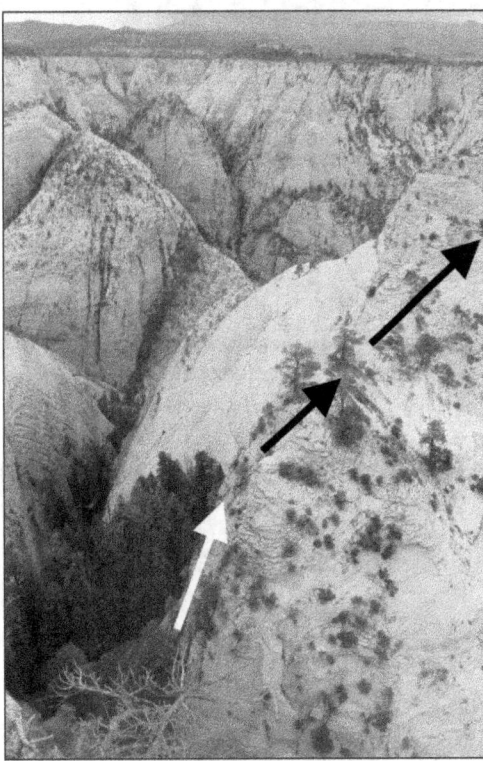

Left: the first pitch of the Saddle Route. Right: The Saddle Route as seen from the summit of Big Red.

Cat's Crown

INTRODUCTION Cats Crown lies at the western end of the valley between Gregory Butte and Timber Top Mountain. Technically it might be considered the west end of Gregory Butte. When looking at it from the La Verkin Creek Trail near Camp 2, it appears as a separate and distinct formation.

CLIMBING CAT'S CROWN

1. THE CAVE ROUTE 5.7+ *D Stih and M Dunn, 2025*
EQUIPMENT: Standard free rack.
WATER SOURCES: If it's rained within a few weeks, water might remain at the west end of the creek that runs along the north side of GB, just before scrambling up the final approach to route.
TIME REQUIRED: Best done as part of the Cat Walk - a traverse around the Gregory Butte massif. **THE ROUTE:** Scramble up the face, taking the easiest path into the cave. Exit the cave on the left, climb a wide crack/chimney feature, then traverse back right, to a tree above the cave. The next pitch goes up and right. It looks like a dead end. There are hidden cracks and holds near the end. It exits with a scramble. Continue by walking to a spot where the easiest way to continue is a short rappel off a bush on the south side of the ridge. Pull the rope. Scramble to the summit.

GETTING DOWN: Start walking back down, looking for a gap on the right. Scramble down to a tree. Rappel to another tree and then the ground. Two long rappels. Two 200-foot ropes.

Gabriel

The view from La Verkin Creek Trail, after leaving the trail head at Lee Pass.

INTRODUCTION Gabriel lies between Beatty Point to the south (left), and Nagunt Mesa to the north (right). To the immediate south is a smaller peak known a Icebox Knoll. In the first edition, I named this Peak 7410. That was based on its altitude. At the time, I asked the mountain what it wanted to be called. Nothing came to me. A few year later, when asking for beta about getting to Center Point and the North Eye, a climber asked why I had not given Peak 7410 a proper name. As I was telling the story of the Great White Throne, I remembered Nick had promised to name a peak after Gabriel. I now call this peak, Gabriel.

CLIMBING GABRIEL

1. WEST FACE C1+ OR 5.9+? *FKA D Stih 2020, roped solo*
EQUIPMENT REQUIRED: Standard free-rack. Two (2) 200-foot ropes are required to rappel the route from natural anchors. There are no bolts. Please don't add any.
CAMPING / TIME REQUIRED: I bivied on the large ledge with trees at the bottom of the last pitch, the technical crux. Just because I wanted to. It made for a fun trip.
STARTING POINT: Lee Pass.
THE ROUTE: 1) Climb two pitches up the west face to a pine tree. While this might be

The route. The dashed arrow on the right is the route up the neighboring peak, Icebox Knoll.

The last pitch on Gabriel. Climb the obvious right-leaning crack with the big cave at the top. From the cave it's a hike to the top. The ledge with the tree is huge and nice to bivy on.

mostly a scramble, I was rope-soloing and stuck to the crack system to ensure I could place protection. I thought the bottom was a mental crux due to the uncertainty of where the route goes and how to protect it. 2) From the pine tree, 3rd-class up a big chute to a big ledge on the north face. 3) Climb a right-leaning crack to a big cave. I found this easy to aid. There are good foot holds and a potential it can be freed. 4) From the cave, scramble to the top.

EXTRA CREDIT: If you have time, you may enjoy climbing Icebox Knoll, the peak to north. The route is indicated by the pink dashed arrow. It's a scramble.

FUTURE CLIMBING ON GABRIEL: An alternate route to explore. The crux appears to be climbing face in the middle section. I suspect the section too steep to free-climb, and without a crack to aid. However, I've learned until you come face-to-face with the rock, you never know how difficult a climb might be. High adventure and exposure!

Above: an alternate route to explore to climb Gabriel.

An old section of wire fencing found high on the hill side. Before Kolob Canyons became part of the national park, locals used the area to heard stock.

The east face of Gabriel as seen during my traverse of the Buck Pasture amphitheater. The climbing route starts on right skyline of the west (shaded) face. The bivy ledge with trees is visible, three-quarter up the skyline.

The Droids

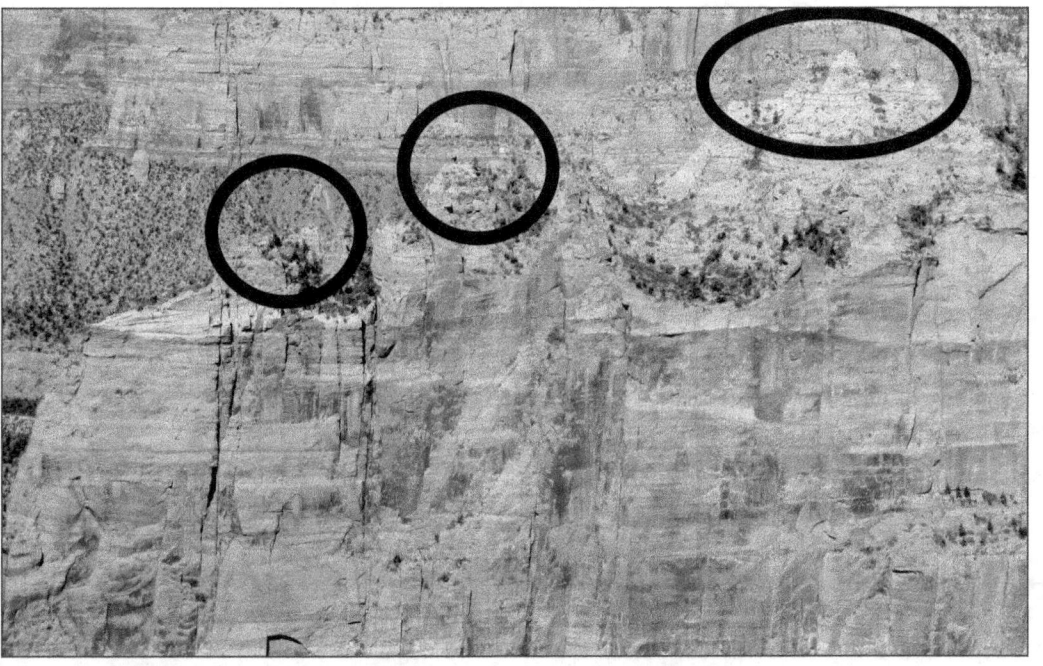

INTRODUCTION The Droids are a series of red hoodo-like formations on the finger that jets out from the western side of the Altar of Sacrifice into Coalpits Wash.

CLIMBING THE DROIDS

TRAVERSE OF THE DROIDS 5.5 *D Stih and M Dunn, April 2022.*
EQUIPMENT REQUIRED: If not a rope, rock climbing shoes will make it less intimidating. We left our gear on the approach to the Altar, thinking the Droids would be scrambles. As luck had it, the highest droid has the most exposure and requires careful down-climbing. As we approached it, it looked improbable and we wished we a rope.
THE STARTING POINT: Explore the Droids as part of the Traverse of the Towers of the Virgin on the way to climb the west side of the Altar of Sacrifice.

Other First Ascents

Clouds in a break in a rain storm on the West Rim Trail.

Nice Line

INTRODUCTION This is a two-pitch climb behind the restrooms at the parking lot / shuttle stop for the Narrows and Temple of Sinawava. If you need to go to the restrooms, they are heated, and only ten steps away.

No Waiting in Line

In 1994. as we drove through the parking lot at the Temple of Sinawava, I noticed what looked like a fun climb near the restrooms. The bottom looked like free-climbing, followed by aid climbing. The best of both worlds. It should have made myself (the free-climber) and Ron (the aid climber) happy. I parked the car, and ran up to get a closer look. I was delighted to see that it looked as if we might get some climbing done, instead of driving up and down the road for the hundredth time, looking for routes through a telescope.

The face at the bottom was blank, but I envisioned a way to protect it. I scrambled up the right side, thirty feet to a tree, clipped the rope around the tree, and went down. If I fell, the tree would shorten the fall. I carefully started to climb up the 5.10 face to reach the start of a crack. It was too difficult. I resorted to direct aid. After a few placements, I felt my job was done - I had climbed the free section. I came down to give the lead to Ron, the aid climber. Ron went up a little way and drilled a bolt. It was not for a belay. It was Sunday. We had to drive home to be at work on Monday morning.

The following weekend Ron spent with his girlfriend, so I drove to Zion by myself. I intended to go up the rope and climb higher. It's always warmer in Phoenix, Arizona, and I was wearing the shorts I had on when I left Arizona. As I got to Kanab, the last town before Zion, I realized it was too cold to climb in shorts. It was dark and getting late. Kanab was my last chance to find a pair of pants or anything warm to climb in (There weren't any outdoor clothing stores in Springdale/Zion in the 90s). The Levi's store was closed. I pulled into a local grocery, relived to find it was open. *Surely, I can find something to wear in there*, I thought.

The only thing I found were pantyhose. I recalled that in the 1980s they wore lycra and spandex when climbing. It seemed to me that pantyhose was similar. I bought two pairs of the largest size, thinking wearing two would be more durable.

I finished the drive to Zion, slept in my car, got up in the morning, and walked towards the bottom of the climb. On the way, I stopped in the restroom to put the pantyhose on. Immediately I got a run. I put my shorts over the hose and walked outside to test how warm they were.

Not very. *It's freezing*, I thought. *This is not going to work*. I got in the car and drove back to Phoenix.

The following weekend I returned with Ron. This time I bought warm pants. Ron went up to the high point. This is where a big argument occurred over my disappointment in our climbing styles. (In Ron's defense, his attitude is shared by a lot of climbers - they see nothing wrong with drilling bolts). As a team, I would have come to terms with this attitude, and understand that it did not matter who did what or how.

"What are you doing?" I yelled up to him from below.

"Drilling!"

"Why!?"

"There's no place to put gear."

"Nail a piton into that crack!"

"I am afraid that might cause a chunk of rock come loose. It could fall and hit the restrooms."

After more bickering I gave in. Maybe he was right. I couldn't be sure that rock fall would hit the restrooms if it came down. I am sure I can be stubborn. The last half of our argument was my ego making it clear I was unhappy with the number of bolts he was placing.

Dan on the first pitch.

Our lifestyle was one of constantly driving back and forth in order to keep jobs in Phoenix, Arizona. When Ron reached the top of the pitch, he came down. He left with a rope attached to the belay, waiting for us to come back.

We returned two weeks later. As I approached the rope, I noticed a note curled up, like a miniature scroll, tucked into a hole in the rock at the bottom of the climb.

"Look," I said to Ron, "Someone left us a note."

"What's it say?"

I read the note out loud:

Nice line. Where does it go?
If you must bolt, please camouflage your bolts.
No hard feelings. Come by the Bit and Spur later and we can talk.
- Conrad Anker

We knew who Conrad Anker was. He wasn't yet the Capitan of the North Face climbing team. There wasn't yet a North Face climbing team. Conrad was

Ron, on the second pitch.

living in Salt Lake City, and like us, came to Zion to look for new routes.

We were not familiar with the Bit and Spur. We didn't eat in restaurants when we came to Zion. Dinner was what was whatever we found at the last gas station we had stopped at. We didn't have smart phones and didn't know where it was located. .

I went up to our high point where I climbed a series of roofs, up to where the crack ends. There, I realized what Conrad meant. The crack ran out. There was nothing but a blank face.

When I had first noticed the climb, I imagined I might be able to use hooks to scale the upper section. Now, face-to-face with the nothingness, I had my doubts. I set an anchor for a belay for Ron to come up to meet me.

When Ron got to the belay, I started climbing before he could talk. I did not want him telling me there was no place to go. I became a tyrant. It was my route, and I had a plan. Or so I thought. I clipped my foot ladder into the belay anchor we were hanging, and carefully worked my feet up in the rungs until they were in the top step. It was awkward. I tried to not fall backwards.

"Nope, can't free-climb it," I said. "I'll use hooks."

I had an assortment of hooks. *Surely*, I thought, *one of these will fit onto one of the small flakes of rock on the face.* I picked one and set it onto a flake. As I put my weight onto it, the hook slid off. The flake was too small and sloping. (I didn't realize a Yosemite climber might have used a chisel to enhance the rock, and cut an edge large enough for the hook to sit securely. I didn't have a chisel. If I had I wouldn't have used it. I prefer to climb a mountain - not alter it to suit my desires.)

I placed another hook. This one I thought would be good. But I had forgotten how fragile sandstone can be. The rock crumbed and I fell. Frustrated, I gave up. We rappelled to the ground and left the rope hanging. I didn't know how were going to finish the climb.

A few weeks later, we came back to take our rope down. Something looked different. I couldn't tell what. I started going up the rope, trailing a second rope to use to for rappelling. As I ascended the rope, I noticed it twenty feet before I reached it: 150 feet off the ground, the rope was coming apart, almost completely torn in two. It was not the rope we had left.

I had two choices: continue going and get past the bad spot in the rope, or go down, yo-yoing on the rope, and spending more time on a bad rope than if I continued upward. I decided to continue. It was all I could do to not think about the rope breaking. I slid my jumars up over the frayed section, holding my breath, and reached the high anchor.

We gave up on finding a way to finish the route. There's no shame in having a route that does not go to the top. Desert Shield is an example of a route that does not go to the top. There are tons of routes on the Apron in Yosemite that do not go to the top. We pulled the ropes and left the route as it is, a fun and moderate free/aid climb. Maybe you can make it to the top. If you do, feel free to give the route a new name, perhaps "It Goes."

CLIMBING "NICE LINE"

1. NICE LINE A2+, 5.10
D Stih and R Raimonde 1994

THE ROUTE Scramble up and right on a ramp towards a tree. Half-way up the ramp, look for a bolt on the face to the left. Clip the bolt and carefully climb the face sideways (5.10) left and then up to the bottom of a crack that is aided (A1+) to a bolt, an intermediate belay. Don't belay there. Haul the aid rack and continue up to a bolted belay. The next pitch goes up and around a series of small roofs (A2+) to a bolted belay at the end of the crack. That's the end of the line. Rap the route. It's 220 feet to the ground.

EQUIPMENT REQUIRED: Aid rack. Hangers for 3/8" bolts.

FUTURE CLIMBING The last (unfinished) pitch could be made a sport route by rap-bolting it. I think the route can be finished by climbing up the large crack on the left side of the route, and then climbing up the west (right) face at the top, from which the normal finish to the route could be rap-bolted.

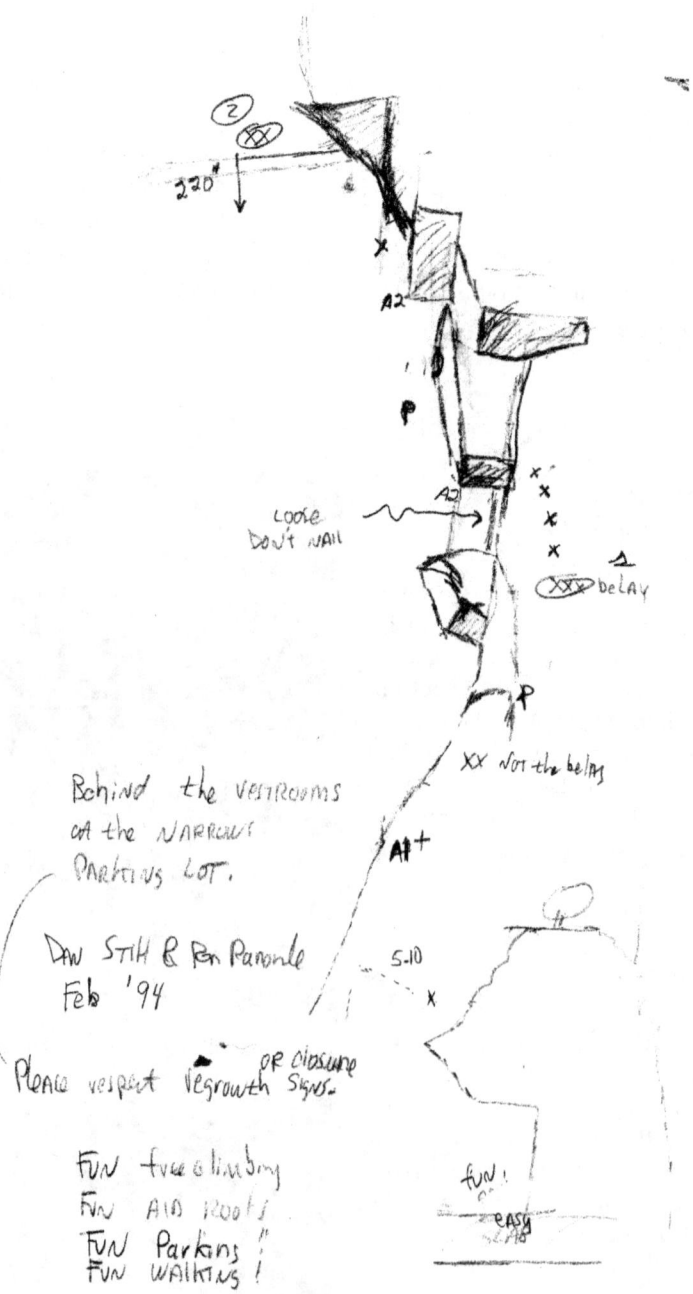

The East Temple Direct

HISTORY It's always been about tourism. The State of Utah began to promote Southern Utah as a scenic destination in the early 1900s. The area was set aside as a national monument in 1909, and became a national park in 1919. The canyon road was extended to the Temple of the Sinawava for access to the Narrows in 1925. The same year, the Gateway to the Narrows, Lady Mountain Trail, and The West Rim trails were built. The Zion lodge was built in 1925. In order to bring more people into the park, construction began on the east tunnel in 1927. Rock climbing is said to have come to Zion in 1931, with the first recorded ascent of the Great White Throne. The West Temple was climbed in 1933, the East Temple in 1937, and the Sentinel in 1938.

In 1997, Ron suggested we climb the East Temple. The guidebook at that time listed only climbing routes on the bottom half of the East Temple. There was no information as to where the 1937 route might be. After scrambling up the approach slabs, we began climbing straight up the easiest way we could find. I think if we had continued around the corner we would have found the 1937 route. Instead, being strong, I just headed up what I thought would get us to the top. It was difficult (5.10+R). I came to a spot where the only way to continue was to use tension. I placed a knife blade piton, clipped my rope into it, and did what's called a tension traverse. I kept my weight on the rope, as Ron slowly let rope out, and I moved sideways to easier ground. We left the piton in place for others to use. We then climbed straight up, pawing at completely blank and unprotected face. We weren't carrying a bolt kit. Why would we be? If we couldn't have climbed it we would have come down and looked for another way.

Modern climbers (in the 2000s) placed bolts on the 1937 climbing route. I don't know why. Modern climbers have better ropes and technology than climbers in the 1930s did.

The State of Utah continues to partner with the federal government to promote Zion National Park. It and the Mormon Temple in Salt Lake City are the state's top two tourist attractions.

The approach from the Overlook Trail.

FUTURE CLIMBING I speculate future climbers will create a new sport that involves removing bolts placed by modern climbers. This could be done for the original routes on the East Temple and West Temple, restoring historical climbing routes and mountains to their original conditions, so that climbers can experience how climbing these mountains originally felt.

CLIMBING THE EAST TEMPLE

SEASON: We climbed in October when weather was perfect for a long day without the need to carry an excessive amount of water. Spring might be pleasant if the snow has melted and the rock is dry.

TIME REQUIRED: A long day, round-trip from the parking lot.

STARTING POINT: Park at the Canyon Overlook Trail parking lot on the east side of the entrance to the big tunnel. Hike the Overlook Trail. At the end of the trail, hop over the fence and hike north, then northwest, up steep slabs toward the south side of the East Temple. As you get close to the mountain, traverse left (west) along the bottom. When it appears you will have to lose altitude to continue, look for the start of the Direct Route. If you are interested in climbing the 1937 route, continue around the corner, losing elevation.

1. THE 1937 ROUTE *A Sierra Group led by Glen Dawson?*

The original 1937 route is around the corner from the Direct Route. In *Zion National Parks: Summit Routes*, the author writes, "Scramble to the top of a huge "V" feature, then to drop a bit." Gain a steep chute on the other side of the V, and go to the hoo doos (circled). The normal 1937 route, and a variation of it called the Casual Route, list the required gear as two 60m ropes, several long slings, carabiners, and a set of quick draws to clip bolts.

2. THE EAST TEMPLE DIRECT, 5.9+ R III AKA THE RIDGE ROUTE
D Stih and R Raimonde 1997

Ron and I didn't want to lose elevation, and started climbing straight up once we had traversed across the bottom of the mountain from the Overlook Trial. Our Direct Route climbs straight up a loose crack with bushes until it becomes impossible to climb higher. From that point, I traversed across a delicate and blank face, leaving a fixed knife-blade in the middle of the traverse. I used the piton for tension, as I went sideways to easier ground. From there, we stepped around a corner (like a ridge) and continued straight up on steep and blank face, to the plateau on which the summit cap sits.

I remember the route being run out, and the protection on the relentless and steep slabs, limited to slings around bushes. Although I marked in my journal 5.9+, it may be 5.10 and possibly X instead of R, depending on your luck and skill with slings around bushes.

When Ron and I reached the base of the summit cap, I got impatient. The guidebook printed in 2009 says "Continue east on the

Left (dashed) arrow goes up standard route. Right arrows (solid) are the direct "ridge route"

Circled are the hoodoos encountered if you pass up the Direct route and continue to the normal (1937) route. Bottom: Ron on the summit; Opposite top: The route we took is marked in (blue) marker. The normal route is marked with (pink) arrows. Opposite page bottom: The first pitch of the route we took. In the middle of the traverse we left a fixed knife-blade piton. Below right: The left arrow goes up slab and around the corner to the "Casual Route"; The right arrow is our "Direct route" that gains up the ridge.

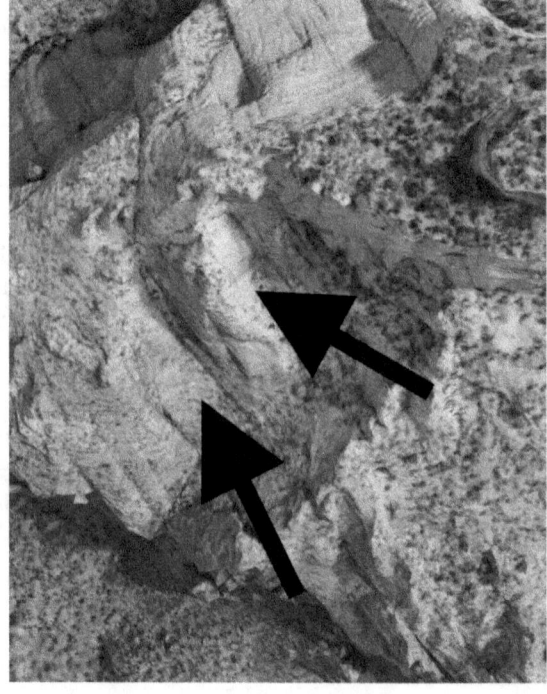

The "East Temple"
5.9+R III
Oct '97

Starts at trail before tunnel. Scramble from E to W along base. Then chimneys difficult face climbing for several pitches

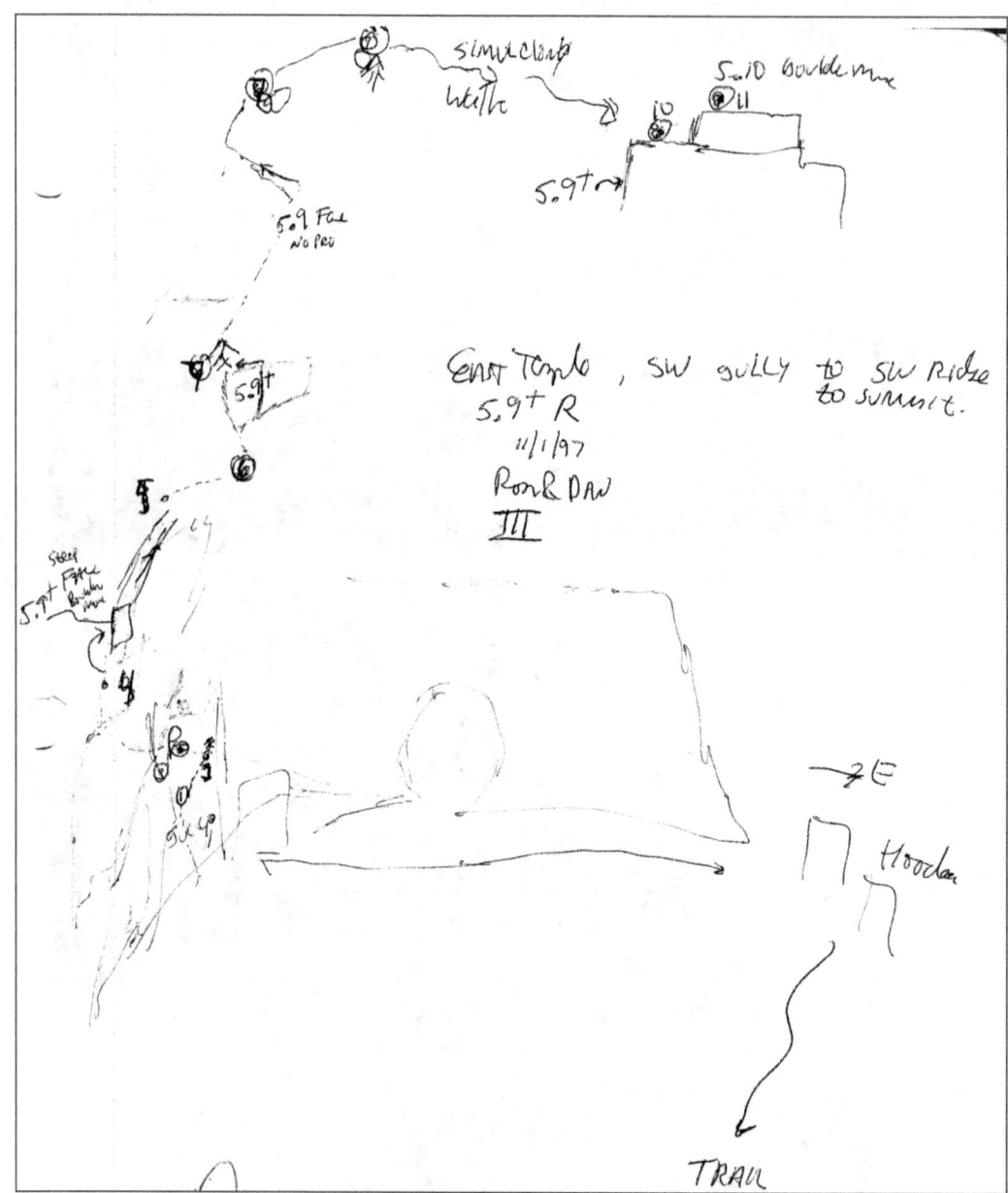

My original drawing of the topo for the Direct Route on the East Temple.

north side, through a beautiful patch of ponderosa, to a low-angle ramp that breaks though the summit cap." Ron and I walked a short way, didn't see an easy way, picked a crack, and just climbed up it. It was wide and overhanging. From the summit, we reversed our route and rappelled off trees and bushes.

Several years later, I tried to repeat our route with the idea to do a traverse of other mountains in the area. I met a climber where I was living in Prescott,

Bridge Mountain viewed from our route on the East Temple. B/W print film. Below: View of The Court of the Patriarchs.

Arizona. He was a guide working for the local college, teaching rock climbing. He seemed capable and strong. He started to complain after we left the Overlook Trail as we were hiking to the bottom of the East Temple. I was moving fast. He complained about heart rate. He said at the rate we were going we'd be out of breath (he was) and that we needed to slow down. I was going fast because I was scared. I was worried I wouldn't be able to keep up with him! He was a guide, and getting out on a regular basis. I was a couch potato, working as a handyman. I might have started like a race horse a bit fast out of the gate.

When we reached the bottom the Direct Route, I was scared. I struggled up the bottom part. As I got to where I needed to begin steeping sideways across the blank face to reach the fixed knife blade piton, he panicked. As I tried to find a place to put my feet, he screamed from below, yelling what I was doing was not OK, and that if I fell, I would pull out all my protection and the belay. His concern and worry caused me to become concerned. I was already having a difficult time. He wasn't sending encouragement. I decided to come down. I lowered off a bush. You might find a sling.

The Sentinel - The North Face

INTRODUCTION This is a ridge that comes down from the NW corner of the Sentinel into Birch Creek. To the north-east (on the west side of the Red Sentinel) are Sentinel Canyon and Princess Spire; to the west is Triangle Peak. **HISTORY** On a visit to Zion in 2019, hanging at the coffee shop and chatting with local climbers, someone mentioned the idea: "Why not climb the Sentinel, go down the other side into Birch Creek, and climb everything around Birch Creek once you get there?" It's a creative idea, one Ron and I attempted in spring of 1998. Ron suggested we climb the 1938 route on the Sentinel, go down the other side, and fix ropes at the top of the Birch Creek waterfall. That would allow us to come back and climb everything at our convenience. We climbed the 1938 route and went down the other side, to the waterfall at the end of Birch Creek. When our ropes did not reach the ground in the Court of the Patriarchs, we were faced with a dilemma - wait for a rescue or try to climb back up the north face of the Sentinel. We choose to climb. We didn't have rock shoes, pitons, bolts, or a drill. I was wearing stiff mountain boots.

We did the second ascent of the north face during our Traverse of the Court of the Patriarchs. We had pitons then, and I placed (and left) a lost arrow at the first crux. This reduces the commitment from X (death) to R (runout), depending on if the piton, a down-ward facing lost arrow in a shallow crack, holds. Please leave it.

1938 in 1998

The Sentinel was first climbed in 1938. Therefore, we expected it would be easy. (Rumor has it the 1938 route was bolted in the 2000's by climbers who thought they were off-route.) I wore the boots I wear in the Alps for climbing ice. We didn't take a drill, nor a hammer or pitons. We took three ropes. We expected that to be enough to reach the ground in the back of the Court of the Patriarchs.

The mountain boots I wore to climb the 1938 Route and then the NW face of the Sentinel.

Although word is that the Sentinel was first climbed in 1938, that's all we knew. There is no known record of the route taken by the climbers. Ron and I assumed the easiest way would be to zig-zag up big ledges with bushes and trees on the east face. It started to rain as we were in the middle of the mountain. As the rain came down harder we paused, wondering if we should stop and turn around. After standing in the rain for twenty minutes, the rain seemed to not be getting worse, so we continued.

The most difficult section is three-quarters up when you come to a what appears to be a dead end. The key is to go sideways, out onto a blank face, then climb up once around the corner. (Sometime after approximately 2010, climbers placed two bolts on a variation to the left. I was told they thought rock fall must have destroyed the original route and therefore they had to do what they did. They are mistaken). Once committed and around the corner,

Left: The crux on the 1938 route. Starting from the lower left, one comes to a dead end at a corner. To continue, go sideways right. It takes commitment to turn the corner and continue higher once hanging on the face around the corner. Alternatively, climb the variation to the left where two bolts were added by climbers who thought they were off route. Right: On the summit after climbing the 1938 route in the rain, wearing mountain boots, in nylon pants.

there are thin holds and sloping feet. You're not sure if it's the right way to go. The drama only lasts for ten feet. Then you grab bigger holds, get protection, and the angle lessons. It's fun - if you're a climber.

From the top of Sentinel, we went down the other side, smooth, white sandstone. Where there were no bushes to use as rappel anchors, we down-climbed by the seat of our pants. We kept a short section of rope tied between us in case the other fell. It started to snow as we were half-way down. We reached a flat section with a cave. Since it was getting late, we went into the cave. I didn't have a sleeping bag. I laid in the dirt.

The next day, we finished rappelling and down-climbing to Birch Creek. There we stood at the edge, where Birch Creek turns into a waterfall. Our motive had been to fix ropes down the waterfall. We were expecting it to be dry, as the desert usually is. It was not. It was Spring, and water was flowing. But it wasn't water that stopped us from going down it. We didn't have enough rope. We had three ropes, a total of 450 feet. We needed 700 - 800 feet to reach the ground.

As the ropes did not reach the ground, we were faced with a dilemma - how to get down. We had rappelled nearly a thousand feet down the back, NW face of the Sentinel, and weren't planning on climbing back up it. We

The Sentinel (left) with the NW ridge coming down. We bivied in the cave-like, overhanging section of red rock in the center right (the east face of Triangle Peak).

didn't have rock shoes or much climbing gear of any sort other than slings.

We discussed our options. We could try to climb back up or wait for a rescue. We couldn't call for help. We didn't have a cell phone. It might have been a long time before Ron's girlfriend reported him overdue and a search was initiated. We decided to try and climb back up it.

We scrambled a few hundred until we were stopped by the first obstacle - a blank, smooth face. I climbed onto a pedestal to get a better look.

"Can you climb that?" Ron asked.

I didn't know so I ignored him. I believe in the power of the spoken word. If I said "No," it would mean that we would have to wait for a rescue. I didn't want to say anything until I was certain.

We had been climbing long enough together that Ron knew if I didn't answer I was assessing things. He knew there was hope, and looked for something to anchor himself to in case I decided to start moving. He found a small bush, sat down, and tied himself to it. The bush, if it didn't pull out, would keep Ron from being pulled over the edge. If I fell, I'd go over the edge.

I began on top of a pedestal of rock, high above Ron. The rope was not clipped into anything in between us. Standing on my tiptoes, I felt above my head for a hand hold. I found one. It was small. After ten minutes of looking, I

The route up the north-west face of the Sentinel, starting from Birch Creek. Circled is the first crux. The second crux is at the top of the highest arrow, just below the summit.

The crux on the lower half of the route is climbing a blank section of face off a flat pedestal with bushes. In the background is the top of Princess Spire.

concluded t it was the only one I would get. I gripped it tight and pulled myself up to get a better look at what was above, moving my feet onto the face.

I was on the rock. But I couldn't see what was above my head. I couldn't tell how hard the climbing might be, or if it was possible. From where I was standing, if I fell, it would be long and bad fall. If I survived I might not live to see the rescue. I could not feel or see holds for my fingers or boots above my head. I remembered something a climber taught me when I was a teenager - speed is safety. Make up your mind and do what you decide. Don't linger. The longer you stay in one place, the more tired your arms and fingers become. If you stop moving you will fall. If decide to come down you'll be too tired to climb down. It's better to give yourself a chance and come down or go for it.

In a moment, something other than my brain made the decision. Perhaps it cells in my body that did not want to perish as my mind tried to figure out what to do. I found myself moving, upward, without thinking, without knowing what I was putting feet on, without apparent hand holds. I pawed the rock like a kitty cat, and just kept moving my feet. I'm sure my guardian angel and a few helpers were giving me a boost. A psychic once told me, "In that case (the kind of dire straits I was in) he (your guardian angel) calls for re-enforcements."

The upper section of the NW face of the Sentinel. The crux is at near the top, just below the summit.

That wasn't the end of the difficulties. The hardest part is a few feet from the top - another blank section. At that point I wasn't scared. My heart beat had returned to normal. I was cautious and careful, and moved slowly and deliberate. There was a key element that may be missing - a dead tree branch laying on the rock sideways, a few feet above my head. I reached the branch on my tip toes (I am 6"2') and carefully used it for balance, as I walked my feet up to reach a better hold. The climbing was 5.11 face. The last piece of protection was a sling around a small, dry bush, fifty feet below. From the top of the Sentinel, it was piece of cake to go down the 1938 route. We retraced our steps and arrived at my van at 9pm, a few minutes after dark.

CLIMBING THE NORTH FACE OF THE SENTINEL

NORTH-WEST FACE 5.11 X *D Stih and R Raimonde 1998*
April 25-26. One bivy. Without sleeping bags.
EQUIPMENT REQUIRED: We used only 4 long slings to protect the entire ascent, strapped around small bushes into which the rope was clipped.
WATER SOURCES: Birch Creek always has water.
THE STARTING POINT: Birch Creek. One way to get there is to climb the 1938 Route on the Sentinel, and rappel and down-climb the NW face. It's mandatory to down-climb sections where there are no natural anchors. Have a partner who is proficient in simul-down-climbing. The other approach is from Phantom Valley, going past Battleship Rock, to Abraham Canyon, and down to Birch Creek.
THE ROUTE: From near the waterfall at the top of Birch Creek, scramble south up a loose dirt hill to a broken ridge of red rock. Climb half-way up the ridge to the first crux. This is just past a rest spot, a large flat ledge on which to belay. The crux is a few feet off the ledge, where the angle steepens and the face above is not visible. Clip the fixed lost arrow. It's the best possible placement. Think carefully before committing. After a few desperate moves, the angle lessens, and the climbing becomes easier. A few hundred feet of scrambling reaches the middle section, a flat mesa. From there walk to the upper section. As you walk towards the Sentinel, on the west face of Triangle Peak is a large cave that can be used for shelter if you need to bivy. Climb the upper section by taking the path of least resistance. Do to expect to find bushes or means to set belays. The crux (5.11) is 100 feet below the top, a blank face that requires delicate and deliberate foot placements for balance, far above the last bush slung for protection.
GETTING DOWN: Descend the 1938 route to the Sand Bench Trail. It's recommended to climb the 1938 route before attempting the NW Face of the Sentinel to become familiar with the descent. It traverses and zig-zags. If you go straight down the east face, expect to get lost and to have a long and epic descent.
Alternative Exits: If you cannot climb the NW Face of the Sentinel, the alternative exit is to go down to Birch Creek. Once there, rather than go down the water fall (dry in the fall) I suggest the rappel route next to the SW face of Abraham (The Squirrel Route). It's the shortest to the ground with the least number of big drops.

It may be possible to escape the area of Birch Creek by climbing Nipples Peak (the peak on the north side of Birch Creek, and west of Abraham). Follow the top of it north, then drop into Abraham Canyon. Say high on the upper Nipple Peak as far north as possible before descending. If you come down too soon you will end up in Abraham Canyon too early, and below drops that are not possible to climb out of. From the summit of Nipples, aim for the saddle between Church Mesa and Battleship Rock. From the NW side of Battleship Rock, scramble down into Phantom Valley. From Phantom Valley, hike west towards the Inclined Temple, then south through the pass between the Sanctuary and Inclined Temple. Head towards the Bishoprics. Finish by exiting towards Cougar Mountain and hiking to Kolob Terrace road. This is long end epic. If I got to Phantom Valley I might ask for a rescue by friends. Tell them bring a 70-foot static rope that's beefy (11-mil) and a 300-foot 8-mil static. They can fix these down the normal rappel off the West Rim for the start to Heaps Canyon. The 70-foot piece should be used at the top. From the bottom of the first rappel, they should scramble down to another tree where the 300-foot can be fixed.

Jacob - The North Face

NORTH FACE 5.10+ OR 5.11- *D Stih and R Raimonde March, 1999*
It's difficult to get to the top of Jacob. We took the easiest way. Two pitches, it has it all: difficult hand and finger cracks, and a chimney.
EQUIPMENT REQUIRED: Traditional free-climbing rack and climbing shoes.
1 of each cam sizes #0.5, 1, 2
2 of each cam size #3 (2 -3")
Small aliens (micro cams), i.e., two each sizes 3/8" and 1/2"
CAMPING / TIME REQUIRED: Unless you are doing it as part of the traverse around the Court of the Patriarchs, this is a day climb.
STARTING POINT: Hike Old Lady Mountain Trail to the saddle between the north side of Jacob and Lady Mountain. At the saddle, look for the easiest way to climb Jacob.
THE ROUTE: The first pitch climbs up to a pedestal where a belay is set. The crux is a few feet off the belay, a small crack. I stuffed my toe inside it and stood on one toe in order to reach my fingers higher into the crack. It was a desperate balancing act. I was trying so hard not fall, the ink used to dye my leather climbing shoes left

marks inside the crack. Higher up, the route goes up to an over-hanging, roof-like section that is turned on the right. Although it's wide and awkward, there are good hand and foot holds, and it's easier to continue to the top than to stop and place gear. If you stop to place gear you may need a few large pieces, i.e., #4 and #5 cams. If you can free-climb the crux lower down, it's likely you're a good enough climber you won't need the bigger gear.

GETTING DOWN: From the summit, rappel the route back to the saddle and hike down the Old Lady Mountain Trail.

Isaac - The North Face

HISTORY In the 1974 *American Alpine Journal*, George Lowe (not related to Jeff Lowe) wrote the following:

> *Isaac, South Face, Court of the Patriarchs, Zion.* Over the Memorial Day weekend, Jeff Lowe and I climbed the crack system which follows the east side of the south face of Isaac. Two dirty, bushy pitches marred the otherwise clean route. Descent was via a long ledge system, where we traversed north into the canyon east of Isaac and then down the canyon. NCCS V, F9, A3.

This was likely the first ascent of Isaac, and the first descent of what modern canyoneers are calling Jacob Canyon. Modern guidebooks incorrectly give credit to other climbers for doing the first ascent of Isaac in 1993. One of these climbers is said to have said that Lowe was mistaken, and that he climbed a different mountain. Lowe has since admitted to having confused Abraham with Isaac, due to a road sign in the park that listed them in reverse order. However, based on the description for the route and descent, he ultimately appears to have reported the information correctly.

In March, 1999, Ron Raimonde and I did the first ascent of the North Face of Isaac during our traverse around the Court of the Patriarchs. To reach Isaac, we did a descent into Jacob Canyon from the west side of the saddle between Jacob and Lady Mountain. After climbing the north face of Isaac, we went north, doing the first ascent of what is, on early maps of Zion National Park, labeled as Cliff Dwelling Mnt.

CLIMBING THE NORTH FACE OF ISAAC

THE NORTH FACE *D Stih and R Raimonde 1999*
EQUIPMENT REQUIRED: Slings. Two 150-foot ropes.
WATER SOURCES: Isaac Canyon.
SEASON: Spring or Fall. We went the last week of March, and had no trouble staying out of water and avoiding pools. If you finish by exiting down Jacob Canyon. Information on canyoneeringusa.com states: "It does not hold water. Wetsuits are not required." Winter is harsh and icy. Fall may be perfect, but unless it rains a few days before your trip, there is the possibility you won't find water to drink.
CAMPING / TIME REQUIRED: This could be a fun day-outing for those who are only interested in climbing Isaac. A canyoneer with an alpine rack could attempt a one-day ascent/descent, and not need to carry additional gear than what's required to do the descent of the canyon. It would be best to do a day trip in the summer, when there are long hours of daylight and warmer temperatures in case of a forced bivy.
STARTING POINT: Start across from the Zion Lodge. Hike the Old Lady Mountain Trail to the saddle between the north side of Jacob and Lady Mnt. The trail is officially closed. There are sections of 5th class. Constructed in 1925, it was most technical climb in the

Our route on the north face of Isaac.

On the summit of Isaac, during our traverse of the Court of the Patriarchs in 1999. Note the 9-millimeter, 150-foot rope on my back. In order to go light, it was our lead line. We supplemented it with a 7-mil static for long rappels.

park at the time. The first fatality was in 1930. It was closed in the 1960s. From the saddle, scramble down the other side (west, towards Jacob Canyon) until you reach a cliff where it's impossible to go further without rappelling. We wrapped our ropes around a big tree and rappelled into the canyon. At the end of our ropes we drilled a bolted rappel station (fixed angles). One more rappel (hanging rap station) reaches the bottom of the canyon. Once in the canyon, we hiked south towards Isaac, until we reached a drainage that comes down from the north side of Isaac. We filled our bottles, left Isaac canyon, and headed up to north side of Isaac.

THE ROUTE: From the bottom of Isaac, we climbed the NW face, simul-climbing (climbing at the same time). We kept a rope tied between us in case the other fell. I was impressed with Ron's free climbing. He was primarily an aid climber and typically I led the harder free-climbing pitches. I could barely keep up with him, as I tried to not trip on the slack. To get down, we reversed our route and down-climbed.

DESCENT: Go back into Jacob Canyon and follow the canyon to a drop into the Court of the Patriarchs. See Tom Jone's *Zion: Canyoneering* guidebook and information on Canyoneering sites for information on the canyon descent.

Good Times on the West Temple

Above: Parking on the side of a dirt road in Springdale to go on a 4-hour ascent of the West Temple. Left: Ron on the West Temple.

In February, 1998, Ron and I climbed the West Temple in the fashion we had climbed the East Temple. Before there were guidebooks, internet, and bolts, knowing only the mountain had been climbed, we set off from the Jolly-Rodger Cemetery. After trudging up the steep talus slopes to the bottom of its west face, we climbed straight up in order to reach the ridge that is normally reached via a long traverse. The route I took us up is at least 5.10. Ron kept complaining, telling me to take the easi-

est way. I just wanted to make sure we got to the top. Modern topos show an easier route, one that traverses the mountain sideways.

When we got to the last bit below the summit, we protected it with cams in a crack left of where there are now bolts. Someone has since added bolts to the 5.6 crux near the top. Today it's rated 5.8 on the internet. It's not that hard. I suspect future climbers will remove the bolts and restore the mountain to its original condition. The crack next to bolts takes gear.

The modern and normal (solid arrows) way to climb the West Temple starts from the Anazazi Trail in a residential area to the south, and traverses up the face in a diagonal, taking the easiest way. Ron and I started at the cemetery (dashed lines). I don't recall our exact line. We took the most direct course possible, preferring not to lose elevation. From the top of the drainage behind the cemetery, we hiked up the most direct path to the base of the wall. Upon reaching the wall we climbed a direct line to access the ridge, intercepting the normal route somewhere north of the notch.

The old log book, a glass jar, can be found inside the modern plastic log box on the summit.

Zion

DON'T JUMP!

At 7,810 feet, the West Temple is the highest peak in Zion National Park. Its north aspect has a spot with a sheer drop of almost 2,000 feet, terminating in the open expanse of Oak Creek canyon. In March, 2014, an experienced BASE jumper arrived in Zion. When he reached the top, he figured he was at the place to jump. [Dangerous Dan does not jump and does not condone base-jumping. His motto is why jump off a perfectly good mountain.] It's likely he had not climbed the West Temple before. The highest point does not have the biggest drop. A series of shorter peaks connect to the West Temple at that point: the Three Marys. To get the 2,000 feet of clearance, he needed to hike down the other side, almost to where it is not possible to continue further. The jumper leaped from the worst place possible. As soon as he jumped he probably saw the ground. There was no time to deploy his chute.

Cathedral Mountain
Iron Curtain 5.10 A2+

INTRODUCTION On July 25, 1931, despite the heat, Ronald C. Orcutt, tried to climb Cathedral Mountain. He had just completed the second ascent of the Great White Throne. When he didn't return by dinner, the trail crew went on a search and found his body. To carry the body out and down the canyon required placing ropes with drops as big as sixty feet (*Death, Daring and Disaster*, p. 112).

In 2017, after telling him about my traverse of the mountains surrounding the Emerald Pools, CP, author of one of the guidebooks, asked why I had not included Cathedral Mountain and Mt. Majestic. The only thing he was not certain about was the white face near the top of Cathedral Mountain. I looked at the face on a satellite image and confidently said, "I can climb that!" My younger brother wasn't so sure. He said it looked terrifying.

Behunin Canyon is the normal place to start the traverse around the Emerald Pools. Starting with Castle Dome (from Behunin Canyon) it is a fun adventure that requires minimal gear. Instead of repeating the route I established on Cathedral Mountain, future parties doing the traverse around the Emerald Pools may wish to start in Behunin Canyon as normal. Leave packs and gear near the bottom of Behunin Ridge, scramble to the summits of Mt. Majestic and Cathedral Mountain, then return to Behunin Canyon to finish the rest of the traverse (see the chapter on traverses for details). That way you won't have to carry a large rack or worry about not having enough water while climbing Cathedral Mountain.

Mold Mouth

I drove through the night and arrived in Zion at 5am. I parked at Flanagan's and slept in the back of my Jeep. The restaurant opened for breakfast at 7am. I had breakfast there. I therefore didn't get to the backcountry office until 8am.

It took me a long time to get a permit. It was a busy weekend. Add to that the day before the rangers had not given out any permits because of rain. Everyone had to come back.

After getting a permit, I waited in line for the shuttle. It was noon when I got off the shuttle at the Grotto.

I expected the climb to take two days. Therefore, I left with only two liters of water. I couldn't carry any more, as I was carrying two ropes, a rack of climbing gear, a sleeping bag, and a stove. I hiked the West Rim Trail, the one people normally take to get to the top of Angels Landing, and left the trail at the start of Walter's Wiggles, where I scrambled down into Refrigerator Canyon. From there I tried to find a way to climb out onto the other side. It was difficult. The rock was loose, steep and treacherous. It might not be difficult for a hiker. I was carrying a heavy pack.

Once I got on the ridge, it seemed like I might be going the wrong way. It took me all day to get the base of my climb. When I got to there, I found myself looking directly across at hikers on top of Angels Landing.

At a garage sale, I had purchased a used Jet Boil stove. I thought I'd use it to

Top left: the bottom of Walter's Wiggles on the way to Angels Landing. I left the trail there, went down, crossed over the canyon, and climbed up the other side. Right: The cliffs that must be negotiated to get out of Refrigerator Canyon and onto the ridge leading up the start of the climb.

make coffee and eat dehydrated food. It was an all-in-one design. The cup attaches to the burner. I had to lite the stove, then attach the cup. Only the newer models have an ignition switch that allows the cup to be attached *before* lighting the stove.

After I lit the stove, I found I had not turned the flame down far enough before attempting to attach the cup. As I tried to attach the cup to the stove, the fabric insulating the outside of the cup burst into flames. I shut the stove off and tried blowing out the fireball. The fabric continued to burn. After the flames went out, I waited a few minutes to allow the cup to cool, added instant coffee to the water, and put the cup to my lips.

The cup was so hot that I spilled hot coffee on me and my sleeping bag, burning the skin on my thighs and crotch. I took my pants off and accidentally dropped the stove. The stove fell apart as it hit the ground. The burner rolled down the hill and jetted over the side of the mountain. I have an extreme leave-no-trace ethic and will continue to try to look for it in the canyon. The burns I received were serious. I'm going back to old school methods: bread instead of dehydrated food. I thought this would be a quick trip. The fun was just beginning.

Starting at the bottom, I climbed three long pitches (lengths of rope), that required climbing out of the top of my aiders (foot ladders) to link sections where the cracks disappears or the rock became rotten. In one spot, I could feel a detached flake I was standing on vibrate. Just as I thought a placement for protection was secure, the flake cracked across the middle and separated in two. I would have preferred to thrown the top piece off, except that it was ten feet tall and above my head. To avoid getting clobbered, I stepped left out

The lower part of the route at the start of the climbing, after coming up the ridge from Refrigerator Canyon

Looking up at the first pitch. I had just rappelled back to the start to clean it.

onto the face and climbed around it. At the end of my rope, the ground leveled, and I slept for the night.

The next day I realized it was taking me longer than anticipated to climb the route and I considered I might run out of water before I finished. It was 85F, sunny, without a cloud in the sky. Heat reflected off the white sandstone like being in an oven. I began to ration my water to two cups per day, and gambled on it being easier to get to the top than to go down. I hoped I could finish the next day. I wondered if I got heat stroke or become dehydrated, what that might feel like. *Would I need to be rescued?* I felt like a rabbit in the middle of the highway as it tries to decide which way to run. I thought if I tried to go down, I might make a mistake while rappelling or down-climbing into Refrigerator Canyon or have difficulty getting out of the canyon and back to the trail.

A golf ball sized blister had developed on my right heel due to my socks

At the top of the bottom half of the route, looking south.

being wet with sweat. Scar tissue from previous blisters had gotten soggy and tore. I was grateful my foot wasn't swollen or infected. I had tried to stop and take socks off and let my feet dry, but that was hard to do while hanging on the side of a mountain. I once dropped my shoe doing that and had to finish a climb barefoot.

    The top section was difficult. There are only a few hand holds. I fell fifty feet, slid back down to the start, regrouped, and checked my body. I had hurt my shoulder. I became scared and started to worry. It was hot and I was running out of water. I can't remember the last time I drilled a bolt. I drilled one on the blank face before I reached the crack coming down from the top. I cleaned the bolt (angle pounded in hole). The hole may make it easier for future parties to free-climb this section. As I limped upward, my eyes locked on a target: a small tree growing out of the crack, thirty feet from the top. I thought if I could get to the tree, I would make it to the top.

    When I reached the tree, I wrapped a sling of webbing around it and clipped my rope to it. I used it for leverage, wiggled up the crack, one foot on the crack, the other on the tree. As I stepped off the tree, the tree fell out of the crack it had been growing. My rope was still attached to it. Fortunately it didn't pull me off the mountain.

    I slept on top of Cathedral Mountain. I was out of water. Listening to my

A small tree that pulled out of the crack with my rope still attached on the last pitch, just below the summit.

recorded message, speaking into my camera, I kept repeating, "I am so... tired." My brother texted me on my satellite communicator. He said it must be cold where I was, since it was 70F in Phoenix. I laughed. In an effort to conserve every drop of water in my body, I was sleeping naked in my sleeping bag so I wouldn't sweat.

In the morning I went to the summit of Mt. Majestic, then north to a spot where you can sit and watch hikers coming up the last switchback on the top of the West Rim Trail. After people-watching, I scrambled down into Behunin Canyon. (*Zion National Park: Summit Routes* refers to this ridge as Behunin Ridge.)

I was so tired and desperate to get to water, I threw my pack down when I reached the rappel slings and down-climbed. My pack tumbled, picked up momentum, bounced, and almost went over the edge and into the canyon on the wrong side of the ridge.

In Behunin Canyon, I found water. After resting and rehydrating, I hiked up the canyon to where it meets the West Rim Trail, and hiked down to the Grotto.

Back home I found the roof my mouth was painful. I woke at 3 am to an incessant pain on the top of the roof of my mouth. I first noticed the pain on the third day of climbing. In the evening when I would eat something without water to drink, it got sore. Dehydrated chicken teriyaki particularly made it painful. As did goo packs. I was able to eat dehydrated maple-oatmeal out of the bag and not have a problem. That gave me energy, probably from the sugar. My thought was that my glands were fighting off stuff. Like from all cuts on my body and a weakened system from not drinking enough water.

A week later my left shoulder still hurt. The cuts and blisters on my hands were healing. I emailed my older brother: "Today's brain teaser: what does the

On the summit of Mt. Majestic, watching hikers coming up the last switchback on the West Rim Trail; Below: on the way down.

uvula, that thing in the back of your throat do? Mine is swollen. For the last few days the roof of my mouth has been painful. When it gets really bad, I get chills and get tired. Last night it felt like my head was going to explode from pressure and pain. I took an 800mg IB left over from the dentist. You know I never take pills. What do you suppose is wrong? I eat lots of dirt as it came down on me when I was cleaning the cracks I was trying to climb."

I went to urgent care. Their diagnosis was candidal stomatitis, a fungal growth. They gave me nystatin to treat the fungus. I wore Birkenstocks and sprayed the open blister on my heel with Benzalkonium Chloride. Bacteria on the heel, mold in the mouth. The only thing for certain was ibuprofen. It gives me new appreciation for those who suffer from migraines.

CLIMBING IRON CURTAIN

IRON CURTAIN A2+ 5.10 *D Stih 2017* September 15-18. Roped solo. 7 pitches.
There's a ton of mixed climbing. There is mandatory free climbing to link sections where the rock is rotten or the cracks too shallow to place gear. The hardest aid is found on the last pitch on the lower section. The hardest free climbing is the first pitch of the upper section (the white face near the top).

EQUIPMENT REQUIRED: (2) of each cam 0.5, 0.75, 1, 2, 3; (1) #4 cam; (2) yellow Aliens 5/8"-3/4"; (3) knife blades; (5) baby angles #1 and #2; a few longer and bigger angles; a few thick blades such as bugaboos; tie offs; long slings for bushes.

WATER SOURCES: Carry water from the Grotto. There is no water between the start of the climb and Behunin Canyon.

SEASON: Since the optimal season is not dependent on finding water (there is none), heat is the important variable. The south white face of the upper part of the mountain can be unpleasantly hot, in even mildly warm temperatures. Fall is best. In the winter there will be snow to melt on the route to make water. In winter carry ice cleats.

CAMPING / TIME REQUIRED: It took me a 1/2 day to approach the route. I spent two days on the route. On the fourth, I descended into Behunin Canyon and hiked up to the West Rim Trail.

STARTING POINT: The Grotto. Hike the West Rim Trail towards Angels Landing. Leave the trail at the start of Walter's Wiggles, the bottom of the switchbacks that go up to Angels Landing. Go down into Refrigerator Canyon, then find a way to scramble up the other side, and onto a ridge that goes up and left (south) to Cathedral Mountain. The scramble out of the canyon is steep, dirty, and loose. You should be going south, back towards the Grotto. It's a long way of scrambling before you are sure you're not going the wrong way. The climbing route is not visible until you are high on the ridge. As you reach the bottom of the climbing route, you will be looking directly across at hikers on the summit of Angels Landing.

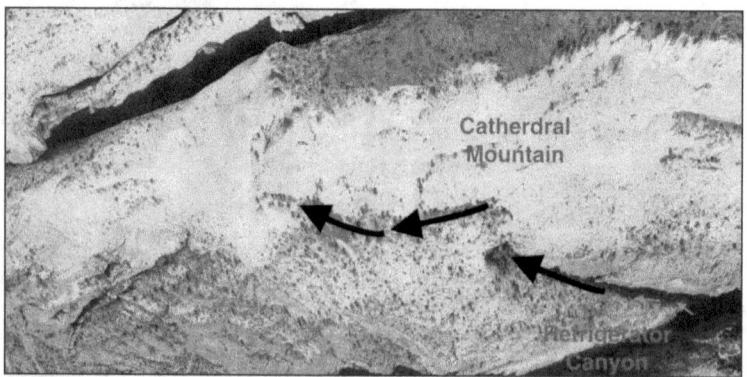

THE ROUTE: From the base of the route, climb three long pitches, the most difficult being the third (A2+) to a bivy where the white rock flattens. From the bivy, climb two more pitches, the first straight up, the second west across steep and airy face to the final white headwall. The final section has two pitches. The bottom is 5.10 face, protected with holes drilled for angles. The holes may have washed out and be large enough to

 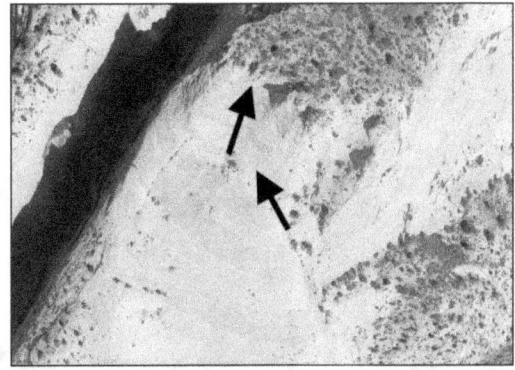

Left: the lower part of the route. Right: the upper portion of the route.

provide pockets for handholds. The final pitch is an enjoyable crack that looks difficult but is actually well-protected and a scramble to the summit.

GETTING DOWN: After going to the summit of Cathedral Mountain (an adventure of its own), hike across a land bridge that connects Cathedral Mountain to Mt. Majestic. Climb to the top of Mt Majestic, then hike NW, aiming for Behunin Ridge, a ridge that can be scrambled (5th class) south, down into Behunin Canyon. You should find water in Behunin Canyon. To continue on the traverse around the Emerald Pools, climb Castle Dome next (see Traverses). To exit and go home, walk the canyon upstream to where it meets the West Rim Trail, and hike back down to the Grotto.

Red Arch Mountain (By Descent)

Looking at Red Arch Mountain (end of the arrows) from Castle Dome.

INTRODUCTION An alternate way to reach the top of Red Arch Mountain.
HISTORY In *Guide to Zion National Park*, author Ron Kay writes that on July 11, 1973, an Air Force F-111 crashed above the Zion Lodge below the rim of Deertrap Mountain. According to Kay, the pilots ejected to safety in a capsule and landed west of Lady Mountain. Wew! That's a rugged place to land.

CLIMBING RED ARCH MOUNTAIN

DESCENT TO RED ARCH MOUNTAIN *D Stih and CP 2016*
EQUIPMENT REQUIRED: Slings, two long ropes, Jumars (ascenders) and a set of etriers for each climber. It is not possible to lower equipment to the second.
CAUTIONS / SPECIAL DIFFICULTIES: In addition to a lead line, bring an 8-mil, 300-foot static rope for fixing. Thin ropes can jump out of a jumar. After putting jumars on the rope, clip a locking carabiner through the top hole on each of the ascenders to prevent the rope from coming out.
THE STARTING POINTS: We started at the pullout on the side of the road used to park if climbing Mountain of the Sun, a pullout east of the big east tunnel (overlook tunnel). From the pullout, we scrambled to the top of Deertrap Mountain. There are at least two other starting options to reach Deertrap Mountain. Using a longer approach may cause

you to have to turn around for lack of daylight. One is to start hiking the trail when it's dark from a trail head at the Ponderosa Hunting Club. The other is Kay's route, which starts on the west side of the smaller tunnel at the east entrance. This may be a shorter, but more rugged, approach than coming from the Ponderosa Club. Kay's description suggests it's a 10-hour trip and to bring survival gear in additional to a rope.

THE ROUTE: From the final peak on the traverse (after Deertrap Mountain), CP and I down-climbed until it became necessary to use a rope to rappel. From that point, a big tree, I made a short rappel down 5th class terrain I thought I would be able to scramble back up without a rope. I pulled the rope, then scrambled down to where it became necessary to rappel again. From the top of a big wide, ugly gaping crack, I fixed the rope to rappel. The rope did not reach the ground. Although I am six-foot three inches, my feet barely reached a hold on the side of the mountain, as the end of the rope slid though my rappel device. CP got to witness the possession that over takes Dan when he sees a summit, gets a vision, and thinks he can do it. I hoped the rope stayed in place, as I finished down-climbing, then scrambled to the summit of Red Arch Mountain. (To avoid having to down-climb this, bring a 300 - 350 foot static rope to fix).

GETTING DOWN: Go up the fixed rope and reverse your approach.

CP, traversing north after descending Deertrap Mountain.

The last mountain descended before reaching the saddle, south of the summit of Red Arch Mountain. The circle marks the end of my rope. From there, I down-climbed.

References: *Ron Kay's Guide to Zion National Park*. Ron Kay. 2008.
Credits: An air-to-air left front view of an F-111 aircraft during a refueling mission over the North Sea. Author: Master Sgt. Patrick Nugent. Public Domain. Wikipedia.org. Sept 2019.

CP on the way back up to the top of Deertrap Mountain. Below: a piece of wreckage.

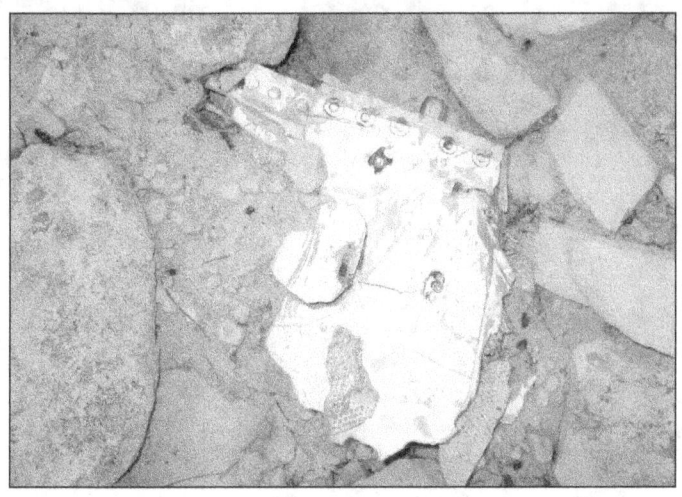

Looking down from the summit of Red Arch Mountain. This may be what Kay refers to a the "Grotto Drainage" and crash site.

Other Notable Ascents

Checkerboard Mesa

INTRODUCTION Find yourself without time or equipment to do a big wall, wanting to do a free climb, but can't climb 5.11? Would you like to do something more significant than a pitch or two? Sure, there are longer free climbs, but most require 5.10 to 5.11 and are serious undertakings. What about a moderate, multi pitch free route? I've got you covered. I call Checkerboard Mesa the "Fairview Dome of Zion." It's six pitches (850 feet) of 5.8 with great views and is generally moderate except for a few runout and tricky sections. It's a park and climb. You can eat breakfast in Springdale, climb an awesome route, and have time to relax at the end of the day.

Anything For You

I was on a camping trip with my girlfriend, her brother Kevin, and his new wife, Carrie. I told him I would climb anything he wanted to. Coming into the park, Checkerboard Mesa was the first thing he saw. We parked, got the ropes and climbing gear out, and went to the bottom.

The girls sat at the bottom, watching Kevin and I climb. My GF was used to watching me climb. His wife, on the other hand, was a babe from the woods. She was young, had grown up in a small town, and had never seen anyone climb. No sooner had I left the ground, she became worried about her husband following me. Instead of words of encouragement, the conversation on the ground was about how dangerous I was being. As I climbed higher, I found the grooves difficult to place protection in. My feet slipped as I struggled to hold on. I was starting to believe his wife might be right - perhaps it was foolhardy to think we could just park, and with no guidebook or route description, climb Checkerboard Mesa.

I reached the end of my rope and set an anchor with two large camelots (spring-loaded devices). After setting up the anchor, I pulled up the slack in the rope, as Kevin climbed up to meet me. When his wife asked how he was doing, he told her he was scared. He should have faked it. It was like letting the dogs out. We never got them back. With every move he took, she yelled at him to come down. This was her hun, her new husband. They were supposed to be starting a new life together.

Low on the route.

By the time Kevin reached me at the anchor, it was certain he needed to go down to calm his wife. I lowered him, then thought about how I was going to get down. The white sandstone is too soft to drill a bolt. I placed a #3 cam in the groove, and lowered myself to the ground.

The following year, I returned with a normal climbing partner, Brian Dede. As we were at the bottom, a car pulled up with two climbers. As I struggled to find way to start, they started climbing a few hundred feet right of us. I looked over at the leader who was a hundred feet off the ground and asked him if he knew where he was going.

"Is this Checkerboard Mesa?" he said.

Looking down higher up on the route. I marked the route I climbed on this postcard. Photo by Mark Fay.

In other words, the mountain is littered with grooves. He just picked one and started climbing. He was strong, crazy, or both.

Brian and I reached the top, climbing the route I chose. The cam I left the year before was gone.

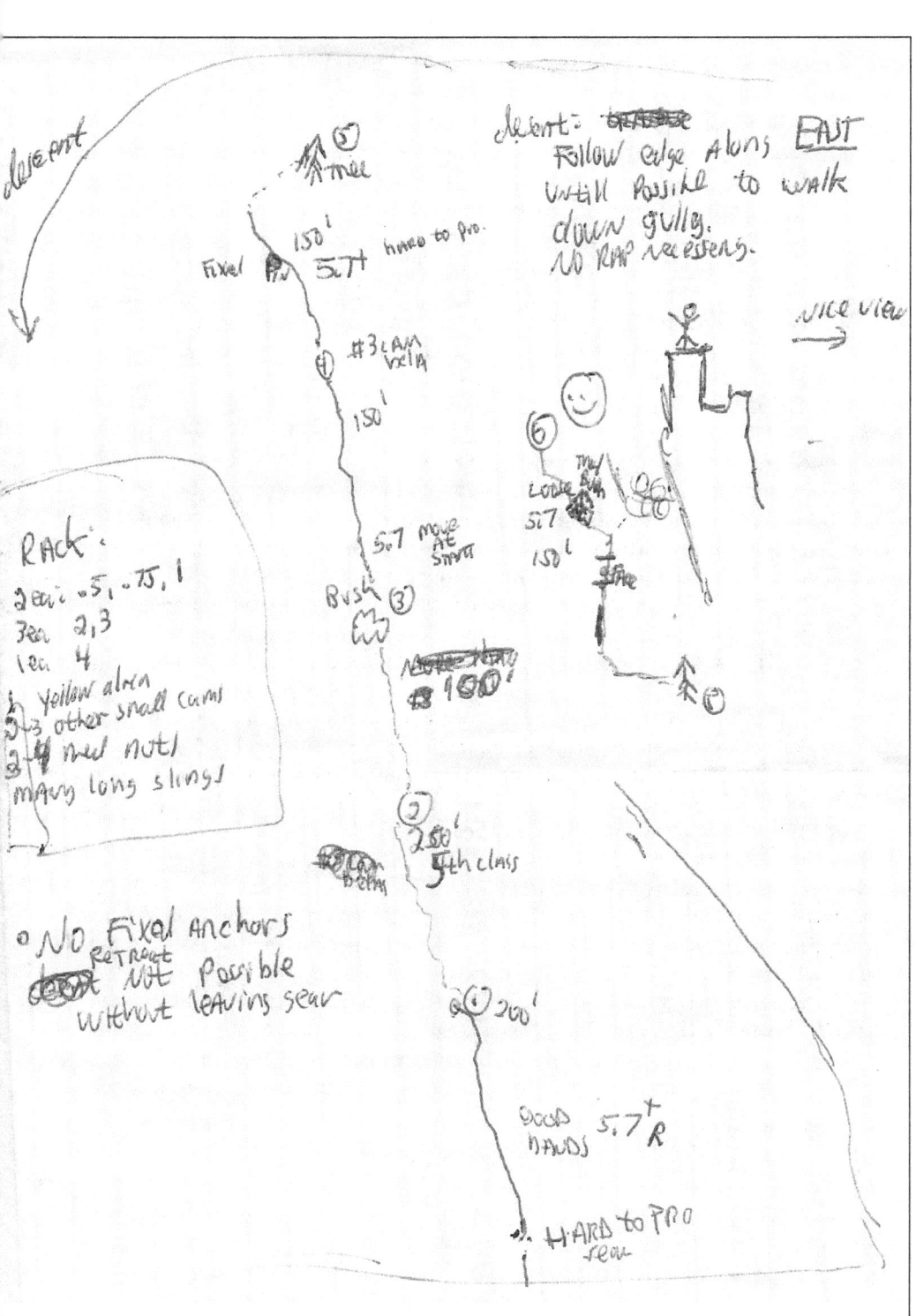

CLIMBING CHECKERBOARD MESA

ERECTION PROTECTION 5.8 *Dan Stih and Brian Dede 1997*
This was not the first ascent of the mountain and may not have been the first ascent of the route.
EQUIPMENT REQUIRED: (2) each camelots # 0.5, 0.75, 1; (3) each camelots #2, #3: (1) #4 cam; a few small cams in the 3/8 and 1/2 inch sizes; (3 or 4) medium sized nuts; many long slings. The route can be climbed with a single 165-foot rope. Take a windbreaker. High up it can get nippy and colder than on the ground.
CAUTIONS / SPECIAL DIFFICULTIES: The route is not recommended for those not proficient at placing natural protection. When available, the cam placements are good, but you must be careful to place them in a downward direction. Semi-horizontal placements can rip out in sandstone. Place protection when you can get it, even when the climbing seems easy. There are no fixed anchors. The bottom is the crux. It's slippery and difficult to protect. If you need to bail you will need to leave a large cam, a #3 or #4. If you can climb the first fifty feet, you'll make it.
SEASON: Checkerboard Mesa is in the high county, as you come into the park from the east entrance. It faces north and holds snow. We climbed it in late March.
TIME REQUIRED: This is a park and climb, a day trip.
THE STARTING POINT: The big parking lot a few hundred feet down the road or a pull-out with room for two or three cars in front of Checkerboard Mesa.
THE ROUTE: From the top of Checkerboard Mesa, follow obvious cracks in the center, straight down the face. There are several ways to start. The easiest is two cracks to the right of the main crack. All are washed out water grooves with sparse protection (5.7 - 5.8 R). All lead to solid hand jams with bomber #3 cam placements fifty feet higher.
1. Pick a crack (groove). Run out the rope 200 feet and belay from large cams. Carry a few extra #2 and #3 sized cams.
2. 5th class 200 feet and belay from a large cam.
3. Continue on 5th class. Go towards a large bush at the base of the main crack in the center of the wall. A few moves of 5.7 may be required to reach it.
4. It's 5.7 off the bush belay. It looks harder than it is. Go up 150 feet and belay from #3 cams. Do not pass up the cam belay or you will end up in an un-protectable section on the next pitch.
5. 150 feet. 5.7+ leads up and left to a fixed pin (I placed and left). Continue up and left, then back right to a large tree. Belay from the tree.
6. Walk straight left from the tree, then face climb up past a bush, unprotected until another bush is in your face. From it, traverses left (more difficult and loose) up and around to the top.
GETTING DOWN: Walk south along the east edge of the summit until it is possible to walk down into a gully on the east side. Rappelling is not required.

September 4, 1997

Dan Stihl
1104 S. Mill Ave.
Tempe, AZ. 85281

Dear Dan,

Thank you for submitting your article, "Rock and Ice Classic," about the Checkerboard Mesa in Zion, to *Rock & Ice*. Unfortunately, though your ideas are very interesting, we will be unable to use the manuscript.

We appreciate you sending us your work and look forward to any other articles you might submit.

We wish you the best of luck in future ascents. Thanks again for thinking of *Rock & Ice*.

Best regards,

Ryan Hart
Editorial Assistant

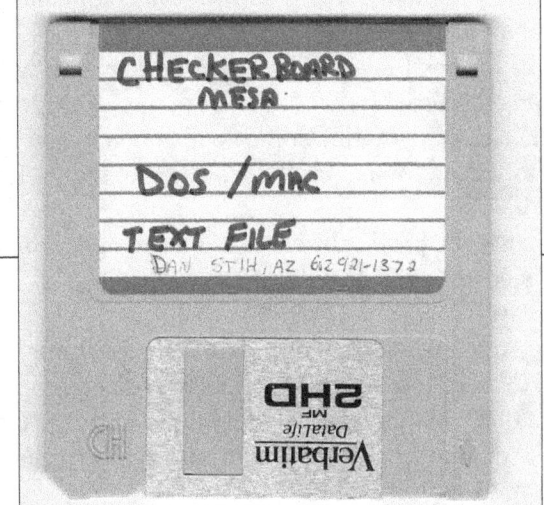

Hidden Canyon

INTRODUCTION Hidden Canyon is normally approached by hikers and tourists from the bottom. Starting at Weeping Rock, walk up switchbacks toward Cable Mountain. As the trail levels off, there is a detour to the right called Hidden Canyon Trail. The pavement soon turns to dirt. All turn around when confronted with the first impasse - an overhanging chasm.

Canyoneers start at the top and go down Hidden Canyon. This requires a long hike through the back county and skill in finding the correct canyon. The high county is level ground, such that the canyon is not readily visible, thus its name. The following is based on interviews with psychics, family members, and hospital records.

Summer of Love

Decades earlier, Nick had died climbing in the Swiss Alps. He was a good man, and had been given his wings. He was going to be a guardian angel, and was waiting to be assigned to a mortal. He prayed it would be someone with lofty climbing goals. Then he got the news: Dangerous Dan was going to be born the following month.

Nick wasn't sure why Dangerous was going to be born in the desert - Phoenix, Arizona. But he had been assigned to Dangerous and was dedicated. He started thinking. *Where will we find big mountains in the desert to climb?* He got an idea: Zion National Park. Modern rock climbing had not yet come to Zion so Nick took a bold step and asked a senior staff member for help - Archangel Gabriel.

"Gabriel, can you find some good climbers and tell them to do a big climb in Zion. I need to prepare the way so that the park rangers are used to people there."

"It's not my job," Gabriel said. "I have bigger things to work on. That's why I'm called an 'arch' angel'."

"Please."

The Archangel looked at the newbie and thought for a moment. Gabriel decided to help. Gabriel went and found some of the best climbers in the world. While the climbers slept, she told them in their dreams, "Go to Zion. Take your climbing gear. Climb something big. If the park superintendent won't allow it, be persistent."

"What should we climb?" the climbers asked.

Gabriel thought for a moment. The throne of God came to mind. "The Great White Throne."

The climbers drove to Zion. "Our car mysteriously guided itself," one of the climbers later wrote.

After they started the climb, it began to rain. The rain persisted for weeks. Nick prayed the climbers would finish before the baby was born.

The Great White Throne

"What's taking them so long?" Nick asked Gabriel.

"They say the rock is soft."

"Tell them to use pitons." Nick had used pitons to climb loose rock in the Alps.

"Way ahead of you," Gabriel said. "The climbers I choose brought pitons."

"Then what's taking so long?" Nick inquired.

"Rain."

The baby was born and the climb wasn't finished.

"I've got to go and help them," Nick told Gabriel. "I've got to help the climbers finish. Can you find me a babysitter?"

"You can't leave," Gabriel said sternly, "You're on duty now. You're supposed to watch over baby Dangerous. But I could tell the doctor to put him someplace safe for a week."

Baby Dangerous was placed in an incubator.

Nick left and went to help the climbers.

"He's too big!" the head nurse said, glaring at the doctor when she saw the baby in the tube. "What's that baby doing in there?"

"God told me to do it," the doctor said. "Keep him in the incubator for a week. Doctor's orders."

Meanwhile, guided by Nick, the climbers inched their way up the mountain. Progress was slow, and still hampered by rainy weather.

"Gab," Nick pleaded to heaven, "Can you ask God to please turn the rain down?"

God appears to have granted that request. The climbers finished a week later, just in time for Nick to return to the hospital as the baby was being taken out of the incubator and given to his mother to go home.

"No more breaks," Gabriel instructed Nick. "Keep him safe." She smiled before leaving for more important business. "Oh ya - name a climb after me."

Circa 1990

I, Dangerous Dan, was in the reserve section at the Phoenix Public Library, reading out-of-print books, searching for information on climbs, when I read Pat Callis's story of the first ascent of The Great White Throne. He climbed it with Galen Rowell and Fred Becky in 1967. It rained. A lot. Although they waited two days for the rock to dry, when they continued, they found the rock to be moist and soft. Callis wrote: "The climbers below the leader heard a series of bitter exclamations as the leader drilled a hole to place a bolt. A substance, not unlike brown sugar, was exuding from the hole which was considerable larger in diameter than the drill bit."

The climbers took a break and went to do the first ascent of the Pulpit. There, they made an important discovery. Callis had brought ice screws. It was found that if one were screwed into a 3-inch hole drilled in soft, moist rock, the efforts of three strong men could not budge it. Since reading their story, I have carried an ice screw in my pack when doing first ascents in Zion. I've never had to use it.

November, 2001

I was still trying to find a way to climb the Meridian Tower when Brian meet me in Zion after Thanksgiving. When we got there and saw how cold it was, I was honest. I explained to him that I wasn't sure where we were going, it might take a several days, and to go light, we would have to not take sleeping bags. Brian didn't try to talk me out of it. He simply said, "No thanks."

My backup plan for us to have an outing was to find a way to put up a new route on The Great White Throne. I was looking for an easier way.

Callis and his team had not been the first to climb The Great White Throne. That award goes to William H. Evans. In 1927, after climbing to the top, Evans fell while coming down. He was found at the bottom, alive, several days later. I knew Evan had taken the easiest way. I suspected I would find easier routes on the back side.

As Brian and I discussed what to do, climbers were being rescued off Hammer and Sickle (VI A3+) on Cable Mountain. They had been stuck below the summit after an ice storm made climbing the final pitch impossible.

The following day, Brian, James (a friend of Brian's), and I set off to explore Hidden Canyon in search of a place to put up a new climbing route on the Great White Throne. There was ice in the canyon. We didn't have crampons. We walked until we were met with the first obstacle - an overhanging chasm. To get over it required climbing a bomb-bay chimney, a wide opening requiring full-body stemming (5.9X). Imagine climbing inside a chimney in a house, with the walls leaning inward. It was impossible to get foot holds. I had to wedge myself inside it and wiggle my body up, hoping my feet didn't slip and fall out.

After getting over the chimney, the canyon returned to a normal hike except for a few short climbing sections. Near the end, it was difficult to climb out of the canyon, not because of the rock climbing, but rather the canyon walls were covered with ice. I had to pull on bushes and look for places to put my feet that didn't have ice.

We came out of the canyon eye-level with the ground. I turned and looked back. The Great White Throne seemed a mile away. We had passed it a long time ago, while we were in the canyon. It became obvious there was no way to climb the Great White Throne from Hidden Canyon. We turned around and went back down. I later read that Hidden Canyon was "discovered" by rangers in 1927, when they were looking for Evans. He wasn't there. The "easy" way is reached by descending the next canyon over to the west.

Summer, 2006

Starting in the high country, I walked past Hidden Canyon where Brian and I had been, and kept walking towards Deertrap Mountain. I left the car when it was dark. By mid-day I was frustrated at not being able to see the Great White Throne, as I kept an eye out for the proper canyon to descend. When it seemed I had hiked too far on the trail, I backtracked and started down a gully that seemed to be the only possible route. It lead me down to the south face of the Throne.

The easiest way to climb the face of the Throne appeared to be on the right side of its south face. Someone was supposed to have placed bolts on a route there a few years earlier. I scoured for the bolts. Without bolts, there would be no protection. Not that those that came before me had any.

In August of 1946, 19-year old, Zion Lodge cook, Roger Club, had climbed to the summit of the Great White Throne, continuing after his friends turned around. He didn't have time to get down, and spent the night on top. In the morning, a rescue party arrived, It was determined that the only safe way to get to him was to drill 3-inch holes in the sandstone, insert steel pins into the holes, and step on them. As they got close to the top, they tied a string to a rock and threw it up to Club, from which he pulled up a rope.

I couldn't find the bolts. On the left side of the face there are cracks. Cracks can be protected with modern climbing gear, so I got out the rope and tried to climb one of the cracks. I struggled and hemmed and hawed, and took a short fall. As I hung on my rope, I heard a great thunder and felt the earth shake. Coming down the gully I had come down to reach the throne, running at a full speed, was a heard of mountain goats. Without stopping, they ran up the rock face on my left, traversed across my head, and dropped rocks on me, taunting me as their feet propelled them to the top.

Surely if they can do it I can, I told myself.

I came down and went back to look for the bolts. Twenty feet up, I found one. I clipped it, and climbed to the top. Getting down was the problem. I had brought only one rope. From the top, I lowered myself until I was almost at the end of the rope, and at a bolt. It is dangerous to rappel off a single bolt. If it pulls out you're dead. As fate had it, the only way I could lower myself to the ground was by stopping at the bolt. It was loose and spinning in its hole. I figured if the guys in the 1920s and 1930s could climb without a rope or bolts, I could down-climb using the bad bolt. I put the rope through the bolt hanger and used the bolt for balance, as I walked my feet down, carefully placing them on good foot holds. I reached the ground safely.

Note: Two ropes are required to get down this single pitch, 5.8, bolted sport route on the south face of the Great White Throne.

CLIMBING UP HIDDEN CANYON

UP AND DOWN 5.9 X *D Stih, Brian DeDe, James 2001*
Starting from Weeping Rock, a full ascent of Hidden Canyon to Deertrap Mountain Trail, then a descent of the canyon back to the Weeping Rock shuttle stop.

EQUIPMENT REQUIRED: Free-climbing rack with a few extra-large pieces. Two ropes if rappelling back down the canyon.

CAUTIONS / SPECIAL DIFFICULTIES: In *Zion: Canyoneering*, author Tom Jones writes of Hidden Canyon: "Very exposed, not for those with acrophobia." He gives a time of 5 to 7 hours to descend it from the top. Climbing up will take longer. He writes that the canyon has been the scene of numerous broken legs and difficult extractions from people who tried to ascend it, and that "bolts pop up in a few places." When we climbed it (2001) we didn't find any bolts.

CAMPING / TIME REQUIRED: A long day.

STARTING POINT: Weeping Rock shuttle stop.

THE ROUTE: From Weeping Rock, hike the trail towards Cable Mountain to where it branches off to Hidden Canyon. After a short way, the official trail ends and climbing begins. The 5.9X bombay chimney crux is near the start. After that there are a few pitches of scrambling, interspaced with climbing, and it becomes more of a hike. Near the end (top) of the canyon, grab bushes and trees to yank yourself up slabs that lead up to the plateau on the SE side of the Great White Throne. The Throne will be far in the distance to the north.

GETTING DOWN: Reverse course. We rappelled back into the canyon from trees on the west side of the mouth of the canyon. We made two, double rope rappels through a forest on the side of the canyon wall. We continued by down-climbing and rappelling off natural anchors (trees, logs jams, bushes.) Alternatively, from the top of the canyon, you could walk dead south and run into a hiking trail that, going right (east) will lead to the east entrance.

Arch Gully

HISTORY In July, 1954, Philadelphia climbers Victor Fritz and George Riley tried to measure the span of the arch by climbing to the top of the plateau. To get there they tried to climb a gully to the east. They almost reached the top of the gully. They turned back as it was getting late in the day. A few weeks later, in August, 1954, Fred Ayres and A.E. Creswell were first to reach the top of the plateau. (See *The American Alpine Journal*, 1954). They too climbed the gully to measure the span of the arch. The 1980s saw two more attempts to measure the arch. According to "Measuring the Span of the Great Arch at Zion National Park, Kolob Section" (The Blake Paper), one was in July, 1983,

another in May, 1984.

My first attempt to climb the gully was in May, 2016. The gully had water flowing down it. I played hopscotch to place my feet on dry holds but it was futile. I returned in 2016, a few days after the fourth of July, and over six was successful in climbing the gully as well as doing the first ascent of Gregory Butte. Although not clearly prohibited, I did not step onto the arch.

Someone removed the fixed pitons Ayres and Creswell placed in the gully, and one of the bolts on the final pitch. They gave them to the Zion History Museum where they are said to be in a display case. The gully is treacherous. Falling may result in death. Please do not remove old gear when you find it. It is safer to have old gear, than to have no gear.

CLIMBING ARCH GULLY

ARCH GULLY, 5.9 R *Fred Ayres and A.E. Creswell, August, 1954*
First know solo: D Stih, 2016 and a 2nd solo in 2024.
CAUTIONS / SPECIAL DIFFICULTIES: The gully is old school 5.9, wet, hard to protect.
EQUIPMENT REQUIRED: Two 200 foot ropes. Alpine free rack (1 each 0.5, 0.75,1,2,3)
WATER: Fill up at the creek at Arch View point. At the top of the gully, head toward the arch. Just before the arch there are pools. How much water depends on the season and if it has rained within a month.
SEASON: Due to water dripping from snow melting and seeps, it may only be possible to climb the gully beginning in July/August. If there has been a big rain within a week it's not likely possible.
CAMPING / TIME REQUIRED: A fast party familiar with the approach (how to get into the bottom of the gully) can do this in a day, hiking in and out on the La Verkin Trail by headlamp. It will help to be familiar with the approach. Do a day hike to explore how to get into the gully prior to planning to actually climb the gully.
STARTING POINT: Lee Pass trail head. Start by headlamp. It takes about 3 hours to hike to arch view point. Hike the La Verkin Trail to Arch Trail, and to the end of arch trail (Arch view point). Scramble up to the bottom of the gully: From Arch View at the end of Arch Trail, at the big old tree, cross the creek in font of the big tree and turn right, up the ridge lying between the two brooks. Zig-zag as needed. From the top of the cliffs, head east and traverse slabs towards the gully, staying high above the tree line to avoid brush below. If you are too low you will find entering the gully difficult to impossible.
THE ROUTE: Pitch 1: The first pitch is long (200+ feet), run out, mossy, slippery, often wet, sometimes dripping. The fern filled crevasse in the back is shallow, bottoms out, and won't take gear. Pitch 2: The Cave Pitch. Belly crawl into the cave. Pitch 3: Exit the cave. Step out onto an airy ledge and move along the wall. Notice where the first party that attempted the gully (Victor R. Fritz and George H. Riley in August, 1953) placed expansion bolts (remains of holes). The second ascent of this pitch, and the first to successfully climb the gully (Fred Ayres and A.E. Creswell, August 1954) avoided using them by driving angle pitons into the overhead crack. Modern climbers can get large cams in this crack. Haul yourself up past the chockstone and belay at a large tree. Next, scramble up the gully through brush several hundred feet to a point where the gully divides into two branches. Several boulder problems are encountered along the way.

Every few years a major flooding washes large tress and debris down the gully, changing the path you might have taken and creating new obstacles. If, towards the end of the gully, you miss the proper junction, you will end up at a dead end, having taken the right branch. Go back and take a left. As you do, look for the "Friction Pitch" a face climb on a smooth aerate. Pitch 4: "The Friction Pitch" There are a few bolts. The slope is 50 degrees, 5.9. Belay when you run out of rope. Another short pitch of scrambling is recommended to reach a place to safely untie and finish scrambling up to the valley.

The "Friction Pitch" on the ridge between the two branches of the gully. Photo by A.E. Creswell. The climber is Fred Ayres. Circa 1954.

GETTING DOWN: From the top of the Friction pitch, scramble up and left to a safe (untie) location from which you're at the top of a drainage with trees that can be used to rappel

Opposite: Looking down the gully after coming out of the "cave". Top: walking along the bottom of Gregory Butte, above and behind the arch.

Old tat in the gully outside the cave, used for descent by earlier parties. This can be avoided by using two 300-foot ropes and rappelling from a tree at the top of the lower section in the gully (top of the airy pitch climbed after exiting the cave). Or stop here at the cave, and replace the tat.

Don't fall! An old star bolt, found on the last pitch in the gully. Still good. They don't drill 'em like they used to.

down to the start of the friction pitch. If you break this up into two rappels, (2) 200 foot ropes are sufficient. From there, scramble back down the gully to the big tree at the top of the pitch after the cave pitch. Rap back into the cave where there's tat outside the cave, used for descent by earlier parties. Replace the tat (tied around a chockstone) and finish rappelling. Be careful. It might be a reach at the bottom or require some down climbing. It's about 250 feet total from the top. The rock in the gully is not good for bolts so don't count on being able to drill them.

FUTURE CLIMBING On the wall to the right of the arch there are two potential aid routes that could be climbed to get to the top of the plateau. I call them West Seam and East Chimney (5.10 A2?). I made two attempts on East Chimney. After I bailed I went back a week later and tried again. (And failed). The piton placements are thin (bird beaks). I think free-climbing is required. Once above the chimney I believe it will be easier. West Seam (A3?) is closer to the arch, has spectacular exposure, and may require thin placements up overhanging and possibly loose rock. It may be the preferable and shorter choice.

I left the aid rack hanging by a hook on a flake to allow me freedom of movement in the chimney.

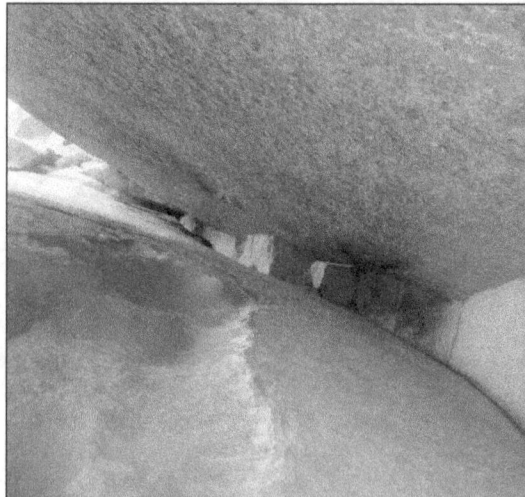

Looking up where I bailed on the chimney. It may not be possible to nail the corner. Free climbing may be required. There are good foot holds on the left face.

The Traverses

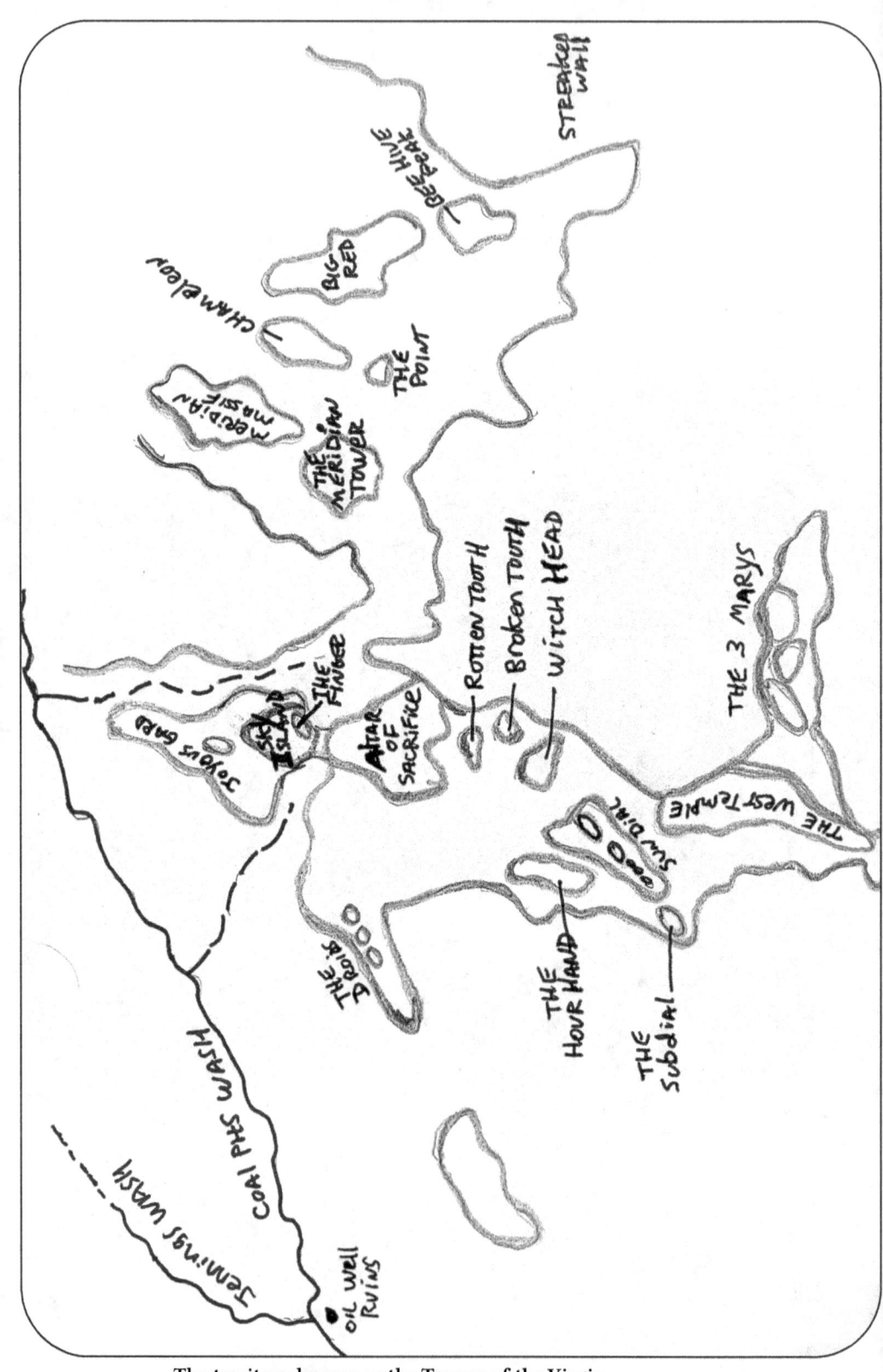

The territory known as the Towers of the Virgin

Traverse of the
Towers of the Virgin

The Towers of the Virgin. Left to right: West Temple, Sun Dial, Witch Head, Broken Tooth, Rotten Tooth, Altar of Sacrifice.

INTRODUCTION & HISTORY This traverse includes climbing the Towers of the Virgin. Much of the difficulty is found in down-climbing and rappelling. Ron drew a topo and placed it in the history books kept by the park service. Because his last name was Raimonde (Italian), or more likely because he rated the climbs using the international alpine system, for two decades the locals believed the traverse had been completed by a group of visiting French climbers.

 The first repeat of this traverse, was done by Mike Dunn and Arthur Herlitzka in March 2021. After reaching the summit of the Altar, rather than rappelling the NE face, they rappelled into the notch between the Altar and Sky Island and went down the first two pitches of Left Crack to reach the plateau. They then climbed the Red Cap of the Meridian Tower massif from the east side after going down to Birch Creek, then added to what Ron and I had done, by climbing Chameleon Peak, the Point, Big Red, and Bee Hive Peak, before descending the descent used for the Streaked Wall. to the Museum They did not go to the second summit of the Sun Dial (I hadn't told them about it yet), Sky Island, nor the tower proper of the Meridian Tower.

In winter of 2023, the day after days of heavy rain and snow caused the road to be closed at the East Entrance due to rockfall, James Barrow and Conner Baty set off on an ambitious attempt. They climbed Cowboy Ridge and Kinesava to reach the West Temple, then climbed Broken Tooth, Rotten Tooth, the Drioids, and the Altar. A looming forecast led them to bail after reaching the summit of the Altar of Sacrifice.

In April 2024, Barrow and his partner made a second attempt. Starting from the bridge in the Anasazi HOA, they climbed Cowboy Ridge and Kinesava to reach the West Temple, rappelled the West Temple, tagged the Subdial, climbed the Witch Head, did the traverse of the Time Machine, climbing the Sun Dials, Cogs, and Hour Hand, climbed Broken Tooth, Rotten Tooth, the Drioids, the Altar of Sacrifice, Sky Island, the Finger, Avalokiteshvara Temple, the red cap on the Meridian Tower, Chameleon, The Point, tagged Big Red, the Beehive, and went down the descent used for the Streaked Wall, ending at the Museum. Similar to Dunn and Herlitzk's attempt, they did not climb the tower proper of the Meridian Tower.

There have been other attempts before and after those mentioned. The peaks climbers fail the most on are the Sun Dial (due to ice and snow) and the Meridian "Tower" (it looks intimidating and improbable). To date there has not been a second ascent of the "Tower" on the Meridian Tower. Ironically, these are two of the most prominent peaks on maps in the area known as the Towers of the Virgin.

Virgin Voyage

The following is a transcript from my journal in 1998. To stay light, I didn't carry a sleeping bag and took only power bars for food. Ron and I had tested this tactic by climbing in Colorado in the winter without sleeping bags.

Friday, March 20, 1998. We parked my van at the Jolly Rodger Cemetery, named after the Jolly family and the Rodger family, pioneers and early settlers of the town of Springdale. We trudged up the long, steep, loose dirt hill for what seems like a mile to get to the bottom of the West Temple. We carried minimum climbing gear and climbed wearing our packs. **1 PM**: We reached the saddle on the West Temple where the traverse across the top ridge begins. Looking straight down, you can see Dan's Direct Variation, a 5.10 loose face and chimney route that is a straight-up approach to the saddle instead of climbing the standard route on the West Temple. We had climbed it on a previous trip, in order to find a way to climb the West Temple. (There was no

guidebook at that time). That was before I started listening to Ron when he said, "Take the easiest way." **3 PM:** We were on the summit of the West Temple. The hardest move, 5.6, we climbed wearing our packs. We signed the register and checked the radio tower, a small solar-powered tower placed there by park rangers to communicate. We trudged across knee-deep snow to the north side. There, we did two controlled clasades, slides down snow, to the first rappel. The first rappel was off a bush so small it could have easily pulled out. To prevent it from being pulled out, we kicked steps down the snow, and only used the rope (anchored by the bush) for balance. **5 PM:** We traversed

Rappelling the West Temple into the saddle between it and Sun Dial. Although I marked where, at the time, I thought we went down, Ron and I likely didn't go down that way. Later, Mike and I did. James reports not having to, rather his team scrambled up higher NW, and came down (rappelled) white slabs, finding ample brushes. That may have been what Ron and I did, as we only had a 150 lead rope and 200 foot tag line.

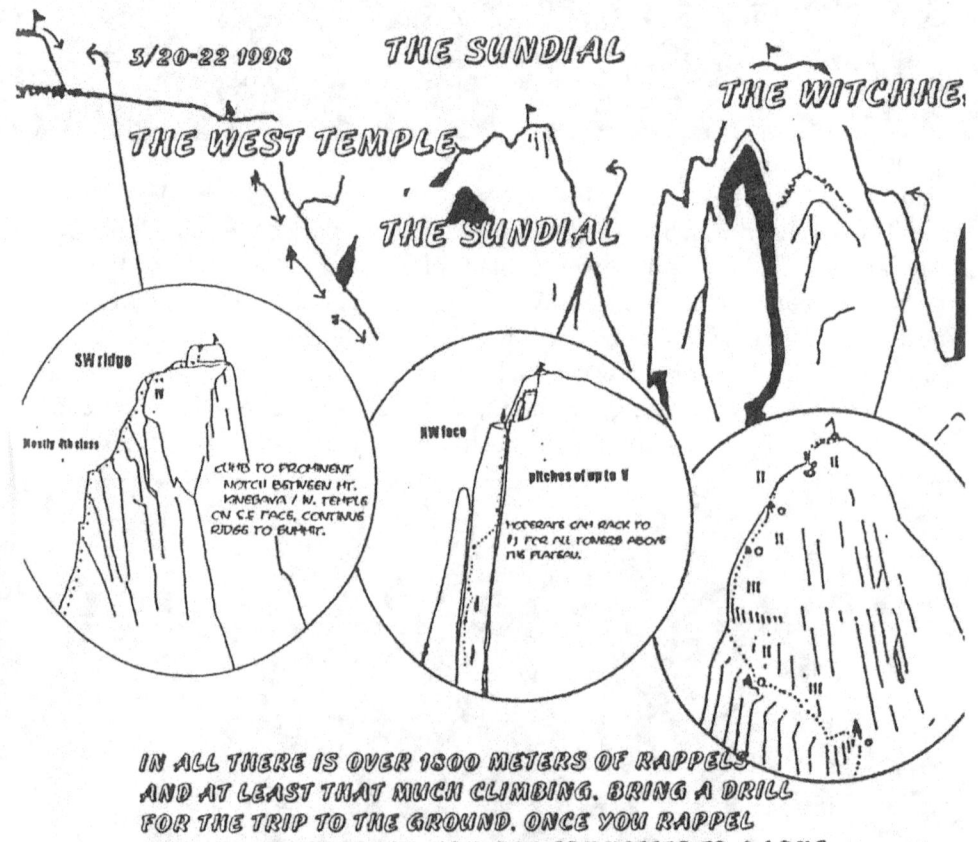

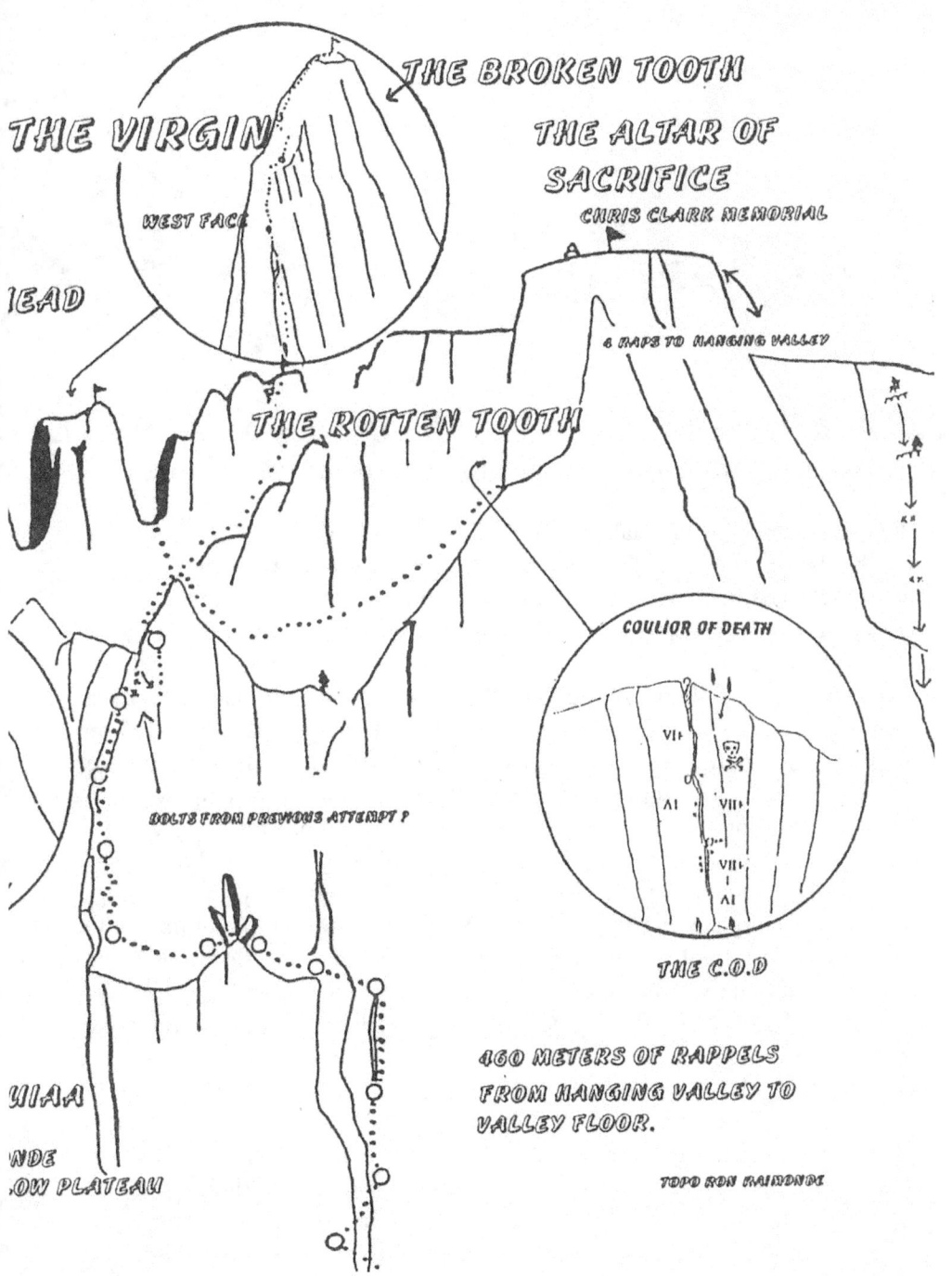

Rappelling of the West Temple into the saddle between the West Temple and Sun Dial.

the east face of the Sun Dial, and pitched camp on "the flats", an area north of the Sun Dial at the base of the Witch Head. This was our first bivy.

March 21. The first day of Spring and my younger brother's birthday.
6:30 AM. I guess we were in a hurry, cold, or both. We kicked steps in the snow up the Sun Dial. There was so much snow, we didn't need to climb the rock. We couldn't. On the first part of the route, we took a variation from our original ascent, climbing directly up the north face. **11:30 AM:** We signed the summit register on the Sun Dial that we had installed on our first ascent. We rappelled the NE side, something quicker than the way we came up, something we could only do because there was snow. We climbed Witch Head. I found it still to be a nasty, loose, 5.10, run out, and dangerous (without protection). Then we climbed the central tower without difficultly and the Broken Teeth, taking a direct route up the SW face as a short cut. That proved to be more difficult than anticipated, and loose. **3 PM:** We rappelled off Broken Teeth, and began an exploration of the area around the SW and then the NW side of the Altar. On the far NW side we found an easy way to the summit, a gully. The start was the crux. We kicked steps up steep snow for what seemed like hundreds of feet to where the snow met a rock cliff. There I had to climb a short section of the cliff, wet from dripping snow, without protection. I was beat from plodding up the snow ramp. The short section of cliff looked like it should be 5.5 (easy). Wearing a pack and in wet conditions without protection, it seemed like 5.10. Perhaps it was because I was tired. We had blasted up dozens of hard pitches of climbing that day. As I had been doing all the leading, I was beat and surrendered the lead to Ron. He went ahead, quickly plunging though snow, yanking on bushes and trees, up to the summit.

When we got to the summit, I had to sit and rest. Ron continued, and went

Ron at our bivy on the edge of the Altar of Sacrifice. Below: Ron rappelling the east face of the Altar of Sacrifice.

to look for possible ways to rappel the east face of the Altar to continue our traverse. We decided to bivy on the summit of the Altar. I was too tired to continue, and the summit is an amazing place to sleep. We slept near the edge. I did not bring a sleeping bag. Ron brought a stove. I can't remember what he cooked. I was too beat to care. I ate the dinner I rationed myself - a power bar - and curled up in my bivy bag (plastic sac), and went to sleep.

Sunday, March 22, 7AM. This should have been an easy day. Ron found a spot he believed there to be trees down the face of the Altar to rappel. Before heading down, we stopped to refill our water bottles at a puddle in the red rock on the summit. Some kind of animal foot prints led to the edge of the pool. Rabbit? Squirrel? They looked like big prints. Ron says rabbit prints can look that way due to the way they walk. There were two types. One looked rabbit, the other big paws. I

wonder what draws these animals to the summit. Perhaps it's the same forces that draw us. I wondered how they get down and considered, maybe they did not want to.

From the summit of the Altar of Sacrifice, we rappelled its east face onto the hanging valley between it and the Meridian Tower. We did not leave slings. It might be difficult to locate and it's not recommended. If you do go this way, look for the logical, that which is the shortest to the ground, the first rappel will be from a big tree down to another big tree on a ledge. The next rappel goes over the edge onto the blank and overhanging face. At the end of the rope, if you find the way, you will come to a hanging anchor with fixed pins. Rap to another set of drilled angels and then to the ground.

When we got to the bottom of Meridian Tower, I couldn't find a way to climb it. I was tired and gave up. Ron, not as tired, trudged up the gully on its west side to get a better view. He came back and told me it was not possible - the larger massif did not connect to the tower. I believed him. Although to me it's possible to climb anything you put your mind to, I was tired and wanted an excuse to go down.

We descended what I call the standard decent from that area - a large gully on the west side of the Meridian Tower that empties into Oak Creek Canyon. Ron and I came down the gully without drilling bolts. Today the gully has been bolted (fixed angle pitons were added on subsequent trips. I am astonished and in dis-belief we rappelled off such tiny bushes and down-climbed at the time.) While I was disappointed in not climbing the Meridian Tower, that would be the genesis to power a decade of additional explorations. Had I been successful, I would not had spent so much time coming back and climbing other peaks and canyons nearby.

TRAVERSING THE TOWERS OF THE VIRGIN

TRAVERSE OF THE TOWERS OF THE VIRGIN A2, 5.10
D Stih and R Raimonde, March 1998.
EQUIPMENT REQUIRED: Alpine rack.
CAUTIONS / SPECIAL DIFFICULTIES: A crux used to be rappelling the overhanging north face of the West Temple to reach the saddle between the West Temple and Sundial. Ron and I rappelled off natural anchors i.e., small bushes and down-climbed. The trees have had time to grow. Retreat anywhere between the West Temple and the Altar of Sacrifice is difficult. Do not expect to find webbing at natural anchors. We left nothing. It used to be a palm slap was required to negotiate getting around the east face of the Sun Dial into the wash on its north side. It was what likely stopped Trapier from accessing the Altar of Sacrifice and Sun Dial. Erosion must have made what was once improbable, easy passage. Now it's just a hike. The note and carin left by Tapier are gone.
WATER: Snow is your friend. Unless there is snow, there is no water on the West Temple or the south side of the Sun Dial. Unless there is snow to melt, you will need to traverse across the east face of the Sun Dial to reach water. In spring, there is water on the north

Rappelling off the West Tempe in 2022 when Mike Dunn and I did the Traverse of the Time Machine. I didn't remember it being so overhanging and spooky!

side of the Sun Dial. Snow collects in a couloir on the north side of the Sun Dial, providing a stream into the first week of June if there is normal snow fall in the winter. In early season (March - early April) there may be snow banks on the west side of the Altar of Sacrifice after you traverse around its back (west) side. If there is no snow, it's likely you are climbing late in the season or there wasn't a lot of snow. In that case the water situation could become serious.

After you rappel the Altar to the hanging valley between the Altar of Sacrifice and Meridian Tower, water, might be found in a large pool far down the white slabs heading down from the notch between Sky Island and the Altar. The only other place water might be found is in a creek next to the west face of the Meridian Tower on its southern end if there's been a heavy amount of snow that year. If there's no water, you're out of luck until you reach the ground or hike up and down along the west side of the Meridian Tower down to Birch Creek. This is, therefore, the recommended route to take to climb the Meridian Tower - go down to Birch Creek and either climb the north face, as Dave and I did, or a ramp on the east face, as subsequent parties are doing.

SEASON: Mid-late March through mid-April, depending on snow.

CAMPING / TIME REQUIRED: Four days for a fast party that has previously climbed the West Temple and climbed up the descent used for the Streaked Wall, such that you are familiar with the start and descent. Those unfamiliar with the terrain may require more.

THE STARTING POINT: We parked just past the cemetery in Springdale. As Zion (Springdale) becomes developed, the city may not allow that. In that case, ride bicycles or get dropped off close to the east side of the West Temple. When you get down, be sure to walk back to where you started do a fair job of it all.

THE ROUTE: Climb the 1938 route on the West Temple. From its north edge rappel onto the white slabs between the West Temple and Sun Dial Massif. Tag the summit of the Sub-Dial before scrambling down the white slabs. Traverse across the lower east face of the Sun Dials. Turn the corner and go west to access the climbing route for the Sun Dial. Drop your bivy gear and do the Traverse of the Time Machine. Pick up bivy gear and proceed towards the west side of the Altar of Sacrifice, climbing the Witch Head, Broken Tooth, and Rotten Tooth on the way. Before heading up to the west face route on the Altar (a long trudge), drop bivy gear (and climbing gear) take water and rock shoes, and traverse the Droids. After summiting each of the Droids, return to your gear and head up to the summit of the Altar. The west face

The blank east face of the Altar of Sacrifice.

The east side of the Altar of Sacrifice, showing the valley between it and Meridian Tower. The wall in the center below the forested cliff is the Beehive Wall, a wall Ron and I once tried to climb. A descent gully, if needed, is on the left (west) side of it.

route is a scramble except for the first pitch, a grunt (5.8 - 5.8+). On the summit (an excellent place to bivy), sign the register. It's tucked inside a tall carin on the NE edge overlooking the old Visitor Center (now the History Museum). Walk to the opposite, south end of the summit and down-bush-wack to locate the rappel into the notch between the Altar of Sacrifice and Sky Island. Rappel into the notch, then climb the last pitch of the original route on Sky Island (last pitch of Left Crack). At the top of that pitch you will come up at the base of the Finger. Tag the summit of the Finger (one short pitch), then continue towards the summit of Sky Island. A red cliff band blocks the summit. It's fairly easy. Down-climb or rappel the red cliff band and goto the area between the Finger and Sky Island. From there, bushwhack down the drainage to a set up a double-rope rappels that go down the ascent for Right Crack (Sky Island). From the bottom of Sky Island, walk to the Meridian Tower. Before you get there, hike to the summit of what CP named after a buddha figure. As you reach the Meridian Tower, hike north upward along its west face to the top of a saddle, then descend the other side down into Birch Creek. There you can get water and start the original route to climb the main

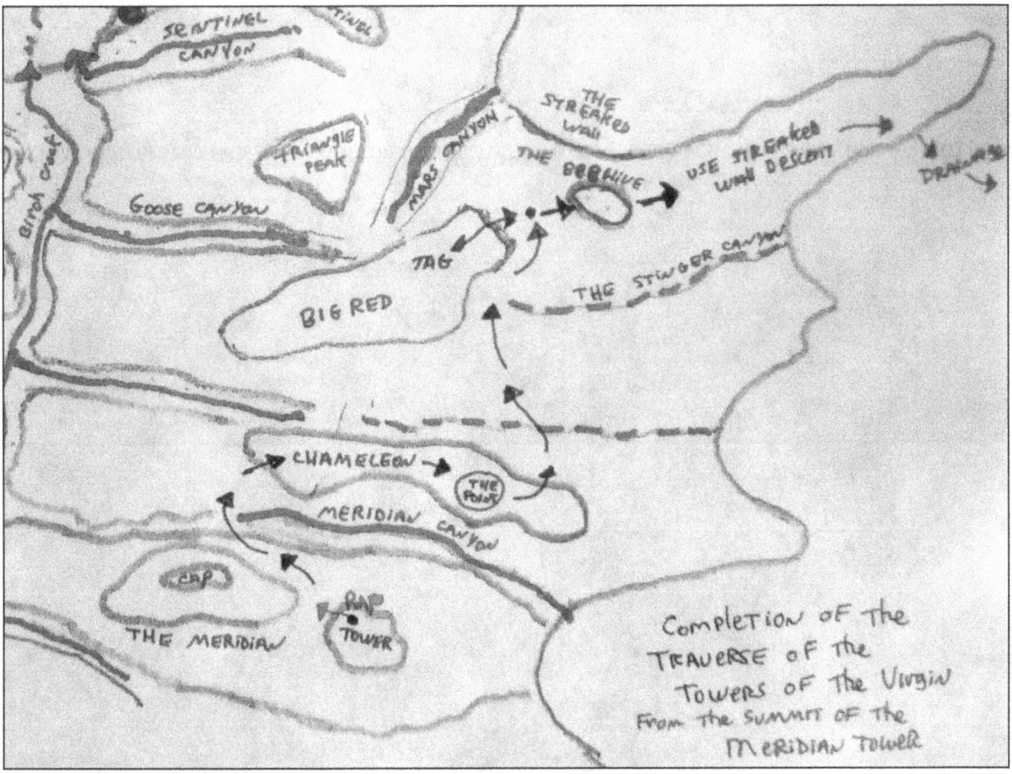

Mike Dunn and Arthur Herlitzka on the summit of the Altar of Sacrifice, March, 2021, the first visitors since Ron and I were there in 1998.

The completion of the traverse after reaching the Meridian Tower.

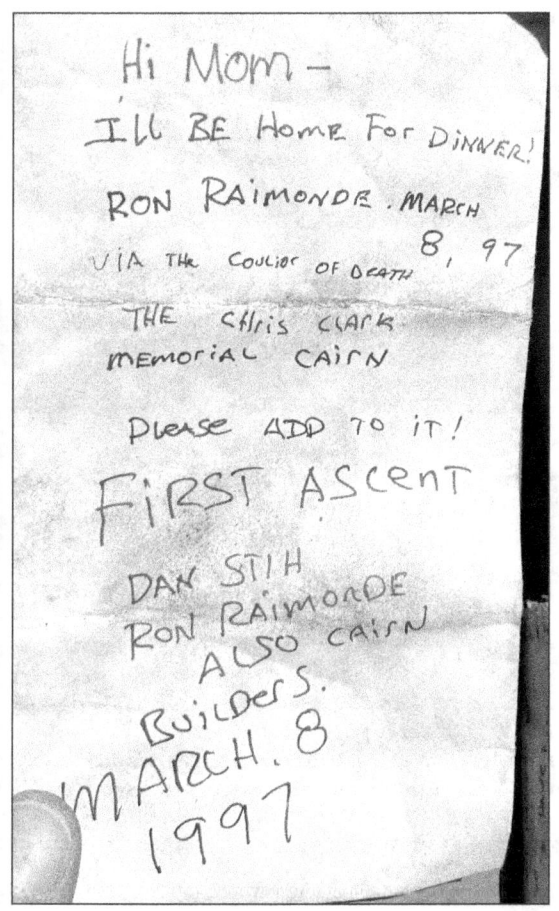

What was left of the Chris Clark Memorial carin after twenty-five years. (Photo Mike Dunn, 2021). It was rebuilt by Mike and Arthur. In 2007, an article in *Climbing* magazine said "the traverse had been repeated just once." Mike found no evidence of a repeat. The confusion may be due to Ron drawing "Coliour of Death (COD)" on his topo for the traverse. We climbed the COD on the first ascent of the Altar. We did the second ascent of the Altar by climbing its West Face during the traverse. Hence perhaps why it was thought the traverse had been repeated. Left: the note Ron and I left inside the register we left on the Altar in 1998. Opposite page: The Altar of Sacrifice as seen from the plateau on the way to climb the Meridian Tower.

massif of the Meridian Tower. Alternatively, you can go a short way down Birch Creek and scramble up a ditch to access the east face of the Meridian Tower where a ramp can be scrambled to access the summit of the main massif. After reaching the summit of the massif (boulder moves to climb the red cap), rappel into the notch between it and the tower. Climb the tower, then rappel east from the notch between the two summits of the Meridian Tower. Scramble up the west ridge of Chameleon, hike to its far southern end and descend. Climb the Point, then scramble down into the valley between the Point and Big Red, traversing around the bottom of Big Red to stay out of Stinger Canyon. Tag Big Red, a scramble. From the base of the Bee Hive, it's a scramble up white slabs to tag the summit of Big Red. Although Big Red may not be a Tower of the Virgin, why not. Come down and scramble up and over Bee Hive Peak, heading SE to descend to civilization using what those who climb the Streaked Wall use to descend into Oak Creek. Hike out to the old Visitor Center (History Museum). Walk back to your starting point. If you get a ride or ride your bike you didn't do the traverse. To date, those attempting this ambitious adventure got a ride from a vehicle waiting in the parking lot at the visitor center. See other chapters for details on the various peaks mentioned here.

Descend from the saddle (the notch) of the Meridian Tower (upper left) to the tree covered ledge on the east side of the Meridian Tower. Traverse north (right) to the saddle between the Meridian Tower and Chameleon, and get onto the north ridge of Chameleon.

The Point (L) and Chameleon (R). From the summit of Chameleon, hike to its south edge (left), and descend to the Point.

Between Big Red and Beehive Peak, stay high to avoid Stinger Canyon. Work around the south corner of Big Red into the valley between Big Red and the Point.

FUTURE CLIMBING
Do the "traverse".
To date, no one has included the Three Marys in their traverse of the Towers of the Virgin. I think the perfect solution is to start by climbing the Three Marys, then hike over to the 1938 route of the West Temple. Rappel off the West Temple and finish the travererse as it's normaly done, coming down the descent by the Streaked Wall. Walk back to your starting point. If you include the Three Marys in your traverse, in my opinion you will have done the first real and complete traverse of the Towers of the Virgin.

The cave visible under the south rim of Big Red that can be seen from Springdale. It can be reached by climbing up the descent used for the Streaked Wall and traversing west, or by rappelling off the SW corner of Big Red, or by climbing the Point and coming down into the valley to the east.

Traverse of the
Court of the Patriarchs

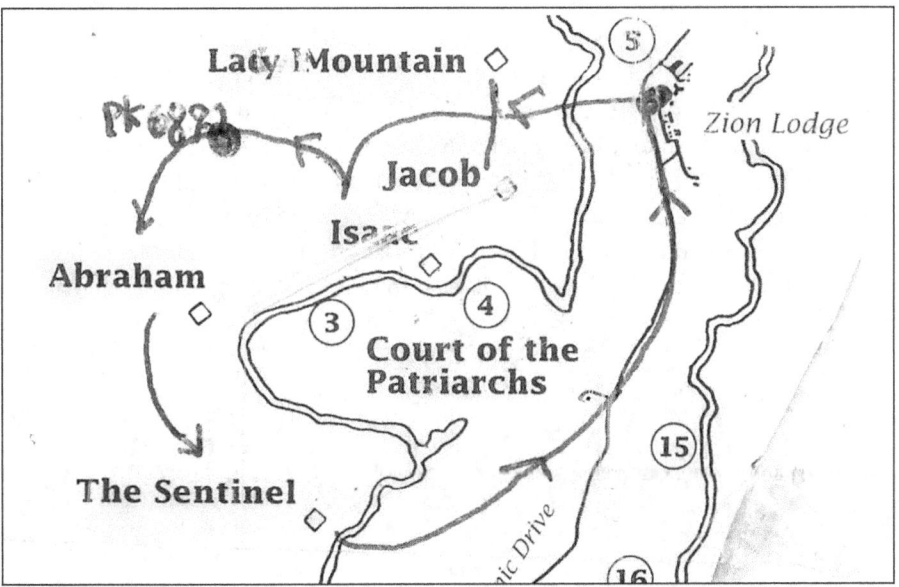

INTRODUCTION This is a "closed loop traverse" (the route starts and ends at the same point) of the mountains surrounding the Court of the Patriarchs, including Jacob, Lady Mountain, Isaac, Cliff Dwelling Mountain, Abraham, and the Sentinel. The traverse is more difficult and dangerous than the traverse of the Towers of the Virgin, and requires mandatory 5.10+ climbing with scant protection.

The Alps Come to Zion

I learned about traverses from Ron Raimonde. Each summer Ron quit his job in Phoenix, Arizona, and went to Switzerland to climb in the Alps. In traditional mountain climbing, it's common to traverse a series of mountains. Sometimes the only way to get to the top of a mountain is to climb others on the way. The following is from my journal:

March 27 - 29, 1999. A traverse of all the formations in the Court of the Patriarchs, each by a new route. Two bives. No Sleeping bags. Cold! Iodine tablets. Two, 2-liter water bottles carried. We would re-fill them when we stumbled across water.

Rack (Jacob): 1 each: #0.5, #1, #2 cams; 2 each #3 cams, small Aliens
Rack (Lady Mountain): Nada
Rack (Isaac & Abraham): Slings
Rack (Sentinel): Slings

We were stumped as to how to begin. We knew we wanted to do a traverse but could not see a way to get started. When you drive down the road towards the Zion Lodge, and look up at the east face of Mt. Lady Mountain, it looks steep and improbable. It doesn't look like there could be a way to climb it. We parked on the side of the road and walked up and down in front of Lady Mountain. Back and forth. It was cold. We were stumped. I suggested we get coffee in the Zion Lodge. That was not our normal routine. We were hard men, and it would be uncool to join tourists in the warm Lodge. I had to twist his arm. We didn't have anything else to do except go home.

Lady Mountain, as viewed from the Zion Lodge. Incredible as it might seem, a trail, closed since the 1960s, meanders up the middle.

As we sat drinking coffee sitting at a table on the second floor, looking out a big window at the mountain, our waiter noticed our focused attention and stuck up a conversation. He told us about the Old Lady Mountain Trail, one that ascends the otherwise blank face. He also told us to be careful. Someone had recently died on the trail. The rock had been wet and slippery. We politely

A spike remaining where a cable used to be attached to the mountain for a handrail.

agreed to be careful, not disclosing that we planned on running across the street and looking for the trail as soon as we finished our coffee.

Warm and excited about finding a way, we exited the Lodge, walked across the road, and started bushwhacking up the mountain, taking the easiest way. We ran into the trail. Officially closed, it's a testimony to the old days. They don't build trails like they used to. It's in disrepair. Occasionally we lost the trail.

After reaching the top of Lady Mountain, we went down to the saddle between Jacob and Lady Mountain. From the saddle we picked the easiest route to get to the top of Jacob. It turned out to be a 5.11- hand/finger/chimney crack. After reaching the top, we rappelled back the saddle.

Back at the saddle, we rappelled into the canyon between Jacob and Isaac. We had two 50-meter ropes. We started from a tree on the NW edge. We did

Ron on the Old Lady Mountain Trail.

Isaac (right of the tree in the foreground); Cliff Dwelling Mnt (Right), as seen from Lady Mountain.

not leave rap slings around the tree. It was our ethics not to leave slings unless the ropes would not pull. We drilled one hanging station on the bank face to finish descending into the canyon. Ron drilled it. I always let him go first when rappelling if looked scary and uncertain. Ron drills solid anchors.

    Once in the canyon, we went South towards Isaac, to where it meets a drainage coming from the north between Isaac and Peak 6892 (as marked on the Trails Illustrated map, and also known as Cliff Dwelling Mnt.) We found water there, a trickle to fill our bottles. We left the canyon there, and headed up the drainage to the north side of Isaac. I suppose if someone (a canyoneer) wanted to, you could continue south and exit what's probably a water fall (when water is flowing) between Isaac and Jacob / Mt. Moroni. [Later I learned this is Isaac Canyon and was used by Lowe as a descent when he did the first ascent of Isaac.]

    We climbed the NW ridge of Isaac, simul-climbing as fast as one can while managing a rope. I was impressed with Ron's free climbing. He's primarily an aid climber. Typically I led the harder free pitches and he led the hard aid. Here he took off. I could barely keep up while managing the slack in the rope between us. To descend, we reversed the route, down-climbing and rappelling. We worked fast and efficient as a team. We didn't need to talk. We knew what needed to be done, what the other was capable of, and when it was time to use the rope. The history of mountaineering has a few similar matchings of partners. Like a good rock band, there's a chemistry between members that can't be replicated. I compare Ron and myself to Reinhold Messner and Peter Habler. We were doing on sandstone what they had done on the ice.

The NW ridge of Abraham was our next objective. We weren't sure how to get there. A deep canyon, the Gunsight, separates Isaac from Abraham. We couldn't go down into it and expect to climb out. The canyon walls are hundreds of feet high on each side. There was water there in the bottom in a place the sun doesn't shine. If we went down into that canyon we would be swimming in ice cold water.

We hiked north, along the side of the canyon we had come down into get to Isaac. Half-way up the canyon, we found ourselves heading to the top of another mountain - Cliff Dwelling Mountain. At first the climbing was easy. Then we ran into a road block. We found ourselves at a blank, steep wall. There was but one weakness, a crack that looked not too steep that we could not climb it. We roped up. I went first. Half-way up, I began to grumble as I climbed a 5.8+ squeeze chimney. A squeeze chimney is a crack not wide enough to fit your body, but too wide to securely place hands and feet. It's awkward and makes you grunt. I was wearing a pack. This was the first

Looking at the rappel that is normally used to get into the Cross Roads from Phantom Valley. We climbed up it to get out of Heaps Canyon and reach the north side of Abraham. On the right is a ridge leading up to the Middle Cathedral.

The north ridge on Abraham. Our route starts on the lower left corner, where the sun meets shade. There may appear to be a ramp leading up from the lower right side where there is a red, tree-covered hill in the foreground. It does not connect to the upper part of the mountain.

known ascent of Cliff Dwelling Mountain.

When we got to the top of Cliff Dwelling Mountain, we were not sure where we were going. We hiked north across the summit. We hoped we could climb Abraham when we reached it. From our vantage point, the North ridge of Abraham looked steep and intimidating. As we descended Cliff Dwellings and got closer, Ron kept asking, "Does that [Abraham] look climbable?"

I always answered, "Yes," even though I had doubts that boarded on, "No." I never allowed those thoughts to take verbal form. I didn't know what would happen if we got stuck. We didn't have a backup plan. Half way down it became too difficult to down-climb, and we started rappelling. After the first rappel, there was no way we'd be able to climb back up to the top of Cliff Dwelling Mnt. As it grew dark and hard to see, we found ourselves at a ledge big enough to sleep on. We bivied, on the side of the mountain, on the descent down the west side of Cliff Dwelling Mountain.

Day 2. In the morning we finished rappelling into the canyon between Abraham and Cliff Dwelling Mountain (the Gunsight). There was water in it. We walked up stream to where it meets the Cross Road, and that's where things got interesting. I didn't know there was such a thing as canyoneering, a sport

On the north side of Abraham, as we made our way across the top.

people go down canyons for simple sake of experiencing the canyons. As we reached the Cross Roads, I was astonished to find foot prints in the sand. I felt like we had traveled to the moon and found footprints.

    Standing in the Cross Roads, Ron and I stared at Abraham. It looked too steep to climb. We needed to keep going, to hike towards it and not worry. We hiked past the Phantom Valley Narrows, to the base of NW corner of Abraham. To get there we free-climbed the rappel route canyoneers normally use to go down to get to the Cross Roads from Phantom Valley. It was a two-hundred-foot cliff. We didn't know we were climbing up, what others rappel down, unroped, and wearing our packs.

    On flatter ground, we got out of the canyon, and walked towards the north side of Abraham. Unlike the steep, vertical east face we had been looking at, the north side had slope to it. It had potential. There was hope we might be able to climb it. If we couldn't, we had no idea where we were or how we might get back to civilization.

    We started climbed Abraham. After a few hundred feet of easy climbing we

The west face of Abraham where the descent from the top comes down into Abraham Canyon. Rugged, steep and complex. An easy place to get stuck.

came to a section that was 105 degrees steep and blank. The crux was 5.10. The climbing moves were protected by a micro-cam twenty feet below my feet. I could not see where I going, or if there were good holds above. A short distance later the angle eased and we went back to simul-climbing. If you believe the first person to stand on the highest point is the first to climb a mountain, we had done the first ascent of Abraham.

We took a break and ate lunch. After lunch, we began to try and find a way to go down the west face to continue the traverse. It was complicated. We found no rap slings or evidence of a previous descent. It was easy to find the wrong way. We ended up at a dead end and had to climb back up. After starting over in a different spot, several rappels lead to easy ground. We followed this to more easy ground, but ended up stuck and had to climb back up. We traversed NW and finish rappelling. We had to drill one hanging rap station to reach the ground, Abraham Canyon.

After reaching the ground we scrambled down Abraham Canyon to Birch Creek, and the valley between the Sentinel and Abraham. We were in familiar

Bottom arrow: the north-west ridge leading from Birch Creek up to the Sentinel, and the first crux; Top arrow: the north face of the Sentinel. The second crux is at the tip of the arrow, just below the summit.

terrain, having climbed the north side of the Sentinel and gone down the 1938 route on the other side, the previous year. We took a break and filled our water bottles.

The Sentinel was the hardest of the climbing on the traverse. It has several mandatory run-out sections on loose, steep, sandy terrain. This was our second ascent (See "North-West Face of the Sentinel"). Instead of being easier, we found ourselves in awe. Many of the belays are slings wrapped around small bushes that would not hold a fall. You have to count on your partner using his body weight to hold a belay stance, and not fall. This time we had a hammer and a few pitons. I placed a Lost Arrow at the start of the first difficult section. It was pointed downward in a shallow crack. We left it there.

We bivied at the "cave," a feature cut in the north face of Triangle Peak. The only food we had left was one Power Bar. Ron gave it to me in exchange for me agreeing to sleep there. I would have preferred to finish the traverse and get home in the dark. Ron was tired. He built a fire to kill time. I didn't have a sleeping bag. I was cold, tired, and hungry. We found water from snow melting.

In the morning, we finished climbing the Sentinel, descended its east face, and walked the Sand Bench Horse Trail back to the Zion Lodge, back to where we had started. A true traverse. We were not assisted by mountain bikes or other means of transportation.

A one-paragraph description of our traverse was published in *Rock & Ice* magazine No. 93. I felt like Jimmy Page when *Rolling Stone*, not appreciating the significance of the first Led Zeppelin album, gave it one paragraph.

TRAVERSING THE COURT OF THE PATRIARCHS

TRAVERSE OF THE COURT OF THE PATRIARCHS 5.10+ R
D Stih and R Raimonde 1999
EQUIPMENT REQUIRED: We used only slings to protect the routes on Isaac, Cliff Dwelling Mnt, Abraham, and the Sentinel. We used a normal free-climbing rack to climb Jacob (See Jacob). In order to get our packs light, we didn't take sleeping bags, and used iodine tablets to treat water. We climbed with a 150-foot 9-millimeter dynamic rope, rated as a 1/2 rope, and a 200-foot 7-mil static to supplement the dynamic for rappels. (At that time the thinnest rated rope was 10.5-mil, too heavy to consider.) Using 150-foot ropes was lighter and worked better than a longer rope. Much of the climbing is scrambling and simul-climbing.
CAUTIONS / SPECIAL DIFFICULTIES: Climbing Abraham is difficult. Getting down is as difficult. The descent on the west face of Abraham is difficult to locate. There are huge drops into Abraham Canyon. The north face of the Sentinel is steep, unprotected 5.10+ face climbing. If when you get there you can't climb it, the escape is to rappel into Birch Creek. It helps to be familiar with the 1938 route on the East face of the Sentinel so that when you reach the top of the Sentinel you know the descent.
WATER SOURCES: Jacob Canyon (between Jacob and Isaac), The Cross Roads (between Cliff Dwelling Mnt and Abraham), and Birch Creek (before climbing the Sentinel).
SEASON: Spring when there is water from snow melting. Summer is too hot. Late fall may be pleasant if you can find or carry adequate water. There's always water in the Cross Roads and Birch Creek.
CAMPING / TIME REQUIRED: Several days.

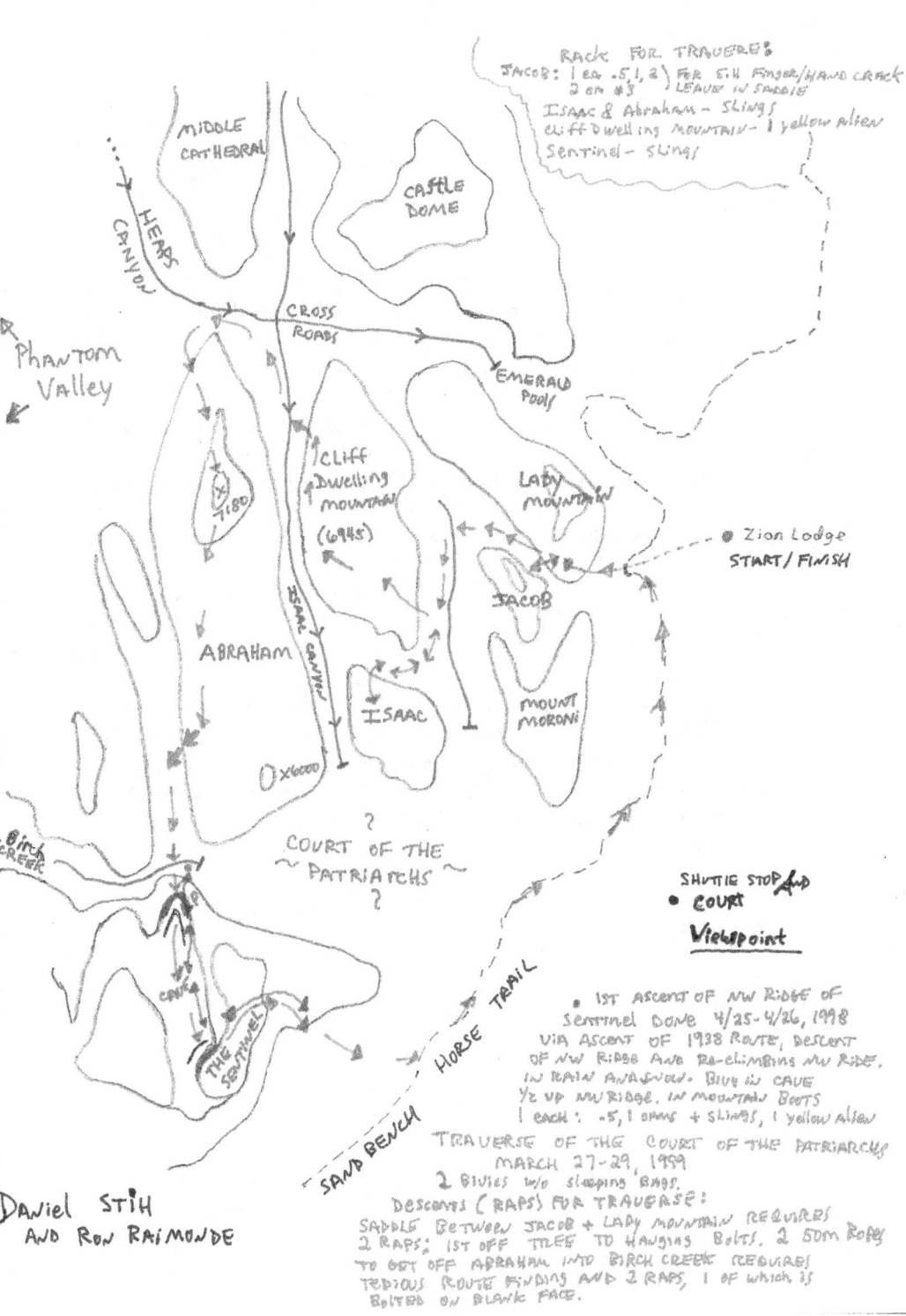

THE STARTING POINT: The Old Lady Mountain Trail (Zion Lodge).

THE ROUTE: Hike the Old Lady Mountain Trail to the summit of Lady Mountain, then descend to the saddle between Jacob and Lady Mountain. Climb the north face of Jacob to its summit. Rappel back to the saddle. Scramble down the other side of the saddle towards Jacob Canyon. To get into Jacob canyon requires two rappels: the first off a big tree, the second (and possibly 3rd, I don't recall) from drilled angles on a blank face of the canyon wall. Once in Jacob Canyon, hike down stream until you reach a drainage on the right that comes down from the north face of Isaac. Go up the drainage to the base of Isaac and climb its north face. Descend the route.

From the bottom of Isaac, work north around the east side of Cliff Dwelling Mnt, taking the easiest path to the summit (5.8-5.9). From the summit, down-climb and rappel its NW corner into Gunsight Canyon, just south of Cross Roads. At the Crossroads, head up Heaps Canyon and climb up the right side of the rappel canyoneers use to get from Phantom Valley to the Cross Roads.

Once in Phantom Valley, get out of the creek and head towards the north ridge of Abraham. Climb the ridge to the summit (5.9+ R). Stand on the summit, then walk across the top to the south end. From the southern tip, backtrack and look for the easiest way to scramble and zig-zag down the west face and rappel into Abraham Canyon. (See the chapter Abraham for details.) Walk the canyon to Birch Creek, then up a dirt hill on the south side of the creek to the next objective: the north ridge of the Sentinel. One of the cruxes of the traverse is on the way to climb the Sentinel. Half-way up the ridge, where the red blocks meet white face. (See the Chapter, The North-West Face of the Sentinel). Look for a fixed lost arrow that is clipped by standing on a pedestal. Pull up on thin holds over 100-degree face to easier climbing. Hike to the bottom of the North Face of the Sentinel. The next crux, and probably the most difficult on the traverse, is several rope lengths up: a blank, 5.11, white face, without protection, a hundred feet below the summit. From the summit of the Sentinel, down-climb and rappel the 1938 route, then hike the loose dirt hill down to the Sand Bench Trail. Walk back to the Zion Lodge where you started. Don't take the shuttle or ride a bike. Doing so would mean you didn't do a complete traverse.

The east face of the Sentinel, and the final descent at the end of the traverse. On the far left, Bird Beak Spire is visible. The 1938 route is on the right.

FUTURE CLIMBING Do the traverse in reverse. Start by climbing the 1938 route on the Sentinel and rappelling and down-climbing its north face into Birch Creek. Go a short ways up Abraham canyon. Climb out of the canyon onto the east face of Nipples Peak when it get too difficult to continue. Head towards Battleship Rock. From Battleship Rock, descend towards Phantom Valley to access the route on the north face of Abraham as described earlier in this chapter. From the summit of Abraham, reverse the route, heading back into Phantom Valley and follow the creek / canyon for Heaps, rappelling or down-climbing as needed to reach the Cross Roads. From the Cross Roads, climb Cliff Dwelling Mountain as described in the chapters Cliff Dwelling Mountain and Traverse Around the Emerald Pools. From the summit descend, towards and then climb Isaac. From there, either climb back to the summit of Cliff Dwelling Mountain or find another way to climb up to the saddle between Lady Mountain and Cliff Dwelling Mountain. It may be possible to climb up Isaac Canyon. The next objectives are Lady Mountain and Jacob. From the summit of Jacob, you can add to what's previously been done by depending the south side of Jacob and climbing Mt. Moroni for a complete traverse around the cirque referred to as the Court of the Patriarchs.

Traverse of the Bishoprics

INTRODUCTION This is a one-day traverse of the three Bishoprics (North Bishopric, East Bishopric, West Bishopric) and the formations around the Bishoprics (the Entry Pawns, Gate Keeper, the Blob, and Hamster).

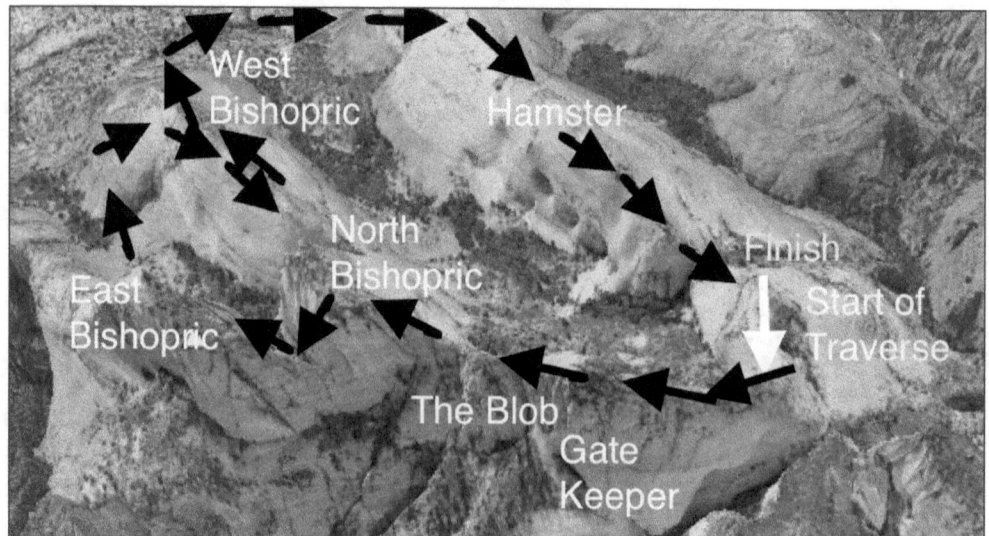

The Three Bishoprics

I slept in my jeep, on the side of the road at Canyon Junction. I got up at midnight and rode my bike (not motorized) up the road to the trailhead at the Grotto. The ride in the middle of the night was quiet, lit by the end of a full moon cycle. It was gorgeous. Deer occasionally crossed the road, probably as startled as I from the break in the silence. An occasional whisper of wind blew through the tall grass and oaks. I had not known the ride was going to be up hill. At times I thought of giving up. In the lowest gear, I seemed to barely be making progress. My legs were on fire. My brother, an avid rider, would have laughed at how tired I was after the five-mile ride. He'd just ridden 100 miles in a race. But he wasn't wearing a haul bag and has a nice bike. I've had the same bike since 1990.

When I reached the Grotto, I looked for the bike rack, stashed the tire pump in a pile of dead leaves, locked the bike, and headed off to the start of the trail. In places the trail was rocky and beat from erosion. I followed the trail in the faint moon light without using my headlamp. I carried a gallon of water in one hand, the idea to drink as I hiked to hydrate. At times that seemed silly because I passed running water from snow melting. My bag weighed 70 pounds. It contained a rope, rack, shoes, warm clothes, food, sleeping bag, and so forth. When I got the top of the West Rim it was still dark.

The Entry Pawns.

 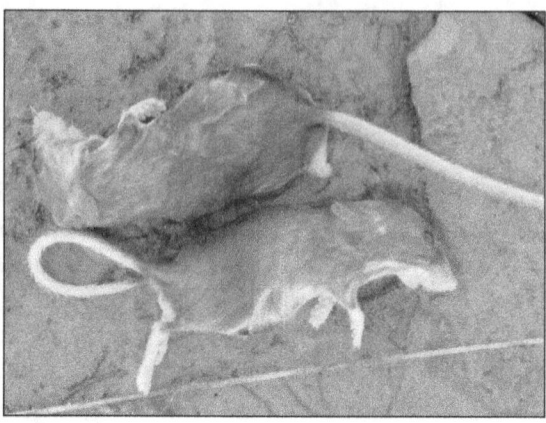

Mice got into my water bottle.

Normally it would be unsafe, and unproductive (you'd get lost) trying to do the 300-foot rappels into Phantom Valley in the dark. I've done the descent so many times during previous adventures, I have it memorized. Although it was cold, in the high 30s, my tee-shirt was soaking with sweat. I changed into a thermal and put on a wind breaker. Feeling warmer, I reached the ground in Phantom Valley as it became light enough to see.

My plan was to hike to the Bishoprics and do the traverse the following day. I had the whole day to get to them. Since that would only take half the day, I took time out and hiked to the bottom of the Sanctuary, a big peak on the left side of Inclined Pass. I envisioned doing a traverse of the mountains around it on a later trip, and wanted to familiarize myself with it. The only known route on the Sanctuary is Rat Salad. In my hiking boots, I free-climbed the first pitch, looking for the fixed pin that is supposed to be on it. I didn't find one. I went as far as I could without a rope, came down, and proceeded to finish hiking to the Bishoprics. When I got to my camp near the Bishoprics, my calfs and legs were blown.

Food didn't help to restore my energy. I needed time to recover. For the rest of the day, I didn't do anything except to lie still, in the shade, under a tree on the south end of the ridge that leads up to the Gate Keeper. I hoped I would have the energy to climb the next day. My hips and knees were hurting. I hoped I could climb with all the gear I would have to carry. To solo, you have to carry everything yourself - rope, rack, protection, water, jacket, and so forth. As I rested under the tree in the shade, I prepared a pack with the gear I would need. While it seems silly to carry two packs, I had carried a large haul bag with climbing gear, sleeping gear and such; and a smaller, book-bag size backpack to use on the climb. The smaller pack is what I call an assault pack.

In the morning, I felt better and ready to go. At the first hint of daylight, I made coffee. I know that's bad. You're supposed to stay hydrated. If I should ever be sponsored, it could be by Starbucks. Their instant coffee is just what I needed. Two goo packs and a Cliff Bar rounded my supplies for the day. I cautiously started hiking toward the start of the climb, checking my body to see

The descent off the summit of the North Bishopric goes down a corner with a dihedral just right of the left skyline, to reach the saddle between the North Bishopric and East Bishopric (barely in sight on the left).

how the legs and feet felt. I seemed to have recovered. At least I was not in pain or dreadfully tired and weak. I climbed the two peaks between the North Bishopric ridge and the Hamster, naming them the "Entry Pawns." As they are not difficult, it's possible early settlers scrambled up them.

After climbing the Entry Pawns, I scrambled to the top of the Gate Keeper and then over to the rappel to reach the bottom of Troubled Youth on the Blob. I trailed the rope, free soloing the Blob. When I reached the North Bishopric, I roped up. I reached the top of the North Bishopric early in the morning.

The decent from the North Bishopric scared me. It would be the scariest thing I had to do on the traverse. *What if I go down the wrong way or the rope, the only one I have, gets stuck when I try and pull it? What if the rope isn't long enough?* I didn't have a bolt kit or a drill. I looked down and saw a big ledge, twenty feet wide. I rapped off a tree onto that ledge. Once on the ledge, I pulled the rope, committing myself to fate. I looked for another tree, one near the edge to set the rope around. There wasn't one. I needed to go sideways to the north, not straight down the big, white, east face. The white face was loose, smooth, and without bushes.

From a vantage point on the ground, I had seen a crack on the north side that might have bushes. If I went down it, I thought, and the bushes were too small, in the worst case I could leave gear in the crack. I'd have better chance of getting down that way. The issue was exposure. The north face was windy and dropped a thousand feet. I only needed to go down a few hundred, then I could hop sideways onto the saddle between the North and East Bishoprics. I just needed to keep my head on. I put a sling around a branch on the tree, six feet off the ground. I wanted to make sure the rope pulled. I didn't want it to get caught on rocks or branches laying on the ground. I went over the edge, rappelling almost to the end of the rope. There I found a small bush. I pulled the rope, rappelled off the bush, and made it to the saddle safely.

The hardest, most dangerous part of the traverse was over. It was just a matter of time. I needed to keep moving if I was going to finish by dark. I scrambled up the NW corner of the East Bishopric. I lost my way near the top, and did some exposed, thin face climbing to get back to course. When I got to the top, even though I had been there before, I had forgotten what it was like. There are lots of thick, thorny manzanita. It was a struggle to walk to the other side. There I found the cairn I had built on my last trip, and what seemed like a trail from other climbers or animals. The faint trail helped expedite my cruise down the south toe. Compared to what I had climbed, it seemed like a deer trail. I ran down it.

From the bottom of the East Bishopric, I hiked sideways to the West Bishopric. I filled up on water on the way. My strategy was to fill my bottle whenever I found water. It takes twenty minutes for treatment tablets to take effect. I would rest for twenty, gulp water, and re-fill the bottle with dirty water before I left. Twenty minutes later I'd start drinking again. I saved half a bottle to add the instant coffee to. That kept me hydrated and gave me caffeine.

The West Bishopric, when done right, is a cruise. I left my rope and pack at the bottom and free-soloed it. There's a section of 5th class near the top, a ten-foot section that's perhaps solid 5.5. Two moves. Then it's a long walk to the north end, the summit, and back.

Back on the ground, I hiked over to the Hamster, and scrambled to its summit. On the way I stopped to fill my bottle from a stream created from snow melting in the chasm between the North and East Bishoprics. In early season (Early April) there will be water flowing down a small creek there.

To complete the traverse I went down the other side of the Hamster. It required two rappels. The first got me to a large ledge, an oasis of tall pine trees. There was plenty of daylight remaining, so I took a break, thankful for the oasis, a special place that can only be reached the way I came down. It's likely no one had been there before. After a good rest and gratitude, I made a final rappel to the ground, arriving on the other side of the Entry Pawns. I coiled the rope, put it in my pack, and walked around the corner, and back to camp. I had no time to rest. The next day I did a traverse of the Sanctuary, the King, and the Queen.

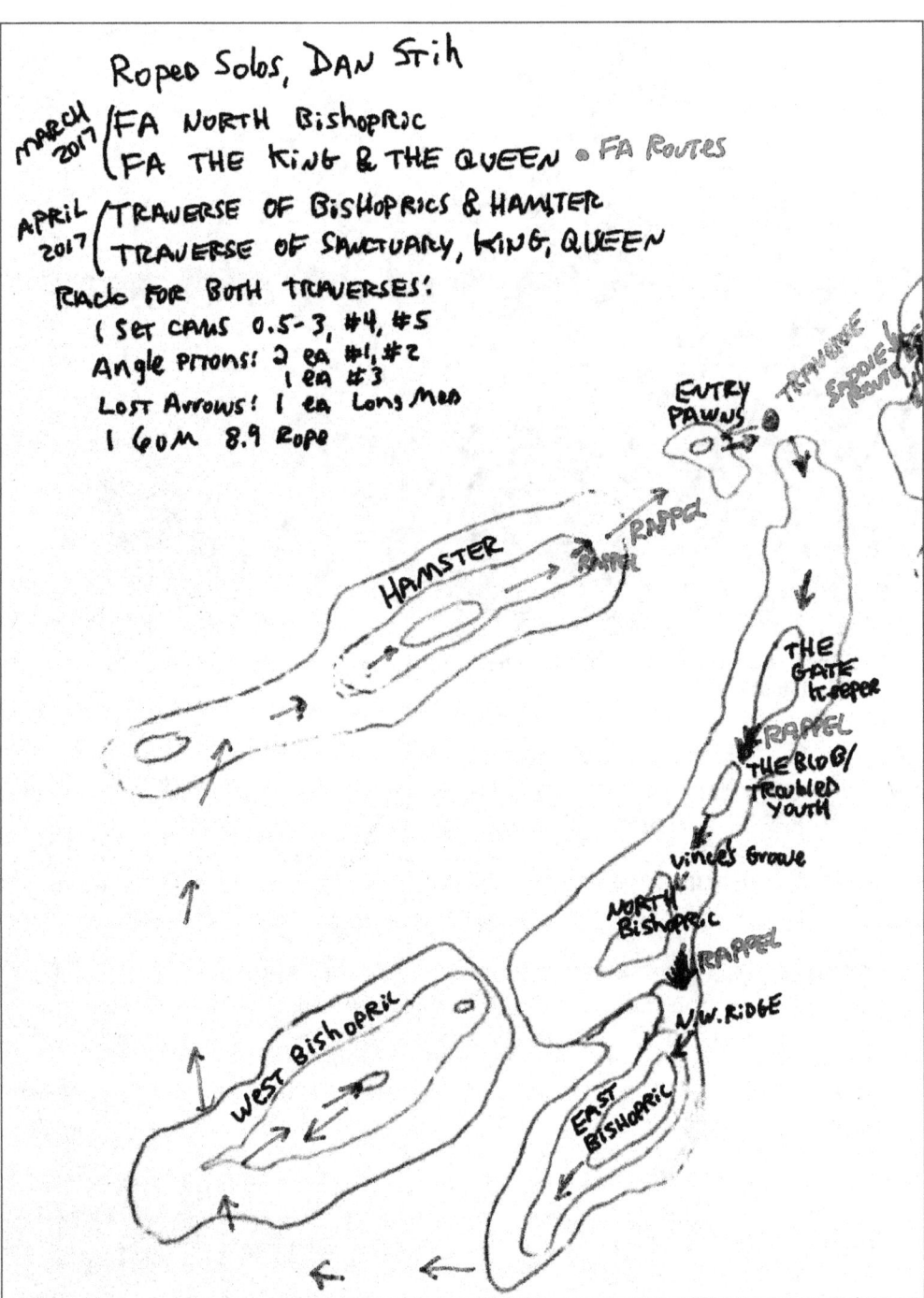

Looking back at the Hamster after rappelling its north side (in the shade), at the completion of the traverse.

TRAVERSING THE BISHOPRICS

TRAVERSE OF THE BISHOPRICS D Stih 2017
This is a "closed loop traverse" - the route starts and ends at the same point.
EQUIPMENT REQUIRED: Standard alpine rack. Take free-climbing boots for Vince's Groove. It's fun. All of the mountains, including the rappels, can be done using a single, 60M rope.
CAUTIONS / SPECIAL DIFFICULTIES: The rappel off the North Bishopric into the saddle between the North and East Bishoprics is not for those easily frightened by exposure. It requires careful route finding, commitment, and using bushes and tree branches for anchors.
WATER: Done the right time of year, you can re-fill at the bottom of the descent of the East Bishopric as you head toward the West Bishopric. You can also re-fill at the bottom of the West Bishopric on the way to the Hamster.
SEASON: Spring is a nice time as water is flowing from snow melting in-between the peaks. The traverse can done in the fall, going a few days after a big rain to ensure the big pool near camp on the south side of the area, between the Hamster and West Bishopric, has water.
CAMPING / TIME REQUIRED: A minimum of three days. It will take one day to get to the Bishoprics and a day to hike out. If you've have not previously visited the area of the Bishoprics, once you get there spend a few days becoming familiar with the moun-

tains before attempting the traverse. Spend a day climbing the ridge to the summit of the North Bishopric, and descend via Nate's Tree Descent. Spend a day hiking up to the saddle between the North and East Bishoprics, and scoping the rappel line used to get off the North Bishopric during the traverse. From there you can scramble up the NW ridge of the East Bishopric to its summit, and descend its south toe (the normal ascent route). As you hike up to the saddle between the North and East Bishoprics, look for the pitons I placed on the east face of the North Bishopric when I attempted an aid route. I left the pitons to remember where the route started. When I came back they were buried under a ten-foot snow drift. Time permitting, scramble up the West Bishopric and the Hamster. Take a rest day. Then do the traverse, starting with the Entry Pawns.

STARTING POINT: Begin at the saddle between the Entry Pawns (to the west), and the end of the ridge coming down from the Gate Keeper (to the east). In early spring (late March) there may be snow allowing for a camp there. When the snow has melted, camp must be near large pools and a creek at the south tip of the valley between the Hamster and West Bishopric. If you camp at that creek, start by hiking north up the valley. At the end of the valley, scramble up and left up slabs between the Hamster and Entry Pawns. At the top of the slabs walk NW then NE around the corner to reach the saddle between the Entry Pawns and Gate Keeper, the start of the traverse.

THE ROUTE: Climb the two Entry Pawns, then come down and walk to the ridge that forms the NW toe of the Gate Keeper. Scramble up and across the ridge to the summit of the Gatekeeper. Descend the other side (a hike) to continue along the ridge towards the Blob. A short rappel is required to reach the Blob. Climb the Blob, then continue along the ridge toward the North Bishopric. The crux on the North Bishopric is the first pitch, Vince's Groove. From the top of Vince's Groove scramble to the summit. Sign the log book found inside the summit carin.

From the summit of the North Bishopric, four rappels (using a single 60m rope) are required to reach the saddle between the North and East Bishoprics. AVOID rappelling down the steep, white, east face. The shortest route to the ground is on the NE corner. Walk to the NE corner. Look for a cairn on the NE edge. The first rappel is off a tree near the cairn. The tree is actually on the north edge of the mountain. I rappelled off a branch that sticks out south. I didn't leave a sling. Look down the east face and you will see a large ledge 100 feet down with another big tree. That's where you need to be. It's committing. You won't be able to climb back up once you pull your rope.

The next rappel is off said big tree. I left a sling. Similar to the first rappel, don't rappel straight down - rather, rappel sideways to the north. You're aim is to get onto the north face. It might seem crazy to go out on the north face, but you will be in a dihedral with a crack that angles down into the saddle, a dihedral with good rock and bushes to use as anchors as needed.

The next rappel is off a bush. I placed a piton in the crack two feet above the bush, but didn't have enough webbing or patience to equalize it with the bush. I gave up, rappelled off the bush, and left the pin for others to work with. The fourth and final rappel is off another bush. Aim for the saddle.

From the saddle, the hard parts of the traverse are over. From there it's full speed ahead and fun scrambling. Scramble up the NW corner of the East Bishopric to its summit and run down its south face. Walk over to the West Bishopric. Leave your pack at the bottom. A rope is not required to climb the West Bishopric. Scramble to the summit (5.5) then down-climb back to your pack. Walk over to the Hamster. Take your pack and rope. You're not coming back. Climb to the summit of the Hamster. From the summit, make two rappels on the far north side, down to a large, tree covered ledge, where you can unrope and take a break in the shade. When rested, rappel the north side to the ground, a saddle between the Hamster and Entry Pawns. Walk around the corner back to the start.

Congratulations!

Th 5.5 pitch on the East Bishopric. Just a scramble.

Traverse of the
Sanctuary, King, and Queen

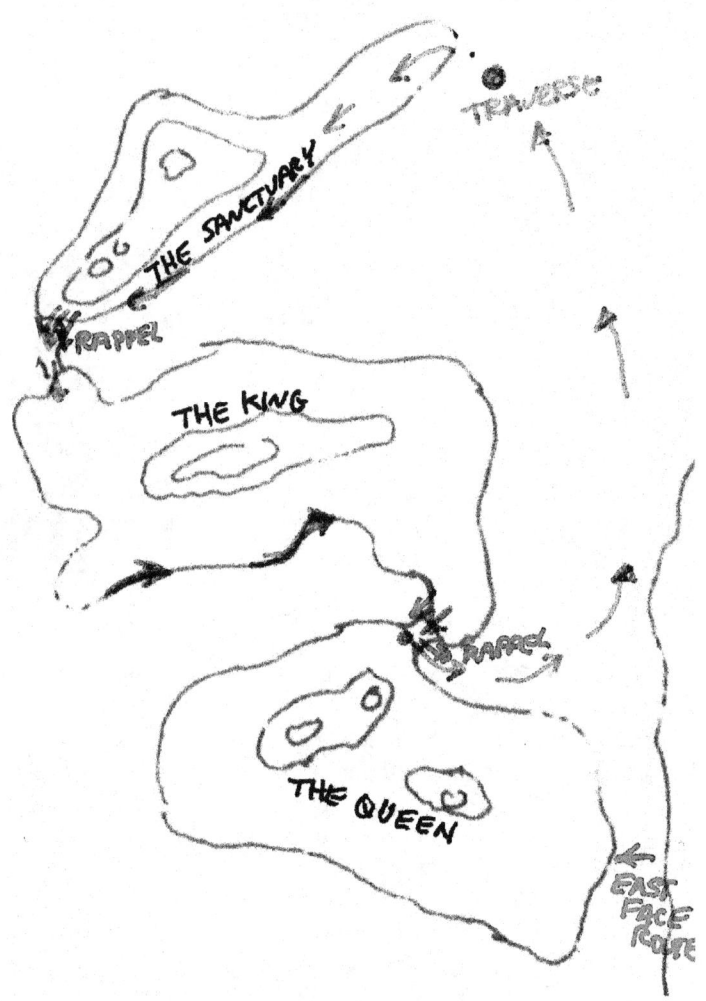

INTRODUCTION Starting from the bottom of the Sanctuary, this is a one-day traverse of the Sanctuary, the King, and the Queen, arriving full-circle back at the Sanctuary.

444
TRAVERSING THE SANCTUARY, KING, AND QUEEN

TRAVERSE OF THE SANCTUARY, KING, AND QUEEN *D Stih 2017*

This is a "closed loop traverse" - the route starts and ends at the same point.

A one-day solo traverse of the Sanctuary (by possibly a new route on its north face), the King, and the Queen (by a new route on its north face).

EQUIPMENT REQUIRED: A standard free-climbing rack. One of each cam up to #3 may suffice. Doubles are plenty. At least a dozen or more long slings. The only roped climbing, other than on the Sanctuary, is to get to the summit of the Queen.

WATER SOURCES: Spring is a nice time to go. There will be water on the west side of the Sanctuary from snow melting. Water is often in pools and pot holes in Phantom Valley on the approach. In late season (Summer and Fall), it may be prudent to wait until after it has rained a few days before starting, to allow pools to re-fill. In early season (spring) there will be water in the canyon between the Queen and Church Mesa, to re-fill bottles on the way back to the Sanctuary. In late season this canyon will be dry.

Snow melting on the west side of the Sanctuary in March.

CAMPING / TIME REQUIRED: Three days. A day to get to the Sanctuary, a day to do the traverse, and a day to hike out.

STARTING POINT: The bottom of the Sanctuary.

THE ROUTE: Start by climbing the north face of the Sanctuary (It's an RNA so stay off the summit proper). After soloing several hundred feet, I traversed right on a good ramp-like ledge to get under a crack system with bushes and trees. I climbed three pitches. The cracks were surprisingly good and took cams. No bolts or pitons were required. Down-climb its south side, making a short rappel near the bottom to reach the saddle which connects the Sanctuary to the King. From the King, scramble down its SE edge to the rocky saddle that connects the King to the Queen. Continue up the other side to the summit of the Queen. A short pitch is required at the rim of the Queen. Tag the Queen, then rappel from a bush on the rim back to the saddle. From the saddle, down-climb and rappel east into a canyon. Follow the canyon down to where it meets a canyon running north-south between the Queen and Church Mesa. Turn left and start down that canyon. After a bit, get out of the canyon and scramble up and across slabs and through brushes, back to the base of the Sanctuary.

View of the Sanctuary from the north side. To start, scramble left up the ramp to the trees. From the trees, climb straight up, then traverse right onto the face to get under one of the major crack systems.

There are the two major crack systems with trees and bushes, what I refer to as Left Crack and Right Crack. I climbed the Left Crack.

Above: On the Sanctuary, looking down at the ridge that connects the Sanctuary to the King. Below: a short pitch is required to reach the Queen.

Traverse Around the Emerald Pools

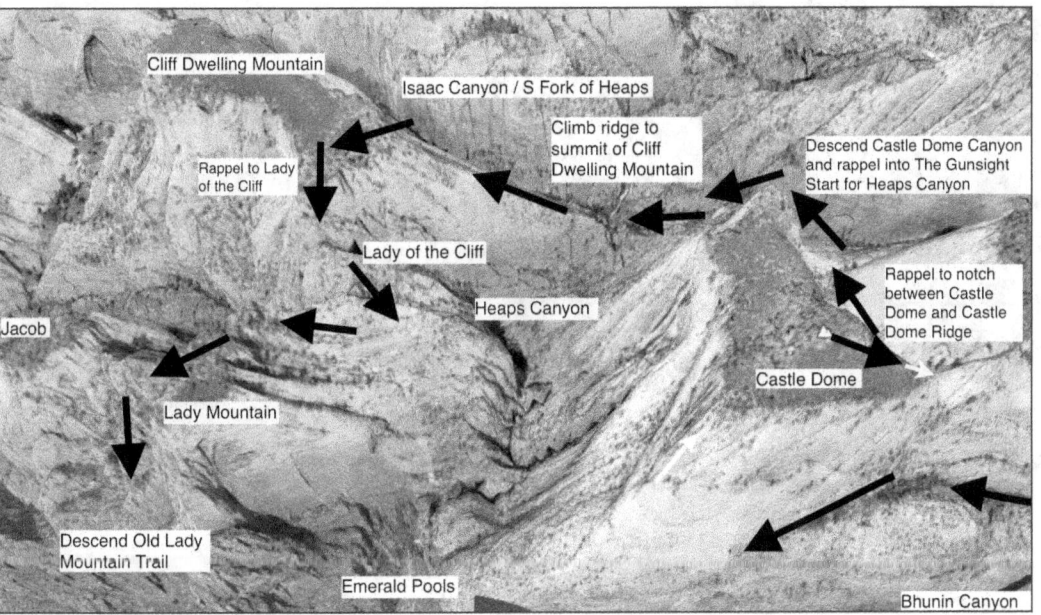

INTRODUCTION The traverse around the Emerald Pools includes climbing an aid route on Cathedral Mountain, followed by Mt Majestic and Castle Dome. The adventure is just getting started. A blind rappel into Gunsight Canyon follows. Depending on the time of year and amount of water, you may find yourself wishing you had an inflatable raft. The canyon is descended to the Cross Roads and the crux - climbing out of the canyon, and up to the summit of Cliff Dwelling Mountain. A less difficult, but long descent, leads to Lady Mountain and then down to the Zion Lodge.

HISTORY Since doing my first "traverse" with Ron in the 1990s, the creative side of my brain has been on the lookout for possibilities. I got the idea for this one as I was climbing Castle Dome with CP and AR. We were near the top, looking over at Lady Mountain, when I shared an idea to do a traverse of the mountains surrounding the Emerald Pools. I was shy to speak of it, not sure it was a genius or ridiculous idea. One or both of them were quick to say, "It's not possible." They were matter-a-fact about it, as if it was a no brainer it can't be done. That inspired me to try.

A Trip Through Emerald City

Above: Lady Mountain (L), Lady of the Cliff (center), Cliff Dwelling Mnt (right) with its north ridge heading right, down into the Cross Roads and Heaps Canyon. Gunsight Canyon is on far right. Photo taken on the descent down Castle Dome Canyon.

My climbing partners said it could not be done. That inspired, and worried me. For almost two years, their opinion nagged at me, as I planned to do what they said could not be done. I thought about backup plans and what to do if I got stuck, what kind of gear to take, and what the best time of year to try such feat should be. The first crux would be to have a light pack. I needed enough rope and climbing gear to climb the difficult sections, but needed to keep my pack light enough to climb while wearing it, unroped, on the upper section of Castle Dome. Easy is relative. Pack too heavy and something easy becomes difficult and dangerous. To keep it light, I planned to take only one rope. That limited potential backup plans. Reading Tom's classic canyoneering guide book, a potential emergency exit would have been Isaac Canyon. But a 280-foot rappel is said to be required. My single rope would only reach 100 feet. If I had to go that way, I might need to drill an intermediate anchor on the way down. But I was not going to carry a bolt kit.

I planned to be cold. I wouldn't take a sleeping bag or a foam pad. (I wish I had taken half a foam pad. The sand was so cold ta night I couldn't lay flat on the ground). I would take a sweater, a plastic bag to sleep in, and a warm hat.

There were other uncertainties. A big concern I had was how much water might in the canyons. Wet suits are normally worn when going down these canyons. I could find myself in a deep pool where the sides are slippery when wet. It had been raining a lot. Which was good. That's a reason I choose to go in the summer. The water level would be low, but there'd still be drinking water.

I am not a swimmer. I lived in San Diego for two years, and only went in the water twice. One evening, at the Wind and Sea Beach near La Jolla, I went for a swim. The water was shallow, the waves were breaking near the beach, so I ventured out further. When I was waist deep, I turned around to look at the beach to see how far out I was. As I turned back toward the ocean, I saw a wall of water, a fifteen-foot wave, just before it clobbered me. It knocked me to the bottom so hard I felt I had nearly drowned. When I surfaced, I staggered to the beach with a hand on the side of my head. It felt like I had a concussion. The pockets in my shorts where filled with sand from being drug on the ocean floor. That was it for me in water. I know - there's no surfing in Zion.

I thought about other exit and backup plans. Another backup plan would be to scale the rappel route at the Crossroads, get into Phantom Valley, and then hike out Coalpits Wash to the highway, where I could hitch-hike. That's assuming I could get to the Crossroads, and was not stuck in water at the start to Gunsight canyon.

In 1980, Reinhold Meisner, an Italian mountain climber, did the first ascent of Mt. Everest without using bottled oxygen. At the time it was a mental barrier. Most told him he was stupid for trying to climb at that altitude without having bottled oxygen, and that he would get permanent brain damage. He ignored their criticism and did it anyhow. Now it's a common. Climbers know it can be done. My traverse was similar. Plan as I did, ultimately one can only plan so much.

I patiently waited for the right moment to go. There were three cities on my weather app: Santa Fe, where I lived, Hurricane (close to Zion), and Springdale (very close to Zion and the Emerald Pools). As summer arrived, I checked daily for a day below 90F. My gear was packed and ready to go. In August, I canceled a trip to climb in the Wind River Range in Wyoming. My heart wasn't into it. I wanted to have my adventure in Zion. It was September when a cool spell was finally forecast. Cool weather (85F) was expected to begin on a Tuesday. Anxious to get out of the house, I drove to Phoenix, Arizona, on Sunday, and spent it with my brother and his family, where I told my brother and sister-in-law of my plans, and waited for their responses, a type of non-verbal communication that helps me gauge weather I'm planning something difficult or stupid.

On my brother's computer, one with better resolution than mine, I showed him what I intended to climb on satellite images. That's when I started to have doubts. The bottom part of Cliff Dwelling Mountain looked like a vertical maze of steep and broken rock. My emergency exit plan - Isaac Canyon - had walls that looked steep and vertical. There would be deep water for sure.

Why? You might be wondering, *why*. Why I don't I get a partner? Meisner did not have a partner when he climbed Everest. Was it because he couldn't talk someone into going with him? No. There is something spiritual about being on a mountain alone. Partners change the vibe, for better or worse, depending on what kind of experience you're hoping to have. Having a partner introduces new liabilities. If your partner gets scared and wants to exit, things can go bad. A frightened partner doesn't think clearly and makes bad decisions. The actual real reason is I am selfish. I want the experience that comes with climbing by yourself.

Monday morning, as my brother was getting ready to go to work, I went online, and used a tarot card service. I asked for a sign as to if should I go climbing, and pulled a card. I pulled the Death Card. When my brother came back down to leave for to work, I said, "I can't go."

'Why?" he said.

"I pulled the Death card."

Without hesitating he said, "You can't believe that thing! It's a computer game."

That was enough. It was onward. I felt better driving to Zion, knowing I was headed where I belonged. I told myself that this time, it was not just a drive, hike-see, and go home. A month earlier, I had made an attempt. I drove to Zion, got a permit, hiked up to Castle Dome, looked at the first canyon, and said no. I tried to talk myself into continuing. Each time I took a step forward, I felt no. It was no use. I hadn't even uncoiled the rope. I turned around and went home.

The only way to know how difficult something is, is to try. I had to go into that canyon. It was the only way I'd ever stop thinking about it. Later, a friend told tell me that the Death card means getting over your fears.

The other thing my bother suggested, and I did, was activate my inReach, an emergency satellite phone that allows you to send and receive text messages. I thought about the weight it would add, and that I might not get a signal in the canyons. He also told me to get a permit for an extra night. That way I could take my time.

When I got to Zion, I took the last shuttle up the canyon road to the Grotto. It was 8 pm. My plan was to bivy (sleep in the open) at the base of Castle Dome, as close as I could get to it in the dark. There was no moon. In the

Castle Dome Canyon on the way to where it drops into Gunsight Canyon.

dark, it was challenging. Hiking the trail was easy. Once I left the trail and started down Behunin canyon, it was treacherous. It had been raining. The normally barren canyon was overgrown with bushes. In places the water was deep and I had to leave the canyon, scramble to high ground, and come back down into it. I often was not sure if I was in the right place. The closest I could get to Castle Dome was the junction where the canyon opens, and the creek makes a sharp turn towards a water fall for the first rappel down Behunin Canyon. There was a place to sleep up high out of the water on flat sand. I was tired and anxious to rest.

I pulled things out of my pack to get ready to sleep. That's when I noticed it. Flashing at the top of the screen on my InReach satellite device, in big, bold, red and yellow capital letters, was the message: "SOS IN PROGRESS." Somehow it had turned on and then sent an SOS. To send an SOS, a safety switch must first have been clicked sideways from locked to open. Then the SOS button had to have been pressed and held down for a few seconds.

Maybe, I thought, I can turn it off. I pressed and held down the power button.

It responded with: "SOS in progress. Can not turn off until SOS canceled." I was in the canyon with poor reception. I tried scrambling up the side of the canyon to get a clearer view of the sky. At first, no luck, then, unbelievably, I

View of the Gunsight, a narrow and wet canyon.

got the message: "SOS has been canceled".

At the same time, I received incoming messages. The International Emergency Response Coordination Center in Montgomery, Texas, had called my emergency contact the moment my SOS had been received. My emergency contact had been on the phone with them for hours. In preparation, they had called local authorities and the national park service. The parties were waiting until morning to stage a rescue. Unless the SOS button had been pushed again. If that had happened, they would have gone in the middle of the night. Good to know the system works. Wish the unit was not capable of sending false SOSs.

At first light, I stood up, put the rain jacket I had been wearing to stay warm in my pack, and hiked to the start of the climbing route on Castle Dome. I went as far as I could before stopping to rope up. I traversed, climbed sideways, then up to easier ground, where I fixed the rope around a tree.

There's a lot of extra work to do when you climb by yourself. After I tied the end of the rope around a tree, I had to go down and untie the other end from its anchor, a bush. Then I had to climb back up to the tree, pulling myself up the rope. Back at the tree, I untied the rope and put it in my pack. I climbed to the top without using the rope again.

At the top, I searched for a way down, into the canyon called Castle Come Canyon. There were no trees with which I could secure the rope to lower off.

Blank cliffs on the north-west side of Cliff Dwelling Mountain where it touches the Cross Roads. I needed to find a way to climb up them.

I had to climb down to reach a bush to wrap the rope around it and rappel. Several rappels followed to reach the canyon. It was quiet and peaceful there There were big pools with willows growing. Further down, the water petered out as the canyon walls got steep, and the water emptied into Gunsight Canyon.

    I attempted to navigate down into Gunsight Canyon without rappelling. In the end, I had to do two rappels from trees, and couldn't see if my rope reached the ground until after I started lowering myself over the edge. The rope barely reached the ground. And, thank God - I found myself in a dry section of the canyon.

    I took it slow and stopped to drink. I had two bottles. When I came to water, I would drink as much as I could to empty a bottle, then re-fill it and put tablets in it to treat it. I then would drink from the bottle with older and cleaner, treated water, until I got to the next pool at which that bottle would be empty. This way the purification tablets had time to work and I was always drinking. It was a hot, cloudless, day. I never took water for granted. I didn't want to have to backtrack. There were enough obstacles. I didn't' want running out of water to be one. I kept thinking ahead to how I would get out of the canyon and onto Cliff Dwellings Mountain when I got there. When I did there would be no more water.

The steep face of Cliff Dwelling Mountain (center).

    Parts of the canyon were narrow and full with water. Just as I thought I might have to swim, I found I could scramble up the side, hike along the side of the canyon, and come back down to a dry section. Sometimes, when I found water, I took my shirt off and poured water over my head. I had to be careful. The geology made for quick sand. Near the end of the canyon, I scrambled towards the rappels used to get to the Crossroads. I had made it to the next step.

    It would be the last opportunity to fill water bottles. I decided not get on Cliff Dwelling Mountain until I drank so much I would not need to drink for a while. The strategy was to get on Cliff Dwellings with two full liters. Standing in the Crossroads, I looked up at the mountain. The easiest way to climb it, the only way I could imagine, was to get on to a ridge that sticks out into the Crossroads. The bottom where I stood was vertical.

    I walked past the Cross Roads and down Isaac Canyon, looking for an easy place to get out of the canyon. This was the area that concerned me when looking on my brother's computer. I became frightened. Only a short way down, the canyon walls got steep and pools of deep water blocked progress. When I stepped in what looked like a dry spot, the sand was wet and I sank quickly. I couldn't see the mountain for all the trees and bushes growing. It was a jungle.

    I noticed a ditch coming down from Cliff Dwelling Mnt. Desperate to go anywhere but down the canyon into water, I scrambled up the ditch, grabbing bushes to pull myself up it. I worked my way up through a loose, vegetated path, and just kept going, following an overgrown gully. My gosh, I thought to myself, I'm getting pretty high.

Next thing I knew, the vegetation cleared, and I saw the red rock face above. I wasn't sure I was going the right way, a way that would take me to the top. But there was nothing ahead that seemed insurmountable and no other way to go. I jogged left, then right, then back left again, weaving.

A small pack. It contained everything to climb, eat, and sleep for three days.

At one point, carrying the pack was a bit much to climb with. I tossed it up over my head onto ledges. I couldn't muster pulling myself up while wearing it. I placed gear in cracks to protect myself if I fell. Instead of using a rope, I clipped myself directly into the protection using long slings, and reached down and took the gear out once I moved higher. I made it to the white section, the lower angle slabs near the top. I was home free. From there I scrabbled to the summit of Cliff Dwellings, the rope still in my pack.

I explored the summit. There are no cliff dwellings, no ruins of any kind. The top is a sea of thick manzanita bushes that made exploration frustrating, and consumed energy in the hot sun. It was like post-holing in snow. It took a lot of work to step over or plow through the manzanita. High steps. The summit is big!

I could have continued. There was enough daylight. But I wanted to slept on the summit. In hindsight, I'm not sure that was the best idea. I didn't have a sleeping bag or a foam pad, and didn't realized how cold sand can be at night. Laying flat on the ground, the heat got sucked out of me.

In the middle of the night, I realized I would be warmer if I didn't lay flat, and pulled my knees to my chest. That wasn't a position I could sleep in. I got up and went to look for a tree I could lean against. There are only a few trees on the summit. In the dark, cold and tired, I found one. I sat down, leaned my back against a tree, and dozed off immediately.

I woke to the smell of ants- on the tree bark, on me, and my clothes and gear. I got up and walked back to the flat sand patch near the edge of Lady of the Cliff where I had set my rope for the rappel in the morning. I went back to a miserable night suffering on the cold sand.

When I woke up in the morning, I stood on the edge and looked around. I was dizzy. I stumbled and thought I just needed a moment. The dizziness persisted. I fought to keep my balance, as I stumbled along the edge. I realized I need to fall to the ground before I fell over the cliff. I turned myself away from the cliff, and let myself fall forward. I landed in a patch of cactus. I saw the cactus before I fell, but figured I could live through that. The dizziness lasted a minute. I don't know what it was about. Maybe being cold, not sleeping, or blowing my nose too hard to get all the dirt and sand out of it.

On top of Lady Mountain. Almost done with the traverse. All I had to do was get down.

 Rappelling Cliff Dwellings Mountain wasn't difficult. I rappelled into the notch between it and Lady of the Cliff. One of my big fears had been that it might be difficult to climb up other side. On their attempt to climb Cliff Dwelling Mnt, climbers had rappelled off Lady of the Cliff in order to get to Cliff Dwelling. I would need to climb up their rappel route. I climbed up to the rappel slings they had left around a large tree, cut the old webbing off the tree, and put it in my pack to throw in the trash.

 The climb to the top of Lady Mountain was easy. On the summit I thought it would be piece of pie from there. It was hot and I wondered what the symptoms of heat exhaustion might be. I thought maybe it was because my legs were tired. All the ups and downs carrying a pack. Being fifty, every time I go to the gym I get hurt. So I save my body for climbing. Maybe I'm being too hard on myself. I had hiked up the West Rim Trail in less than three hours. When you're scarred and use your muscles more. Back to wondering about heat exhaustion... what does it feel like? Would there be nausea? Dizziness?

 Because I was tired and it was hot, the descent seemed long and difficult. There were no clouds. It was 92F with 2 mph winds. I kept losing the trail. And I'd been up and down the trail to the top of Lady Mountain twice before. Being a climber, when the going gets rough, I just kept going. In one section I got lost when I missed a turn and kept going straight down. I ran into old posts, anchors, and coils of wire. I finally realized that the relics had gotten swept down the mountain by an avalanche of rock fall. It might explain why hikers and tourists hadn't carried them out. I may have left my rope there to become a relic.

Rest and water were not enough. I had this sense I needed to get down fast, even though it seemed I was doing the right thing by stopping to rest. When I got lost, it took me a while of going back up and down and sideways to find the trail again. The trail had taken a sharp turn where it pinches down to a narrow path obscured by bushes. When it widened, I was walking on bare rock. It was hard to know if the rock was the trail or not. I didn't realize I was off the trail until the path petered out into a void.

Somewhere along the way I dropped my rope. It fell out of my pack. I didn't notice it missing until I was two-thirds down the mountain, stopping to rest in the shade and drink the last of my water. My pack still seemed heavy. I backtracked to look for it. I couldn't find it. I decided to continue down. The rope was trying to save my life. Someone (my guardian angel) had taken it off my pack when I wasn't looking.

The further down I went, the easier it became to stay on the trail. The carins were not helpful. Half-way down, there are two shinny bolts. I could not imagine what for. They go down the wrong way. Later I leaned they were placed by a SAR team performing a rescue and lowering a litter. Someone gotten hurt on the trail.

I got to the bottom and reached the river. I changed into my bathing suite.

Dangerous Dan after completing the traverse. He doesn't look that tired.

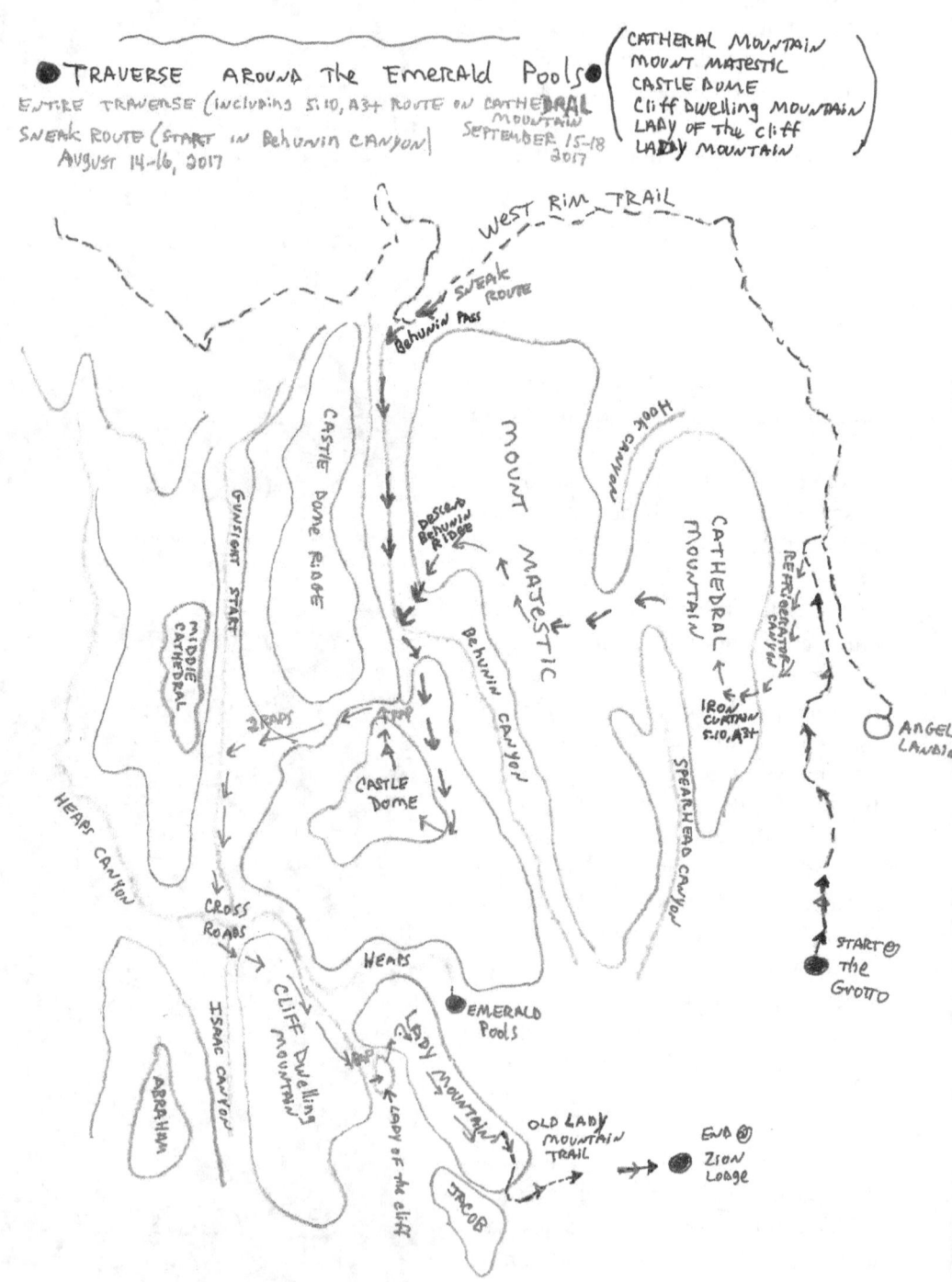

When I removed my harness, I found it as heavy as my pack. I had clipped a lot of stuff to my harness, things that would not fit inside the pack. I went into the river and sat. I laid down and submerged my body, forcing my head underwater. When I was done, I walked upstream, crossed the bridge, and went to the Zion Lodge. I dropped my pack and laid down on the tall, cool green grass under a big tree.

When I'm in a shopping mall, or on the beach in California, or playing guitar in a bar, no matter how much I try, sometimes I feel like I don't belong. When I was in the canyons and on the sides of the cliffs, I felt I belonged there.

After laying in the grass and reseting, I got up and went and drank from the fountain near the bus stop. I got on the shuttle and took it back to the Visitor Center to take care of business in the following order:
- Text my brother I'm back safe
- Drink Gatorade
- Eat ice cream
- Drink water
- Buy a large Diet Coke. It's a long drive home.
- Check phone messages
- Start driving

I drank a full gallon of water on the drive home.

TRAVERSING AROUND THE EMERALD POOLS

TRAVERSE AROUND THE EMERALD POOLS *D Stih 2017*
This is a "closed loop traverse" - the route starts and ends at the same point.
HA (High Adventure) on a scale of NA (No Adventure), MA (Moderate Adventure), and HA (High Adventure). August 14-16, solo (with a rope). It included the first descent of Castle Dome Canyon into Gunsight Canyon, and climbing a new route on the north face of Cliff Dwelling Mountain.
EQUIPMENT REQUIRED: A true believer in leaving adventure and nothing else, I didn't drill bolts or leave any webbing at the rappels.
CAUTIONS / SPECIAL DIFFICULTIES: If there is high-water in Gunsight Canyon you may need a wetsuit. Put it on before starting the blind rappel at the end of Castle Dome Canyon.
WATER: I did the traverse in August, and found low water in Behunin Canyon, just enough to drink. There was water in Castle Dome Canyon to drink. It had been raining within a few days of my trip. There is always water in Gunsight Canyon (deep water south of the Cross Roads) and at the Cross Roads (pools).
SEASON: Unless you have canyoneering skills, spring is probably not ideal, as a wetsuit and dry bags may be required if the Gunsight has high water. I climbed it in August, and found pools of water to collect for drinking, but could walk around the pools and didn't need to swim. Conditions in Fall are likely to be similar.
THE ROUTE: I descended Behunin Canyon until just before the first rappel, then left

the canyon and climbed onto Castle Dome (see Castle Dome). From the summit, I rappelled and down-climbed north into the notch between Castle Dome and Castle Dome Ridge, the ridge that leads out from the West Rim. Five rappels were required with a single rope. I then descended west, down Castle Dome Canyon. At the bottom of the gully/canyon, two rappels were required to descend into The Gunsight Start to Heaps Canyon. I was lucky to land in a dry spot. These were blind rappels. There was water in the canyon.

Once in Gunsight Canyon, I followed it downstream to where it feeds into Heaps Canyon at The Crossroads. Just before I got there, I scrambled high on the right. Perhaps that's why I didn't find the bouldering moves or the rappel in Gunsight Canyon that Tom Jones mentions in his guide book on canyoneering. I continued a short way into Isaac Canyon before climbing onto the north ridge of Cliff Dwelling Mountain, which I climbed to the summit. From the Summit of Cliff Dwelling Mountain, I made several rappels to Lady of the Cliff, then climbed up Lady of the Cliff, what appeared to be the rappel route Buzz Burrell and Jared Campbell used on their descent from Lady of the Cliff to reach the east face of Cliff Dwelling Mountain.

According to "Tales from the Backcountry" in CP's guidebook, Buzz and Jared attempted a new route on the east face of Cliff Dwelling Mountain. They retreated and reversed course. I removed the webbing left there around a large tree. I then rappelled east from the summit of Lady of the Cliff and climbed to the summit of the lesser crag between it and Lady Mountain, then onto the northwest ridge of Lady Mountain. I scrambled to the summit of Lady Mountain and descended the Old Lady Mountain Trail to the Zion Lodge.

ALTERNATE EXITS: Reference Tom Jones' *Zion Canyoneering* for maps and details regarding canyons in this area.

Traverse of Kolob Canyons

The scenery makes the adventure worth the pain.

INTRODUCTION Starting at the parking lot at Lee Pass, I hiked the La Verkin Creek trail past the junction to the Kolob Arch Trail and climbed up to Death Point. From Death Point, I hiked to Buck Pasture mountain, then across to Beatty Point, a virtual island in the sky. From there, I down-climbed and rappelled to my truck parked at Lee Pass.

FUTURE CLIMBING From Buck Pasture mountain, one might continue past the finger that leads to Beatty Point, to the finger that leads to Paria Point, or even the finger that leads out to Tucupit Point. To get there requires walking around the mouth of the Middle Fork of Taylor Creek Canyon to stay off private property. There appears to be a small section of BLM (Taylor Creek Wilderness) around the mouth of the Middle Fork that would allow such an adventure. Descending Paria Point appears to more difficult, with longer and steeper rappels, than what's encountered descending Beatty Point.

Success Story

This was my second attempt. I obtained a permit for five nights. I hoped it would only take two or three. I left the car at 4 am, when it was 37 F. With holes cut out in the back of my shoes, blisters could not be an obstacle. I'd have to free-climb everything wearing the boots, however, and hoped that was possible. Since it had not rained in a long time (the locals said it had been ninety days) I didn't count on finding water at bottom of Death Point. I carried a water bottle in addition to two, empty 2-liter coke bottles which I planned to fill at the creek on the way. The moon was full. On my last attempt I had not brought a sleeping bag. I had slept in my clothes, wrapped in a space blanket. Now, night temperatures were in the 30s, so I carried a down bag. It was so cold when I left the

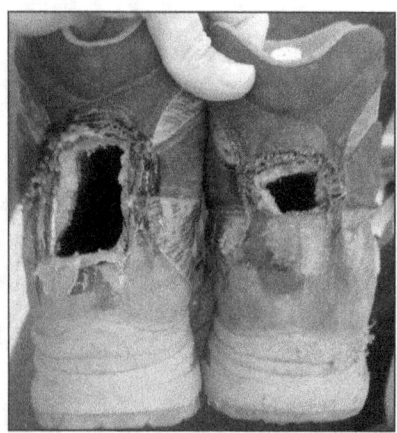 

car, I was comfortable hiking in a down jacket and wearing fleece gloves. I reached my turn off, the canyon leading up to Peak Inaccessible, a few minutes after it became light. The moon was still on the west horizon, high in the sky. The yellow and red fall colors, a perfect clear blue sky, the sound of the creek, and the red rock walls in the twilight of the early sun, made me pause.

At the creek, I filled the coke bottles and guzzled water. One and one-half gallons. That was to be my supply from that point. They say you should drink two quarts a day. I planned to cut that in half in order to stretch my supply to four days. I wasn't sure how difficult the climbing might be. I was prepared to stick it out and do whatever it took. I had plenty of climbing gear. If I ran out of water, however, well that would be the end of the trip.

I wasn't looking forward to climbing the gully. My pack was heavy with the water bottles filled. The brush was thick and thorny, the canyon gully steep. There was no trail. I kept a positive attitude. At the top of the gully is a cliff that must be climbed. It was the second thing I wasn't looking forward to. It can only be climbing by scaling a dead tree that leans against it. I used the stubs on the tree where branches had broken off for foot holds. Near the top, I grappled for something I could pull myself to the top. There is a big, dead log laying on

The starting point, the trail head at Lee Pass.

the edge at the top of the cliff. It appears to heavy and secure, but it moves if you pull on it. The dirt under the log has washed out. The log is barely hanging onto the cliff. I might have gently pulled on the log, except it was extra imperative to not let the log shift. At its far side, the log has a short piece like a hockey stick protruding. The top of the tree is resting on the hockey stick. If the log shifted, the whole kit and caboodle might tumbling down. Terrified, I made it to the top.

From the top of the cliff, I hiked across the plateau towards Peak Inaccessible. As I got close, I hiked down a weakness, a section of steep leaves and brush, into a canyon to the east. In the bottom of the canyon, I scrambled up loose rock and brush to the top of another plateau, from which I could see Death Point. It was longer and harder to get to the bottom of Death Point than I remember it on my previous attempt.

At the bottom of Death Point, I found my gear as I had left it when I retreated months earlier. I was elated to discover I had left a Cliff Bar. I wondered where the map was. The map showed the way down, once I got to the top. Good thing I had memorized it. I pleased to find that I left a full bottle of water. Although it was three months old, it, tasted better than the "fresh" water I had collected from the creek on the hike in.

I got the rope out, tied it to tree to self-belay myself, and set off to see if I could climb without wearing rock shoes. I could. I reached the bail sling I had tied around a bush on my previous attempt, and climbed past it to a tree. The day was off to a good start.

When you are climbing by yourself, you have to do things twice. At the end

The approach to Death Point as viewed from Death Point. Note the two canyons that must be crossed to reach Death Point from the southern side of Peak inaccessible (just out of sight on the lower far right).

of my rope I found a good tree, tied the rope to it, and went down. At the bottom I untied the other end and went back up the rope carrying my pack. The first two pitches were the hardest. After that the route got easier. But because the rock was loose, and I wasn't sure how difficult the route would be, and because the pack was heavy, and because although I'm Dangerous Dan, I'm careful and don't take unnecessary chances, I stayed roped up the entire way. When the going was easy I just got to the end of the rope faster.

Day 2. I know you're not supposed to drink coffee when it's hot and water is limited. I couldn't help it. I was so tired. Mid-morning, I added two instant Starbucks coffee packs to the last bit of water in one of my bottles and shook it up.

On the third pitch, an easier one with some bushes, I got the feeling to look down. I saw a grasshopper, sitting still in a bush. They say grasshopper is a symbol of good luck. Its abil-

ity to connect and understand sound vibrations is a symbol of your inner voice telling you to trust it. I went around grasshopper, making sure the rope didn't touch the bush.

Towards the end of the day it became windy as the sun went down. I got to a good ledge I could sleep on. It had a divot to keep me from rolling off in my sleep. Although it was only 4pm, I decided to stop. I was tired and needed a rest. And I wanted to enjoy the space. I enjoy siting and sleeping on a mountain. I sat there until it got dark. Then the moon came up and entertained me. As it got cooler I tucked myself into my sleeping bag.

Although the most difficult part of the climb was over, I didn't know that yet. In fact, I didn't know if the route went to the top. There was the chance I'd get close and find the top blank, rotten, impossible. If that happened, I would have to go down. Once in a while I'd step around the corner to see if there was another way. There wasn't. The rock dropped off on either side. I was lucky choosing the route I had. When I was at the bottom, I had wondered if there might be an easier way. I had almost decided to take a different way, then remembered not to second-guess myself. *You choose this way for a reason. Stick to it.* I constantly thanked the mountain for my safety and passage.

As I got near the top, I saw what I had envisioned - a single path, on a slope of loose rocks that allowed passage. On either side were vertical drops, and impossible to climb walls that fell to the ground. As I made the last few steps, I came face to face with a short, brown, metal pole. For a moment I thought someone else had climbed the mountain before me. Then I realized it was as a survey marker, and remembered that Death Point can be reached on foot from private property. I walked past the marker to a tree and secured my rope to it. I didn't feel death. I felt an endless, needless suffering to what I was doing.

After going back down to get my pack, I came back up to the tree, untied my rope, and packed it away. Now, I thought, it should be piece of cake. Maybe I can get down tonight. I thought I saw foot prints. I hoped there was a trail. Death Point got its name during a cold spell when a group of cattle froze to death. But that was a long time ago. There was no grass. The whole place was overgrown with tall, thick manzanita bushes. It was slow and painful to walk-through the bushes to reach the top of Death Point. I fought way through bushes. By 4 pm I was exhausted and on the verge of crying when I saw a clearing, a flat spot of crushed white limestone on the ground.

I went to the clearing and unpacked, made camp, got in my sleeping bag, and looked forward to the sun set and moon. I tended to my feet and examined them for blisters. I mended holes and tears in my pants and shirt with duck tape. I built a wonder-woman bracelet to protect my arms from bleeding. I planned to use it when I forced my way through the sharp brush the following day. Dinner

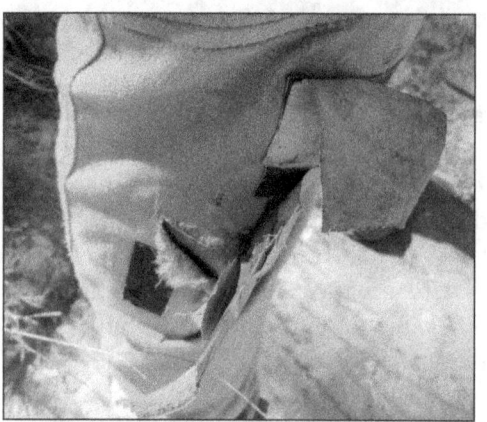 

was a bag of Turkey Jerky. I had one Cliff Bar and two goo-packs remaining. Goo are sugary, energy snacks, 100 calories. It was water I thought of most. I was drinking 1/2 gallons a day, more than my ration. In the middle of the night I got hungry and ate the Cliff Bar.

Day 3. The morning started in good spirits. I got up at the first sign of light. I wanted to start moving when it was cold, so that I could wear my gortex jacket and fleece gloves to protect my arms and hands as I battled through sharp bushes. It was heartbreaking to see how far I had to go. I spent the entire day bushwhacking. The only thing that kept me going was the thought that I had to. The end point wasn't moving. My destination was a still point on a map. So

The North Eye (center) as viewed after reaching the top of Death Point.

long as I kept moving, I would get there. If I didn't keep moving I felt I'd die, perhaps lie down in the thick brush, never to be seen again.

    Near the end of the day, I reached the end of a finger and stared down at the ridge known as Beatty Point. At the bottom was parking lot and my car. It looked to be 4th to 5th class, and normally would been cake to go down. Carrying a heavy pack, however, the loose rock made it difficult and scary. At one spot I set my pack down to explore ahead to see which way I should go. On the way back, I passed my pack and lost it. I hiked up and down the ridge twice before I found it.

    As I carefully made my way down, I came to a spot where I thought I should rappel. It seemed too dangerous to down-climb wearing a pack. I got the rope out, set it around what I thought was a good bush, and put the rope though my rappel device. I put my pack on, placed my weight on the rope, leaned backward, and heard a crack. The main branch had split, almost in two. I decided to climb down without using the rope.

    Near the end of the day, I saw the road where my truck was parked. It looked so close. I thought I might make it down before dark. Instead, at 4 pm, exhausted, I stopped on top of a point where the views are spectacular. I built up a spot with flat rocks to make a sleeping platform. I had a cup of water left and drank it. I ate the last of my food. There would be no breakfast or water tomorrow. As the sun went down, a group of hawks and eagles played in wind, circling above me. Although I was tired, I strained to stay awake and not miss the show.

Day 4. I thought this would be an easy day. I had spent a year studying photographs of the mountain from different angels. I thought I knew which ways to not go down, ones that would put me on the side of a blank wall. I knew where I should aim for, a place I could hopefully get down with a single rope. Climbers normally bring two ropes. To save wright, I had only one. If I started down something and didn't reach another anchor before I ran out of rope I could be stuck. My pants had big holes in the knees and the seat. My shirt was torn. I was out of duck tape. Full speed ahead.

I wondered why I was being so mean to myself, why I didn't love myself. *Why are you doing this to yourself?* Of course, I didn't know it was going to be like this. I had envisioned a classic, easy way to climb Death Point, a fun walk across the top, and a quick walk down to the car. Instead, I was having a horrid time. I had to keep my wits together and focus on two things: not falling off the mountain. The rock was loose and I was wearing a heavy pack; and choosing the best course. If I missed a turn or went the wrong way, I could find myself stuck, hanging from my rope. It felt beyond pushing. I was being punished. I was punishing myself. There seemed no point to the pain.

After I went down as far as I could scrambling, I got the rope out and started to rappel. At one point my rope ran out when I was on the side of the mountain. Fortunately there was but one small crack. I pounded in an angle piton into it and lowered to a flatter area, where I walked sideways across a big ledge.

On the ledge, I remembered that based on what I studied in photographs, I needed to avoid the temptation to go straight down. There were big, tall cliffs directly below, ones my rope would most certainly be too short to overcome. I hiked sideways to where I expected to find shorter cliffs. When I got there, I became worried. I couldn't see a way down. That's when I noticed them. I was practically standing on them.

Just as I was about to give up and cry, I looked down and saw three old bolts. Someone had probably climbed up Beatty Point or started high on private land and went down it. They were star bolts, a type used in the 1970s. An old piece of rope was tied to the bolts, through which the previous climbers had threaded their rope. The decrepit piece of rope crumbled when I pulled on it. I left a sling and carabiner of my own. I couldn't tell if my rope reached the ground until I was on rappel and leaning over the edge. My rope reached the ground. Just barely.

There was still a maze of cliffs and hills to navigate before I reached the highway. I had cramps. I attracted them to worries, but it was probably dehydration. The salt tablets I had tasted so bad I spit them out. There was another 1/4 mile of bushwhacking, navigating canyons and cliffs, before I reached the road. I reached my truck at 1 pm. I drank 1/2 gallons of water on drive to town. I was beat and broken. A break was in order.

TRAVERSING KOLOB CANYONS

TRAVERSE OF KOLOB CANYONS *D Stih 2019*
This is a "closed loop traverse" - the route starts and ends at the same point.
EQUIPMENT REQUIRED: See Death Point.
CAUTIONS / SPECIAL DIFFICULTIES: The top of Death Point and Buck Pasture Mountain are covered by heavy stands of oak, serviceberry, and manzanita. In 2006, crew members inventoried the Buck Pasture Mountain area and reported it difficult to see more than a few feet. They walked the rim where the brush was less dense, and reported the remainder too thick to be walked. In the event of an emergency, seek high ground or a known reference point for those who are trying to find you.
WATER: See the chapter Death Point. In dry seasons, water is not available after leaving

the La Verkin Creek Trail. In early season (spring) and perhaps only in wet seasons, a pool can be found near the bottom of Death Point.

SEASON: Due to the lack of water sources, it would be difficult and unpleasant to attempt the traverse in the summer or when the temperature is above 70F.

CAMPING / TIME REQUIRED: A minimum of two days, possibly three. I took four, but I was by myself, rope-soloing. It's more difficult to rope-solo 4th class than climb A5. My pack was heavy, making down-climbing Beatty Point treacherous. If I had a partner, I suspect we would start at 3 am at the car, in order to be ready to leave La Verkin Creek Trail at first light, at the location where the trial meets the canyon that leads up to Peak Inaccessible. I suspect it would take until mid-morning to get from there to the base of Death Point. If we were fast, we might reach the top of Death Point (the rim) before dark on the first day. It's likely we'd have to bivy on top. The manzanita bushes are painfully thick. There are only a few open and flat spots. It's more pleasant, given the opportunity, to bivy on the route. Consider a bivy on the route close to the top, such that you give yourself a good start in the morning to conquer the manzanita.

THE STARTING POINT: Park at Lee Pass.

THE ROUTE: From the parking lot at Lee Pass, hike the La Verkin Creek Trail (6.7 miles) past the Kolob Arch Trail, to its junction with Hop Valley Trail. At that point, stay on the left side of the creek and continue past the junction. In a short while you will see a faint path in the dirt on the left, which leads up and around the corner to the right, into a drainage/canyon. Once in the drainage/canyon, hike up to its end, a saddle. On the right you will see a dead tree leaning against a wall. You must climb to the top of the wall using the tree. A crack on the left side of the tree takes cams. Do not use the log at the top of the cliff to pull yourself up. The tree will move, as it's resting on the log at the

☐ VISITOR CENTER

① PARK AT LEE PASS HIKE LA VERKIN CREEK TRAIL TO THE JUNCTION W/ HOP VALLEY TRAIL

② LEAVE THE TRAIL AND GO UP THE CANYON USED TO GET TO PEAK INACCESSIBLE

③ CLIMB THE TREE ONTO THE PLATEAU

④ BEFORE REACHING P.I. DESCEND INTO CANYON TO EAST

⑤ CLIMB OUT ONTO ANOTHER PLATEAU.

⑥ DESCEND TO DEATH POINT

⑦ CLIMB 6 PITCHES OF TECHNICAL CLIMBING ON THE SOUTH FACE OF DEATH POINT

⑧ HIKE TO BUCK PASTURE MOUNTN

⑨ HIKE TO THE WEST POINT OF BEATTY POINT

⑩ DESCEND BEATTY POINT TO PARKING LOT

THE TRAVERSE
KOLOB CANYONS

Roped Solo
Dangerous Dan
4 Days, October, 2019
UIAA GRADE VI (5.6/5.7)

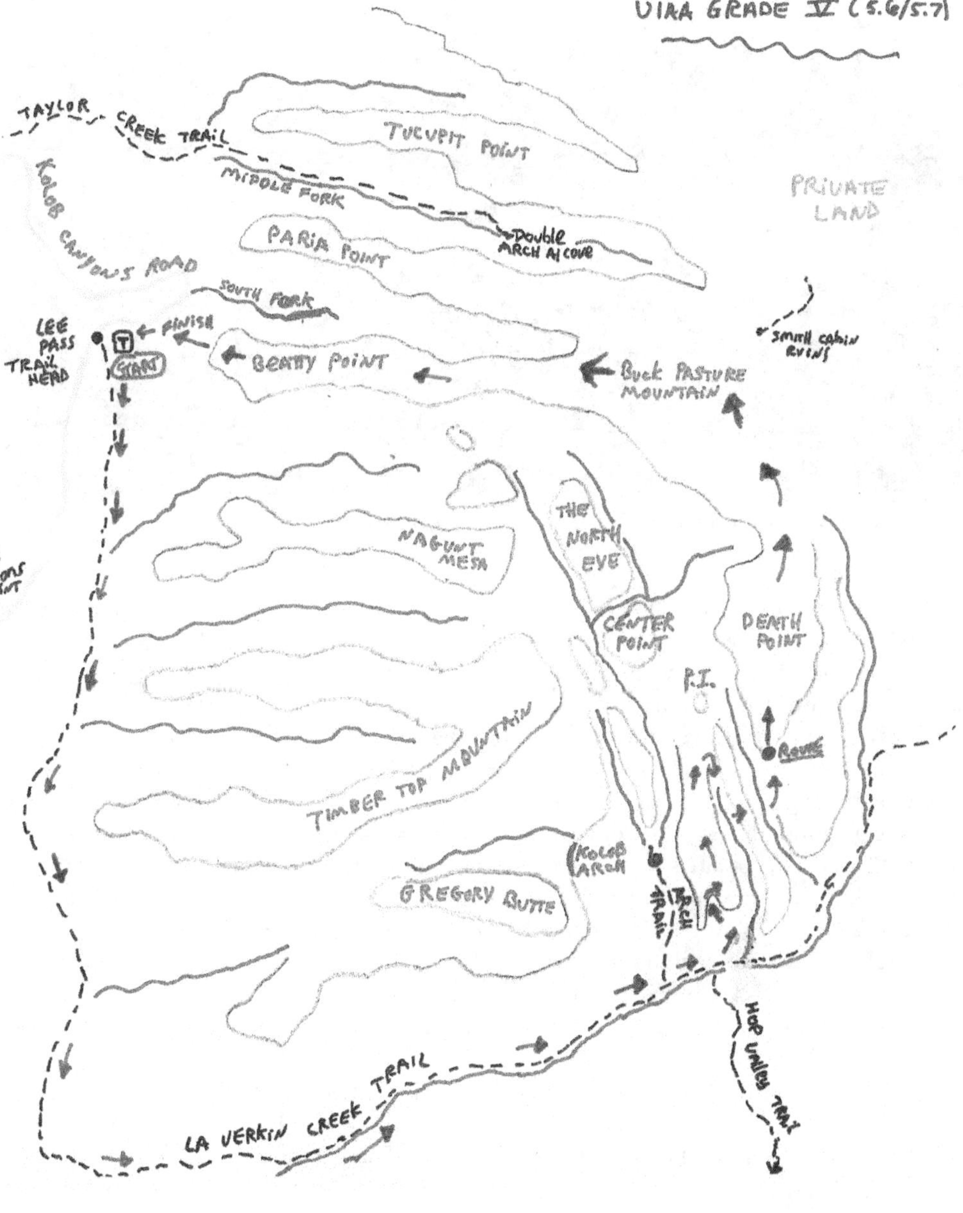

Hiking through Manzanita bushes on the finger leading to Beatty Point.

top of the cliff.

From the top of the plateau, walk towards Peak Inaccessible, staying close to the EAST edge of the plateau. As you get close to Peak Inaccessible, you will see a place where it's possible to hike down into a canyon to the east. As soon as you get to the bottom of that canyon, start looking for a way to scramble out the other (east) side. After getting out of the canyon, avoid the urge to immediately climb up and over to the other side. Walk south to the southern tip of the obstacles, where it's possible to walk around rock outcroppings that block the top, instead of climbing over them. From there, start descending into the next canyon. In early season there will be water in the canyon at the bottom. Fill up. In late season you should have filled up before leaving La Verkin Creek.

Hike up the base of Death Point. The route starts in the middle of the south face. Take a look at the first pitch in the photo in the chapter Death Point. The best way to check you're in the right position is: when you think you are at the start, continue around the corner to the east. You will find the wall steep and blank. Go back and start. If you find the correct start, the route is obvious. It's about six pitches. The first two are the most difficult. After that it's a scramble.

From the top of Death Point, hike to Buck Pasture mountain, then west across a finger to Beatty Point. Beatty Point is mostly a 4th class down-climb. The crux is near the bottom where one or two rappels are required. Hike back to the car at Lee Pass.

Traverse of the Beehives

INTRODUCTION Modern maps have the peak above the Streaked Wall labeled as Beehive Peak. Older maps did not differentiate it from the other beehives that litter the tops of the cliffs between the Streaked Wall and the Sentinel. "The Beehives" is written on older maps. This is a traverse of all of the possible bee hives.

Zion National Park Brochure with the caption "The Great West Wall, Beehives (above), and the Sentinel (right) as seen from Zion-Mount Carmel Highway." United States Department of the Interior, 1957.

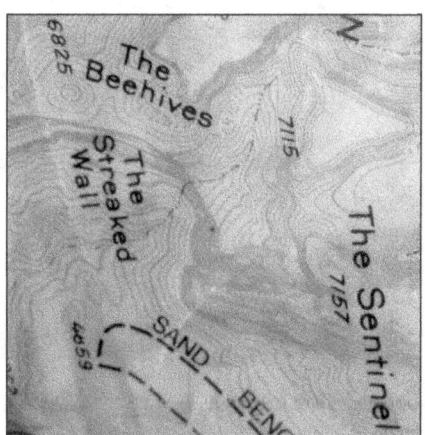

Trails Illustrated topo map, 1988. Big Red is clearly a hive.

Above: An interpretive sign in back of the History Museum (previously the Visitor Center), pointing to Triangle Peak with the caption, "Beehives 6904ft 2104m".

TRAVERSING THE BEEHIVES

TRAVERSE OF THE BEEHIVES *D Stih and Mike Dunn 2020*
Completed over three days in record hot (88 F) October weather. It included descents of Mars Canon, Goose Canyon, and Sentinel Canyon and climbing all the hives between the Streaked Wall and the Sentinel. No bolts were placed. Please don't add any.

CAUTIONS / SPECIAL DIFFICULTIES: We carried two 320-foot 8-mil static ropes to do the rappels between Big Red and Triangle Peak, and descend Goose Canyon. As we climbed up the descent for the Streaked Wall, we used one of the statics as the lead line, placing a screamer (shock-absorbing sling) between the leader's harness and tie-in point to buffer the impact in the event of a fall. In late season, the water in Birch Creek (the only location water will be found) will be stagnant, but drinkable. Goose Canyon requires technical down-climbing and the frequent and creative use of natural anchors for rappelling such as dead-men.

WATER: In early season, the top of Big Red is saturated with water and there is a spring flowing on its summit near the rim on the east side. In early season, snow is likely to be present in the saddle between Big Red and Triangle Peak. Water for drinking can be found in Birch Creek in any season. In late season (starting in May depending on the snow that season) do not expect to find water until you are in Goose Canyon, almost finished with the traverse.

THE STARTING POINT: Start by climbing up the descent used by those who climbed the Streaked Wall. It is approached from behind the Museum (the old Visitor Center). Walk the service road until the first large gully on the right. Hike the gully to its end, then scramble to a notch between the main wall on the left (west), and an outcropping on the right (east). The crux is several pitches up, 5.6-5.7, a few moves at a small roof. This is the most difficult of the climbing encountered on the traverse. The foot and hand holds are good.

Map of Zion National Park 1929 showing "Bee Hives" written between peaks 69500 and 6900.

THE ROUTE: After climbing up the descent for the Streaked Wall, climb the big hive (Beehive Peak). Scramble up it and down the other side into the valley between Beehive Peak and Big Red. From there, scramble up the white slabs on the south face of Big Red to its summit. Climb the hives on top of Big Red. Most of them are scrambles. The exception is the prominent hive on the east edge. The route on this hive is on its south face. It's a loose scramble with bushes to tie-off for protection. Down-climb the route.

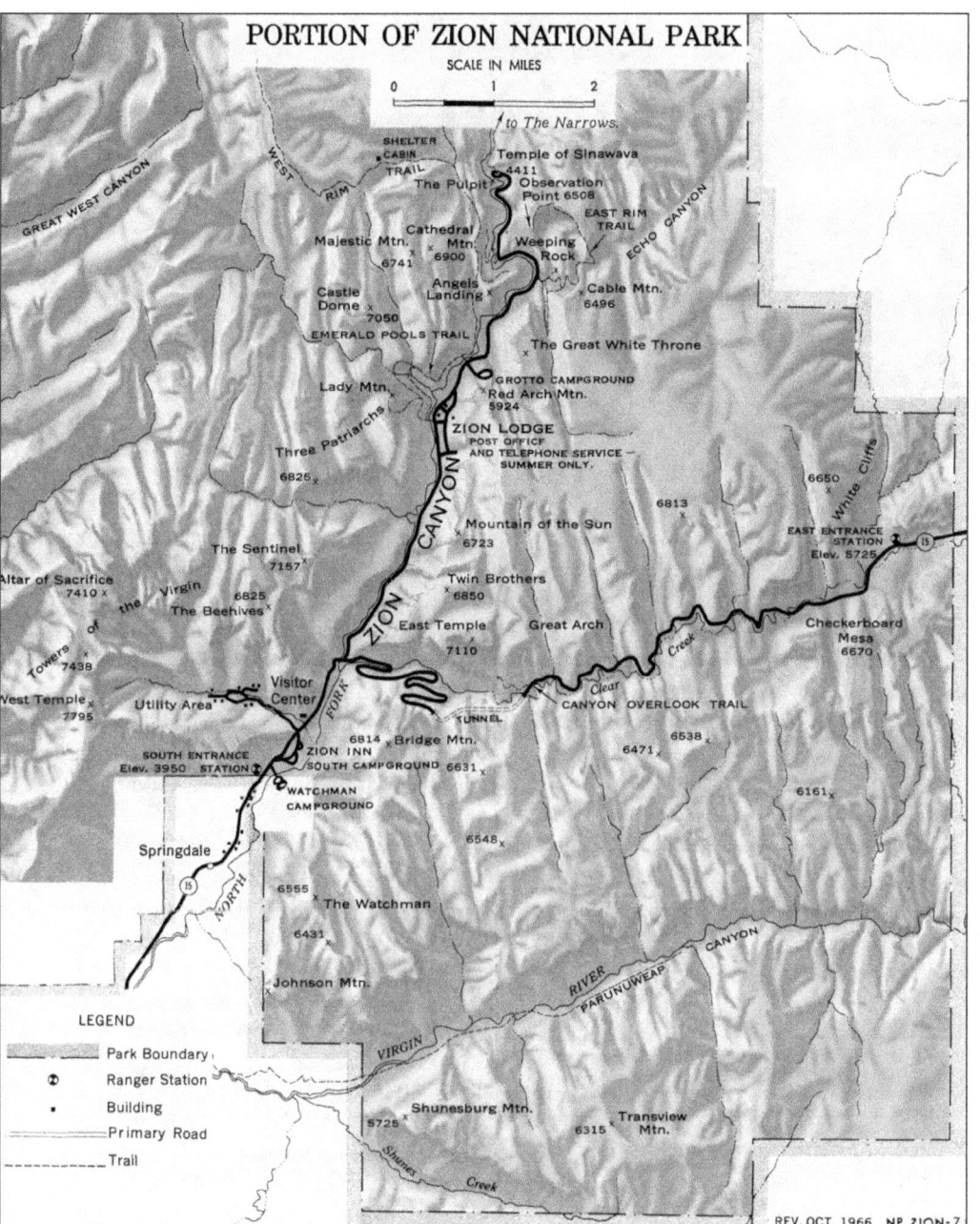

Excerpt from the brochure, *Zion,* **published by the U.S. Department of the Interior National Park Service, 1966, showing "Beehives" written next to peak 6825.**

Walk along the east edge of Big Red to its midpoint, a place where there's a drainage leading to a waterfall (or dryfall). Rappel into the saddle between Big Red and Triangle Peak. Start at a big tree on the east edge of Big Red at the top of the drainage. A 315-foot rappel from the tree goes down steep face. Near the end of the rappel, aim for another big tree to the left (north). From that tree, about 230 feet will reach the ground, the saddle between Big Red and Triangle Peak.

On the north side of the saddle is Goose Canyon. On the south side is Mars Canyon,

The approach and start of the route after hiking up the gully behind the old visitor center. Start up it, then work toward the wall on the left.

a canyon that drains onto the white slabs between the Streaked Wall and the Sentinel. Descend Mars Canyon. Expect a scramble with a few short drops that require short rappels.

At the bottom of Mars Canyon, walk NE around Triangle Peak, towards the Sentinel, at which the easy way up Triangle Peak can be found: low-angle white slabs. Climb Triangle Peak (see Triangle Peak), then climb the hives on top. The most difficult is the prominent hive on the east edge just before the proper summit. As you near the summit of Triangle Peak, the route on this hive is on the left (north) corner. It's a scramble and can be down-climbed.

For a true ascent of Triangle Peak, continue to the summit and climb the highest of the numerous red boulders that litter it. It requires a boulder problem. Down-climb the boulder with a spot. That's the end of the hives. Now all you have to do is get down.

GETTING DOWN AND ALTERNATE EXITS: The fastest way to get back to civilization might be to rappel Triangle Peak, the way you climbed it, back to the bottom, and then hike north through a notch between Triangle Peak and the Sentinel. After exiting the notch, climb up the NW face of the Sentinel (see the North-West Face of the Sentinel) and descend the 1938 Route to the Sand Bench Trail. The face on the Sentinel is difficult (5.11 R). If you have not previously climbed the 1938 route, this exit is not recommended, as you may get lost on the descent.

An alternate exit is to descend Sentinel Canyon from where Sentinel Canyon meets the west edge of the NW face of the Sentinel. Sentinel Canyon empties into the Court of the Patriarchs.

The other possible exits go down Birch Creek. One is to rappel the drainage between Sentinel Canyon and Triangle Peak into Birch Creek.

Another, the recommended descent is: from the summit of Triangle Peak hike to its SW corner and down-climb and rappel into the saddle between Triangle Peak and Big Red. From there go down Goose Canyon which empties into Birch Creek. At the end of Birch Creek, you may choose to descend Birch Creek into the Court of the Patriarchs OR traverse into Sentinel Canyon and descend it into the Court of the Patriarchs OR if you want a descent without big air, hike to the south-west corner of Abraham and go down the Chipmunk descent into the Court of the Patriarchs (See Alternate Descents and Abraham).

Top left: Technical climbing near the bottom of the climbing route that goes up the descent used by those who climb the Streaked Wall. Top right: the crux on the ascent up the Streaked Wall descent.

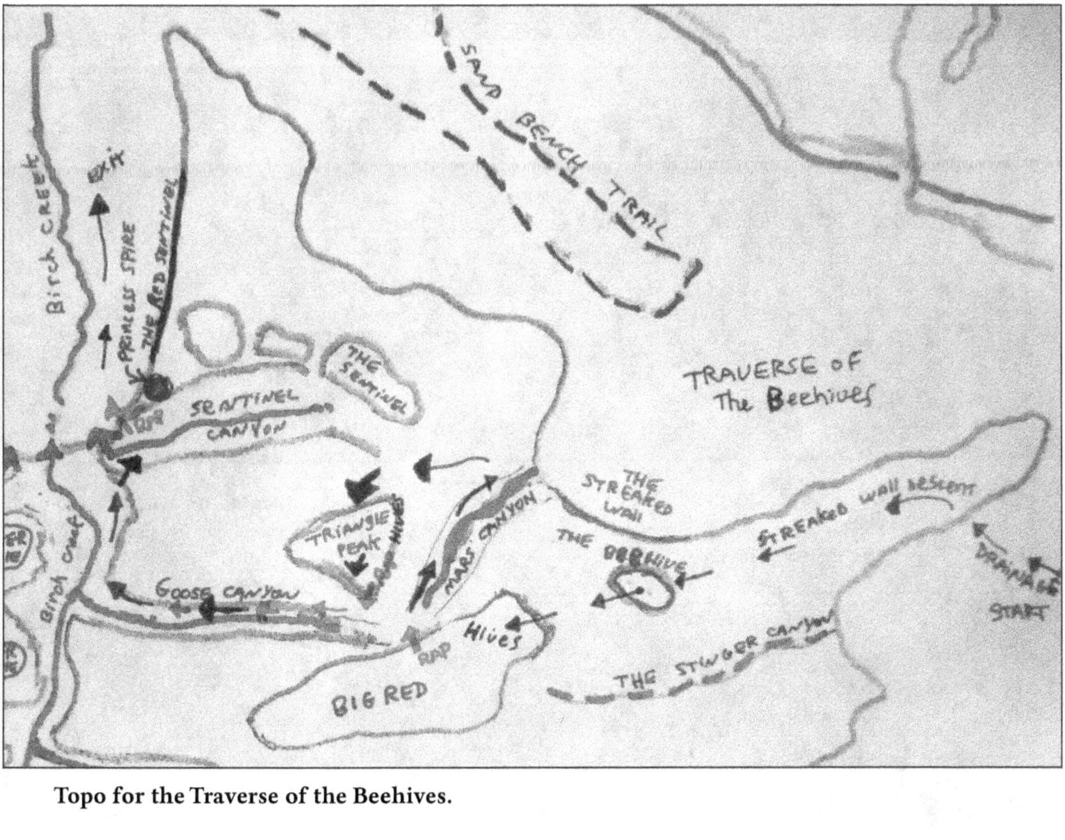

Topo for the Traverse of the Beehives.

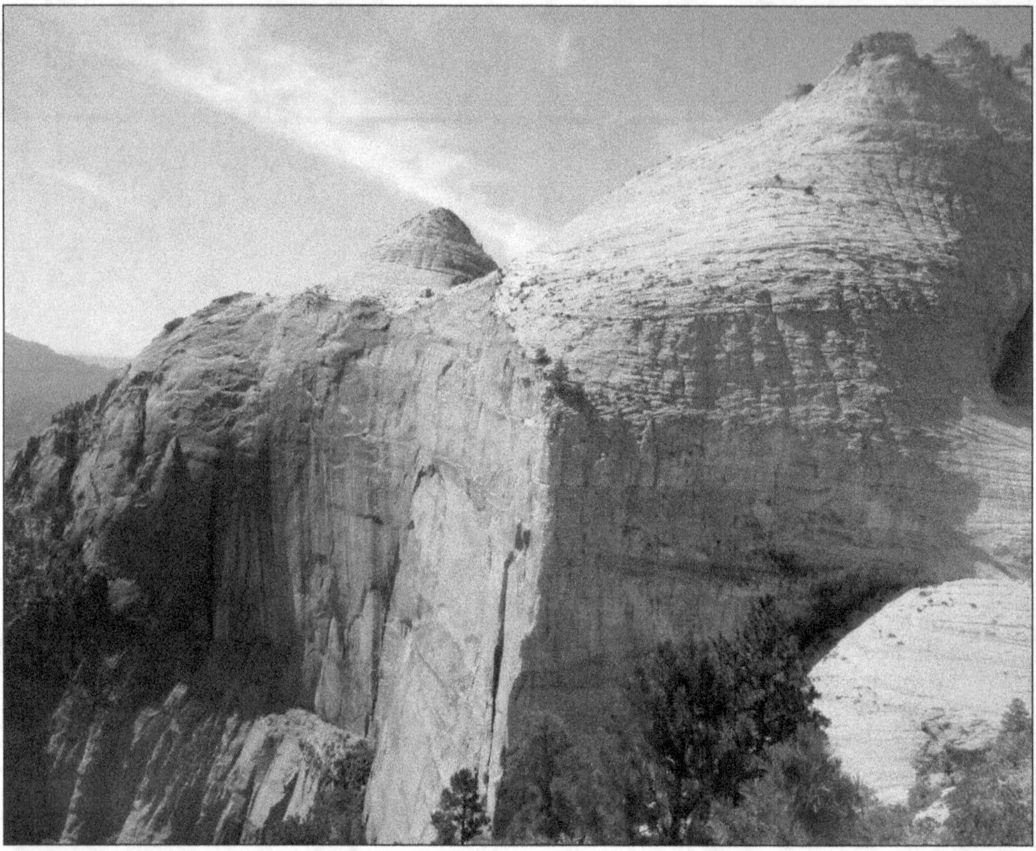

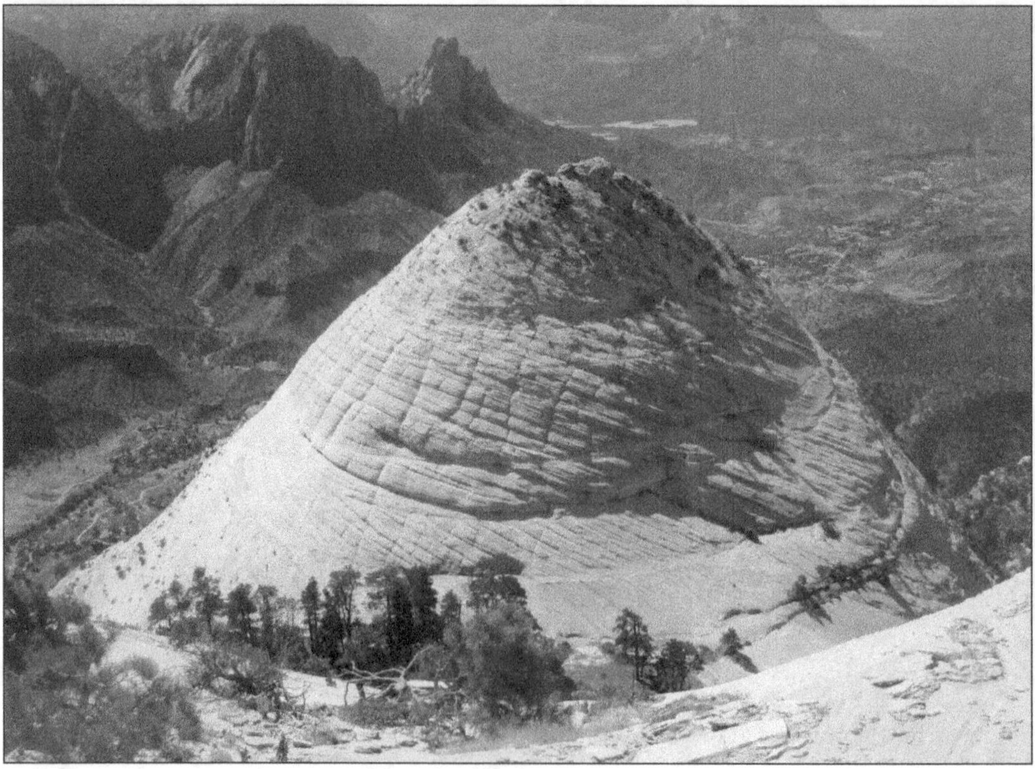

Above: The crux hive on Big Red. To surmount it, traverse the middle of the south-east (shaded) face along a ledge with bushes, before climbing straight up at the right (SE) corner.

Right: The descent from Big Red into the saddle between it and Triangle Peak. At the end of the obvious black streak, aim for the big tree on the right. A pair of 320 foot ropes is required. Another long rappel from that tree reaches the saddle.

Opposite page top: View of Beehive Peak above the Streaked Wall and the beehives on top of Big Red, as viewed from the bottom of the east face of Triangle Peak.

Opposite page bottom: Beehive Peak above the Streaked Wall, as viewed from the scramble up to Big Red.

Top: the hives on Triangle Peak, as seen on the approach from the bottom of Mars Canyon; Bottom: the crux hive on Triangle Peak. The easiest route is a scramble on the left side.

Traverse of the Time Machine: The Sun Dial, Cogs, and Hour Hand

The Truth Will Set You Free?

Some may have noticed in Ron's drawings of our route to climb the Sun Dial and the Traverse of the Towers of the Virgin, he drew only one summit for the Sun Dial. In my opinion, the Sun Dial has two summits. Both times Ron and I climbed the Sun Dial (the first being our first ascent of the peak; the second during our traverse of the Towers of the Virgin), we went to the SE summit, the first high point reached after climbing the only possible route on the formation. When we got to the top, Ron pointed toward the other summit and asked, "Should we go to that one too?"

    I had been looking at the other summit before he asked, wondering how we'd get there and how I would climb it if we did. It looked blank, steep, difficult, hard to protect, and scary. I would have had to lead it. I was afraid. Heck, I was afraid of how we would get to it. It appeared we might need to rappel, which

Left to right: the Cogs, 2nd summit of the Sun Dial, 1st (Original) summit. As seen from the West Temple.

meant we wouldn't be able to reverse course if we found it too difficult to climb.

"No," I replied, knowing I wasn't being honest. "We don't have to."

At the time, there was no way of exploring the mountains from space. We couldn't use Google Earth or a software program to look at the mountain from different angles and from the comfort of our living rooms. There was only one way to explore mountains back then- go and look. Touch them. From where we were stood it looked impossible. Add to that, we had an alpine rack consisting of =a few cams and slings, not the amount of gear climbers normally carry.

Not going to the second summit would not have bothered me expect that a newer topographical map shows the second summit to be a few feet higher. Altitudes on maps are not 100% accurate and change with subsequent editions. The map at the time we climbed the Sun Dial showed only one summit: the one Ron and I had reached. A later map showed elevation markings on both summits, with the second 50 feet higher. Both summits are now shown as one-hundred feet higher than noted on previous maps. For a long time I schemed on going back to climb the second summit. It was only after a long study of satellite images that I saw what I believed to be a climbable route on the NW side of the second summit, a side Ron and I could not see from our vantage point.

Turns out it's easy to climb the second summit once you reach the first. I climbed it with Mike in April, 2022, during The Traverse of the Time Machine.

TRAVERSING THE TIME MACHINE

THE SUN DIAL, COGS, AND HOUR HAND 5.7-
D Stih and M Dunn, April 2022

EQUIPMENT REQUIRED: Two 200 foot ropes, the second for rappelling. Natural anchors or fixed pins are in place for the rappels from the Sun Dial massif onto the Hour Hand.

CAUTIONS / SPECIAL DIFFICULTIES: The descent from the Sun Dial massif onto the Hour Hand takes courage. The anchor at the end of the first rappel is at the end of the rope.

THE STARTING POINT: The logical way to get there is by rappelling north off the summit of the West Temple as done for the Traverse of the Towers of the Virgin. Tag the summit of the Subdial, then come back and scramble down the east face of the white slabs between the West Temple and Sun Dial massif. Traverse across the east face of the Sun Dial massif to access the hanging valley its the north side.

THE ROUTE: Begin by climbing the original route to the first summit of the Sun Dial. Sign the original summit register made by Ron Raimonde. Scramble down west, down a cleft of scree, then south and around the south face of the second Sun Dial summit to reach a weakness on its NW side. Climb to the top of the second Sun Dial summit then downclimb it. Walk up and tag the various formations on the far western portion of the Sun Dial massif - the Cogs. These sit on what from the towns of Virgin and Rockville appears to be a shield, an impressive and formidable wall of white sandstone. Come back to edge on the middle of the north face of the Sun Dial massif, where it's required to rappel to continue. Using natural anchors (bushes), rappel the Minute Hand, a steep ridge that connects the Sun Dial massif to the Hour Hand. The anchor at the end of the first rappel is at a ledge at the end of the rope. The second rappel is equally long. The remainder of the traverse, across the Hour Hand, is mostly a scramble. Congratulations!

GETTING DOWN: Continue on the Traverse of the Towers of the Virgin towards the Altar of Sacrifice.

Descending the Minute Hand from the Sun Dial massif onto the Hour Hand.

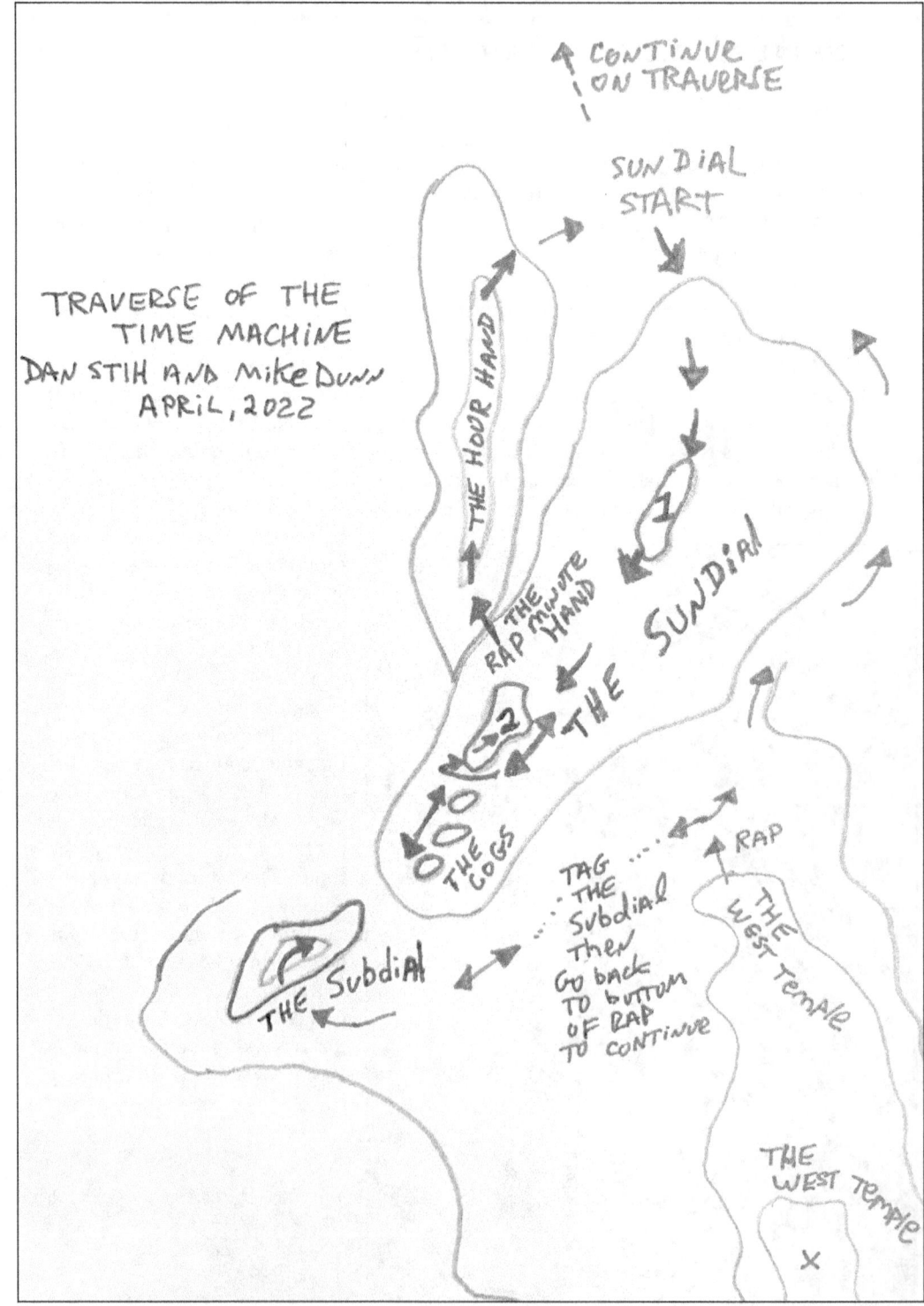

The Cat Walk:
A Traverse Around the Gregory Butte Massif

View of the arch from the Seat at the edge near the Emerald Pool

INTRODUCTION The traverse provides an exploration of a rarely visited and magical place. It requires less gear (no aid) than what's required to do a route on Gregory Butte and is therefore more "fun." Cats, a Guardian, lives in Cats Forest. After climbing Cats Crown, hike to Cats Ridge by walking around the Forest, staying high on the slabs above it.

THE CAT WALK

TRAVERSE OF THE CAT WALK, 5.9 R
This is a "closed loop traverse." The route starts and ends at the same point.
D Stih and M Dunn, 2025

CAUTIONS / SPECIAL DIFFICULTIES: The gully is old school 5.9, wet, hard to protect. Going down the ridge is tedious and requires rappels off natural anchors (we left no trace), short pitches of 5.8+, is loose and can be hazardous.

EQUIPMENT REQUIRED: Alpine free rack (1 each 0.5, 0.75,1,2,3) a dozen biners and lots of long slings may be sufficient. Thown in a few doubles as preferred. Two (2) 200-foot ropes are required to rappel the Cave Route and, if you need to, bail down the gully.

WATER: From the top of the gully, water can be found in pools near the arch and along the north side of Gregory Butte depending on rain and season.

SEASON: Due to water dripping from snow melting and seeps, it may only be possible to climb the gully starting in July/August.

CAMPING / TIME REQUIRED: Two days.

THE STARTING POINT: Lee Pass trail head.

THE ROUTE: Hike the La Verkin Trail to the end of the Arch Trail. Climb the approach gully used to get to Gregory Butte (See: *Arch Gully*). From the top of the gully, to find water and a nice rest spot, hike around the rim of the cliff in the direction of the arch. Just before the arch, near the edge, there are fantastic pools. Spend a rest. Take a nap. Drink water. Take a moment to sit on the Seat at the edge and gaze at the arch.

Onward: Hike west, down the valley. Near the end, as you follow the drainage, if it's rained within two weeks, water might remain. Fill up. This is the last place you will find water on the traverse. Climb the Cave Route on Cat's Crown. (See *Cat's Crown*). Come back down to the valley. Traverse Cats Tail Ridge to the Tipping Point and descend the ridge to the La Verkin Trail, exiting near Camp #2. (See *Cats Tail Ridge*.) Walk the La Verkin Trail back to the car.

Cat's Tail Ridge as viewed from slabs at the bottom of the Cave Route on Cats Crown.

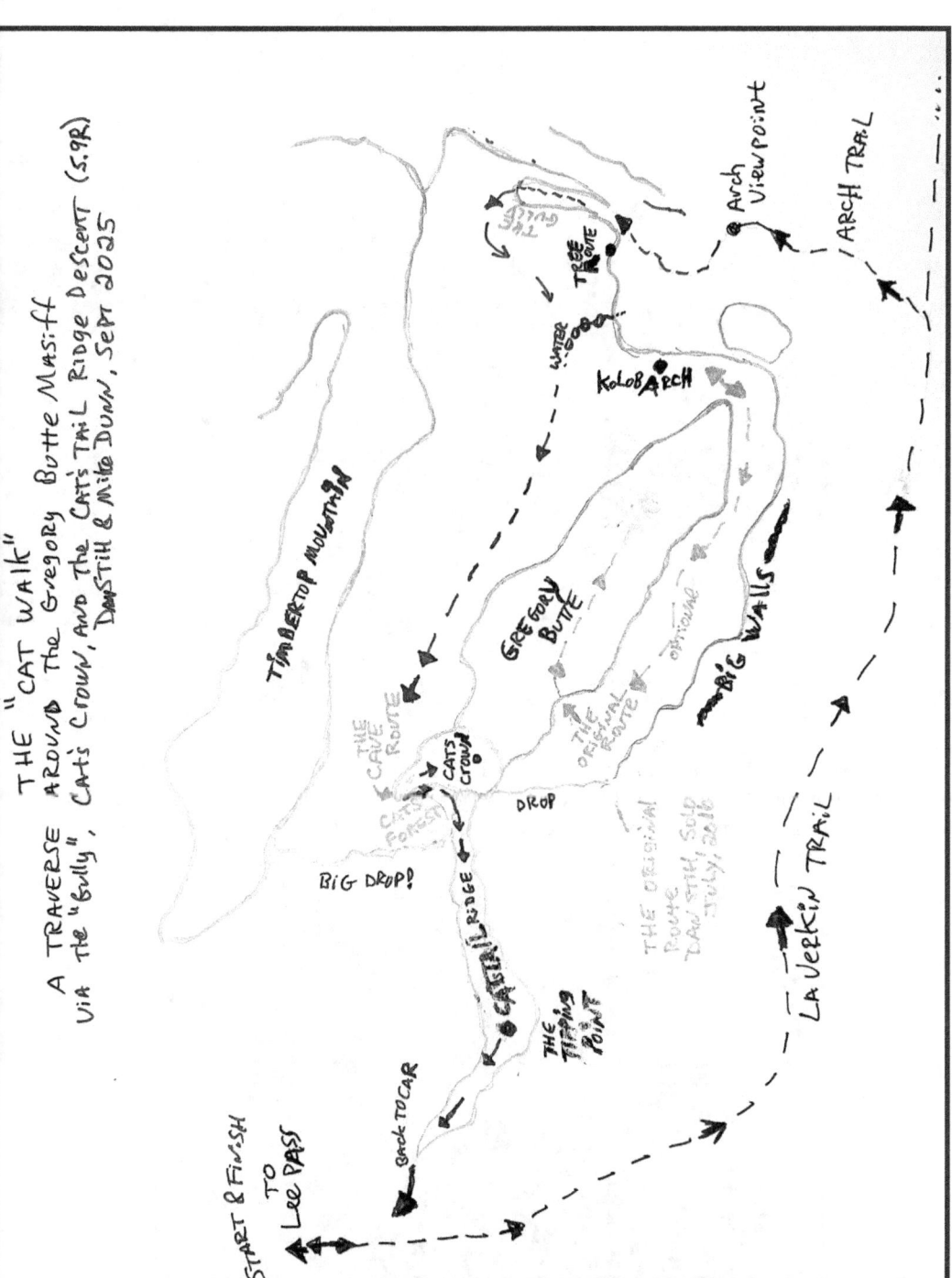

Seat at the Edge

FUTURE CLIMBING: Do the traverse in reverse: instead of climbing the gully near Arch View, climb up Cat Tail Ridge from the La Verkin trail starting near Camp 2. You'll miss the classic experience of climbing Arch gully. Descending the ridge required many rappels so there's a bit of climbing involved. In Mike's opinion, "It's climbable".

Emerald Pool

Canyon Descents

Inclined Canyon
(North Side of Inclined Temple) & Inclivins Canyon

INTRODUCTION Inclined Canyon is on the immediate north side of the Inclined Temple. It drains into a canyon below Ivins Mountain. This could be used as an alternate start to the Subway for those wanting a less traveled route. Start from the Grotto and use the rappel anchors on the West Rim at the start of Heaps Canyon to get into Phantom Valley.

It is possible to go down Inclined Canyon, explore the canyon, and come back to Phantom Valley. You might find this a side adventure if you are camped near the Bishoprics and want to explore more before returning the way you came. Leave ropes fixed in the gully/canyon for returning to Phantom Valley. You would need a 300-foot rope and be OK cutting the it up into a few small sections and have prussic or jumars. I dropped my helmet while climbing Ivins You may find it in the canyon, a traditional type with stickers.

DESCENDING INCLINED OR INCLIVINS CANYON

INCLINED CANYON D Stih and M Mower 2013
EQUIPMENT REQUIRED: Rappel using natural anchors. Bring additional equipment as required, depending on the exit you plan to take.
CAUTIONS / SPECIAL DIFFICULTIES: Once you pull your rope on the first rappel down Inclined Canyon you are committed to finishing via the subway or trying to get out of the canyon by hiking up Wildcat Canyon to the trail and Lava Point. Wildcat Canyon is rugged and difficult to navigate. Cell reception at Lava Point is spotty.
WATER SOURCES: Water is almost always present in pot holes in Phantom Valley as you cross the valley towards Inclined Canyon. Depending on the season, puddles to deep water might be in Inclined Canyon.
THE STARTING POINTS: Leave a car parked the normal exit for the Subway. Carpool back to the Visitor Center. Take the shuttle to the Grotto. Hike the West Rim Trail to the top, and find the rappel anchors on the south rim used as the start for Heaps Canyon. Once in Phantom Valley, hike towards Inclined Temple, aiming for the north side of the Inclined Temple.
THE ROUTE: From the top of the gully on the north side of the Inclined Temple, scramble down the gully until you become uncomfortable down-climbing. Two or three short

The view from inside the canyon after rappelling the gully on the north side of Inclined Temple. A 300-foot cliff blocks the view of Ivins Mountain on the right. Above the arch is the end of Inclivins Canyon/gully.

(single rope) rappels are required, depending on your comfort level. The bottom of the canyon is wide. A wetsuit was not required (in November, for that part of the canyon). Except for a few spots where our shoes got wet, we were able to walk around water.

ALTERNATE ROUTE: From Phantom Valley or the Bishoprics, approach the back (south) side of the Inclined Temple by way of Incline Pass. Traverse along the west side of Inclined Temple and climb Inclivins Point. Go down its south ridge to access the mouth of Inclivins Canyon (the canyon between the Inclined Temple and Inclivins Point). Descend that canyon (expect a big drop).

Inclined Gully/Canyon (left). Inclivins Gully/Canton (right).

EXIT: In the bottom of the canyon, after a short way, you will find yourself in a flat, sandy wash that can be walked NW towards Wildcat Canyon. You will intersect the middle of the Right Fork Route of the Subway between the Giant Staircase and Black Pool. If you have a permit, you can finish by descending the Subway. If you do not, you must find a way to climb and scramble up Wildcat Canyon to a trail on its west end.

Meridian Tower Plateau into Oak Creek

(The Gully on the West Side of the Meridian Tower)

The Altar of Sacrifice (left). The Meridian Tower is to the right, with snow on its left side. The descent gully is in front of the snow patch on the Meridian Tower.

INTRODUCTION From the plateau / hanging-valley between the Altar of Sacrifice and Meridian Tower, this descent terminates in Oak Creek and can be taken to the service road behind the old visitor center (history museum). Ron Raimonde and I established it during our Traverse of the Towers of the Virgin in 1998. We left no trace - no webbing, no bolts. We rappelled off small bushes. In places we down-climbed instead of rappelling. Fixed pins and webbing have since been added.

DESCENDING MERIDIAN GULLY

THE STARTING POINT AND ROUTE: Likely requires two ropes. There is a set of fixed angles on the last rappel. There is an intermediate ledge in the middle of the last rappel which may provide for a descent using a single rope, something I have not attempted. From the west side of the Meridian Tower, walk SW towards the cliff overlooking Oak Creek. At first it may not seem the way. It becomes obvious as you start down it, descending loose scree down the center of a gully. The first rappel is not encountered until a long way down the gully. The last rappel goes over the edge into space. Once on the ground, the hike down cliffs into creek is epic. Find a way to scrabble down cliff bands into the creek. Several wet and dry falls are encountered. Alternatively, from the bottom of the last rappel, heading west towards the approach to the Altar of Sacrifice before heading down into Oak Creek is less dramatic.

Matt installing fixed anchors on the second descent, at a spot where Ron and I down-climbed. Right: The last rappel down the gully on the west side of the Meridian Tower into Oak Creek. Below: Navigating Oak Creek from the bottom of the last rappel.

Chipmunk Cliff
An Alternate Descent from Birch Creek into the Court of the Patriarchs

INTRODUCTION Birch Creek is a serious canyon. The final drop is longer than 300 feet, hanging in space ten feet from the wall. It was spooky for me. Therefore, when I returned to so first ascents in that area, I wanted to find a new way to get down, one with less exposure and fewer big drops. The way I went down (the Chipmunk route) there are ample bushes and small trees to stop and rest at when using ropes of standard length (200-feet). It is possible to descend this in all seasons without getting wet, including when Birch Creek and Abraham Canyon are flowing. I named it Chipmunk Cliff as there was a steady flow of Cliff Chipmunks going up and down it in the corner. As they scrambled up, they would leap into the air to grab holds, as if doing 5.14 dyno moves. I scared the first one, and he or she turned around and hid in a crack in the corner. I waited quietly, hanging on my rope. When it came out of hiding, three others followed. I knew there was a fourth. I didn't want him or her to be lonely. I continued hanging and quietly waited. Finally, the last one came out of hiding. It looked like the baby.

DESCENDING CHIPMUNK CLIFF

CAUTIONS / SPECIAL DIFFICULTIES: A negative of this descent is loose rock.
STARTING POINT: From the waterfall at the end of Birch Creek, hike NE up a hill to the SW side of Abraham, crossing over Abraham Creek (a small stream that will be dry in late season). Scramble up a short hill on the other side of Abraham Creek and touch the south face of Abraham.
THE ROUTE: 1) From slings around a patch of bushes near at the top, rap down low-angle, loose scree, 150 feet, to a stance at a bush on the edge before a drop. Note: The first rappel is low angle. The rope will be in the dirt, making it difficult to pull. Alternatively, go down about 40 feet to the end of the dirt slope where a nice stance is found next to solid rock. Drilling an anchor on the side of Abraham there may facilitate pulling the ropes easier. 2) Go down 200 feet (might be less) to a stance in a corner with a bush for an anchor. Stay as close to Abraham as possible. Avoid going straight down, as that will make the trip longer and will put you on the blank face used for Abraham Canyon. 3) It's 300 feet to the ground. It's possible to rap to the ground but not advised. Go down over the edge close to Abraham. Pass a <u>very loose</u> section and end at a bush on a large ledge that cuts sideways across the cliff. Rather than stopping here, the first person going down should walk sideways (staying on rappel) in the direction of Abraham, to a safe place to stay of the way of rock fall when the second person rappels. Stop at a bush on the east end of the ledge, one with rappel slings. 4) From the bush on the east side of the ledge, it's 200 feet to the ground. There is a faint climber's trail. Stay high and out of the creek. Traverse loose terrain sideways across the top of the canyon. The trail gets better and more obvious as you reach the approach used by climbers for Abraham. At that point follow it across and down to the Sandbench Horse Trail.
ALTERNATE EXITS: See Sentinel Canyon, also dry and less traumatic than the water fall at the end of Birch Creek.

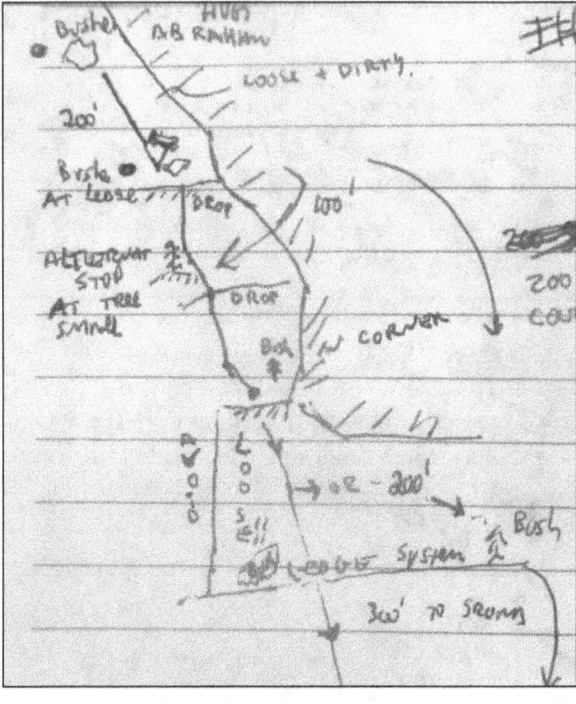

Jacob's Ladder
Descent from the Saddle between Jacob & Lady Mountain into Jacob Canyon

Lady Mountain (left), Jacob (right).

INTRODUCTION This is an alternate way to get into Jacob Canyon for those wanting to explore the canyon, and then exit into the Court of the Patriarchs. Ron and I established this in 1999 during our Traverse of the Court of the Patriarchs. At that time, we left no webbing around the tree at the first rappel. Others have since descended this route and may have left webbing.

DESCENDING JACOB'S LADDER

THE STARTING POINT: Scramble up the Old Lady Mountain Trail to the saddle between Jacob and Lady Mountain. Keep toward the north side of Jacob and avoid the unnecessary extra work of going to the top of Lady Mountain unless you want to visit it.

THE ROUTE: From the saddle between Jacob and Lady Mountain, scramble down loose screen towards Jacob Canyon, until it's not possible to scramble further without rappelling. Rappel from a tree on the NW edge of the saddle, down to a hanging rappel station (two drilled angle pitons) on a bank face. We used two 50M ropes. Rappel to the ground in Jacob Canyon. See canyoneering guide books for details on Jacob Canyon and descending it into the Court of the Patriarchs.

Goose Canyon

INTRODUCTION On a trip to explore the mountains on either side of Birch Creek, I came to a fork in Birch Creek. I took the fork, and walked up the canyon between Triangle Peak and Big Red. Half way up the canyon, laying in the sand, was a dead Canadian Goose. The book *Animal Speak* says geese fly in formation, so each has an unobstructed view, and reminds us not undertake a quest without having a full view of what it entails. It says we should be open to new ideas and are about to start a new path. I took the goose as a sign that I should wait until I had a climbing partner to descend this canyon.

When, with a partner, we descended it, half-way down we found a bolted anchor. Based on the types of bolts and hangers we found it appears to have been drilled in the 1960s or 1970s. How the first-descent party reached Goose Canyon is unknown. They may have come down from Beehive Peak (Big Red) or, more likely, the top Triangle Peak. They may have reached Triangle Peak by climbing the 1938 route on the Sentinel and descending its NW face.

Looking up Goose Canyon after scrambling a short way up it from Birch Creek. It's *much* longer than it appears.

DESCENDING GOOSE CANYON

GOOSE CANYON *D Stih and Mike Dunn 2020*
(The first descent party is unknown.)
CAUTIONS / SPECIAL DIFFICULTIES: Goose Canyon is, as Mike said, "a proper canyon." It is steep and narrow, holds water, requires copious use of natural anchors (dead men), and has sections of difficult and mandatory down-climbing. Only expert canyoneers should attempt it. Be self-sufficient. Standard length ropes may not be adequate. Please keep the canyon in its current state. Do not attempt it if you feel you may have to add bolts. Before you attempt it, become proficient at using natural anchors and down-climbing tricky and exposed terrain.
WATER: In late season (Sept-Nov) the bottom of the canyon is dry except for one pool near the bottom. That pool can be negotiated by a pendulum off a fixed pin on the wall above. There's always water in Birch Creek. In the driest of seasons, there are pools for drinking a short distance down Birch Creek from the exit of Goose Canyon.
SEASON: If you're the type of canyoneer who enjoys getting wet and experiencing a canyon in its flow glory, April to May may be best. Fall provides a drier experience for those less appreciative of water, or not wanting to carry wet suits. We did it in October when it had not rained in several months, and found it almost completely dry, save for one section at the bottom.
STARTING POINT: The saddle between Triangle Peak and Big Red. (See Mars Canyon).
THE ROUTE: Start by scrambling down loose, thick, rotten and dirty, woodsy debris to reach the edge of a big drop. If you head straight for the middle of the mouth of this drop, expect a BIG drop. If you prefer a shorter drop for which you can expect to land on good footing and not have to drill bolts, get as close to Big Red as possible before making the first drop off a patch of bushes on the edge.
EXIT: At the bottom of Goose Canyon, finish your journey by descending one of the descents at the end of Birch Creek.

Sentinel Canyon

When viewed from the back of the Court of the Patriarchs, the chasm/notch visible is the end of Sentinel Canyon.

INTRODUCTION From the back of the Court of the Patriarchs, only the end of this canyon is visible, causing it to appear as a chasm instead of a proper canyon. I explored the middle section of Sentinel Canyon (and named it) during my ascent of Princess Spire. On a later trip, with Mike Dunn as a partner, we did several short pitches to climb UP the canyon, before descending it into the Court of the Patriarchs. At the tree used as an anchor for the big drop into the Court of the Patriarchs, we found grooves in the rock that might be rope burns from those who had done a previous descent not left webbing.

Third Time's Not a Charm

It had not rained in a record number of days. That suited me. I just wanted to do the canyon descents. I don't like water. The wet suit and boots I bought last year are still in their boxes. Unfortunately, dry conditions meant it was hot. It was 89F without clouds.

We had started from the parking lot at the Museum, with three gallons of water, and reached the top of Triangle Peak the end of our first day. We were doing the Traverse of the Beehives. Subsequently, we slowed and enjoyed our location, spent a half-day exploring Birch Creek by climbing up it, and bivied, before coming down into Sentinel Canyon the following morning.

It seems I was destined to be rescued from this area. In 1998, my partner, Ron, and I had avoided a rescue (See the North Face of the Sentinel) when our ropes didn't reach the ground. Law Enforcement had been lenient on me when, in 2018, when my emergency device failed to turn on, and a helicopter searched for me for two days during my ascent of Princess Spire. I had been wanting to do Sentinel Canyon since. Therefore, after completing the Traverse of the Beehives with Mike, and I chose Sentinel Canyon as the way to get back to civilization.

There is a nice, healthy tree at the top of the chasm, around which we wrapped our two 300-foot ropes. Mike went down first, going down to the end the ropes, where he reached lower-angle, bushy ledges and ramps. When I reached Mike, we pulled the ropes, tossed them down for the next rappel, and I started down. I should have gone straight down. I felt safer sticking to the ramps and ledges with bushes. I could not see if the ropes reached the ground.

At some point I heard a branch snap. The ropes, unknown to me, had been going over

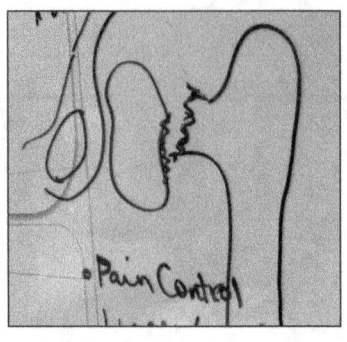

Dan, being lowered to the ground as he used trekking poles to make sure his leg with the fractured hip bone didn't touch the rock.

a bush. I found myself swinging. I have experience swinging, and know that it's better to keep moving your feet across a face than to try to slow things down or try to grab on to things. Then I felt a G-force and my stomach drop. *Wow, I'm moving pretty fast.* As I swung around a corner, my left side slammed into a corner, one there was no way to avoid. In an instant I went from sixty to zero.

It hurt. Fortunately, I found myself just a few inches above a good ledge, big enough to lay down on. I unclipped from the ropes and yelled that I was off rappel.

When Mike got to me, he found a good, thick-girthed bush he used to set up an anchor. I couldn't see over the edge. I couldn't stand up. It seemed we were still at least 200 feet above the ground.

Stand up, I told my self. *You have to get to your feet.*

I couldn't. I didn't yet know that the impact had broken the ball of my femur in half, and that the ball had then lowered itself inside my the flesh of my leg. I felt tingles from nerves that didn't seem to be in the right places, tendons than squeaked and popped. My foot seemed to dangle and move in the opposite direction from what I wished it. I couldn't tolerate putting weight on my leg.

Mike and I each had one trekking pole. Using the poles as canes, telling myself I had to get up, I stood. But I didn't know how I'd get over the edge and to the ground. Fortunately a bush was at head level. Mike clipped me into one end of the rope and ran the rope up through the bush like a pulley. As I used the poles to keep the foot on my bad leg from touching anything, he lowered me, inch by inch, to the bottom. At the bottom was a small patch of sand in the otherwise steep and rocky moat. I was lucky to land in it, and not in the trees.

"Leave me here," I said to Mike when he reached me on the ground. I had a sleeping bag and a bottle of water. "Just go for help."

Before Mike left, he fixed the rope to a tree and threw it down the steep

hillside. I spent the next hour trying to get into my sleeping bag. An hour later I heard voices. A few moment later, I saw the rope move. Someone was coming up. It was Mike, followed by two of the SAR (Search and Rescue) team.

I had luck. The best of SAR had come. One of them checked my vitals and tried to give me an IV for pain, but although I have good veins, my pipes would not allow it. The vessels closed as soon as poked. I settled for a few IBUs. They assessed it was too dangerous to move me further, as my femur artery was close to my injury. It was late in the day. We slept where we were.

The next day, a helicopter came and hovered above us, less than 20 feet from the side of the mountain. After reconing our position, the copter flew away. An hour later, it returned, towing a guy on a cable. The man on the cable was lowered to us. He had the packaging kit. The helicopter left as we got me packaged. When I was inside the kit, an inflatable litter, the SAR team used a hand pump to blow it up so it held me tight. Then copter came back, towing the cable again. I was clipped to the cable and lifted into the air. The parking lot at the Zion Lodge had been cleared for my landing. Blacktop. I wondered how soft the landing be.

It was soft. The copter gently lowered me to waiting hands. They unclipped the cable, and with help from two strong shoulders to lean on, I hobbled to Mike's van. He drove me to the hospital in St George. The surgeon

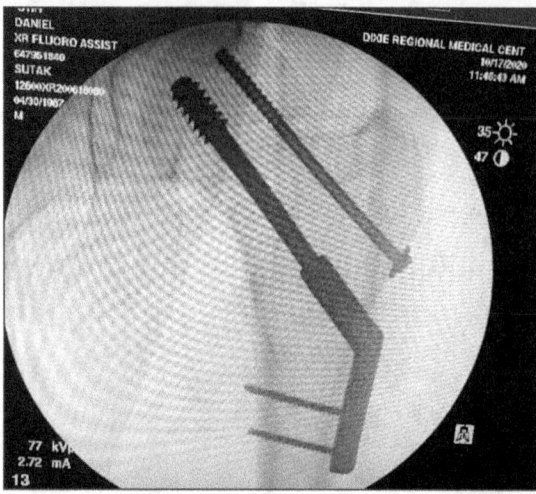

Not the recommended to exit: Daniel, being short-hauled during a rescue after an accident descending Sentinel Canyon.

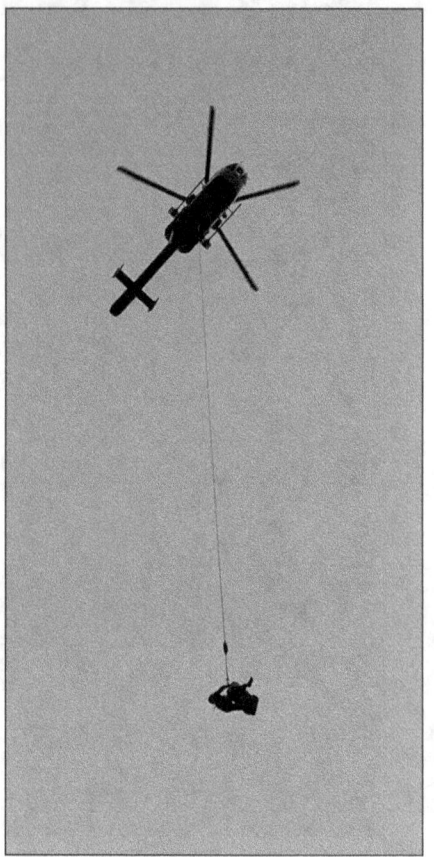

decided it was better to fix me with screws, than give me a new hip. He said I'd have better flexibility with my old bones, that a hip replacement could pop out when I was climbing.

The day after surgery, I tried walking down the hospital hallway using a walker. I moved at the pace of a turtle and felt shooting pains whenever I twisted my hip. I wondered if that was because of the screws, or tendons and nerves that got scrambled. The next day I was released from the hospital. I didn't have health insurance and wanted to leave as soon as possible.

Two weeks later, I returned to see my surgeon. I stayed in a hotel in Springdale. My morning ritual was eating pancakes at Porter's. I had trouble sleeping and was up early. As I went to get breakfast, I found the restaurant burning down. No one was hurt. I took it as a sign to move forward. The restaurant would be rebuilt, better than before, and so would I. It was a world-class, professional rescue. My deepest gratitude to those who assisted.

DESCENDING SENTINEL CANYON

SENTINEL CANYON *D Stih and Mike Dunn 2020 (First Known Descent)*
EQUIPMENT REQUIRED: We had two 300-foot, 8-mil, static ropes, which we found to be helpful for the big drop into the Court of the Patriarchs. Your feet are always in contact with the face, and there are intermediate places with stances and cracks that could be used if descending with a pair of 200-foot ropes.
WATER: There is no water in this canyon. Wet suits are not be required. In early season (spring) the back of the canyon will have a chute of snow where it meets the Sentinel that can provide drinking water if carrying a stove.
STARTING POINT: From Birch Creek, traverse a tree covered ledge as if approaching Princess Spire.
THE ROUTE: Once in the canyon, it's easy going. It's mostly a hike. The technical sections are the big drops getting into the canyon (if you're doing one of the future suggestions, instead of traversing into the canyon from Birch Creek) and the final drop into the Court of the Patriarchs.
POSSIBLE FUTURE DESCENT An alternative approach is to rappel into Sentinel Canyon from the saddle between the Sentinel proper and what's called the North Sentinel (Red Sentinel). The drop looks big. Have gear to do 300+ foot rappels. Climb the bottom half of the 1938 Route of the Sentinel. Half way up you'll come to a saddle between the main summit of the Sentinel and the lower summits to the north that are referred to as the Red Sentinel and the North Sentinel. Head toward this saddle.

The saddle between the outcropping to the north (left) called the North Sentinel and the Sentinel proper (right). Descend the obvious treed area in the saddle to a big drop.

POSSIBLE FUTURE DESCENT Another alternative approach is climb the 1938 Route on the Sentinel to the top of the Sentinel, and then descend the north face to the west side of the top of Sentinel Canyon. Drop into the canyon from there. A BIG drop!

Sentinel Canyon as viewed from top of the North Sentinel. The massive white face is Triangle Peak. The NW ridge of the Sentinel is on the left. Drop into the canyon as you come down this ridge. The closer you can get to the Sentinel, the more complete a descent would be.

View of Sentinel Canyon after traversing across to it from Birch Creek. Note the steep wall on the left, one that could be descended if rappelling into Sentinel Canyon from half-way up the 1938 route. Note the huge drop if coming directly off the summit of the Sentinel.

Mars Canyon

INTRODUCTION This canyon is visible between Big Red (the Streaked Wall) and Triangle Peak (left of the Sentinel). A good view is from the switchbacks coming down from the big tunnel as you enter the park from the east.
FUTURE DESCENTS At the end of the canyon, future explorers could get back to town by continuing down the water course (wet or dry depending on the season), rappelling the blank drop where black streaks mark the mountain.

DESCENDING MARS CANYON

MARS CANYON *D Stih and Mike Dunn 2020 (First Known Descent)*
CAUTIONS / SPECIAL DIFFICULTIES: The canyon is not technical. The cruxes are reaching it and getting back to your car.
WATER SOURCES: In late season, the canyon is completely dry. In early season there may be a trickle of water. It's very narrow and a bad place to be if it rains.

The big fall in wet conditions, as seen from the main canyon road.

Looking back at Big Red (left) and Triangle Peak (right) from the end of Mars Canyon.

STARTING POINT: The saddle between Triangle Peak and Big Red.
There are two ways to get there:
Via the Sentinel: Climb the 1938 route on the Sentinel, descend its NW face, and scramble to the summit of Triangle Peak. From the top of Triangle Peak, down-climb and rappel the NW ridge into the saddle between Triangle Peak and Big Red.
Via the Summit of Big Red: To get to the top of Big Red, either climb my aid route that starts from Birch Creek (see Big Red) or scramble up white slabs on the south side of Big Red from the north side of Beehive Peak. From the top of Big Red, rappel 315 feet from a big tree in the middle of the east side where there is a water course. In spring it will be flowing. By summer it will be dry. Aim for another big tree, down and left. All of 315 feet of rope are required. A second rappel (250-300 feet) reaches the saddle.

THE ROUTE: From the saddle, a single rope is sufficient to descend the canyon. There are only a few short drops from natural anchors. It's otherwise a hike.

GETTING DOWN: At the exit of the canyon you will find yourself on big, smooth slabs at the bottom of the east face of Triangle Peak, right of the Streaked Wall. Get back to town either by rappelling the blank fall (a feat that may not have been done and may have BIG drops) or traversing around the bottom of Triangle Peak towards the Sentinel. Hike through a notch between Triangle Peak and the Sentinel. On other side consider descending Sentinel Canyon into the Court of the Patriarchs, starting from where the canyon meets the north face of the Sentinel (expect big drops) OR hike north towards Birch Creek. A few rappels and down-climbs are required to reach Birch Creek. Finish by descending Birch Creek.

Time for a Break

My blisters were healed. So I drove back to Zion. I wasn't sure what I wanted to climb, so I packed my truck to the gills with all the ropes and rack I owned. Ten ropes. You never know what you might start climbing. It was cold in Zion, freezing at night, but perfect in the October daytime. The issue was the days were short, and it didn't warm up until 11am. Or at least that's my excuse for not getting anything done.

After getting a permit for three nights, I hiked out, got lost, missed a turn, and walked an extra ten miles. I got to a spring, one where I was hoping to find water. I was greeted by a shallow, stagnant pool. The bottom was coated with white lime. If I wanted to continue, I would need to fill up the plastic, 2-liter, coke bottles I was carrying. I wondered what drinking it would do to my insides. I just wasn't into it. I turned around.

The next day I went to recon a different climb. I walked out behind the old visitor center and motored up the cliffs to the north-west. Half-way up, almost stuck, I found a way up the cliff bands by slipping though a hole in the red bands of rock. After squeezing though the hole, I thought I might be on level ground. Instead, I found more cliff bands. I moved sideways, then up, then back sideways. I wondered if I got stuck again if I would remember how to get down. I wasn't carrying a rope.

When I got to the top of the cliff bands, I took my pack off to change out of my down jacket and get my hiking pole out. The collapsible pole, one I've used on countless adventures, would not go together. It seemed a part was missing or broken. I tried to pry what ever piece was loose inside of it out, and ended up breaking the pole. Guess that was another sign. I looked for a big stick to use as a hiking pole.

As I went higher, I wasn't feeling the vibe. My feet felt fit and secure. My body felt strong. I moved fast and nimble, like a cat. My mind was not scared.

It was my heart that didn't feel it. *Knowing* was missing. That's the most important thing to being successful and safe - feeling and knowing you are doing the right thing on the right path. You can overcome obstacles such as blisters, aching hips, and sprains. You can think your way out of precarious situations. You can not, however, change *knowing*. The logical mind does not know why something is or is not best.

I felt like I was running on two out of three cylinders. Without the knowing, it was like driving a car with a tire low on air, wondering how long it

There's a reason for the earthquake that destroyed homes built on the east side of the West Temple. And a reason a cougar lives in the basement of one of the leveled houses. An occasional sip from the well is permitted, but not a continuous sucking of the energy. If it were not this way, the energy might run out. The well might run dry. It needs to recharge from the Power Source in order for things to remain in balance.

would be before it was completely flat. Feeling like an old car, I said to my guardian angels, "Just one last time, give me a way down." Then I told myself, *let's find the way down and go home.*

I followed my feet. I didn't think about which direction I should go, or when and where I should start going down. I let my feet do the thinking. I allowed the feet to keep moving. They intuitively knew the best route. Heart, the flat tire, kept doing it's best, transmitting data to the mind, which sent it to the feet. If I had paused and thought, "Which way should I go now?" I don't believe I would have gotten down safely. A short time later, I found myself at the bottom, where, I made a decision with my mind: It's time to go home.

Bibliography

Death in Zion National Park: Stories of Accidents and Foolhardiness in Utah's Grand Circle. Randi Minetor. Globe Pequot, 2017.

Zion National Park: Summit Routes. A Hiking and Climbing Guide to Zion National Park and Southwest Utah. Courtney Purcell, 2015.

Zion: Canyoneering: Trail Hiking and Technical Adventures in & Around Zion National Park. Tom Jones. Canyoneering USA, 2006.

Abraham
Zion: National Park • Utah. U.S Department of the Interior National Park Service. U.S. Government Printing Office. GPO: 1966 OF—238-804.

Map of Zion National Park 1929.

Mountain Review 5. Issue 5: November / December 1993. OTE Media Services, London.

http://canyoncollective.com/threads/jacob-canyon-april-2017-new-bolts.24872/#post-107494. Cited on-line, July, 2021: "From Jeff: 'What is properly called Abraham, which harbors the radiator wall, was first climbed by George Lowe and me in 1972, via the huge corner system on the right side. The formation properly known as Isaac, was climbed by Wick Beavers, Mike Weis, John Weiland and me in 1971, I think. The article in *Ascent* starts with: 'The roadside plaque reads Isaac, Jacob and Abraham - The Three Patriarchs.' He named them incorrectly based on a roadside sign. That kept folks confused for years."

https://www.canyoneeringusa.com/zion/technical/Isaac. Cited on-line July, 2021: "Isaac Canyon runs between the Abraham and Isaac peaks into the Court of the Patriarchs. First known descent: Walt Shipley and John Middendorf, February 1990, descending from the first ascent of Abraham via the Radiator route."

Yosemite: Half a Century of Rock Climbing. Alex Huber and Heinz Zak. Menasha Ridge Press, 2002.

Royal Robbins: Spirit of the Age. Pat Ament. Adventure's Meaning Press, 1992.

http://canyoncollective.com/threads/new-route-north-face-of-abraham-via-phantom-valley-narrows.18185/#post-72858.

The Inclined Temple
"Eight days, 1,000-year rain, 100-year flood." John Aguilar and Charlie Brennan. Daily Camera, 2013. Cited-on line: [https://www.dailycamera.com/2013/09/21/eight-days-1000-year-rain-100-year-flood/].

Gregory Butte
"Measuring the Span of the Great Arch at Zion National Park, Kolob Section". Referred to as *The Blake Paper.* Zion Park Museum Collections.

"Kolob Arch - Fred D. Ayres and A.E. Creswell". *American Alpine Journal.* American Alpine Club, 1954.

Desert Magazine. May, 1966.

Cable Mountain
Zion National Park: Cable. Rev. 07/94.

Death Point
You Can Heal Your Life. Louise L. Hay. Hay House, 1984.

Animal Speak: The Spiritual & Magical Powers of Creatures Great & Small. Ted Andrews. Llewellyn Publications, 1993.

Red Tooth
Exploring the Backcountry of Zion National Park: Off-Trail Routes. Known as *The Green Book.* Thomas Brereton and James Dunaway. Zion Natural History Association, 1988.

Isaac
American Alpine Journal. American Alpine Club, 1974.

Mountain Review 4. Issue 4: September / October 1993.

http://www.bigwall.com/fainfo.html. Cited on-line, 2021: "ISAAC: Southeast Buttress a.k.a. The Lowe Route (FA) Jeff Lowe, Wick Beavers, John Weiland, Mike Weis, 2/72."

Cathedral Mountain
Death Daring and Disaster - Search and Rescue in the National Parks. Charles R. "Butch" Farabee Jr. Roberts Rinehart Publishers, 2001.

Red Arch Mountain
Ron Kay's Guide to Zion National Park: Everything You Always Wanter to Know About Zion Nation Park But Didn't Know Who to Ask. Ron Kay. The Countryman Press, 2008.

Hidden Canyon
"A Brief History of Climbing in Zion." cited on www.bigwalls.net/climb/Zionhis.html. This appears to be the same text as printed in *Desert Rock: Rock Climbs in The National Parks* by Eric Bjornstad, Chockstone Press, 1996.

Traversing of Kolob Canyons
Zion National Park: 2006 Inventory of Invasive Non-Native Plants and Endemic Plants. Northern Colorado Plateau Inventory and Monitoring Network, 2006.

Traverse of the Beehives
Zion: National Park • Utah. United States Department of the Interior., U.S. Government Printing Office. Reprint 1957-O-434341.

214 Zion National Park. Utah. Trails Illustrated, a Division of Ponderosa Publishing Company, 1988. Revised 1995.

Other Maps, Books, Brochures, Pamphlets, Articles
Zion National Park. Trails Illustrated Topographical Map. National Geographic Society, 1988, Revised 2012.

Zion National Park. Trails Illustrated Topographical Map. National Geographic Partners, LLC, 2018.

Zion: National Park • Utah. U.S Department of the Interior National Park Service., U.S. Government Printing Office. Reprint 1955 O-F—335748.

Zion National Park: Sanctuary in the Desert. Nicky Leach. Sierra Press, 2000.

Zion National Park: A Geological and Geographical Sketch. Arizona Highways, 1949.

A History of Southern Utah and it's National Parks. Angus M. Woodbury, 1950. Reprinted by the Zion Natural History Association Inc, 1997.

The Zion Tunnel: From Slickrock to Switchbacks. Donald T. Garate. Zion Natural History Association Inc, 1991.

"In Pursuit of the Golden Dawn." Ron Olevsky. *Rock and Ice*, June, 1987.

"Northwest Face of the Great White Throne." Pat Callis. *The American Alpine Journal.* The American Alpine Club, 1968.

Selected Climbs in the Desert Southwest: Colorado & Utah. Cameron M. Burns. The Mountaineers, 1999.

"Earth, wind, and Rubble: Ridge Climbing in the Heart of Zion". Fitz Cahall and James Q. Martin. *Climbing*, Issue #255, February, 2007.

"Red Sentinel, Human Centipede V". Rob Pizem and Brian Smoot. *The American Alpine Journal 2017*, The American Alpine Club, 2017.

About the Author

Visit www.danielstih.com.

Daniel Stih

Pioneer, Innovator, Explorer

Daniel Stih has done the first ascents of ten mountains officially named on maps of Zion National Park (one of his favorite places to climb), more than any climber in history. These include the Altar of Sacrifice, Sun Dial, Gregory Butte, the Bishopric, Abraham, the Meridian Tower, Inclined Temple, Ivins Mountain, Castle Dome, and Cliff Dwelling Mountain. A true believer in the spirit of adventure and leaving no trace, most of Daniel's climbs do not have bolts. Daniel is a speaker on the topic of success and how to find and do what has not been done before. For questions or to book Daniel to give the keynote at your event, email daniel@danielstih.com

Also by Daniel Stih

Because You Can
*How to Succeed Under Difficult Circumstances :
Lessons Learned From Climbing Mountains
That Had Never Been Climbed*

The rate of change in people's lives is faster than ever. There are people looking at mountains that need to be climbed, and for various reasons, they may not think they can climb them. They may be scared or not know how to get started. In *Because You Can*, Daniel outlines how the same principles used to climb mountains can be used to:

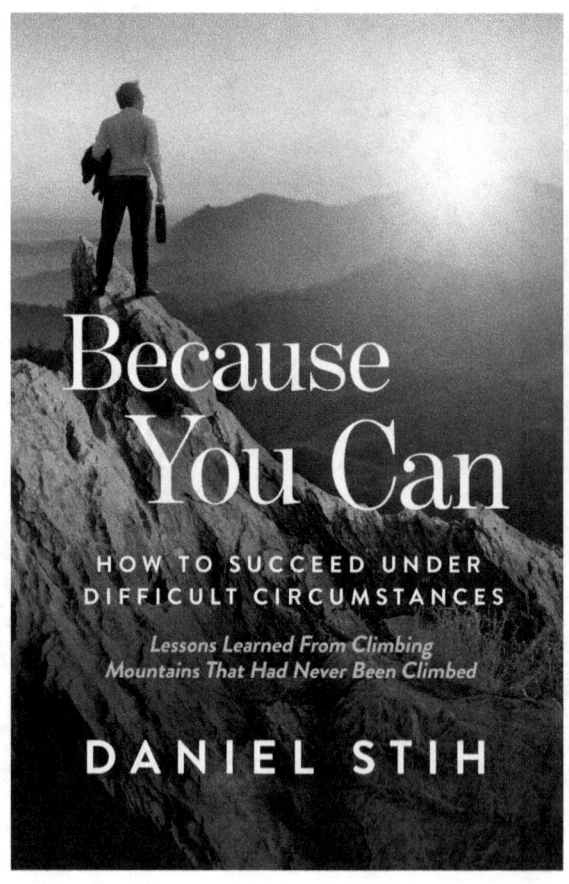

- Overcome fear so you can pioneer your own way

- Understand the secret to making no-lose decisions

- Take on a new challenge

- Master the art of transforming uncertainty into positive action

- Create a personal roadmap for attaining success

www.ingramcontent.com/pod-product-compliance
Lightning Source LLC
Chambersburg PA
CBHW050828230426
43667CB00012B/1918